"... superbly researched, well annotated, and written in a lively, entertaining style. It makes a fine addition to the canon of colonial American history."
—*American History* magazine

"... a Baedeker for a terribly bloody dispute across Massachusetts, Rhode Island, Connecticut, and Maine."
—*The Boston Globe*

"... superb and gripping ... *King Philip's War* is exceptionally well-organized, with a cogent history of New England at the time the hostilities began and with chapters devoted to each battle location."
—*The Worcester Phoenix,* Worcester, Mass.

"... does much to reestablish the conflict's importance for popular historical study of the area."
—*Library Journal*

"... presented in a clear, concise form that makes the conflict and its implications easy to understand ... [a] highly informative and painstakingly researched book."
—*The Patriot Ledger,* Quincy, MA

"*King Philip's War* is an unbiased account of the traumatic events of this war of survival on the sacred landscape of our aboriginal ancestors ... a well-written work that uniquely identifies key historic sites for the modern reader."
—Russell Gardner, Great Moose, Wampanoag tribal historian

"During my own research in the late 1940s, I visited many of the sites mentioned in *King Philip's War,* including Wheeler's Surprise and the place where Mary Rowlandson spent the first night after her capture, but Eric Schultz has done this exploration more thoroughly and intelligently than anyone before or since. He has made it possible for anyone to find and visit these interesting places. This original and praiseworthy book will be useful for years to come."
—Douglas Leach, author of *Flintlock and Tomahawk*

"A significant contribution to the historical literature on colonial wars, *King Philip's War* corrects misperceptions and answers many historical questions about an important seventeenth-century conflict. A valuable narrative history and a wonderful guide to the actual sites of ambushes, raids, and battles, this book will appeal to both academic scholars and general readers."

—Patrick Malone, author of *The Skulking Way of War*

"That King Philip, whose head was paraded around the streets of Plymouth in a barbarous show of triumph, was the son of the Wampanoag chief who celebrated the first Thanksgiving with the Pilgrims in 1621 adds to the irony and tragedy of the events, whose memory this well-researched book deservedly keeps alive. . . . The authors make abundant use of maps and photographs of old sites to enable the reader to follow the course of the war: the book forms an exhaustive guide for the armchair historian or anyone wishing to visit the monuments and battlefields today."

—Editorial Reviews, Amazon.com

"Schultz's and Tougias' evocative descriptions, along with maps, photographs and drawings, would make history come alive to any hiker venturing out to these hallowed grounds."

—*The Sun Chronicle,* Attleboro, MA

"Every battle and historic confrontation is described, and the maps showing sites, illustrations and old engravings contribute to a work that history buffs should prize."

—*Times Argus,* Barre VT

"New England history buffs will love using this book to track down hard-to-find King Philip's War sites, each of them a story in itself."

—Jill Lepore, author of *The Name of War*

KING PHILIP'S WAR

The History and Legacy of America's Forgotten Conflict

Eric B. Schultz

Michael J. Tougias

THE COUNTRYMAN PRESS · WOODSTOCK, VERMONT

Library of Congress Cataloging-in-Publication Data
Schultz, Eric B., 1957–
King Philip's War : the history and legacy of America's forgotten conflict / Eric B. Schultz,
Michael J. Tougias.
p.   cm.
Includes bibliographical references and index.
ISBN 0-88150-434-3 (hardcover : alk. paper)
1. King Philip's War, 1675–1676. 2. Indians of North America—New England—
History. 3. Indians of North America—Government relations—To 1789. 4. New England—History–
Colonial period, ca. 1600–1775. I. Tougias, Mike, 1955– . II. Title.
E83.67.S38   1999
973.2'4—dc21   99–23481
CIP

ISBN 0-88150-483-1 (paperback : alk. paper)

Text design by Dean Bornstein
Jacket design by Glenn Suokko
Page composition by Melinda Belter
Maps by Jacques Chazaud © 1999 The Countryman Press

"A Map of New England," reproduced here on the jacket and elsewhere in the book, was
produced by John Foster of Boston around 1677. It was the first map to have been published in the Britsh
colonies and may have been the first map published in the Western Hemisphere. (Courtesy of the John
Carter Brown Library, Brown University.)

The jacket portrait of King Philip—date and artist unknown—is reprinted courtesy of the
Haffenreffer Museum of Anthropology.

The authors and publisher are grateful to the following people for permission to reprint the archival images
used in this book: The Haffenreffer Museum of Anthropology and The John Carter Brown Library, both
Brown University; the Hadley Historical Society; the Old Dartmouth Historical Society/New Bedford
Whaling Museum; the Peabody Essex Museum; New England Financial Corporation; and the Collections
the Library of Congress. Specific credits are given with each image on the page where it appears.

Published by The Countryman Press, P.O. Box 748, Woodstock, VT 05091

Distributed by W. W. Norton & Company, Inc.
500 Fifth Avenue, New York, NY 10110

Printed in the United States by Versa Press, Peoria, Illinois
20 19 18 17 16 15 14 13 12 11

To my parents

—E.S.

· Contents ·

Chapter 5: *King Philip's War in Central and Western Massachusetts*

PART III · THE DIARIES AND
EYEWITNESS ACCOUNTS

We Americans are the best informed people on earth as to the events of the last twenty-four hours; we are not the best informed as to the events of the last sixty centuries.

— *Will and Ariel Durant*

· *Preface* ·

ERIC SCHULTZ WROTE THE MAJOR SHARE OF THIS BOOK; I came on the scene after most of the hard work was done. I thought the reader might be interested in the story behind our collaboration.

When my historical novel about King Philip's War, *Until I Have No Country*, was released in 1997, I received a congratulatory note from Eric, who was a total stranger at the time. Attached to the note was the table of contents of a book he was working on, titled *Discovering King Philip's War*. Being a pack rat, I stuck the note and the table of contents into one of the thousands of files I keep in my messy office, and forgot all about it.

A year later I began work on a short book about the war, which would include maps, roadside history suggestions, and eyewitness accounts. (I'd given dozens of narrated slide presentations to historical groups about the war, and people would always ask for directions to battle sites or express curiosity about what diaries I used in my research. These requests were what prompted my project.) After writing about a third of the book, I vaguely recalled Eric's table of contents, and after a couple hours of searching I located it. I quickly realized the book he was working on was similar to my own. Maybe, I thought, I should meet him and see if we couldn't split the research and writing. I called him, suggested we meet for coffee in a couple weeks, and asked him to first send me a portion from the book.

When his manuscript arrived, I was stunned. It was fantastic—well written, impeccably researched—the kind of book I go out of my way to buy for my own use. In a smooth style he had pieced together some of the lesser-known events of the war and even solved some mysteries.

His manuscript was also largely completed. It really didn't need much editing, so I merely did proofreading and fact checking and outlined a promotional plan. All I could offer was to add the diaries and the maps and then find us a publisher.

When we met for coffee, Eric was probably wondering just how much reworking would be involved in this collaboration. He later told me it was music to his ears when I said, "Don't change a thing—I'll just add maps and diaries." And so the expanded version of *Discovering King Philip's War* was launched. Even before we found a publisher I did an interview with the *Boston Globe*, where I raved about his research and how the book was fun to read. Now I know what a literary agent feels like when he knows he has found something special.

A great many people helped me with my research for this book and my novel, particularly Native Americans, who went out of their way to give their time. My gratitude goes to them, and it's my hope that this book increases the awareness of what really happened so many years ago.

Michael Tougias
Franklin, Massachusetts
1999

· Acknowledgments ·

THIS BOOK WAS WRITTEN IN FITS AND STARTS over eight years beginning in 1990, and I owe thanks to many, many folks who spent time with me during the book's research and preparation.

The late Nanepashemet of the Wampanoag Village at Plimouth Plantation was, from the beginning, enthusiastic in his support and helpful in sorting fact from fiction about King Philip and his people. Likewise, Russell Gardner, the Wampanoag tribal historian, helped enormously, especially in interpreting the period and events around Massasoit's and Wamsutta's deaths. I was honored to have Douglas Leach, whose 1958 *Flintlock and Tomahawk* is still the standard text on King Philip's War, offer his wisdom and enthusiasm to my manuscript. Patrick Malone of Brown University also made time amid his own hectic schedule of teaching and writing to offer helpful ideas and overall encouragement. William Turnbaugh of the University of Rhode Island and Joseph Granger of the University of Louisville were both generous in sharing material on the Narragansett generally, and on the Great Swamp Fight specifically, that was otherwise inaccessible to me. Audrey Milne and Emerson Baker III of the Dyer Library and York Institute and Museum in Saco, Maine, provided invaluable information on the King Philip's War sites in that state. Maggie Stier of the Fruitlands Museums assisted me with my work on King Philip's War Club, Mark Choquet of the New England Historic Genealogical Society with Massasoit's genealogy, Douglas Kelleher of the Massachusetts Historical Commission with Woodcock's Garrison, and Nate Fuller with a personal tour of Smith's Castle.

In Rehoboth, Lydia Carswell and Deborah Cahoon Didick, former directors of the Carpenter Museum, E. Otis Dyer Sr., E. Otis Dyer Jr., and Robert Sharples were most helpful in all respects, but especially on the topic of Anawan Rock. Helen Pierce of Swansea spent the better part of a day guiding me to the King Philip's War sites in that town, as did Herbert Hosmer in Lancaster, Francis Rowland in Mattapoisett, Gary Brown in Marlboro, and Rosa Johnston in Northfield. Byron Canney of Whately spent an afternoon searching with me for the site of the Battle of South Deerfield, while Maryanne MacLeod took me to several locations in Sterling related to the Waussacum Pond ambush. Richard Colton of the Montague Historical Society helped me to reconstruct the Fight at Turner's Falls and provided valuable insights on seventeenth-century warfare. Jeff Fiske's excellent grasp of local history and knowledge of sites and landmarks in New Braintree enabled me to examine the locations related to Wheeler's Surprise and the Nipmuc camps at Menameset. John Pretola of the Springfield Science Museum shared with me his work on the Fort Hill Agawam Indian site. Edward Nash of Leominster helped me to locate one possible site of the Quaboag Old Fort and challenged me on a number of issues surrounding the Great Swamp Fight (including, but not limited to, how to locate ticks in my socks after a day's tramp through the swamp).

In several other towns people were generous with their time and information: Paul Hurd of the Medfield Historical Society; Jane Lopes of the *Middleborough Antiquarian;* Robert Beals of the Middleborough Historical Commission; Charles Crowley, a city Councillor and local historian in Taunton; Lila Parrish in Great Barrington; Becky Warren of the Chelmsford Historical Society; Mary Conley, the Ipswich town historian; Robert Hanson of the Dedham Historical Society; Pamela Toma and Terrie Korpita of Historic Northampton; Dorothy Russell of the Hadley Historical Society; Ruth Loring of the Ossipee Historical Society; Isabel Beal of the Groton Historical Society; Carl Congdon of the Pettaquamscut Historical Society; Mary Lou Cutter of the Hatfield Historical Commission; Ruth Warfield of the Massachusetts Archaeological Society; C. Carlton Brownell of the Little Compton Historical Society; Christina Kelly, town historian in Schaghticoke, New York; Susanne L. Flynt of the Pocumtuck Valley Memorial Association in Deerfield; Mary Soulsby of the University of Connecticut; E. Pierre Morenon of Rhode Island College; Ann McMullen of Brown University; Jill Lepore of Yale University and now Boston University; Jane Beebe of the Berkshire Museum; and Gary Bremen of the Roger Williams National Memorial in Providence.

Finally, in my indoor pursuit of King Philip's War, I had valuable assistance from Albert Klyberg and Linda Eppich of the Rhode Island Historical Society; Barbara Hail of the Haffenreffer Museum; Paul Robinson of the Rhode Island Historic Preservation Commission; Norman Fiering of the John Carter Brown Library; and the staffs of the Rhode Island Historical Society Library in Providence, the Old Colony Historical Society in Taunton, and the Massachusetts Historical Society in Boston.

Thank you to my sister, Elizabeth Schultz Dale, who read and improved several sections of the text; to Dan Mandell, for his thoughtful reading of the text and many insightful comments; to our editor, Helen Whybrow, who vastly improved everything long after I was sure it was as good as it could get; and to my wife, Susan, who was patient enough to put up with the travel, the clutter of maps and documents, and all those pictures of rocks, gravestones, and (seemingly) empty fields. And, of course, to Michael Tougias, whose writing enhanced the book considerably, and whose energy allowed it to see the light of day.

Eric Schultz
Boxford, Massachusetts
1999

This illustration, entitled Pometacom, shows a brooding but proud King Philip. (Courtesy of the Haffenreffer Museum of Anthropology, Brown University)

· *Introduction* ·

AMONG THE HANDFUL OF SEMINAL EVENTS that shaped the American mind and continent, King Philip's War is perhaps the least studied and most forgotten. In essence, the war cleared southern New England's native population from the land, and with it a way of life that had evolved over a millennium. The Wampanoag, Narragansett, Nipmuc, and other native peoples were slaughtered, sold into slavery, or placed in widely scattered communities throughout New England after the war. In its aftermath, the English established themselves as the dominant peoples—and in many New England towns, the only peoples—allowing for the uninterrupted growth of England's northern colonies right up to the American Revolution. As important, King Philip's War became the brutal model for how the United States would come to deal with its native population. Later names like Tippecanoe, Black Hawk's War, the Trail of Tears, the Salt Creek Massacre, the Red River War, and Wounded Knee all took place under the long, violent shadow of King Philip's War.

King Philip, also called Metacom, was the son of Massasoit, sachem of the Wampanoag and the man most closely associated with the natives' goodwill toward the struggling Plymouth colony. It seems particularly ironic, then, that Massasoit is seated prominently in our romanticized view of the First Thanksgiving, while the most graphic image of Philip (for those who still study the war) is his severed head skewered on the end of a pike and placed along a major Plymouth thoroughfare for most of a generation. The real tragedy is how we came to embrace one image and lose the other. In removing King Philip's War from our history books, we became, according to the rubric, destined to repeat it. That we did, with a vengeance.

While King Philip died in the war and his people were decimated, the Wampanoag as a group were not exterminated. In places like Martha's Vineyard and Mashpee, Massachusetts, small, courageous groups were able to sustain the Wampanoag culture in the face of overwhelming pressure from their white neighbors. Today the Wampanoag represent a small

I

but important part of New England's population, who regularly come together for governance and to perpetuate their customs and traditions. However, the impact of King Philip's War was so profound that it would be 253 years after Philip's death—1929—before the Wampanoag would hold their first powwow of the modern era.

The war erupted on June 20, 1675, along the southern border of Plymouth Colony, and it is startling to see how quickly two peoples, having lived side by side for a half century, could become consumed so quickly and completely with an intense hatred for one another. A small band of Pokanoket (a people of the Wampanoag) warriors left their camp in present-day Warren, Rhode Island, crossed the Kickamuit River, and raided several farms in the English settlement at Swansea. A messenger was immediately dispatched to Governor Josiah Winslow at Marshfield, who on June 22 sent orders to Bridgewater and Taunton to raise a force of two hundred men for the defense of Plymouth Colony's frontier.

Three days after the raid, twenty-year-old John Salisbury of Swansea shot and mortally wounded a marauding Pokanoket. Within a day Pokanoket warriors had ambushed and killed seven English, leaving the entire Swansea settlement of about forty families huddled in three or four secure garrisons. Plymouth and Massachusetts Bay troops attempted to quell the violence by cornering Philip, son of Massasoit and sachem of the Pokanoket, on the Pokanoket peninsula (Warren and Bristol, Rhode Island). However, as the poorly prepared English troops stumbled around Pokanoket territory, Philip slipped across Mount Hope Bay into present-day Tiverton and Fall River, where he drew additional strength from his Pocasset allies. A short time later he would elude the English again when he abandoned his camp in the Pocasset Swamp, crossed the Taunton River, and streaked toward central Massachusetts and the security of his Nipmuc allies.

A year after the incident at Swansea, Plymouth and Massachusetts Bay Colonies lay in shambles. Mendon, Brookfield, Lancaster, Deerfield, Northfield, Wrentham, Worcester, Groton, Rehoboth, Middleboro, and Dartmouth had all been reduced to ashes and abandoned. Swansea itself was left with six structures standing. Marlboro had been destroyed except for a few buildings maintained throughout the war by the military. Other locations

With the many portraits of King Philip extant, it is important to recognize that no genuine physical description of Philip, either in art or prose, remains. (Courtesy of the Haffenreffer Museum of Anthropology, Brown University)

such as Hatfield, Springfield, Medfield, Weymouth, Scituate, Sudbury, and Chelmsford faced enormous loss of life and property. Even towns such as Hadley, Northampton, and Taunton, which successfully countered Indian assaults, were scarred by a war that led family and friends to their deaths in faraway towns, kept residents in a constant state of fear and uncertainty, and created a standing army that gobbled up food stores and required an endless stream of tax payments for its support.

Rhode Island found itself the victim of a war it had neither instigated nor declared and suffered as much as its Massachusetts Bay and Plymouth neighbors. Providence lost seventy-two homes and was deserted by most of its inhabitants. Warwick was burned to the ground except for one stone house, while places like Wickford and the ancient settlement of Pawtuxet were utterly destroyed. By March 1676, the area south of the Pawtuxet River had been largely deserted by the English,[1] and by the war's end only the village of Portsmouth and the town of Newport had been spared the ravages of King Philip's War. Connecticut's military played a crucial role in the war, and the colony escaped assault with the exception of Simsbury, which was abandoned and burned to the ground. In that part of the Massachusetts Bay Colony that became present-day Maine, however, King Philip's War led to the destruction and abandonment of all English settlements except Kittery, York, and Wells.[2] In all, more than half of New England's ninety towns were assaulted by native warriors.[3] For a time in the spring of 1676, it appeared to the colonists that the entire English population of Massachusetts and Rhode Island might be driven back into a handful of fortified seacoast cities. One historian noted, "No period of the revolutionary war was, to the interior of any part of the United States, so disastrous."[4]

Between six hundred and eight hundred English died in battle during King Philip's War. Measured against a European population in New England of perhaps fifty-two thousand, this death rate was nearly twice that of the Civil War and more than seven times that of World War II. The English Crown sent Edmund Randolph to assess damages shortly after the war and he reported that twelve hundred homes were burned, eight thousand head of cattle lost, and vast stores of foodstuffs destroyed. Thousands of survivors became wards of the state, prompting churches in England and Ireland to send relief ships to New England's aid.

War	Est. Deaths	Est. Population	Deaths per 100,000
King Philip's War			
English	800	52,000	1,538
Native American	3,000	20,000	15,000
American Revolution	4,435	2,464,250	180
Civil War	305,235	35,630,885	857
World War II	291,557	141,183,318	206

(Sources: Department of Defense, Bureau of Census, Francis Jennings' estimates)

For all their suffering, the English fared well compared to New England's Native American peoples. During the war, the English attacked and massacred Narragansett and Wampanoag at the Great Swamp in South Kingstown, Rhode Island, along the Connecticut River in present-day Turner's Falls, Massachusetts, and in locations as separate as the Housatonic River in western Massachusetts and the Pawtucket River north of Providence. Some of the most grisly executions were of native women and children trying desperately to flee the war or surrender. One account estimated that three thousand Native Americans were killed in battle.[5] In a total population of about twenty thousand, this number is staggering.[6]

Many of the surviving natives were sold into slavery in the West Indies as part of a scheme designed to replenish colonial coffers depleted by the war. Others migrated west to New York or north to Canada to seek refuge with neighboring tribes. Those allowed to remain, despite having supported the English war effort, often lost their property rights and individual liberties. Never again would the English and the southern New England Indians live side by side as they had prior to King Philip's War.

The impact of King Philip's War on early America was profound. In Plymouth, authorities would exhibit Philip's skull in public for more than twenty years after his death.[7] A century after the conflict, the country's Revolutionary War generation was still intimately familiar with Philip and "stories of Indian atrocities";[8] Paul Revere himself would engrave the most famous of Philip's many images. Just before the Revolution, and again in the early nineteenth century, a spate of literature about the war appeared. Both Washington Irving and James Fenimore Cooper penned tales about Philip. In 1829 a tragic play about the extinction of the noble savage, *Metamora; or, the Last of the Wampanoags,* based upon the events of King Philip's War, opened to rave reviews in New York,[9] and would become one of the most widely produced plays in nineteenth-century America.[10] Speaking just a few years later at the commemoration of one of the war's worst massacres, Bloody Brook (in South Deerfield, Massachusetts), the renowned orator Edward Everett predicted:

> Ages shall pass away; the stately tree which overshadows us shall wither and fall, and we, who are now gathered beneath it, shall mingle with the honored dust we eulogize; but the "Flowers of Essex" [those young men from Essex County, Massachusetts, killed at Bloody Brook] shall bloom in undying remembrance; and with every century, these rites of commemoration shall be repeated, as the lapse of time shall continually develop, in richer abundance, the fruits of what was done and suffered by our fathers.[11]

Today, Everett's prophecy is only partially fulfilled. While a small group of modern historians carry on a lively debate about the impact of King Philip's War and a few individual towns still commemorate important events associated with the war, the single most cataclysmic event of seventeenth-century colonial New England has become an obscure historical footnote for most Americans. As the typical New Englander races along Route 195 from Cape Cod to Providence, up and down Route 91 in the Connecticut River Valley, or along Route 95 in Maine and New Hampshire, he seldom realizes that the ghosts of King Philip's War cast huge shadows on the landscape all around him.

This book is about those ghosts: the many traditions, sites, landmarks, and eyewitness accounts that still speak to us about King Philip and his seventeenth-century world. Divided into three sections, *King Philip's War* features a brief history of the conflict; those readers wishing to understand the war in context, and follow it chronologically, should begin here. The sec-

Both Alderman, a Pocasset disenchanted with Philip, and Caleb Cook, the English soldier who lost his chance at immortality when his gun failed to fire, are pictured in this version of Philip's death. As a reward for killing Philip, Alderman was given Philip's hand, which he reportedly kept in a pail of rum and showed at taverns for a fee. (Courtesy of the Haffenreffer Museum of Anthropology, Brown University)

ond section, and in some ways the heart of the book, contains a series of more detailed stories and descriptions of the war's sites, including a greater reliance on firsthand and contemporary accounts. This section is chronological by region to assist the reader interested in a particular locale. The final section includes extensive excerpts from the war's eyewitness accounts, primarily those of Mary Rowlandson (held captive by the Indians) and colonial soldier Benjamin Church.

It is in these sites and eyewitness accounts—discovering the scene of an ambush, reconstructing a long-lost battle on current maps, or reading the diary of a participant—that the war again takes shape and substance. It is our hope that *King Philip's War* will resurrect much of a past that has been lost, and we can begin to again learn those things that our history books have forgotten.

A 1900 depiction of Philip's meeting with commissioners of the United Colonies at the first meetinghouse in Taunton, Massachusetts, shows the English gathered on one side of the room and the Pokanoket on the other. Given the strong Puritan bias in accounts of this meeting, this seating arrangement may be one of the few indisputable facts remaining. (Courtesy of New England Financial, Boston, MA)

❧ PART I ❧

A BRIEF HISTORY OF
KING PHILIP'S WAR

The costliest battle of King Philip's War was in December 1675, when English troops attacked a fortified Narragansett village in South Kingstown, Rhode Island. While no illustration of the Narragansett fort exists, this depiction of an 1585 Native American fortified village in Pomeiock, North Carolina, gives a general sense of what the English may have encountered during the Great Swamp Fight. (Courtesy of the John Carter Brown Library, Brown University)

Chapter I ·
New England Before the War

WHEN OUSAMEQUIN, BETTER KNOWN BY HIS TITLE of Massasoit ("great sachem"), died in 1661–1660,[1] it was one more indication that a long, generally peaceful era of English-Indian relations in New England was drawing to a close. Massasoit was leader of the Pokanoket, whose domain encompassed the Mount Hope peninsula in Narragansett Bay, now Bristol and Warren, Rhode Island. Massasoit was also a grand sachem of the Wampanoag, recognizing the allegiance pledged to him by seven lesser Wampanoag sachems.[2] Massasoit's influence was extensive but his power far from absolute. Like other New England sachems, he maintained loyalty only by being a wise, compassionate leader.

The Wampanoag were one of several Algonquian peoples residing in New England in the seventeenth century, related to their neighbors by a common linguistic tradition. The Wampanoag held sway from the eastern shore of Narragansett Bay to the far reaches of Cape Cod, including Nantucket, Martha's Vineyard, and the Elizabeth Islands. Wampanoag peoples included among others, Massasoit's Pokanoket, the Nemasket (Middleboro, Massachusetts), the Pocasset (Tiverton, Rhode Island), and the Sakonnet (Little Compton, Rhode Island). These groups would be important participants in King Philip's War.

The Wampanoag domain lay adjacent to that of New England's most powerful Native American group, the Narragansett, whose various sachems controlled land throughout present-day Rhode Island. In 1675 the Narragansett boasted as many as four thousand warriors,[3] great supplies of wampum, and the ability to construct impressive wartime fortifications. Benefiting from Roger Williams' example, the English showed great respect for the commercial enterprise and military might of the Narragansett, making for peaceful relations between the colonists and natives in Rhode Island. The Wampanoag and Narragansett were less cordial, carrying on sporadic warfare in the early and mid-seventeenth century. By the time of King Philip's War, however, the encroaching English threat would bind these two native peoples more closely together.

The Native American presence throughout central Massachusetts was less cohesive than in either Wampanoag or Narragansett territories, but was equally important to the events of King Philip's War. Central Massachusetts was occupied primarily by the Nipmuc, which included the Nashaway, located along the Nashua River near present-day Lancaster; the Quaboag, who made their home along the Quaboag River and Pond near Brookfield; the Quinsigamond, near Worcester; the Nipnet, around present-day Grafton; and the Pegan, near the towns of Dudley, Webster, Douglas, and Oxford.[4] The Nipmuc traditionally had been allied with both the Narragansett and the Wampanoag, and their relations with the latter were particularly strong on the eve of King Philip's War. Further west, the Pocumtuck occupied land along the Connecticut River Valley. Among this group, the Norwottock (near Northampton) and the Agawam (near Springfield) played vital roles in the war.

The Abenaki included the eastern Abenaki of Maine and the western Abenaki of New Hampshire and Vermont. Among the former were the Penobscot, Casco, Sheepscot, Passamaquoddy, and Androscoggin, all of whom would be caught up in King Philip's War. The western Abenaki included the Pennacook, who had their main camps along the Merrimack River from Lowell, Massachusetts, to Concord, New Hampshire; the Pigwacket, who resided near Fryeburg, Maine; the Sokoki, who lived along the Connecticut River; and the Squakeag, who held territory near Northfield, Massachusetts.

Several other groups of Native Americans had a profound influence on the outcome of King Philip's War. The Mohegan of eastern Connecticut fought gallantly in the war on the side of the English, whose ally they had been for many years. Less visible but still critical to the outcome of the war were the Mohawk, a member of the Iroquois nation. Based in upstate New York, the Mohawk were universally dreaded by New England's native population. The Mohawk War (1663–1680) consisted of random and violent incursions by the Mohawk into western New England, forcing the Nipmuc,

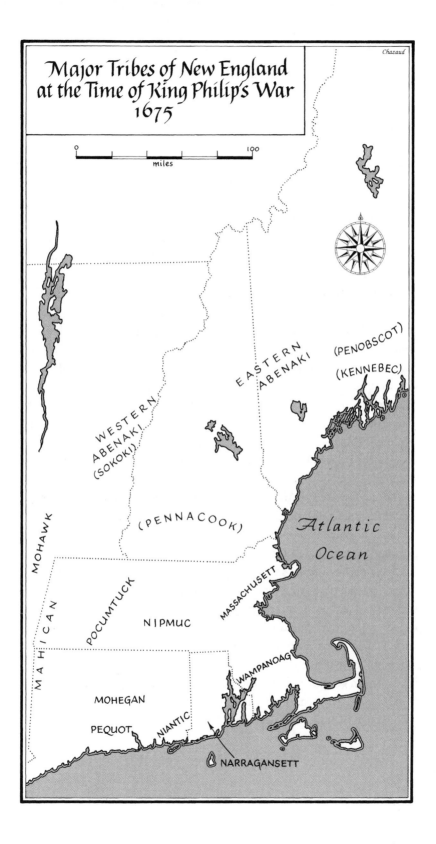

Major Tribes of New England
at the Time of King Philip's War
1675

Chazaud

0   100
miles

EASTERN ABENAKI

(PENOBSCOT)

(KENNEBEC)

WESTERN ABENAKI (SOKOKI)

(PENNACOOK)

MOHAWK

Atlantic Ocean

MASSACHUSETT

MAHICAN

POCUMTUCK

NIPMUC

WAMPANOAG

MOHEGAN

PEQUOT

NIANTIC

NARRAGANSETT

Abenaki, and Connecticut Valley tribes to fight wars on two fronts against two enemies in 1675 and 1676. Had the Mohawk remained neutral during King Philip's War or joined with the Wampanoag against the English, the outcome might have been much different.

Wampanoag relations with the English under Massasoit had been generally peaceful, in part because Massasoit had been instrumental in ensuring the well-being of the Plymouth colonists. In 1622 the sachem had visited Plymouth and negotiated a treaty that would guarantee the colonists the security necessary to establish their settlement. In return, the Wampanoag secured a new ally against the Narragansett.

The strength of this treaty rested initially on the fact that both parties to it were so weak. The Pilgrims arrived in the New World fundamentally unprepared to transplant their own culture on its shores. Historian Francis Jennings believes that, had the Europeans truly discovered pristine wilderness (as North America is apt to be romanticized), "then it might still be so today, for neither the technology nor the social organization of Europe in the sixteenth and seventeenth centuries had the capacity to maintain, of its own resources, outpost colonies thousands of miles from home."[5] For their part, the Wampanoag had been devastated by European disease in the years prior to the Pilgrim's landing, leaving them susceptible to Narragansett conquest.

Indeed, few Native American groups in New England escaped the ravages of European disease, perhaps the single "import" that did more than any other to shape Indian-English relations prior to King Philip's War. One historian has concluded that southern New England's native population may have declined from 90,000 in 1600 to 10,750 in 1675.[6] The Massachusett, a tribe occupying territory around present-day Boston, saw their warriors reduced from three thousand to three hundred in the sixty years preceding the war.[7] These losses were at perhaps twice the rate that the Black Plague killed Europeans in the fourteenth century. This decimated population base distorted every aspect of relations among the various Native American groups, and relations between the natives and the Europeans.

The peace between English and Indian was also supported by the elaborate system of trade that developed throughout the seventeenth century.

European traders were navigating Narragansett Bay by the early 1500s, and by the late sixteenth century hundreds of European ships were sailing into these waters each year for the purpose of trading, fishing, and exploring. The Narragansett came to prize European-manufactured goods for their superior design and usefulness and as status symbols.[8] In return the Europeans demanded furs, encouraging the Narragansett to deemphasize their aboriginal crafts in favor of commercial hunting. By the early seventeenth century the beaver population along Narragansett Bay was depleted, prompting the Narragansett to strengthen their commercial ties with inland native groups capable of providing beaver pelts. The furs continued to flow, more European goods were acquired, and the Narragansett became wealthy "middlemen."[9] Before long some of the European goods that had once been luxuries came to be considered necessities.

The Narragansett also took advantage of their long coastline to exploit the manufacture of wampum, white and purple beads made from shells and used as currency by both native and English. As the seventeenth century progressed, the Narragansett became the "southern mintmasters,"[10] a sign of further dislocation from their traditional way of life. As long as European demand for beaver pelts remained steady and the value of wampum held at the trading post, the Narragansett (and other New England natives) grew prosperous and powerful.

By the middle of the seventeenth century, however, a shift in European clothing styles reduced the demand for imported beaver pelts. This decline lead to the devaluation of wampum. Suddenly the Narragansett found themselves victims of changing fashions on a continent thousands of miles away. The demand for pelts never disappeared, but in a relatively short time the Narragansett role as important trading partners to the English diminished. The colonists increasingly sought not what the Narragansett (and other native peoples) could provide from the land, but the land itself. This radical shift in what had once been a cooperative relationship, more than any other single factor, would eventually lead them to war.

In Maine, a different but equally disastrous economic displacement was occurring among the Abenaki. As the English placed their trading posts in the choice coastal areas of the region, the Abenaki were rapidly driven inland from their traditional fishing grounds and clam beds. This placed an emphasis on hunting, which became an important source of both trade and sustenance. To improve their efficiency the Abenaki gave up their traditional weapons to adopt English firearms. Once the Abenaki were dependent on English technology for the tools of their livelihood, the English gained an important cultural advantage.[11]

The adoption of English weapons by the Indian was commonplace throughout New England. By the start of King Philip's War, most native warriors had flintlock muskets or carbines,[12] as opposed to their more traditional bow and arrow weaponry. Because the English were slower in abandoning their inferior matchlocks[13] and less likely to use their weapons in the daily procurement of food, natives were often more adept with European technology than the English themselves. In addition, the colonists were wedded to European military practices, including the use of single shot and the reliance on volleys,[14] both ill-suited to wilderness warfare. In *The Skulking Way of War*, Patrick Malone notes that "It would take months of defeat before the colonists would admit that the Indians' way of employing muskets in warfare was clearly better than their own."[15]

Over time the native became proficient at repairing English firearms. The Narragansett had their own forge, and the skill to use it. When colonial soldiers raided the native camp at present-day Turner's Falls, Massachusetts, they found and destroyed two forges. Only the ability to manufacture gunpowder eluded the Indian, and it was not until 1676 that the colonists themselves were able to establish a successful gunpowder factory at present-day Milton, Massachusetts.

While New England's Indians eagerly adopted firearms, other aspects of English culture were more at odds with traditional Native American society. Stray farm animals regularly damaged Indian crops and at times seemed intentionally sent to drive the natives from their homes; in particular, cattle required enormous tracts of land and, even when properly fenced by the English, constantly threatened the natives' traditional homelands. Alcohol was a constant source of friction between the two worlds, and some of the more unscrupulous English came to use alcohol as an advantage in their business dealings. The zeal with which English clergy attempted to convert the Indian to Christianity, although only marginally successful, ultimately weakened traditional native culture, drew men from the native community, and threatened the leadership of the *powaws* (spiritual leaders) and sachems. Some of those natives who converted — so-called Christian Indians or Praying Indians — provided invaluable service to the colonial militias during the war. The great majority, however, were mercilessly persecuted by their English neighbors and the colonial governments. By March 1676, in the panic caused by heavy colonial losses, four hundred innocent Christian Indians were forcibly removed to Deer Island in Boston Harbor, where conditions were so wretched that many died of hunger and exposure.

THE QUEST FOR LAND

In *Flintlock and Tomahawk*, Douglas Leach described what an observer might have seen in 1675 had he been able to view New England from the air:

> He would have been most vividly impressed by the almost unbroken expanse of forest which lay over all the land like a shaggy carpet. Here and there the monotonous wilderness was broken by a few acres of cleared land and a small cluster of houses — a village set down in the middle of the forest. New England was a land of isolated villages and occasional towns, interconnected by a network of woodland paths which served as virtually the only means of access to most of the inland settlements.[16]

The "shaggy carpet" of forest, while magnificent, was something less than the dense and impenetrable wilderness of New England folklore. Many forests were set beside extensive open areas that, in places like Boston, might be entirely absent of trees. Indeed, the diversity of the land was remarkable, ranging from open oak woodlands, to wet lowlands, to so-called quaking bogs of densely matted moss, to the sandy soils of the coast, which featured oyster beds a mile in length and clam banks so dense that a person traversing them was showered with spouting water. The

English who settled in New England were struck with the richness of the land—which seemed designed specifically to produce wealth—and the paradox posed by the native, who seemed to live in poverty: "How could a land be so rich and a people so poor?" [17]

Of course, the Wampanoag, Narragansett, Nipmuc, and Abenaki felt anything but poor. As Indian men hunted and fished the land, leaving their women to the domestic tasks and the planting of beans and corn, they wondered why Englishmen took on the female role of working their fields. Meanwhile, English farmers saw hunting and fishing more as leisure time activities, branding the Indian men as lazy and unworthy to "own" the land. English villages were fixed throughout the year, helping to develop a sense of European permanence and ownership; Indian villages prospered precisely by moving with the seasons, establishing a permanence with the environment that the English were unable to comprehend. Ironically, the Indian practice of burning the land, so misunderstood by the English, led directly in its new growth to the abundance of animal species that were so impressive to the English.

These profound misunderstandings in how the New England native and the New England European viewed the land, and the wealth that the land represented, underlay the tensions leading to King Philip's War. Historian William Cronon summarized it as the struggle over two ways of living, expressed "in how two peoples conceived of property, wealth, and boundaries on the landscape." [18] In *Ecological Revolutions*, environmental historian Carolyn Merchant believes that by the time of King Philip's War, an ecological revolution had taken place in southern New England, one that disrupted the Indian gathering-hunting and agriculture production with the introduction of new plants, new animals, fenced lands, and fur and timber extractions. [19]

Thus, while the impact of disease, trade, firearms, religion, and alcohol were all important in defining the English-native relationship, it is impossible to escape the fact that New England Indians were victims of colonial Americans' inexhaustible appetite for territory and expansion. Just two years after the Pilgrims landed, Governor Bradford was bemoaning the fact that his fellow colonists desired additional farmland away from the close-knit Plymouth settlement; by 1627, a second grant of land was made to nearly every resident of Plymouth to satisfy the thirst for expansion.[20] Roger Williams saw the same "depraved appetite after . . . great portions of land . . . This was one of the great gods of New England."[21] Eugene Aubrey Stratton wrote, "Though Separatist and Puritan alike had powerful religious motivation to persuade them to immigrate to New England, anyone who underestimates the importance of land as a like enticement fails to comprehend the value system of these seventeenth-century Englishmen."[22]

Many of the Englishmen who planned and carried out King Philip's War were intimately involved in the pursuit and development of territory. Benjamin Church, Josiah Winslow, and Constant Southworth had designs on land at Sakonnet (Little Compton, Rhode Island); Daniel Gookin, Ephraim Curtis, Daniel Henchman, and Thomas Prentice were involved at Quinsigamond (Worcester, Massachusetts); John Winthrop, Richard Smith, Josiah Winslow, George Denison, and Edward Hutchinson were part of a company attempting to secure lands in Narragansett country.[23] These groups included some of the most prominent and influential leaders in the colonies.

The English were adamant, at least in form, about securing land from New England's natives in a legal manner. Josiah Winslow wrote in 1676, "I think I can clearly say, that before these present troubles broke out, the English did not possess one foot of land in this colony but what was fairly obtained by honest purchase of the Indian proprietor."[24] Some modern historians have echoed these sentiments.[25] However, Francis Jennings and others have identified countless fraudulent methods the colonists employed to exact a seemingly legal transfer of property from an unwilling Indian. Among these were the imposition of absurd fines so that a native would have to forfeit his lands in lieu of payment; allowing livestock to ruin native crops so that the land was "voluntarily" vacated; threats of violence; and inducing drunkenness so that a native would sign a deed he was unable to understand.[26]

If none of these ruses worked, an Englishman desiring a piece of property might simply scout around until he could find a sachem willing to sell it, rightfully or not. In 1633 the New Netherland Dutch purchased land at

Hartford, Connecticut, from the grand sachem of the Pequot Indians; not wanting to lose such an attractive parcel, Plymouth authorities found the sachem who had been driven from the land by the Pequot and purchased the same tract from him.[27] These activities—sometimes honest misunderstandings—were more often nothing less than theft, justified by the Reverend Increase Mather, Boston's minister, who believed that the Puritans lived among "the heathen people . . . whose land the Lord God of our Fathers hath given us for a rightful possession."[28]

Pressure to acquire land and secure new commercial opportunities in the decades before King Philip's War was exacerbated by New England's first baby boom, the result of high fertility and relatively low mortality rates in the 1630s and 1640s. Young Englishmen (now "Americans") coming of age were anxious to secure their place in the New World. A generation after the Pilgrims landed, settlement and incorporation began changing the face of the Native American homeland. Dartmouth (Massachusetts), Kittery (Maine), and York (Maine) were established in 1652, Northampton (Massachusetts) in 1656, Marlboro (Massachusetts) in 1660, Hadley (Massachusetts) in 1661, Westerly (Rhode Island) and Westfield (Massachusetts) in 1669, Simsbury (Connecticut) in 1670, Brookfield (Massachusetts) in 1673, and Framingham (Massachusetts) in 1675. In other areas not formally established until later, like Deerfield (Massachusetts), Little Compton (Rhode Island), and a host of Maine settlements, the English were setting up trading posts, clearing fields, importing livestock, building homes, and making their presence felt among the Indians.

On the eve of the war, Massachusetts Bay's frontier included Groton, Lancaster, Marlboro, Mendon, and Wrentham. Worcester (with six or seven families) and Brookfield (with twenty) were isolated settlements dependent on ancient Indian trails for their ties with the outside world. Even the large, well-established cities of today were fledgling communities: Springfield had five hundred people, Northampton about the same, and Providence about six hundred residents.

Present-day Maine, which did not become independent of Massachusetts until 1820, was a "sparsely settled fringe of coast"[29] stretching from Exeter and Dover (New Hampshire) to the settlement at Pemaquid, east of the Damariscotta River and referred to by Hubbard as the "utmost boundary of New England."[30] There were perhaps five thousand English living in Maine on the eve of King Philip's War.[31]

In Plymouth Colony, the frontier outposts were Dartmouth, Rehoboth, and Swansea. Of particular note, Swansea was established in 1671 on the western frontier of Plymouth's lands, abutting Philip's homeland. The settlement's forty homes were connected with Plymouth by forty miles of Wampanoag trails. Commissioned in 1668 to import tax-free strong liquors and anxious to participate in the Atlantic and Caribbean trade, the town from its beginning had sought a deep-water port.[32] The Pokanoket land to the immediate south in present-day Bristol, Rhode Island, provided such an outlet. "With a port on Mount Hope capable of handling ocean-going ships," historian John Raymond Hall concludes, "Swansea was on the verge of riches. Only King Philip stood in the way."[33]

Rapid acquisition of land, the establishment of frontier communities, and constant friction between English and native prompted the development of a colonial militia system. By 1675 Massachusetts alone had some seventy-three organized companies. Each county maintained a dozen foot companies and one cavalry, while the counties of Suffolk, Middlesex, and Essex fielded a combined cavalry company. Each foot company contained about seventy privates and each cavalry about fifty.[34] Muster days were held on a regular basis, although drilling could not compensate for the fact that New England's defense was dependent on farmers unaccustomed to wilderness warfare. Leading the companies were men like Captain Daniel Henchman, a schoolteacher, and Captain William Turner, a tailor. Some veterans of New England's Pequot War and of England's Civil War would assume commands during King Philip's War, but in most respects, leaders in the colonial militia were as ill-equipped to lead an army as their troops were to fight a war.

The need for mutual support had also led to formation of the United Colonies in 1643. Representatives of Plymouth, Massachusetts Bay, and Connecticut met on a regular basis to maintain order among their colonies and, increasingly prior to 1675, address rumors of Indian conspiracies and provide for the common defense.

EVENTS LEADING TO KING PHILIP'S WAR

Massasoit's oldest son, Wamsutta, thus faced a perplexing world when he became sachem of the Pokanoket at the death of his father. The English in 1661 were far stronger than that struggling band of colonists Massasoit had befriended at Plymouth. The relationship between English and Native American had grown inordinately more complex over forty years. Many of the important personal ties forged among men like Massasoit and Stephen Hopkins, Edward Winslow, and William Bradford had vanished. The old guard was changing on both sides, and with it a sense of history and mutual struggle that had helped to keep the peace.

Shortly after becoming sachem, Wamsutta requested of Plymouth authorities that he and his younger brother be given English names. The request was likely made to signify a new and important period in Wamsutta's life and to assist him and his brother in moving more freely between English and Wampanoag societies.[35] Soon after, Wamsutta became Alexander, and his brother Metacom became Philip.[36]

Alexander quickly proved himself to be more independent than his father. He was first rumored to be discussing war plans with the Narragansett. The English had been haunted by such tales of coordinated Indian uprisings from the moment they stepped ashore in America. Even more disturbing to Plymouth Colony, however, was Alexander's sale of land to the outcast colonies living in Rhode Island. When news of such dealings reached Plymouth, the General Court demanded that Alexander appear before them to explain his activities. When Alexander balked, colonial authorities sent Major Josiah Winslow, the eldest son of Governor Edward Winslow, to force the issue.

In July 1662, Winslow took a small party of men to Alexander's hunting lodge near Halifax, Massachusetts. Winslow surprised Alexander a short distance from the main camp and forced the sachem and some of his party to march to Duxbury under armed guard. The message delivered to the sachem—"if he stir'd or refused to go, he was a dead man"[37]—was very much in keeping with the Puritan tradition of threat and violence toward the Native American.

This marker, placed by the Halifax Historical Society not far from the shore of Monponsett Lakes, designates the approximate site of Wamsutta's capture in 1662 by eight or ten well-armed colonial soldiers under Major Josiah Winslow. (Eric Schultz)

Next we encounter one of the great mysteries of American colonial history. Alexander's band was forcibly marched from Halifax to Duxbury, and then on to Marshfield. After being interrogated there by Plymouth officials Alexander fell ill, but departed for a visit to Massachusetts Bay Colony. Within a few days he returned to Winslow's home at Marshfield, where his illness became incapacitating. Alexander started toward his home at Mount Hope but died along the way, "before he got half way home."[38] The young sachem's men carried his lifeless body to Mount Hope on their shoulders.

No one has ever adequately explained how a young, apparently healthy man like Alexander could sicken and die so quickly. Hubbard opined that "such was the pride and height of his spirit, that the very surprizal of him, so raised his choler and indignation, that it put him into a fever, which notwithstanding all possible means that could be used, seemed mortal."[39] The Pokanoket, including Philip, believed that the English had poisoned Alexander.[40] Indeed, this may have been closer to the truth than the English themselves could imagine. It seems that a Plymouth Colony physician named Fuller, attempting to cure Alexander's malady, administered a "working physic" to the sachem.[41] Maurice Robbins quotes a modern physician who has advanced the theory that Alexander had appendicitis; if so, the "working physic" prescribed by Dr. Fuller may have inadvertently killed the sachem.[42]

More than a decade after the event, sometime around 1674, the minister at Plymouth, John Cotton, wrote to Increase Mather about the circumstances surrounding Alexander's death. Cotton quoted Major William Bradford (son of the governor), who claimed to have been present with Winslow at Alexander's capture.[43] In the revised story, Alexander had freely consented to accompany Winslow, survived the questioning by Plymouth authorities without ill effect, and returned sick to Winslow's home only after having departed Plymouth for Massachusetts Bay. This version, as Cotton related it, was probably an attempt to counter claims that Alexander had been poisoned.[44]

As Alexander was laid to rest about July 1662,[45] Philip became sachem of the Pokanoket. We can only guess how this young man of perhaps twenty-four years might have felt, his father's memory still fresh in mind, watching the erosion of Wampanoag land to a new, contentious generation of English, believing his brother had been murdered by Plymouth authorities, concerned about strained relations with his Narragansett neighbors, and feeling the great weight of his people looking to him for leadership in a time of crisis.

Five years later, in 1667, Philip was at the center of a war scare that had him rumored to be cooperating with the Dutch and French to launch an assault on the English settlers. Philip asserted his innocence and peace ensued. However, in the spring of 1671, Hugh Cole of Swansea informed Plymouth authorities that both Narragansett and Wampanoag again appeared to be readying for war. In April, Philip agreed reluctantly to meet at Taunton, Massachusetts, with representatives of the Plymouth and Massachusetts Bay colonies. At this meeting Philip signed the wholly unsatisfactory Taunton Agreement in which he confessed to planning an attack on English settlements and agreed to give up seventy weapons brought to the meeting, with the surrender of his remaining weapon cache to follow. Few historians today believe that Philip was doing anything but agreeing to English demands in the face of overwhelming pressure. However, the Taunton Agreement, and an agreement signed in September at Plymouth which obligated Philip to pay a fine for refusing to deliver the Wampanoag arsenal, undoubtedly led some Pokanoket warriors to question Philip's ability to resist the English. Hubbard recorded that

> one of his captains, of far better courage and resolution than himself, when he saw the cowardly temper and disposition, fling down his arms, calling him a white-liver'd cur, or to that purpose, and saying, that he would never own him again, or fight under him, and from that time hath turned to the English, and hath considered to this day a faithful and resolute soldier in this quarrel.[46]

While this scene may be apocryphal, the pressure on the young sachem to remain steadfast in the face of intolerable English demands must have been extraordinary.

The next four years were filled with uneasiness and rumor as a kind of "cold war" mentality developed. As one contemporary wrote, "So the English were afraid and Philip was afraid, and both increased in arms."[47] Events finally came to a head in June 1675 when three Wampanoag were brought to Plymouth to stand trial for the murder of John Sassamon. Sassamon was a Christian Indian who had fought alongside the English in the Pequot War, studied at Harvard, and taught at John Eliot's Indian village at Nemasket, near Middleboro, Massachusetts. In 1660 Sassamon returned to Mount Hope to become a counselor to Alexander, and in 1671 was with Philip at the signing of the Taunton Agreement. Few men witnessed so many of the critical events presaging King Philip's War nor traveled as easily between the Native American and English worlds as John Sassamon.

Shortly before the outbreak of hostilities, Philip had dismissed Sassamon from his service, possibly out of distrust for his ties with the English or over a disputed land transaction in which Sassamon had tried to dupe the sachem. In any event, Sassamon's departure was sudden, and shortly there-

While John Eliot was considered a friend to New England's natives, the Christian proselytizing he came to represent was an often unwelcome complication in the Indian-English relationship. (Courtesy of the Haffenreffer Museum of Anthropology, Brown University)

after he came to reside on twenty-seven acres at Assawompsett (in present-day Lakeville, Massachusetts). In January 1675, he visited Governor Josiah Winslow at his home in Marshfield, Massachusetts, with a dire warning that the Wampanoag were planning to wage war against the English. Sassamon returned home and a few days later was found dead under the ice at Assawompsett Pond.

At first the death was deemed accidental, but by June a Christian Indian named Patuckson came forward to testify that he had seen three Wampanoag—Tobias (one of Philip's counselors), Tobias' son Wampapaquan, and Mattachunnamo—murder Sassamon. The fact that Patuckson owed a gambling debt to Tobias notwithstanding, the three were accused, according to Plymouth Colony records, of "laying violent hands on [John Sassamon] . . . and striking him, or twisting his necke, until hee was dead . . . [and] did cast his dead body through the hole of the iyce."[48]

Next came one of colonial America's most infamous courtroom dramas. Douglas Leach describes the "usually placid town of Plymouth . . . alive with excitement"[49] as small groups of colonists met to discuss the upcoming trial: "At the appointed hour the members of the court, sitting in the wooden town house which the settlers had constructed on the slopes above Plymouth Harbor,"[50] marched the three accused Wampanoag before the court. Each denied his guilt and the trial began. Increase Mather, who may not have known fairness to the Indians had it perched on his Bible, noted, "They had a fair trial for their lives, and that no appearance of wrong might be, Indians as well as English sat upon the jury."[51] While there was, in fact, a jury of twelve Englishmen supplemented by an auxiliary jury of perhaps four Indians[52], nobody today is quite sure as to how the deliberations worked. The foreman, however, was clear in saying that the verdict was unanimous among white and Indian. Francis Jennings, who believed the Indians were added to the jury precisely to drive a wedge between Philip's pagans and Plymouth's converted Indians, opined that "this was a show trial staged for political purposes from beginning to end."[53]

Mather went on to note that "only at last Tobias's son confessed, that his father and the other Indian killed Sassamon, but that himself had no hand in it, only stood by and saw them do it."[54] Some twenty years later, Increase Mather's son, Cotton, embellished the story with some of the finest forensic evidence a seventeenth-century Puritan prosecutor could offer: "It was remarkable, that one Tobias, a Counsellor of King Philip's whom they suspected as the author of this murder, approaching to the dead body, it would still fall a bleeding afresh, as if it had newly been slain."[55]

Cotton Mather also went on to describe the confession of Wampapaquan,

John Leverett, governor of Massachusetts, never took to the field during King Philip's War, though he was a veteran of Cromwell's campaigns and active in setting colonial military strategy. (Courtesy of the Peabody Essex Museum)

which can be seen as either a divine act of God or a Puritan ruse to exact a confession from an innocent and unwilling suspect. With ropes around their necks, the three Wampanoag were "successively turned off the ladder at the gallows"[56] on the eighth of June. Tobias and Mattachunnamo died instantly, but Wamapapaquan happened to "break or flip the rope,"[57] hitting the ground to his, and probably his onlookers', amazement. At that point he was questioned again, and seeing no way to further harm his already dead father, undoubtedly felt he might save his own life by delivering the blame Puritan authorities so anxiously sought. (Perhaps, as Leach wonders, he was offered a reprieve in return for his testimony.) In any event, having pointed the finger at Tobias and Mattachunnamo, Wampapaquan apparently enjoyed a month's reprieve.[58] In the end, however, his fate was sealed; he was shot[59] and Puritan authorities completed their farce.

To Philip and his people, as well as many of the English, the trial was a flagrant miscarriage of justice and further proof that maintaining an amicable, respectful relationship between the natives and the English was impossible. Despite some last-ditch political maneuvering on the part of both Plymouth and Rhode Island to mollify Philip, the execution of his people set in motion a war which, by June 1675, neither side could halt.

The attempt by John Easton to maintain peace between the Wampanoag and Plymouth Colony was particularly instructive. Easton was a Quaker and former governor of Rhode Island who captured in his writings a perspective on King Philip's War rarely voiced in Puritan literature. A week before the first bloodshed, Easton met with Philip to plead for moderation, and even suggested the idea of naming the governor of New York and an "Indian King" to serve as arbitrators in the dispute. In response, Philip outlined the list of grievances against the English, reminding Easton that "when the English first came, their king's father [Massasoit] was as a great man, and the English as a little child; he constrained other Indians from wronging the English, and gave them corn and showed them how to plant . . . and had let them have a 100 times more land than now the king had for his own people. But their king's brother [Alexander], when he was king, came miserably to die by being forced to court, as they judge poisoned. And another grievance was, if 20 of their honest Indians testified that an Englishman had done them wrong, it was as nothing; and if but one of their worst Indians testified against any Indian of their king, when it pleased the English it was sufficient. Another grievance was, when their king sold land, the English would say, it was more than they agreed to, and a writing must be proven against them, and some of their kings had done wrong to

The most famous of many King Philip images was done by Paul Revere in 1772 (upper left). It was two hundred years later that historian Brad Swan, visiting the American Antiquarian Society in Worcester, Massachusetts, spotted "Four Kings of Canada," a display of mezzotints first published in London in 1710 shortly after a visit by these Iroquois sachems. In comparing Revere's engraving with two of the Mohawk chiefs, Ho Nee Yeath and Sa Ga Yeath, Swan realized that Revere's Philip was a fabrication that borrowed heavily from their images, including shoes, capes, weapons, postures, and faces. (All images courtesy of the John Carter Brown Library, Brown University)

Ho Nee Yeath Portrait   Sa Ga Yeath Portrait

sell so much . . . the English made them drunk and then cheated them in bargains . . . another grievance, the English cattle and horse still increased . . . they could not keep their corn from being spoiled, they never being used to fence.[60]

Easton noted that Philip found the offer of arbitration appealing, although it was apparently never proposed to the English authorities, and that Philip left their meeting saying that "the English should do to them as they did when they were too strong for the English."[61]

WHO WAS KING PHILIP?

In Easton's writing, we have a singular opportunity to glimpse Philip the man, one of those rare instances when myth does not obscure the sachem's persona. Easton, however, was a lone voice: Philip's larger-than-life presence in colonial New England, the confusion and panic of war, and the one-sided perspective of Puritan historians, have led over the centuries to magnificent inventions of fact. Some relate to how Philip looked and some to his character and disposition. Philip today lends his name to places he never visited and items he never owned; like the Mayflower, whose "authentic" articles multiplied so quickly through the years that they would "freight an Indianman of good tonnage,"[62] artifacts associated with Philip continue to appear long after his death. Discovering the real Philip is a complex task, while debunking the fantasy surrounding him is a lesson in why the best historians are undyingly skeptical.

Perhaps the most famous portrait of King Philip was that done in 1772 by Paul Revere for Ezra Stiles' edition of Benjamin Church's *Entertaining History*. Revere's engraving of the sachem has been deplored throughout the years as being "hideous,"[63] a "neurotic pygmy,"[64] a "grotesque effigy,"[65] and a "terror to children."[66] Antiquarians, who knew that Revere was born sixty years after Philip's death, wondered about his source for the engraving and advised caution as to its authenticity.[67] Indeed, Revere had a reputation during his lifetime for "borrowing" from the work of others, once going so far as to duplicate his brother-in-law's work while crafting his own famous engraving of the Boston Massacre.[68]

Almost two centuries after Revere completed Philip's portrait, historian Bradford Swan was visiting the American Antiquarian Society in Worcester when, Swan explained, he "chanced to wander into one of the balcony alcoves where there were on display mezzotints of the so-called 'Four Kings of Canada,' first published in London in 1710, shortly after the visit of these Iroquois sachems to that city."[69] Struck by the similarity to Revere's engraving of Philip, Swan compared the works and found the detail to be nearly identical. In his monograph, *An Indian's an Indian*, Swan demonstrated that Revere's Philip was a combination of three engravings: two Mohawk chiefs (the dreaded enemy of the Wampanoag), and a group of Ohio Indians originally painted by Benjamin West in 1764. By reading Benjamin Church's book—or at least the passages concerning Philip—Revere embellished Philip's outfit to meet the requirements of the text. Revere's final product, it turned out, had no more resemblance to Philip than if Revere had engraved the sachem from his own imagination.

As an indication that he was, at least, impartial in his artistic theft, Revere engraved a portrait of Benjamin Church at about the same time that was simply a copy of the English poet Charles Churchill, with a powder horn hung around his neck for good measure.[70]

Other illustrations of Philip throughout the years have been better received than Revere's engraving, though none brings us any closer to the real Philip. The simple truth is that not a single likeness of Philip has survived from anyone who ever met or saw him. The few written descriptions we have passed down to us, like Church's "doleful, great, naked, dirty beast,"[71] paint a better picture of the passions of war than they do of Philip.

In fact, we have no satisfactory likenesses of any of the important Algonquian leaders who participated in King Philip's War. The Puritans had little use for painting in general, and less for the painting of such mundane, worldly subjects as themselves and their neighbors. Historians believe that the first portrait of an American Indian painted by a European is probably that of Ninigret II, completed in 1681,[72] after all of the important Algonquian leaders of King Philip's War had died. A statue of Ninigret II's father, Ninigret, who led his people during King Philip's War, is located on

Bay Street at Watch Hill in Westerly, Rhode Island. Like Philip, however, Ninigret was the victim of artistic license: the statue was sculpted in Paris in 1914 and used as its model an Indian from Buffalo Bill's Wild West Show, visiting France at the time.[73]

The character of Philip is even less understood than his appearance. The Reverend William Hubbard, writing during and shortly after the war, in a work sanctioned by colonial authorities, labeled him a "savage Miscreant with Envy and Malice against the English."[74] A second Puritan voice, the Reverend Increase Mather, concurred, reminding his readers that Philip was one of the "Heathen People amongst whom we live, and whose Land the Lord God of our Fathers hath given to us for a rightful Possession."[75] The antiquarian Samuel Drake, who edited both Hubbard's and Mather's works in the mid-nineteenth century, found "that there is ample testimony to his [Philip's] cowardice; being always the first to fly when he fancied his Enemies near."[76]

In time, opposing views began to emerge, in part a result of America's own struggle against the British during the American Revolution and the country's newfound identity. In the early nineteenth century Washington Irving penned *Philip of Pokanoket*, in which he characterized the colonists as being "moved to hostility by the lust of conquest." Irving wondered "how many intellectual beings were hunted from the earth, how many brave and noble hearts, of nature's sterling coinage, were broken down and trampled in the dust!"[77] Philip himself, Irving opined, was "the most distinguished of a number of contemporary Sachems . . . who made the most generous stuff of which human nature is capable, fighting to the last gasp in the cause of their country."[78] Irving concludes with a description of Philip that would be equally befitting of George Washington:

> He was a patriot attached to his native soil—a prince true to his subjects, and indignant of their wrongs—a soldier, daring in battle, firm in adversity, patient of fatigue, of hunger, or every variety of bodily suffering, and ready to perish in the cause he had espoused. Proud of heart, and with an untamable love of natural liberty . . . with heroic

qualities and bold achievements that would have graced a civilized warrior.[79]

The Reverend William Apes, himself a Native American, delivered a eulogy on King Philip at the Odeon on Federal Street in Boston in 1836 which echoed Irving's sentiments. In it, Apes compared Philip favorably to Philip of Macedon, Napoleon, and Washington, calling the sachem "the greatest man that ever lived upon the American slopes."[80] This view, while not necessarily more accurate than Puritan opinion, was indicative of a far more sympathetic interpretation of Philip. By the time of the United States' centennial, Philip's standing as a noble patriot was secure: Antiquarian Samuel Adams Drake wrote, "In his own time he was the public enemy whom any should slay; in ours he is considered a martyr to the idea of liberty not differing from that of Tell and Toussaint, whom we call heroes."[81]

By the early twentieth century, the Reverend George Bodge was exploring a more moderate ground, turning away from both Puritan myopia and noble savagery. Bodge believed that Philip was "a leader of consummate skill, in bringing together the unwieldy and most unwilling forces, and pushing forward other bands of other tribes to bear the brunt and dangers which his own plotting had brought upon them."[82] By 1958, Douglas Leach, whose history of King Philip's War was the first thorough accounting of the conflict in over half a century, wrote that Philip was "more futile than heroic, more misguided than villainous . . . a proud man embittered by the humiliations imposed upon him through superior strength."[83] This interpretation, which had the advantage of avoiding supernatural evil or goodness as explanations for Philip's actions, was bound to run its course. In the mid-1970s a new, revisionist tide was crashing in, characterizing Philip as "the innocent victim of Puritan skullduggeries,"[84] trampled by the so-called Second Puritan Conquest, a willful and illegal land grab.

We are told by some historians that Philip actively sought war and by others that he cried when it came; that he was a valiant warrior riding a black steed into the thick of battle and that he hung back like a coward and was always the first to fly; that he was a master diplomat with wide influence during the war and that he was a minor player pushed to the sidelines throughout most the conflict. Like his portraits, descriptions of Philip's character often more adequately reflected the bias of the times than the life of a real, flesh-and-blood man struggling to adapt to his rapidly changing world.

Philip's dramatic escape from his Mount Hope homeland early in the war ensured that the conflict would spread beyond Plymouth colony to the Massachusetts Bay colony. (Courtesy of the Haffenreffer Museum of Anthropology, Brown University)

· Chapter 2 ·

The Outbreak of War in Southeastern New England

MANY ENGLISH SAW KING PHILIP'S WAR as the long anticipated united Indian uprising. We know today that no single, coordinated plan existed, and that individual sachems experienced great difficulty in holding their people together as the war erupted. While instrumental in the first attacks against the English, Philip himself was unable to draw the Narragansett into the war and had a more limited role in planning native military activity than contemporary Englishmen believed. Awashonks, the squaw sachem of the Sakonnet, was visited by six of Philip's men whose mission it was to convince her people to join with the Pokanoket. Awashonks' response was to send for her English friend, Benjamin Church, who engaged Philip's men in a heated discussion designed to maintain Sakonnet loyalty to the English.[1] Throughout the exchange Awashonks was clearly torn between the desire to side with the English and her fear that the Sakonnet would be split by such a decision. A short time later Church met with Weetamoe, the squaw sachem of the Pocasset, who reported that most of her people had gone to Philip's war dances "against her will . . . and she much feared that there would be war."[2] In the Connecticut River Valley, both the Norwottock and Agawam remained neutral until English military bumbling, or the absurdity of English demands, drove them into the arms of their warring neighbors. William Hubbard wrote that "many of the Indians were in a kind of maze, not knowing well what to do; sometimes ready to stand for the English [and] sometimes inclining to strike in with Philip."[3] For their part, many Christian Indians remained loyal to the English, as did the Wampanoag on Cape Cod. The specter of a single, united Indian conspiracy was less a product of Philip's grand design than of English ignorance and fear.

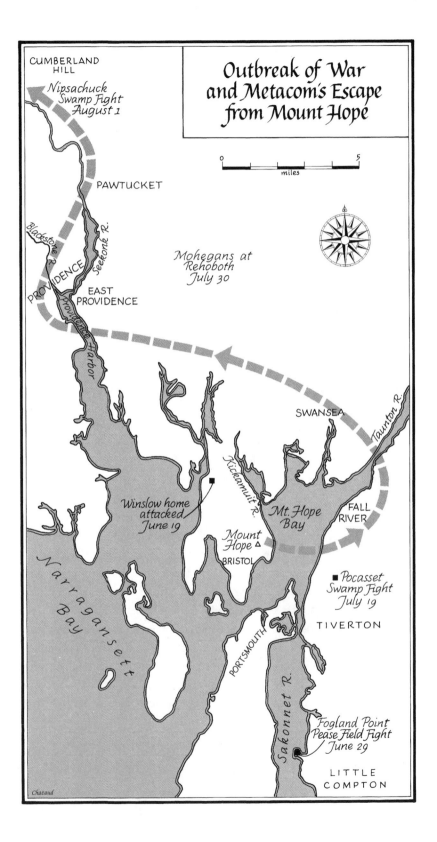

Outbreak of War and Metacom's Escape from Mount Hope

CUMBERLAND HILL

Nipsachuck Swamp Fight August 1

PAWTUCKET

Blackstone R.

Seeronk R.

PROVIDENCE

EAST PROVIDENCE

Providence Harbor

Mohegans at Rehoboth July 30

SWANSEA

Taunton R.

Kickamuit R.

Winslow home attacked June 19

Mt. Hope Bay

FALL RIVER

Mount Hope △

BRISTOL

Pocasset Swamp Fight July 19

Narragansett Bay

TIVERTON

PORTSMOUTH

Sakonnet R.

Fogland Point Pease Field Fight June 29

LITTLE COMPTON

Chazaud

0 miles 5

The English, sometimes accused by modern historians of concocting their own grand scheme to drive the Native Americans from their land, proved to be equally disunited. There was no coordinated effort to prepare for war. Defensive planning in the colonies was haphazard at best in the years after 1671,[4] so that garrisons—those fortified homes, meetinghouses, and blockhouses used for defense by the community—were sometimes inadequately maintained and deficient in number.[5] Throughout the war, bickering among the colonies concerning leadership, troop commitments, and supplies was endless. In 1676, for example, Connecticut threatened to withhold grain from the troops fighting in Massachusetts; in turn, Massachusetts threatened to withhold ammunition from Connecticut troops.[6]

On a larger scale, each colony eyed the other suspiciously over the Connecticut River valley settlements, ostensibly under Boston's administration but with great affinity for Hartford. Rhode Island feared both Massachusetts Bay's and Connecticut's designs on its territory. Settlers in Maine dreaded the heavy hand of Boston authorities and worked actively to maintain their independence. Plymouth was experiencing its own identity crisis as the settlements around Boston and Hartford overtook "the old colony" in population and wealth. Connecticut feared a land grab by the English from New York as much as it feared an Indian attack. New England's paranoia grew as land became more precious, the threat of French and Mohawk incursions mounted, and political leaders contemplated the unpredictable nature of the British Crown. Despite existence of the United Colonies, only the overwhelming loss of life and property during the war fostered true cooperation among the colonies.

The events of Sunday, June 20, 1675, set King Philip's War in motion. A band of Pokanoket, probably without Philip's approval,[7] looted several English homes in Swansea, setting two on fire and forcing the frightened settlers to flee. A messenger was immediately dispatched to Governor Winslow at Marshfield, who on June 21 and 22 sent orders to Bridgewater and Taunton to raise a force of about two hundred men for the protection of Swansea. Meanwhile, Swansea residents retreated to the Bourne garrison house at Mattapoiset, the Miles garrison house at the head of the Pokanoket peninsula, and one or two other protected locations.

Leading the troops assembled at Taunton was Major William Bradford. Here we are also introduced to one of the most dashing figures in King Philip's War, Benjamin Church, who had departed his settlement activity on Sakonnet Point (present-day Little Compton, Rhode Island) to chase rumors of war at Plymouth.[8] There he was drafted and sent south to Taunton.

Church, dubbed by Richard Slotkin and James Folsom "King of the Wild Frontier,"[9] was in some ways the prototype for future American literary heroes like Natty Bumpo and the more mythical aspects of Daniel Boone. Born at Plymouth in 1639, he grew in prominence as both a carpenter and land speculator, taking title in 1674 to property in the Sakonnet territory of present-day Little Compton, Rhode Island. Church was the only white settler there, and he quickly established a friendship with the Sakonnet's squaw sachem, Awashonks. This willingness to form personal relationships with Indians gave Church an advantage among his fellow military officers in incorporating native tactics, in navigating the forests and swamps of New England, and in enlisting natives to the English cause. It also cast suspicion on his advice among the English and, in Church's opinion, often cost him the recognition he deserved for his military prowess.

Church would be present at three of the war's most remarkable events, including the Great Swamp Fight, the death of Philip, and the capture of Anawan. His alter ego, Captain Samuel Moseley, known among his Massachusetts Bay troops for his hatred of and cruelty toward all Indians, was also present—in fact, in the lead—at the Great Swamp Fight, as well as Bloody Brook and other well-known events. Yet, it is Church and not Moseley (nor Appleton, Winslow, or the other notable English commanders) that we remember.

The simple reason is that Church, some forty years after King Philip's War, wrote about his exploits in a book, *Entertaining Passages Relating to Philip's War* (published in 1716). That book—a combination of Church's memory, his journals, and the editing of his son, Thomas—became a staple for King Philip's War students, and its depiction of the war elevated the author to heights certainly unrealized during the war. Historians Richard Slotkin and James Folsom remark, more than a bit facetiously, that in Church's book, "The important battles are the ones in which Church is involved, and only when Church is allowed to succeed does the war move toward an end."[10]

Church was thirty-seven when the war ended. He would go on to fight in several of the subsequent campaigns associated with the French and Indian Wars, develop lands in Pocasset (present-day Fall River, Massachusetts), and become one of the founders of Bristol, Rhode Island. He died in 1717 or 1718[11] after a fall from his horse and was buried with military honors at Little Compton, where his tombstone can be seen today. With the exception of Philip, Church is perhaps the best-known character in King Philip's War, and certainly the one to whom historians are most indebted.

While preparations to defend Swansea were proceeding, Boston authorities prepared to head off a full-scale Indian assault. One negotiating party led by a young trader named Ephraim Curtis traveled west into Nipmuc territory to meet with local sachems and elicit promises of loyalty. Curtis and his men passed through several Nipmuc villages but found each abandoned, a sure sign that something was wrong. Only by capturing a native was the party able to discover the whereabouts of the Nipmuc sachems. A tense encounter followed, and Curtis departed feeling that some progress had been made.

A second group composed of Captain Edward Hutchinson, Seth Perry, and William Powers headed south to Providence, Rhode Island, where they were joined by Roger Williams, whose common sense and respect for the Narragansett would be critical to maintaining peace. The four men departed Providence for present-day Wickford, Rhode Island, where Richard Smith maintained a trading post on Narragansett Bay. From there they traveled southwest to Worden's Pond (in present-day South Kingstown) where the Narragansett leadership, including sachems Ninigret and Quinnapin, met with them to discuss their intentions.

The third party, made up of Captains Thomas Savage, James Oliver, and Thomas Brattle, was given the unenviable task of meeting with Philip. This latter group would never accomplish this objective, for events at Swansea overtook Boston's diplomatic efforts.

There is reason to think that Philip and his warriors believed they could only win the war if the English fired the first shot,[12] which is apparently what happened. Different versions of the outbreak of violence in Swansea have survived the years, but among the most credible is that of the Quaker John Easton, whose *Relation* provided this account of events:

> In this time [Wednesday, June 23] sum indians fell a pilfering sum houses yt the English had left and an old Man and a lad going to one of these Houses did see three Indians run out thereof. The old Man bid the young Man shoot; so he did, and a Indian fell doune, but got away againe. It is reported yet sum Indians came to the gareson, asked why they shot the Indian. Thay asked wheter he was dead. The Indians said yea. English Lad saied it was no matter. The men indevered to inform them it was but an idell Lads Words but the Indians in haste went away and did not hearken to them.[13]

The following day the Pokanoket killed nine Swansea colonists in retribution. Savage's party discovered the bodies of two of these men, ending all hope for a peaceful solution.

By June 24, Major Bradford had arrived at Swansea, as had the Plymouth field commander, Captain James Cudworth. Their strategy to defend Swansea's garrison houses protected only those inside; consequently, Swansea residents were ambushed in several other locations (often trying to retrieve food or possessions from their farms), a sentry at the Myles garrison was shot dead, and men sent to procure medical help were also killed. By June 26 it was clear to Savage and his party that war was on, and they left Swansea to deliver the message to Governor John Leverett in Boston.

Massachusetts Bay decided immediately to aid Plymouth Colony, and by June 26 several companies were gathered on Dedham Plain (the present-day Hyde Park section of Boston) heading to Swansea. One of these companies, made up of an unsavory lot of servants, seamen, and convicted pirates, was placed under the command of Captain Samuel Moseley, described as "an old privateer from Jamaica."[14] Throughout King Philip's War, Moseley would epitomize the cruelty of the English toward the native, sometimes embarrassing colonial authorities with his exploits. His unswerving hatred for the enemy caused him to resist adopting Indian scouts and allies until late in the war, well behind Church and many Connecticut officers. However, Moseley's courageous leadership of men under fire and military success also made him a favorite of the troops, while his marriage to Governor Leverett's niece kept him out of serious trouble.[15] (Had Moseley written a history of the war—which would have included his counterattack at Bloody Brook, defense of Hadley, and lead position at the Great Swamp Fight—it would undoubtedly have kept pace with sales of Benjamin Church's subsequent history of the war. In fact, George Madison Bodge speculates that Church was jealous of the success of Moseley, whom Church fails to mention in his own writings.[16]) In the opening days of the war Moseley would lead his company south to John Woodcock's garrison house in present-day North Attleboro, Massachusetts, to join up with Captain Daniel Henchman's foot soldiers and Captain Thomas Prentice's cavalry.

Over the next several days the troops assigned to Swansea undertook several hapless sorties into Pokanoket territory. On June 30 and July 1, 1675, a large body of English soldiers under the command of Major Thomas Savage swept the Pokanoket peninsula only to find that Philip and his warriors had escaped across Mount Hope Bay into Pocasset country (present-day Tiverton, Rhode Island, and Fall River, Massachusetts). Despite the urging of Benjamin Church to take up active pursuit, Savage and his officers went about the business of building a fort on the peninsula and conducting sorties in the Swansea area. While one Wampanoag band was successfully engaged, the English lost precious time and allowed Philip to join with Weetamoe and her Pocasset warriors. Having gained an important ally and escaped the confines of the Pokanoket peninsula, Philip was now more dangerous than ever.

The English clung to the promise of negotiation. Captain Edward Hutchinson was sent by Boston officials to meet again with the Narragansett, though this time he was joined by Massachusetts Bay soldiers who abandoned their position near Swansea. Hutchinson's meeting, which included, in Captain Wait Winthrop's words, an "order from the Governr to demand hostages from the Narrowgansets or els . . . thay should looke at them as yr enemyes, and abetters with Philip,"[17] might have erupted into outright warfare had not Winthrop been able to defuse the confrontation.

Nonetheless, by attempting to force a treaty of loyalty on the Narragansett, Massachusetts Bay had raised the ire of the thus-far-neutral natives, not to mention officials from Connecticut and Rhode Island, who would bear the brunt of any Narragansett military activity. Among those present at the meeting was Canonchet, a gifted Narragansett sachem destined to play an important role in the unfolding war.

The defense of Swansea was further weakened when Captain Matthew Fuller, Benjamin Church, and some three dozen men left Aquidneck Island to attempt negotiations with Weetamoe. Landing in Pocasset territory, the English met with armed resistance and escaped—just barely—without serious loss, but also without any progress to show for their efforts.

Wampanoag activity was escalating in other locations as well. Taunton was attacked as early as June 27[18] and Old Rehoboth at the end of that month.[19] On July 9, 1675, much of the settlement at Middleboro was burned and the town subsequently abandoned. Another frontier outpost, Dartmouth, Massachusetts, was attacked and destroyed by warriors under Totoson, sachem of the Mattapoisett.

The English grew frantic as they watched the war spread beyond Plymouth Colony to Rhode Island and Massachusetts Bay. A band of Narragansett harassed Providence in July, well in advance of any coordinated decision to enter the war. On July 14, Nipmuc warriors attacked Mendon, the first town in Massachusetts Bay to be assaulted. This foray was led by Matoonas, a former Christian Indian of Pachacoog (near Worcester), who would provide outstanding military leadership during the war. Other Nipmuc sachems were soon drawn into the war: Shoshonin (called Sagamore Sam), sachem of the Nashaway (near Lancaster), who helped lead assaults on Lancaster and Medfield and the ambush of Captain Richard Beers at Northfield; Monoco, who was also involved at Lancaster, Medfield, and Northfield, and led the attack on Groton, Massachusetts; and Muttawmp, perhaps the finest Indian military commander of the war, who played pivotal roles in the natives' most smashing victories at New Braintree (Wheeler's Surprise), Brookfield, Bloody Brook, and the Sudbury Fight.

With a meaningless treaty in hand, the Massachusetts Bay troops under Hutchinson marched north from Narragansett country to rejoin the Plymouth soldiers. On July 19, 1675, the combined army traipsed into the Pocasset swamp, a huge cedar bog better known and more easily traveled by the Wampanoag. The English happened upon several abandoned camps but were able to engage only the Wampanoag rear guard. Seven or eight English were killed and others wounded, and the discouraged colonists gave up their headlong pursuit of the Wampanoag.

Convinced that Philip and his force had been located, however, the English devised a new military strategy intended to trap Philip in the Pocasset swamp and starve his people into submission. Such a strategy required a smaller, faster force, which (not coincidentally) allowed many of the Massachusetts men to return home and get about the pressing business of providing food for their families. Savage and Moseley departed. Prentice and his men marched to Mendon. Cudworth then posted men at the new fort on Mount Hope peninsula, sent others under Captain Daniel Henchman to build a garrison (named Fort Leverett for the governor) in the southwestern region of the Pocasset swamp[20] to block Philip from a water escape, and himself fielded a small force to harass the Wampanoag and destroy their food supply.

Had this new strategy worked, King Philip's War might have ended as quickly as it had begun, all within a short march of Swansea. However, Philip was too savvy a leader and Weetamoe too knowledgeable of the terrain to be trapped so easily. Benjamin Church was openly critical of Cudworth's passive strategy when he wrote: "The army now lay still to cover the people from nobody, while they were building a fort for nothing."[21] About July 29, while Cudworth marched most of his force to Dartmouth to provide relief to those badly shaken settlers, Philip slipped across the Taunton River and fled north past Old Rehoboth, directly into the heart of Nipmuc country. This escape came at a great price; the sachem was forced to leave behind more than one hundred women and children, who soon surrendered and were turned over to Plymouth authorities. On August 4 the colony's council of war concluded that several of the captured Pokanoket had been active in the recent hostilities, "and the rest complyers with them,"[22] so all but a few were sold into slavery.

Philip himself was not yet out of danger. A large force of Mohegan led by Oneko, son of Uncas, had been sent from Connecticut to aid the English military. This fleet band arrived at Old Rehoboth on July 30, overtook Philip, and engaged the Wampanoag in a battle at Nipsachuck (present-day Smithfield, Rhode Island) on August 1, 1675. Philip lost twenty-three of his party, including four chief captains. However, poor decisions and tactical blunders kept the English and Mohegan, numbering 265 men, from capturing Philip and his remaining forty warriors as they huddled in a swamp less than three-quarters of a mile away, possessing only thirty guns and standing ready to surrender.[23] Taking advantage of this lapse, the Wampanoag made good their escape along the Blackstone River. Once safe, Weetamoe and some of her Pocasset headed southwest to join the Eastern Niantic under the leadership of Ninigret. Philip and his warriors continued north to join their Nipmuc allies at Menameset (near present-day New Braintree, Massachusetts).

Outmaneuvered by Wampanoag forces, the English had now come to realize their worst fears. As William Hubbard wrote:

> by this means Philip escaped away to the westward, kindling the flame of war in all the western plantations of the Massachusetts Colony wherever he came; so by this fatal accident the fire that was in a likely way to be extinguished as soon almost as it began, did on the sudden break out through the whole jurisdiction of the Massachusetts, both eastward and westward, endangering also the neighbor colony of Connecticut.[24]

THE WAR SPREADS TO THE CONNECTICUT RIVER VALLEY AND MAINE

Despite the attack on Mendon, Boston authorities had not given up in their attempt to secure Nipmuc allegiance to the English. Fresh from his meeting with the Narragansett, Captain Hutchinson, along with Captain Thomas Wheeler, Ephraim Curtis, and about twenty-five militia and native guides, were sent into the heart of Nipmuc country to meet with native leaders. Leaving Cambridge on July 28, 1675, Hutchinson and his band reached

Quabaug (present-day West Brookfield, Massachusetts) about August 1, the day of Philip's Nipsachuck battle.

Finding the Nipmuc villages still deserted, Hutchinson sent Curtis to locate the natives' camp. He successfully tracked down several of the sachems, whose belligerence and anger should have convinced Curtis that little of use could be accomplished. Nonetheless, he managed to wrangle a promise to meet from the pugnacious sachems. On August 2, as Hutchinson, Wheeler, and their men sought the Nipmuc in present-day New Braintree, Massachusetts, they fell into a deadly ambush known today as Wheeler's Surprise. Eight of the English died. Hutchinson and Wheeler were both wounded but fought their way back to Brookfield led by their native guides. Once there, the remnants of Hutchinson's party and about seventy townspeople barricaded themselves in a single garrison to await the Nipmuc war party. Pouring into town, Muttawmp and his warriors torched the undefended structures and surrounded the garrison, where the English were assaulted for two days before help arrived.

When Hutchinson died of his wounds in Marlboro, Massachusetts, on his return to Boston a few weeks later, a London newspaper reported that it was forty years to the day since his famous mother, Anne Hutchinson, had been killed by Indians.[25]

On August 5, Philip and his forty warriors joined with the Nipmuc at their newly constructed fort at Menameset. The Nipmuc success at Brookfield along with Philip's arrival helped to galvanize the neighboring native groups, attracting additional warriors to the Menameset camp.

On August 22, Monoco led a combined force to Lancaster, Massachusetts, where the group killed seven English and destroyed one home. Fearing the spread of violence to the west, Boston officials moved to fortify the frontier settlements in the upper Connecticut River Valley by establishing Massachusetts, Connecticut, and Mohegan troops at Hadley, Massachusetts. John Pynchon, a prominent citizen of Springfield and son of its founder, was selected against his own recommendation to coordinate military affairs for the region.

On August 25, Captains Thomas Lathrop of Beverly, Massachusetts, and Richard Beers of Watertown, Massachusetts, in command of about one hundred troops, attempted to engage the Norwottock at Hopewell Swamp in present-day Whately, Massachusetts. Nine English were killed in a carefully planned ambush, allowing the Norwottock to escape and join the Pocumtuck. Puritan historians portrayed this so-called Battle of South Deerfield as a victory, when, in fact, another previously neutral group had been turned against the English.

At the end of August, Springfield, Massachusetts, was raided by the Nipmuc, prompting the English to demand the guns of the local Agawam. Neutral and peaceful to that point, the Agawam would soon go the way of the Norwottock, being driven into the arms of their more aggressive Nipmuc neighbors by such heavy-handed English tactics.

A similarly mercurial situation was unfolding in Maine. Here, the battle for land was less intense than in the southern colonies, but other sources of friction would lead just as surely to war. Some of the wealthiest, most influential English traders were notorious for cheating their Abenaki trading partners. Random acts of cruelty against the Abenaki were common, especially their kidnap and sale into slavery. Some of the English were unscrupulous in their use of liquor, and many were quick to demand Abenaki guns at the slightest threat. Few of the sanctions that kept order in the southern colonies were in place in Maine, a rough-and-tumble frontier analogous in some ways to the nineteenth-century American West.

If any leader could have established some measure of order and goodwill in the area, it would have been Major Richard Waldron, an austere Puritan who settled in Dover, New Hampshire, in 1640 and was made sergeant major of military forces in the province in 1674. Unfortunately, Waldron's influence among the Abenaki was limited by his reputation for cheating them at every opportunity.[26]

Shortly after the outbreak of war in Swansea, the settlers of York, Maine, armed themselves and marched to the Sheepscot River to demand that the Androscoggin surrender their weapons. Faced with a history of unprincipled English dealings and the loss of weapons they depended upon for daily survival, the Androscoggin answered on September 5 by raiding Thomas Purchase's trading post above Pejebscot Falls (present-day Topsham, Maine) and killing a few cattle.

On September 9, a party of Englishmen sailing along the north shore of Casco Bay spotted three Penobscot beating on the door of a house. The English assumed the worst and fired on the natives, killing one and wounding another. The Penobscot, under their sachem Madockawando, had been longtime friends of the English and considered this attack unprovoked. Unwilling to participate in any more bloodshed, the Penobscot retired to a fort at Totannock, at the confluence of the Kennebec and Sebasticook Rivers, in present-day Winslow, Maine. In a short time they would be joined by other New England native groups.

On September 12, the isolated home of Thomas Wakely at Falmouth (present-day Portland, Maine) was assaulted, leaving six dead. The retreating English took refuge in Major William Phillips' garrison south along the Saco River.

Everywhere to the east Abenaki came alive under the leadership of Squando, an Abenaki commonly called the Sagamore of Saco. A short time before the war Squando had been touched personally by a random act of English cruelty when his wife and infant son, traveling down the Saco River, were intentionally capsized by English sailors to see if, as legend held, natives could instinctively swim at birth. Despite the mother's best efforts the infant drowned. It was an episode that Squando and his countrymen would never forget.

Also important to the eastern war effort were Mugg Hegone, an Androscoggin sachem who was fluent in English, and Simon "the Yankee killer," a Narragansett and former Christian Indian who was active in the Merrimack Valley before crossing into the coastal towns of present-day Maine.

Throughout the month of September 1675 violence in Maine continued. Two houses were burned, two settlers killed, and two captured at Oyster River (present-day Durham, New Hampshire). On September 18, Captain John Bonython's house on the east side of the Saco River was destroyed. Sensing danger, Bonython had already joined his neighbors from Thomas Wakeley's home in Major William Phillips' garrison across the river. The natives, probably led by Squando,[27] launched a fierce attack, destroying Phillips' mills and nearly capturing the garrison before breaking off their assault. Shortly thereafter five settlers were killed on the Saco River, bringing to thirteen the number of English killed around Saco. At about that time Winter Harbor was abandoned to the Abenaki and burned. When Captain John Wincoll and sixteen men landed there they met with stiff resistance; more than a dozen soldiers and residents of Saco were killed.

The settlers at York were subject to a series of attacks beginning in late September. On October 1, Richard Tozer's home at Newechewannick (present-day Berwick, Maine) was assaulted. Most of the fifteen settlers garrisoned in the structure made their way to safety. On October 16 the Abenaki returned to kill Tozer and his son. In the next few days Lieutenant Roger Plaisted and two of his sons would die defending a nearby garrison. In retreat, the Indians would burn several other houses in the area before traveling to Sturgeon Creek, where two more English were killed. Soon after, seven houses were torched and several English killed at Black Point (present-day Scarborough, Maine), the first of several assaults in that area. The last violent act of the season occurred at Wells, where warriors killed three men and destroyed one home.

In November 1675, the Abenaki withdrew to their winter quarters at present-day Ossipee, New Hampshire; Pequacket (present-day Fryeburg), Maine; and the Totannock fort at Winslow, Maine. In the first phase of the war in Maine, eighty English had lost their lives.[28]

In the early fall of 1675, the warriors gathered at Menameset began to focus their military might on targets in the Connecticut River valley. Deer-field, Massachusetts, came under attack on September 1, perhaps by the same Norwottock engaged by Lathrop and Beers at Hopewell Swamp on August 25. When eight men from Squakeag (present-day Northfield, Mass-achusetts) were killed the following day along with considerable property and crop damage, colonial authorities sent Captain Beers and about thirty-six men to evacuate the settlement. On September 4, Beers and his party ran into a deadly ambush that cost the captain and most of his men their lives. Not until September 6 was Major Robert Treat of Connecticut able to suc-cessfully evacuate Squakeag.

When twenty men were ambushed at Deerfield on September 12, Cap-tain Lathrop was charged with evacuating that frontier town. Despite the lessons of Hutchinson (at New Braintree) and Beers (at Northfield), Lathrop led his ill-prepared party of Essex County, Massachusetts, militia into a lethal ambush set by Muttawmp at Muddy Brook in present-day South Deerfield, Massachusetts. This spot would be known forever after as Bloody Brook. The Reverend William Hubbard, himself a resident of Essex County and familiar with many of those killed, called September 18 "that most fatal day, the saddest that ever befel New England."[29]

With the Connecticut River valley towns being rapidly evacuated, Springfield stood out as the choicest target for Indian attack. On September 26, John Pynchon's mill and other buildings were burned near present-day Suffield, Connecticut. On October 4, the troops guarding Springfield and its five hundred citizens marched to Hadley to join in a new expedition against the enemy, leaving the town virtually defenseless. The following day a combined force of Nipmuc and Agawam burned more than three hundred homes before Treat and Pynchon could arrive to chase them away.

Shortly after this devastating attack on Springfield, Pynchon was replaced by Samuel Appleton of Ipswich, who rode to Hadley and took command of a combined militia of Connecticut and Massachusetts soldiers. After several weeks of unproductive patrolling by the English, the army finally found something to celebrate. On Tuesday, October 19, 1675, Muttawmp and his warriors attacked Hatfield but, in Hubbard's words, "were so well entertained on all hands where they attempted to break in upon the town, that they found it too hot for them."[30] While only a minor skirmish in the overall war, the English touted their defense of Hatfield as a great moral victory and perhaps the first turning point of the war.[31]

In the final days of October, small raids were carried out at Northampton, where two English died and four homes were lost, and Westfield, where three were killed and several homes destroyed. By this time the valley settlements were so ravaged and the flow of refugees to the east so great that on November 12 Appleton had to forbid those left in Springfield, Northampton, Hadley, Westfield, and Hatfield from abandoning the towns without his permission. However, the attack on Hatfield would prove to be the last major native offensive launched in the Connecticut River valley in 1675. As the landscape grew quiet, Appleton worked to bolster the remaining garrisons in the valley. By November 17, the major and his combined militia had orders in hand to break camp and return home. Meanwhile, the combined native force retired to its central winter encampment at Menameset to regroup, plan their strategy, and await the growth of springtime cover so crucial to their military success. Along the way to the rendezvous, one band of warriors stopped to torch the half-dozen houses at Quinsigamond Plantation, a site that would one day become Worcester, Massachusetts.

WAR WITH THE NARRAGANSETT

While attacks by Nipmuc, Pocumtuck, and Wampanoag warriors in the Connecticut River Valley occupied the English military throughout the fall of 1675, the United Colonies remained focused on the threat posed by the mighty Narragansett. Repeated and often foolish attempts to coerce the Narragansett into a peace treaty failed amid growing indications that the Rhode Island natives were headed down the path to war. An October 28 deadline to hand over all Wampanoag refugees was ignored. (Canonchet's eloquent reply: "No, not a Wampanoag nor the paring of a Wampanoag nail."[32]) Reports of Narragansett war preparations began to surface, as did indications that Narragansett warriors had joined in raids with the Nipmuc and Wampanoag. Canonchet, who was reported to command three thousand warriors, came under singular suspicion. Even the venerable Roger Williams found a more belligerent attitude among the Narragansett, some of whom were attempting to wrest Conanicut Island from him. Indeed, of the several Narragansett sachems, only Ninigret still seemed interested in winning favor with the English.

In mid-November the United Colonies voted to send one thousand men into Narragansett country to force the natives to abide by their supposed treaty obligations.[33] Governor Winslow of Plymouth County was selected to lead the army and Major Robert Treat of Connecticut named second-in-command. Even Rhode Island was invited to send a contingent of men, which the colony declined to do, but did agree to provide boats to assist with logistics. The colonies then undertook perhaps the greatest organizational challenge in their history, that of sustaining a thousand-man army in the dead of winter. Soldiers readied their warmest, sturdiest clothing. Food-stuffs and supplies were accumulated and sent on their way to Wickford, Rhode Island, which, with its excellent access to water and location in Narragansett country, was chosen as the base of operations. Even New England's spiritual readiness was addressed with a solemn day of prayer de-clared for Thursday, December 2.

Early on the afternoon of December 19, 1675, the combined army of Massachusetts Bay, Plymouth, and Connecticut attacked a large, fortified Narragansett village located in the Great Swamp (present-day South Kingstown, Rhode Island). The Great Swamp Fight would last for most of the afternoon and become one of New England's bloodiest battles. In the end, perhaps six hundred Narragansett died and Puritan historians de-clared it a great victory; in retrospect, however, it brought the still-powerful Narragansett into the war and so incapacitated the colonial army that it was incapable of continuing the winter campaign.[34]

In Maine, a similar plan to attack the Abenaki in their winter quarters at present-day Ossipee, New Hampshire, failed when the English were un-able to adequately supply themselves for the harsh winter weather.[35] The natives were subject to the same brutal conditions, however, and in early January 1676—racked by hunger and disease—they approached Major Waldron to establish an armistice. Over the next six months Maine would remain relatively quiet, though its English inhabitants would watch with horror as towns to the south and west came under intense assault. The root causes of war in Maine had hardly been solved, however, and these months of relative peace—which would include English atrocities such as the cap-ture and sale of innocent Penobscot into slavery[36]—would only serve to ex-tend the violence.

In southern New England, a cold, snowy December turned into a warmer January and both sides resumed the offensive. On January 27, Pawtuxet, Rhode Island (a village comprised of parts of present-day Warwick and Cranston, Rhode Island), was attacked by Narragansett, who destroyed buildings and stole livestock. On February 1, the garrison of Thomas Eames in present-day Framingham, Massachusetts, was assaulted by Nipmuc; Thomas was away, but his wife and at least three children were killed. Just a few days before, Winslow's refortified army of fourteen hundred started off in pursuit of the Narragansett, who were marching to join their Nipmuc and Wampanoag allies. For seventy miles past Providence, through Warwick to Marlboro and on into Nipmuc country, the English and natives engaged in a series of skirmishes. Poorly supplied from the start, the English were reduced to eating horses and ground nuts.[37] By early February it became clear that a decisive battle would elude the English, and beset by desertions and food shortages, Winslow disbanded the army on February 3 and returned to Boston. This frustrating and unsuccessful pursuit would be known for generations as the "hungry march."

Once at Menameset, the Narragansett would trade information and discuss a more coordinated strategy with the allied tribes wintering there. Ironically, the Great Swamp Fight and "hungry march" had set in motion the very thing they had been intended to prevent: a native alliance built around the military strength of the Narragansett.

Philip played no role in the Great Swamp Fight or in the subsequent "hungry march." By December 1675[38] the Pokanoket sachem was at present-day Schaghticoke, New York, north of Albany on the Hoosic River. There, he hoped to secure supplies and recruit Mahican warriors; instead, the Mohawk attacked him and nearly destroyed his band. In early spring, Philip would return to New England, less powerful and influential than when he left.

WINTER 1676: THE ALGONQUIAN VICTORIES

In late January two Praying Indians, James Quannapohit and Job Kattenanit, returned from a successful spy mission at Menameset with news that the frontier towns of western Massachusetts—Lancaster, Groton, Marlboro, Sudbury, and Medfield—would be attacked within the coming weeks. The plan for attacking Lancaster, the natives' first target, was even described in some detail. Nevertheless, when four hundred warriors under Monoco descended on the town on February 10, only Captain Samuel Wadsworth and his forty men at Marlboro were ready to respond, and even then too late to prevent the destruction of Lancaster's central village and one of the town's six garrisons. Several of the occupants of this garrison, home of the town's minister, Joseph Rowlandson, were killed, and twenty-four others taken captive. One of those kidnapped was Rowlandson's wife, Mary, who would keep a diary of her nearly three months of captivity under the Narragansett sachem Quinapin, who purchased her from Monoco. Published in 1682, this diary became a classic of colonial literature—both for its firsthand account of the Lancaster attack and for its observations of the Algonquian—and the prototype of the American captivity narrative.

The attack on Lancaster, its second devastation of the war, led to its abandonment. Eleven days later, on February 21, a strike at Medfield by three hundred Nipmuc and Narragansett warriors caught the settlers off-guard, despite the presence of one hundred English troops. Some eighteen English were killed and many others were kidnapped. On February 25, the natives burned several buildings at Weymouth, Massachusetts, setting off a panic among the coastal towns south of Boston. It became frighteningly clear to the English that no New England town was safe from the war's destruction.

By early February the United Colonies had turned their attention again to western Massachusetts and the Connecticut Valley, naming Major Thomas Savage to lead a new offensive campaign. Marlboro was designated the main supply base and Brookfield the rendezvous point for Massachusetts Bay and Connecticut troops under Major Treat. (Plymouth Colony, still recovering from the Narragansett campaign, sent no troops.) This new army set out from Brookfield toward the native camps around Menameset on March 2, but was unable to engage the elusive natives. Eventually Savage's force returned to Hadley, discouraged by its lack of success and carrying orders to return east if they could not locate the enemy.

March proved to be perhaps the most successful month of the war for Algonquian armies. Groton was attacked on March 2, 9, and 13, leading to its abandonment. On March 12, 1676, a band under Totoson attacked William Clark's garrison on the Eel River, just south of Plymouth, killing eleven settlers. On March 14 the natives struck at Northampton, Massachusetts, but were driven back by troops under Major Robert Treat and

AWASHONKS

This figurehead of Awashonks was carved for an 1830s Cape Cod whaling vessel, just one small way in which King Philip's War has been commemorated throughout the centuries. (Courtesy of the Old Dartmouth Historical Society–New Bedford Whaling Museum)

Captain William Turner after burning ten houses and killing five colonists; this was one of the few signs of hope for the English amid their steady losses. Two days later the Indians burned all but one house in Warwick, Rhode Island, which was left standing, according to Increase Mather, for the "very good reason that it was built of stone."[39] Soldiers were moved into the Andover and Haverhill, Massachusetts, area around March 19 as natives were spot-

ted and panic set in. On March 26 two settlers were killed and four kidnapped at Longmeadow, Massachusetts. The same day a second warrior
band attacked and set fire to eleven barns and thirteen dwellings in Marlboro, and though Ephraim Curtis led a party that successfully engaged the
raiders, Marlboro was abandoned soon after by all but the military. While
Longmeadow was cowering and Marlboro burning, a third band of natives
torched the already abandoned town of Simsbury, Connecticut.

The worst news of the day was yet to come, however. A company of
Plymouth Colony militia numbering sixty-three, along with twenty natives,
had spent the night of March 25 billeted at Rehoboth. The following morning, under the command of Captain Michael Pierce of Scituate, they set out
along the Pawtucket River in search of the enemy. Marching down the eastern bank of the river, in the present town of Central Falls, Rhode Island,
Pierce's company was ambushed and nearly destroyed. A few friendly Indians managed to escape, but the next day the colonists buried forty-two of
their own at the site of the massacre.

There was little time for the English to grieve. On March 28 Canonchet's band, which had returned south to gather seed corn for spring
planting, attacked Old Rehoboth, destroying forty-five homes, twenty-one
barns, two corn mills, and a sawmill, and capturing most of the settlers'
supplies. On March 29 they burned one hundred structures at Providence,
including the home of Roger Williams, whose long and friendly relationship with the Narragansett proved valueless in their desire to avenge the
Great Swamp tragedy.

With their leaders captured or killed and their tribal alliance dissolved, many New England Indians made the long, arduous trek to the sanctuary of New York or Canada. (Courtesy of the Haffenreffer Museum of Anthropology, Brown University)

· Chapter 3 ·

Spring 1676: The Tide Turns

By NOW THE MASSACHUSETTS FRONTIER was in shambles. Settlers had fled from Springfield, Deerfield, Northfield, Brookfield, Lancaster, Groton, Mendon, Wrentham, Swansea, Rehoboth, and Dartmouth. Marlboro was being maintained solely as a military base. Massachusetts Bay made plans to abandon other towns in the face of angry opposition from their residents; few wanted to give up their homes and farms, no matter how great the risk, especially as planting season drew near. Connecticut, fearful of the war spreading further into its territory, corresponded with Governor Edmund Andros about the possibility of employing Mohawk warriors to fight the Algonquian. Andros, in a biting reply that echoed his own fear that the war might spread into New York, told his neighbors that "they seemed as ignorant in respect to the Mohawk as they did in regard to their own Indians."[1] Indeed, Connecticut's willingness to unleash the Mohawk in New England—a strategy not necessarily embraced by Plymouth or Massachusetts Bay—indicated Hartford's own sense of frustration at the war's prosecution.

Observers in London, who received reports of the war through channels other than the Puritan hierarchy, were entirely unimpressed by the leadership of colonial officials. Richard Wharton, a Boston merchant with close ties to England, reported that military success in the Narragansett campaign had been wasted by political lethargy; the Narragansett had escaped, the army recalled, the frontier towns left unprotected, and Lancaster left to burn despite adequate warning of an attack.[2] Wharton believed that unless "God give greater wisdom to our Rulers or put it into the King's heart to rule and relieve us, these colonies will soon be ruined."[3]

Frustration continued in the field. Unable to engage the enemy, Major Savage left Captain William Turner early in April with defense of the Connecticut River valley and returned to Boston with his troops. With the English offensive curtailed, the Algonquian, racked by disease and hunger, were suddenly given the opportunity to plant, fish, and engage in other traditional springtime activities. This replenished their food stocks and raised their morale, but also created a sense of security that would lead directly to their disastrous defeat at Peskeompskut (present-day Turner's Falls, Massachusetts) in May 1676.

Meanwhile, attacks on English settlements continued. Bridgewater, Massachusetts, lost a house and a barn, foodstuffs, and livestock on April 9. A nearly deserted Chelmsford, Massachusetts, was put to the torch on April 15, while most of the remaining structures in Marlboro were burned on April 17. Captain Samuel Brocklebank of Rowley, then in command at Marlboro, sent a party to pursue the raiders, who were overtaken and attacked in their camp that night.

Also in April, two English were killed and one captured at Andover, Massachusetts, while settlers were killed at Hingham, Weymouth, and Haverhill, Massachusetts, the latter engineered by Simon "the Yankee killer." Towns as distant from each other as Hadley, Worcester, Mendon, Wrentham, Medfield, Billerica, Braintree, and Woburn were assaulted during the month. Even Woodcock's garrison (in present-day North Attleboro, Massachusetts), so central to the colonies' military effort, came under deadly attack.

On April 21, one of the most famous battles of the war took place when as many as five hundred natives under Muttawmp assaulted Sudbury, Massachusetts, burning buildings as the settlers retreated to their garrisons. By day's end, several garrisons remained secure but the main body of English soldiers had been routed. The next day, the victorious warriors appeared at Marlboro and gave seventy-four shouts to indicate the number of English they believed they had left dead in Sudbury. "So insolent were the Indians grown," one Boston observer wrote, "that they sent us Word, to provide Store of good Chear, for they intended to dine with us upon Election Day," May 3, 1676.[4] Officials in Boston were spooked enough by this threat to muster the militia in every town on May 3, though no serious attack took place.

Despite the apparent success of the Algonquian, their plight was growing more desperate daily. This did not go unnoticed by their English captives, like Mary Rowlandson, who recorded a decided lack of enthusiasm after the Indian victory at Sudbury. Of paramount concern was food, a commodity impossible to grow, harvest, or protect when communities were constantly on the move. Recognizing this, the English—though still intent on direct engagements whenever possible—increasingly waged a logistical war designed to deny the natives food and supplies. This involved capturing or destroying food stores and harassing the natives at their traditional fishing locations.

As important, the Indian leadership began to fall. The first and perhaps most devastating loss occurred on April 3, 1676 when Captain James Avery and George Denison of Connecticut surprised a small band of Narragansett warriors at their Pawtucket River Valley camp, near present-day Cumberland, Rhode Island. Among those captured was Canonchet, thought by some to be the shrewdest Algonquian military leader of the war, and instrumental in the victories of the prior three months. Canonchet was sent to Stonington, Connecticut, where he behaved so bravely and honorably at his execution that even Puritan historians were impressed.

The English had other victories as well, made more common and devastating as Massachusetts relented in the use of friendly natives. English technology and manpower, coupled with the Indians' skill in forest warfare, became a formidable combination. In fact, as the war dragged on, it became evident that the natives could inflict more damage on one another— through both skill and deceit—than the awkward tactics of the English could ever hope to achieve. It was, for example, the Mohegan who nearly annihilated Philip's forces in the Nipsachuck swamp; an Indian who led the English to the Narragansett Swamp Fort, and described its one weakness; Mohawk who would massacre Philip's new recruits at Schaghticoke; and natives who would trap Canonchet, Philip, and Anawan. Christian Indians continued to provide inestimable service to the English militia despite their miserable treatment. Had the settlers attempted to prosecute the war with colonial forces alone, the results might have been much different.

Even when the colonists were ambushed or lost a battle—and allowing for the hopeful overestimates of contemporary writers—they still managed to exact a high price from the Indians in men and supplies, higher than a prolonged native war effort could withstand. Among the Indians, these equivocal results led to divided leadership, with some pushing for peace, others seeking the continuance of a raiding strategy, and still others desiring direct, pitched battles. A stream of hungry, sick, disillusioned natives began to surrender themselves to English authorities. As the weather warmed in the spring of 1676, a highly perceptive colonist might have divined that victory was much closer than March's military disasters would indicate.

On May 8 about three hundred warriors under Tispaquin, the "Black Sachem" of Assawompsett (and Philip's brother-in-law), attacked Bridgewater, Massachusetts. Only a soaking rainstorm extinguished the fires set by natives, giving the settlers an opportunity to regroup and drive the Indians from town. On May 11 the few buildings still standing were burned, while eleven houses and five barns were destroyed at nearby Halifax. On May 20, Scituate, Massachusetts, was attacked and nineteen houses burned.

However, by May most of the Algonquian had turned their attention to securing food for their hungry communities. Camps were established at Peskeompskut on the Connecticut River, about five miles north of Deerfield, to take advantage of the falls and its abundant fish. Raiding parties set out to steal livestock and foodstuffs from occupied frontier towns like Hadley and Hatfield. The natives, realizing that the primary English military force had marched east and disbanded, felt secure in their camps and relaxed their defenses, which may have allowed Thomas Reed, captured near Hadley on April 1, to escape the Peskeompskut camp. When Reed reported on the situation to Captain Turner—a man like Benjamin Church in his reluctance to sit idly in a garrisoned town—Turner immediately set about raising a force from the towns of Hadley, Northampton, Hatfield, and Springfield.

On the evening of May 18 Turner and 150 men, young and old, largely inexperienced and incapable of overcoming any significant enemy resistance, mounted and rode from Hatfield north through Deerfield to Peskeompskut. There, at dawn on May 19, Turner's men opened fire on the wigwams, massacring the panicked men, women, and children. Suddenly, warriors from a nearby camp appeared and a devastating English victory became a disorganized retreat. From Peskeompskut to Deerfield the settlers were tracked down and killed. Turner himself died while crossing the Green River. It would take several days before all of the survivors reached Hatfield, and when the final count was made, thirty-nine English had died. Connecticut responded immediately by sending Captain Benjamin Newberry and eighty men to reinforce the valley towns. On May 30 the natives launched a retaliatory strike against Hatfield, killing seven, wounding five, torching twelve outlying barns, and stealing livestock.

By June 1 the United Colonies were ready to begin a new, combined offensive. Massachusetts Bay sent five hundred troops under Major Daniel Henchman to raid the enemy camp at Mount Wachusett and then join up at Hadley with both Connecticut's eighty troops under Newberry and a new force of 440 English and friendly natives under Major John Talcott. As the troops marched to their rendezvous they captured or killed nearly one hundred natives, among these a group fishing at Wausaccum Pond. The Connecticut troops, arriving first in the area, defended Hadley on June 12 from attack by a large native force. This assault on Hadley would prove to be the last coordinated native military action in the Connecticut Valley. By June 16 the combined English force was moving along the Connecticut River, finding only empty native camps. At the end of June the offensive was called off and the frustrated troops returned to their respective colonies.

While a decisive engagement was denied the English, their June offensive proved crucial to ending the war. As the natives fled, they left choice fishing locations and some of the few fields they had been able to sow. With hunger and sickness growing, their leadership debated increasingly desperate measures. In *The Red King's Rebellion,* historian Russell Bourne suggests that, after the Peskeompskut massacre, allied sachems openly discussed the strategy of killing Philip and sending his head to the English as a prelude to peace negotiations.[5] Philip's influence exhausted and his well-being in jeopardy, he headed for his homeland at Mount Hope. The battlefields of western Massachusetts grew silent as the southeastern New England warriors departed and the Nipmuc pondered their future. When Captain Henchman wrote to Boston on June 30 that "all the Indians were in continual motion,"[6] he was describing the final dissolution of the native military alliance.

THE CLOSING CAMPAIGN IN
SOUTHEASTERN MASSACHUSETTS

In June 1676, Benjamin Church, who had quietly spent part of the winter campaign on Aquidneck Island with his wife and children, traveled to Plymouth to see if he could be of assistance in light of the increased native activity near his home. Now more amenable to his aggressive style, authorities restored Church's command and authorized him to raise a new company of English and natives to patrol southern New England. It was on his return trip by canoe, while rounding Sakonnet Point at present-day Little Compton, Rhode Island, that Church spotted a number of Sakonnet engaged in fishing. Church bravely stepped ashore and managed to negotiate a meeting with the squaw sachem, Awashonks, two days hence. When the appointed day arrived—against all best advice—Church met with Awashonks and convinced her and her people to join the English and seek peace terms from Plymouth. With that, eighty or ninety Sakonnet surrendered to Major William Bradford on June 30 and were marched off to Sandwich to learn their fate.

English victories both on and off the field mounted quickly in June and July. On June 12, a large body of warriors was repulsed at Hadley with little damage to the town. A declaration of mercy on June 19 by Massachusetts Bay inspired large numbers of natives to surrender. Narragansett were met and defeated by Connecticut troops twice near the Pawtuxet River. On July 2, Major Talcott turned his Connecticut militiamen north toward Nacheck on the Pawtuxet River, capturing or killing 171 Narragansett.[7] Among those shot was Ninigret's sister, Quaiapen. Eighty Narragansett under Potuck, waiting peacefully at Warwick for terms of surrender after giving themselves up, were massacred by Talcott's men on July 3.

That same day at Dover, New Hampshire, the neutral Pennacooks signed a treaty of peace, securing the area between the Merrimack and Kennebec Rivers. To the south, Ninigret formally delivered his Niantic to the English

Late in the war, separated from his allies, Philip had little choice but to remain on the move, narrowly escaping capture on several occasions. (Courtesy of the Haffenreffer Museum of Anthropology, Brown University)

side on July 15 when he signed a treaty with Massachusetts Bay setting out compensation for the capture or death of Philip. Even Nipmuc leaders petitioned Massachusetts Bay for terms of peace in early July, though the large number of English hostages still being held made negotiations impossible.

Meanwhile, Bradford and his force of 150 English and 50 natives, supplemented by troops under Captains Brattle and Moseley, had turned their attention to the war's greatest prize, the capture of Philip. On July 6, Bradford's troops were able to rescue Jethro, a black servant kidnapped at Swansea a week before. Jethro warned the army of a planned attack at Taunton, Massachusetts, so that the natives' raid on July 11 was easily turned away. During the following week Bradford's men killed or captured several hundred natives around Swansea but always remained one step behind Philip.

Benjamin Church, anxious to establish his own command, rode to Plymouth on July 5 and learned that the Sakonnet would be allowed to serve under him. Church caught up with Awashonks and her people on the shore of Buzzards Bay and there celebrated his new command. By July 11 Church's men, comprised of Sakonnet and English volunteers, captured several groups of natives near Middleboro. Over the next several weeks this highly mobile, savvy military troop would conduct successful operations from Plymouth to Taunton to Dartmouth, always closely following Philip's trail. Together, Bradford and Church began to place a vise around Philip's hungry and disheartened Wampanoag.

In other areas of New England, open warfare turned to clean-up operations; Governor Winslow remarked that, suddenly, "the people in all our towns . . . are very desirous to be ranging after the enemy."[8] In the upper Connecticut Valley and the Mount Wachusett area, English troops launched small patrols—once impossible to operate with safety—to find and destroy native food supplies. On July 25 Pumham was killed and his Narragansett defeated near Dedham. The same day Shoshonin and about 180 Nipmuc marched into Boston to surrender. With them was Matoonas and his son, whom Shoshonin had captured and now turned over to English authorities. Matoonas was shot on Boston Common. During the month of August, Major Talcott mercilessly pursued and slaughtered natives fleeing in desperation across western Massachusetts to New York, which Governor Andros had officially opened as a place of asylum for New England's native refugees in May 1676. On August 15 Talcott's troops hunted down one such group, killing thirty-five and capturing twenty at present-day Great Barrington, Massachusetts. This was to be Connecticut's last military activity in the war.[9]

This is one of the better-known depictions of King Philip's death, the result of a surprise attack at dawn by a party under Benjamin Church. Philip fell, in Church's words, "upon his face in the mud and water, with his gun under him." (Courtesy of the Haffenreffer Museum of Anthropology, Brown University)

On two occasions, August 1 and 3, Church and his band spotted the most elusive prize, Philip, and nearly killed him. Instead, they managed to capture a number of Wampanoag, including Philip's wife, Wootonekanuska, and nine-year-old son, whom authorities sold into slavery after much debate among the clergy.

On August 6 a group of Taunton men captured about two dozen Wampanoag and found the body of Weetamoe in Metapoiset (present-day

Reduced in number by the war, sickness, and hunger, the Wampanoag under Anawan were forced to move almost daily as colonial soldiers sought them in the closing days of King Philip's War. Armed with news of Anawan's whereabouts from a captured native, Benjamin Church surprised the Pokanoket leader at Anawan Rock, a location still marked and maintained along Route 44 in Rehoboth, Massachusetts. (From History and Antiquities of New England, New York, New Jersey, and Pennsylvania, *John W. Barber, 1842)*

Somerset, Massachusetts). She had apparently slipped from a raft and drowned while trying to escape pursuit. Weetamoe's body was mutilated and her decapitated head stuck on a pole on Taunton Green.

On August 11, Church and his party, now resting on Aquidneck Island, received the information that would end the war in southern New England: One of Philip's men, Alderman, whose brother may have been killed by Philip for suggesting surrender,[10] was now willing to lead the English to the sachem's camp, hidden in a swamp on the southwestern side of Mount Hope. There, on the morning of August 12, 1676, Church's men surprised

68

Philip and his people, and in the melee that followed, Philip was shot dead by Alderman. His body was decapitated and quartered and his head was sent to Plymouth, where it was marched through the streets on August 17 and left on display. Alderman received one of Philip's hands as a souvenir.

One last mission remained for Church and his men: the capture of Philip's venerable war leader, Anawan. Patrolling the Mount Hope peninsula, Church captured several Wampanoag parties, soon learning the whereabouts of Anawan. On the evening of August 28, 1676, Church's militia reached the Squannakonk Swamp in present-day Rehoboth, Massachusetts. There, Church and his men silently descended the face of a rocky cliff, completely surprising Anawan and his party. With Philip dead and English patrols relentlessly searching the area, Anawan and his band agreed to surrender. The following day victor and victim marched into Taunton. Despite Church's wishes, Anawan was sent to Plymouth and later executed. Anawan had been a partner and confidant of Massasoit, Alexander, and Philip, and his death truly marked the end of an era.

During the fall of 1676, several small expeditions were launched in the southern colonies to eliminate any remnants of native power. Quinapin, the chief lieutenant of Canonchet at the Great Swamp Fight, was shot at Newport on August 25.[11] Tispaquin, Philip's brother-in-law, surrendered to Church at Agawam (present-day Wareham, Massachusetts) on September 6 on assurance that his life would be spared; Plymouth officials overruled Church's guarantee, beheading Tispaquin and selling his wife and son into slavery. A similar fate befell Monoco, who surrendered to Major Richard Waldron of New Hampshire upon a promise of amnesty and was promptly shipped to Boston, where he was hung on September 26, 1676. Muttawmp and Shoshonin, who had delivered Matoonas to the English, likewise fell victim to Waldron's treachery and were executed at Boston. Also in September, Totoson and his one remaining son escaped capture and attempted to reach their camp near present-day Mattapoisett, Massachusetts; both Totoson and the boy died soon after. As late as December 1676 a band of natives, trying simply to stay alive, was captured near Rehoboth.

CLOSE OF THE EASTERN WAR

In Maine, the July 3 treaty proved to be fragile: on August 11, 1676, the day before Philip's death, Squando led an assault on Cleve's Neck at Falmouth (present-day Portland), Maine, and captured or killed thirty-four English,[12] leading to an abandonment of the general area.[13] On August 13, Richard Hammond's trading post in present-day Woolwich was raided. Hammond was killed and a number of others taken captive in the raid. Also that month the ancient settlement of Pemaquid, Maine, was abandoned and burned to the ground.

From there the warrior bands split. One group traveled north and the other paddled to Arrowsic where, the next day, Thomas Clarke and Thomas Lakes' fortified trading post was overrun and destroyed. By late August 1676 the country east of Scarborough was deserted by the English. On September 3, a group of men, having gone to Munjoy's Island (present-day Peaks Island) to obtain badly needed sheep, were ambushed and wiped out.[14] "In one month," the nineteenth-century historian William Williamson reported, "fifteen leagues of coast eastward of Casco neck were laid waste."[15]

These humiliating losses prompted Boston authorities to place 360 men under Major Richard Waldron, whose job it was to strengthen Maine's settlements and crush the native military. Throughout the region defenses were improved, including the addition of Fort Loyal at Portsmouth, New Hampshire's Casco Neck, supervised by Benjamin Church. However, Waldron, much like Moseley and Talcott before him, unleashed an all-out assault on the native population that failed to distinguish between belligerent and friend, warrior and noncombatant. Among other outrages, his policies sanctioned an English sailor's capture of twelve friendly Micmac at Cape Sable, whose sale into slavery brought the remaining eastern Abenaki into the war.

Waldron himself contributed one particularly treacherous act. On September 6, the day Captains William Hawthorne and Joseph Sill arrived at Dover with about four hundred troops, nearly four hundred Abenaki also arrived, hoping for an end to hostilities and believing they were to take part in a treaty of peace. Feigning goodwill, Waldron convinced them to participate in a military exercise in which the Abenaki were to fight a mock battle against the English. During the exercise, Waldron had the natives fire together into the air; immediately they were surrounded by the English and disarmed. About two hundred of these warriors were sent to Boston, where they were either killed or sold into slavery.[16] Maine historian William D. Williamson expressed the controversial nature of this act when he wrote, "The propriety of this unprecedented course was a subject, which divided the whole community; some applauded,—some doubted,—some censured; but the government approved."[17]

On September 8, 1676, troops under Captains Sill, Hawthorne, and Hunting, now anxious to do battle, marched from Dover to Black Point (present-day Scarborough, Maine) with nothing but frustration to show for their efforts. Frustration turned to fear in October 1676 when the fort at Black Point was surrendered to Mugg Hegone without a fight. This, in addition to the burning of Blue Point the prior year, completed the destruction of Scarborough.

The capture of Black Point caused a stir throughout Massachusetts Bay as the English watched the war—which had supposedly ended with Philip's death—creep farther south. On October 18, 1676, Mugg attacked Wells, attempting a similar ploy to that at Black Point. Undaunted, the settlers held fast and Mugg retreated after killing two persons, wounding a third, and slaughtering thirteen cattle.[18]

On November 1, Captains Sill and Hawthorne set out to attack the Indian fort at Ossipee, New Hampshire, to which it was believed Androscoggin, Pigwacket, and other Abenaki had retreated. The winter had come on fast, and the expedition marched through deep snow and through streams not yet frozen. The soldiers reached the fort, found it empty, and proceeded to burn it. They then began the long march back, returning on January 9 without having encountered a single native.[19]

Mugg used his victory at Black Point, and the unease of English authorities, to initiate a peace mission to Boston in November 1676. The results harkened back to Philip's Taunton Agreement; Mugg was forced to accept terms entirely favorable to the English. These included a return of all English captives, reparations paid to the English for all damages done in the war, government control of the sale of ammunition, and a promise that

Madockawando and his Penobscot would take up arms against other natives if they persisted in waging war.[20] This lopsided agreement virtually ensured that the war would drag on.

As settlements in Massachusetts and Rhode Island went about the task of rebuilding, violence in Maine spilled into 1677. In February, Boston placed 140 English and 60 friendly natives under Waldron's command. On February 21 they skirmished with Squando near Falmouth and then reached Arrowsic, where half of the party set about establishing a garrison. (It was also here that they found the body of Thomas Lake, perfectly preserved despite his death earlier in the winter. Lake was taken to Boston and buried at Copps Hill Burying Ground.) The others went ahead on February 16 to Pemaquid, where Waldron attempted to negotiate a cease-fire (with disastrous results) and instead established a second garrison.

In April, Simon "the Yankee killer" led raids against York, where seven English were killed, and against Wells, where Captain Benjamin Swett lost three soldiers in an ambush. On May 16, the natives under Mugg Hegone again laid siege to Jocelyn's garrison at Black Point; this time, however, Mugg would lose his life and the siege would be broken. The natives withdrew, sending five canoes of warriors back to Wells and York, where seven more English were killed.

On June 29, Captain Benjamin Sweet, Lieutenant James Richardson, and 240 raw recruits from Boston arrived at Black Point with orders to strengthen and hold the garrison. Almost immediately, natives ambushed and killed sixty of their number. Also during the summer of 1677 the natives stole twenty English fishing boats, mostly belonging to residents of Salem, Massachusetts, in the waters of Maine. Massachusetts Bay sent a war ship, manned by forty sailors, to recapture the fleet. The task was made easy by the fact that the Indians had stolen everything of value and abandoned the ships.[21]

In August 1677 the war in Maine came to an abrupt end, but only through an initiative of the British Crown and then only acting in the larger context of its European interests. The duke of York, fearful that the war might allow the French to seize his colonial holdings in the Sagadahock province, authorized Governor Andros to act. Andros, always seeking ways to expand his power, wasted no time in sending an armed expedition to Pemaquid with orders to build a fort, occupy the land, and reopen trade. The New York expedition, finding the natives "pacific and tranquil,"[22] began talks that led to the exchange of captives and gave Maine's warriors the first hope of real peace.

The fall and winter went by peacefully, and on April 12, 1678, English and native signed the Treaty of Casco, formally ending hostilities in Maine. The terms offered by the Crown were far better than Mugg Hegone had been forced to accept in Boston; they included the return of all captives without ransom, and that each English family in Maine extend an annual quit-rent payment of one peck of corn to the Abenaki.[23] The authorities at Boston were appalled by the document, which ended the last chapter of King Philip's War but did little to erase the enmity between English and Algonquian in northern New England.

In practical terms, the natives found English action little changed by the treaty. Hatred festered on both sides, and in the end it took a series of wars and decades of fighting to finally assert the dominance of one side over the other.

SOME NOTES ON THE WAR'S AFTERMATH

Many of the war's political and military leaders passed away soon after its end. Governor John Winthrop of Connecticut and Governor John Leverett of Massachusetts both died in 1676, Governor William Coddington of Rhode Island in 1678, and Governor Josiah Winslow of Plymouth in 1680. Major Simon Willard was struck down by an "epidemical colde" in 1676, and his funeral at Charlestown included a parade of six military companies.[24] Major Thomas Savage, who served in the Second Boston militia for more than thirty years, died in 1682, as did Major James Cudworth, who caught smallpox in London. When Captain Thomas Brattle died in 1683, he was said to have left the largest estate in New England at the time, fifteen hundred pounds sterling, much of which he had loaned to the colony during the war.[25] Captain Thomas Wheeler died in 1686, Major John Talcott in 1688, the Reverend John Eliot ("apostle to the Indians") in 1690, and Captain George Denison in 1694. Major Richard Waldron, aged eighty, died a particularly gruesome death when natives exacted their revenge on him in 1689. Major Samuel Appleton returned to his extensive holdings in present-day Ipswich and died on May 15, 1696. Captain Thomas Prentice, who commanded the guard that would take Sir Edmund Andros prisoner in 1689, died in July 1709 after a fall from his horse. As noted above, Benjamin Church lived to fight in King William's War in 1690 and died in January 1717/18 when, returning from a relative's home, he was thrown by his horse and burst a blood vessel.

Many of the Massachusetts soldiers who survived the war would wage a second battle to secure the land grants promised them on Dedham Plain in December 1675. As they were mustering before the Great Swamp Fight, a message had come from the governor: "If they played the man, took the fort, and drove the enemy out of the Narragansett country, which is their great seat, they should have a gratuity of land, besides their wages."[26] Not until 1685 was the first grant set aside, though the conditions for settling (thirty families and a minister within four years) were too difficult for most to meet. Fifty-seven years passed before Massachusetts officially accepted a list of grantees. However, when a meeting of the Narragansett Swamp Fight veterans and their heirs was held on Boston Common on June 6, 1733, to divide the land, they realized that neither the quantity nor quality of the grant was sufficient. Almost three more decades passed before the claim was finally met, in 1760, and settlement began in towns such as Templeton, Greenwich, and Westminster, Massachusetts; Buxton and Gorham, Maine; and Amherst, New Hampshire. It is questionable whether even one of the 696 Massachusetts men[27] to whom the promise was made lived long enough to see it fulfilled.

Things went more smoothly in Connecticut, though it would still be twenty years after the war's end—1697—before land was granted, and twenty-two before it was assigned.[28]

In 1676 it was ordered that all private persons holding adult male Indian captives in Plymouth colony be required to dispose of them out of the colony or risk forfeiting them to Plymouth authorities.[29] In September 1676 Massachusetts Bay declared that all natives involved in English deaths would be killed and the remainder sold into slavery.[30] Those few friendly natives allowed to remain in New England were often bound into servitude or released to a Praying Town or reservation.[31] This "wholesale perpetual enslavement of the Indians,"[32] as Eugene Aubrey Stratton characterized it, appeared to be the only way the colonists could feel truly secure after the devastation of the war.

Fewer than two hundred of the warring Narragansett survived hostilities, and most of their land was seized by the English.[33] Ninigret died of old age near the end of the war, but his heirs were recognized as the legal owners of all remaining Narragansett land, eventually pared down to a sixty-four-square-mile tract in Charlestown, Rhode Island,[34] under that state's jurisdiction. In 1681, Uncas agreed to turn over most of the Mohegan lands in Connecticut in return for perpetual friendship, equal justice, and sufficient land for his people.[35]

The Wampanoag surviving the war were widely scattered and closely supervised. Awashonks, whose Sakonnet fought bravely with Benjamin Church, was "rewarded" by having her lands reduced to a few small parcels in Little Compton; by 1683, she had disappeared from history.[36] In 1679, Charles II sold Philip's seven thousand acres in Bristol and Warren, Rhode Island, to Plymouth Colony, which in turn sold it to four investors for eleven hundred pounds sterling.[37] By 1774 there were said to be only sixteen Indians in Bristol, and by 1785, only two.[38] The last Indian in Little Compton died in 1827.[39] By the Revolution, many Wampanoag had given up their traditional *weetos* for European-styled homes and their native names for English surnames.[40] Some accepted Christianity. Others learned European trades or married outside of their people. The struggle to maintain traditional cultural values was often waged amid discrimination and poverty. Fortunately, two communities—Gay Head on Martha's Vineyard and Mashpee on Cape Cod—were relatively untouched by the war and would grow in size, clinging to their traditions. In *Behind the Frontier*, historian Daniel Mandell has concluded that the story of the Wampanoag in postwar Massachusetts was not "that of a hapless decent into extinction. While natives declined in numbers and circumstances during the [eighteenth] century, and many villages dissolved, survivors adapted by reshaping their communities while maintaining key elements of aboriginal culture."[41]

For the Abenaki of Maine, the Treaty of Casco was but a temporary respite in a series of five wars against the English, finally ending in the Seven Years' War (1756–1763). Despite their best efforts to prevent occupation of their homelands, the Abenaki would eventually be pushed into the far northern regions of New England and into Canada. Those who remained saw the advent of large-scale hunting and trapping and the destruction of timberland, as well as a new round of European diseases that reduced the population further.[42] By 1820, when Maine earned statehood, the Abenaki were left with only a few thousand acres of land, more of which they would lose when they officially became wards of the state.[43]

Many of the Massachusetts Bay Christian Indians who survived the war were initially scattered in small groups, but eventually came to live at Natick, where a church was established and the town incorporated. In time their numbers dwindled, and the last of the Natick Indians died in 1826.[44]

Despite their military supremacy, political victory for the New England colonists was a more elusive goal. Londoners, who had actively followed the war through letters and pamphlets, were told that "petty, puritan, corporate functionaries . . . had stolen native land, botched colonial defense, and refused aid from imperial possessions lest it compromise their own independence."[45] By March 1676, Edward Randolph was being prepared by Whitehall to visit Boston and compile a record of Massachusetts Bay's real sins, which were bound to include trading illegally with other European countries, enacting laws contrary to those of England, and claiming lands that rightfully belonged to the Crown. This was the opening salvo in a series of royal actions that would reassert English control in New England and return Massachusetts to its status as an imperial province.

When it was finally issued, Randolph's report—biased though it might have been—was devastating. He found Governor Leverett to be openly flaunting English law.[46] He discovered a militia that was weaker than he had anticipated, and poorly trained. He discovered animosity between Plymouth and Boston, and fear throughout the colonies of Massachusetts Bay's aggression. And, Randolph concluded, he had found "the loyal colonies of New Plymouth, Connecticut, New Hampshire and Maine . . . are very desirous of submitting to a general governor to be established by

In the closing months of the war, Philip was primarily concerned with avoiding English soldiers. (Courtesy of the Haffenreffer Museum of Anthropology, Brown University)

his Majestie,"[47] especially if it meant relief from the tyranny of Puritan Boston.

The Crown moved slowly to reassert its authority, distracted by Nathaniel Bacon's rebellion in Virginia, more pressing matters in Europe, and Boston's sudden conciliatory manner. In October 1677, the General Court sent a gift to King Charles that included ten barrels of cranberries, three thousand codfish, and a message from the governor that Massachusetts Bay remained at all times loyal to the king.[48] By 1682 it appeared that Massachusetts Bay's charter might be safe, but in June 1683 Randolph struck again, this time preparing a list of seven articles indicting the leadership at Boston. Among the offenses was the creation of a public mint and the imprisonment of Crown officials.[49]

On October 23, 1684, the High Court of Chancery handed down a decree abrogating the Charter of Massachusetts, and with it the Confederation of New England. In its place, the Dominion of New England was established under Governor Edmund Andros, who would attempt for five years to bring royal authority to the wayward colonies. During this period, Andros would clash with New Englanders over taxation, limits on town meetings, and revocation of land titles. He would even be accused of plotting another Indian attack on the colonies to ensure imperial control. For some colonists, the Andros regime was part and parcel of King Philip's War, one in a series of evils designed to test God's people in the wilderness.

In 1689, Andros was chased from power in the wake of England's Glorious Revolution. Ironically, the governor was fighting Indians in Maine when news of King James II's ouster arrived; his militia mutinied, and when the governor returned to Boston, he found the city in revolt.

Andros' exit, like King Philip's War, was something of a hollow victory. In 1692 a new charter was introduced in Boston, requiring that Massachusetts' governor be appointed from London and that voting rights be based on property and not church membership. While superior in many ways to the arbitrary rule of Edmund Andros, the new charter was still a far cry from the heady days of the mid-seventeenth century, when God's people seemed destined to build their community with little outside interference.

In its first seventy-five years, colonial New England grew in independence, establishing a culture and traditions that were in many ways separate and unique from those of its mother country. King Philip's War violently dislocated this process; the conflict was a watershed event that set in motion forces that would successfully draw the colonies back into close orbit with England. On the eve of the American Revolution, some historians believed, Americans were more English than they had been since the founding of the American colonies.[50] No one who fought King Philip's War would have known it, but from the moment of Philip's death, it would take a full century—and an entirely new war—to return New England to the same level of independence and prosperity it had enjoyed prior to King Philip's War.

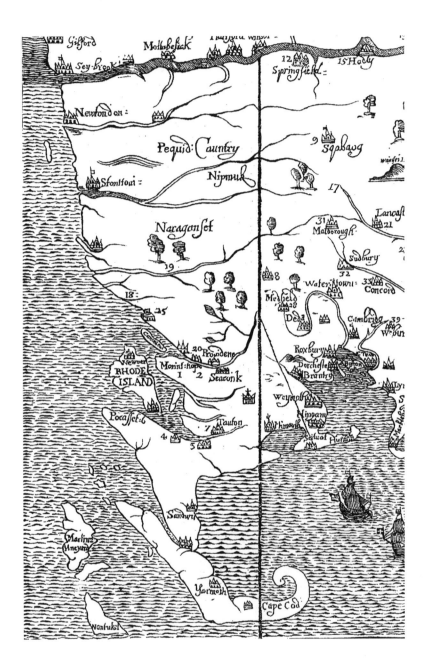

❧ PART II ❧

THE SITES

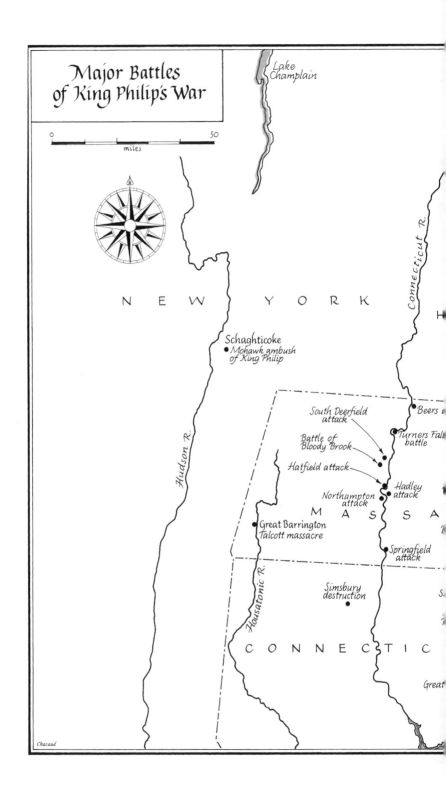

Major Battles
of King Philip's War

0   50
miles

Lake
Champlain

N E W   Y O R K

Connecticut R.

H

Schaghticoke
● Mohawk ambush
of King Philip

Hudson R.

South Deerfield
attack

● Beers

Battle of
Bloody Brook

Turners Falls
battle

Hatfield attack

● Hadley
attack

Northampton
attack

M A S S A

● Great Barrington
Talcott massacre

● Springfield
attack

Housatonic R.

Simsbury
destruction
●

S

C O N N E C T I C

Great

Chazaud

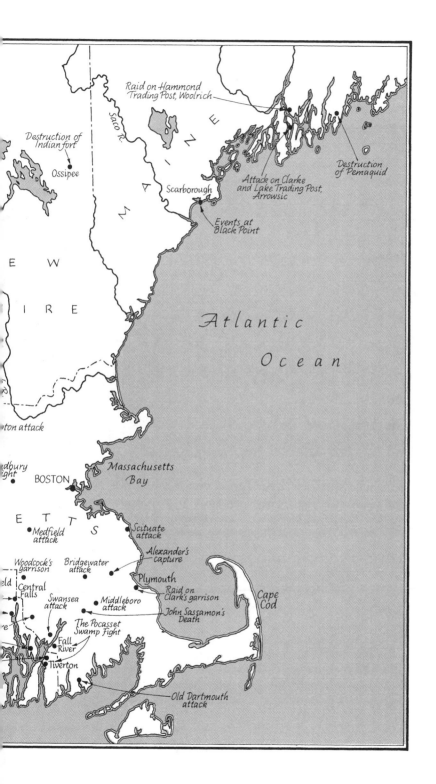

Raid on Hammond
Trading Post, Woolrich

Saco R.

Destruction of
Indian fort

Ossipee

M A I N E

Scarborough

Attack on Clarke
and Lake Trading Post,
Arrowsic

Destruction
of Pemaquid

Events at
Black Point

E W

I R E

Atlantic

Ocean

ton attack

dbury
ght

BOSTON

Massachusetts
Bay

E T T S

Medfield
attack

Scituate
attack

Alexander's
capture

Woodcock's
garrison

Bridgewater
attack

eld

Central
Falls

Plymouth

Raid on
Clark's garrison

Cape
Cod

Swansea
attack

Middleboro
attack

John Sassamon's
Death

The Pocasset
Swamp Fight

Fall
River

Tiverton

Old Dartmouth
attack

The assault of the thousand-man English army on the fortified Narragansett village in the Great Swamp of present-day South Kingstown, Rhode Island, was the single bloodiest day of King Philip's War. (Courtesy of the Haffenreffer Museum of Anthropology, Brown University)

· Chapter 4 ·

King Philip's War in Southeastern Massachusetts

PHILIP WAS AT HOME IN SOUTHEASTERN MASSACHUSETTS, an area he and his family frequented for hunting and fishing and that he also knew from his journeys to Plymouth and Boston. This corner of the Old Colony thus heard the rumblings of King Philip's War several years before its outbreak, in the death of Philip's brother, Alexander, and in the equally infamous Treaty at Taunton. It also saw the start of King Philip's War with the attack on Swansea, and the final passing of native resistance with Anawan's capture at Rehoboth.

ALEXANDER'S CAPTURE, HALIFAX, MASSACHUSETTS

When Major Josiah Winslow set off with, in Hubbard's estimate, "eight or ten stout men . . . well armed"[1] in the summer of 1662 to bring Alexander before Plymouth authorities, he intended to ride to "the said Alexander's dwelling, distant at least forty miles from the Governour's house."[2] Instead, Hubbard reported, Winslow discovered Alexander at a "hunting-house within six miles of the English towns."[3] This has generally been taken to mean the area around Monponsett Lakes in Halifax where Massasoit and his sons kept a summer camp. In 1877, a local resident identified Alexander's specific campsite as being on the southwesterly side of White Island, though the only proof offered was local tradition.[4]

Today, Route 58 crosses White Island along a connecting causeway that separates the two bodies of water that comprise Monponsett Lakes (or Ponds). The Halifax Historical Society has placed a marker at the intersection of Route 58 and White Island Road that reads:

Alexander's party watch in shock and sadness as the sachem dies. His mysterious death was a blow both to his own Pokanoket and to the other Wampanoag peoples seeking leadership after Massasoit's death. (Courtesy of the Haffenreffer Museum of Anthropology, Brown University)

NEAR THIS SPOT
WAMSUTTA WAS TAKEN
PRISONER BY
MAJ. JOSIAS WINSLOW.
AN INCIDENT SAID
TO HAVE PRECIPITATED
KING PHILIP'S WAR
PLACED BY
THE HALIFAX
HISTORICAL SOCIETY

In 1984 Maurice Robbins attempted to reconstruct the Monponset Path, the route by which Winslow probably traveled to reach Alexander's camp. Robbins believed that Winslow would have begun his ride in present-day Kingston, at the junction of Court Street and Wapping Road, traveling west on Wapping Road about four miles to Harrub's Corner in Plympton, where the street becomes Country Road:

> About one and a half miles further the street name again changes to Plymouth Street (at the Plympton town line). Another mile through the town of Halifax brings out to Monponsett Pond at the junction of Route 58, there was in 1662 an Indian site that may have been the location of the hunting lodge where Wamsutta was found.[5]

This site, near the intersection of Route 58 and Route 106, is south of the marker placed by the Halifax Historical Society and is more consistent than tradition with contemporary accounts, none of which suggest Alexander was camped on an island.

THE WINSLOW HOME, MARSHFIELD, MASSACHUSETTS

Governor Josiah Winslow lived in the Green Harbor section of Marshfield at the Winslow family home known as Careswell, the place where Alexander lodged after being stricken by his deadly illness. Historians are uncertain as to whether Josiah and Alexander met in the home built by Josiah's father, the governor Edward Winslow, or in a second, nearby home built by Josiah.[6] Neither structure is standing today. The existing Governor Winslow House, at the corner of Route 139 and Webster Street, was built in 1699 near the location of Careswell. A marker at the house reads:

THE BOWLDER MARKS THE HOME OF
GOVERNOR EDWARD WINSLOW
BORN IN ENGLAND 1595 DIED AT SEA 1655
THIS ESTATE WAS GRANTED TO HIM IN 1632
AND HE GAVE IT THE NAME

CARESWELL
THE FIRST HOUSE WAS BUILT BY HIM IN 1636
AND STOOD SOUTH 34E [TRUE] 865 FEET FROM
THIS
BOWLDER. IT WAS AFTERWARDS OCCUPIED
BY HIS SON GOV. JOSIAH WINSLOW
THE FIRST NATIVE BORN GOVERNOR.
THE HOUSE NOW STANDING IN 1915,
S. 59 W [TRUE] 31 FEET, WAS BUILT BY HIS
GRANDSON MR. ISAAC WINSLOW IN 1699

Archaeologist James Deetz, commenting on findings at the site, reported that the Edward Winslow house:

> had no cellar, and its footings must have been set on the ground and later removed. The only evidence of its presence was a brick smear formed by what remained of the chimney base and small deposits of clay that might have been daubing for the walls. Winslow's son built a substantial house nearby at about the time his father's house was dismantled. Bricks recovered in digging this site were of two types, and some seemed earlier in type than the known date of the later house. The original house built by Edward Winslow was probably cannibalized in the construction of the second house by his son.[7]

Josiah Winslow's grave is located in the Winslow Burying Ground, found on the west side of Winslow Cemetery Road, across from Presidential Circle in Marshfield.

TREATY AT TAUNTON, MASSACHUSETTS

On April 10, 1671, the commissioners of Plymouth Colony and Massachusetts Bay met at Taunton to question Philip about rumors that he was preparing for war with the English. Philip had agreed to the meeting but ever alert to English duplicity, had stopped his party's approach to town at the Three Mile River, about four miles away[8] from Taunton's meeting-house, perhaps in the area south of Westville in present-day North Dighton.[9] The Pokanoket were, according to Drake's *Old Indian Chronicle*, "in con-siderable force, attired, armed and painted as if apprehending a battle."[10]

Governor Prence sent James Brown and "the venerable peace-maker, Mr. Williams"[11] to meet with Philip and guarantee his safety. Encouraged by the presence of old friends, Philip agreed to proceed to Taunton Green, then called the Training Field, but only when Brown and Williams agreed to remain as hostages.

The precise bounds of Taunton's Training Field in 1671 are unknown. However, in 1717 the town voted to enlarge it to eighty-eight acres, with boundaries running approximately as follows: beginning at Neck o'Land, west along Summer and Main Street to the present Taunton Green, north along the west side of Broadway (including the site of Morton Hospital) to Winter Street, southeast to include present-day Plain Cemetery, south along Arlington Street, returning to Neck o'Land via Dean and Prospect Streets.[12]

Philip's party had proceeded from the Three Mile River along a path that eventually intersected and followed present-day Cohannet Street, marching as far as the old gristmill. This mill, built by Thomas Linkon sometime after his arrival at Taunton in 1649,[13] was located on the west side of Mill River, probably near the present-day YMCA. This was un-doubtedly a spot familiar to Philip and to generations of Wampanoag be-fore him, as Samuel Emery suggests in his *History of Taunton*:

> The Indian name for Taunton is Cohannit, at first given to the falls in ye Mill River where the old Mill (so called) now stands, being in the most convenient place for catching alewives of any in those parts. The ancient standers remember that hundreds of Indians would come from Mount Hope & other places every year in April, with great dancings and shoutings to catch fish at Cohannit . . . The first English planters in Taunton found great relief from this sort of fish, both for food and raising of some and prized them so highly that they took care that when Goodman Linkon first craved leave to set up a grist mill at that place, a town vote should be passed that fish should not be stopped.[14]

The mill subsequently passed on to Linkon's sons and was sold to Robert Crossman. It stood until 1823.[15]

It was just before reaching the mill that Philip stopped to place sentinels on a large hill that dominated the surrounding area. The hill, known in the early days of Taunton as Plumbley Hill and Rock Hill, later called Crossman's Hill and Toad Hill, and finally simply referred to as "the gravel hill of Taunton," was bounded by present-day Cohannet and Porter Streets on the west, Barnum Street to the south, High Street on the north, and a continuation of Clinton Street to High Street on the east. The hill was at its highest elevation in the area directly behind present-day St. Thomas Church. The only remaining vestige of Plumbley Hill is the slight rise on which the St. Thomas Church Rectory now sits.[16] Once a landmark of the city, the hill was leveled (in part) to fill the swampland on which the Taunton Mall (and former railroad yard) is now located.

From Plumbley Hill, Philip was probably able to see Taunton's meetinghouse at present-day Church Green and determine if a trap had been set anywhere along his route. Philip recognized that once he left Plumbley Hill, retreat would be nearly impossible, so he dispatched a message to the commissioners asking that they meet him there. "To this the English would not listen," notes the *Old Indian Chronicle*, and the Plymouth men became clamorous to be allowed to attack Philip.[17] Cooler heads from Massachusetts Bay prevailed, however, and several of the commissioners went out to meet with Philip. At that point he agreed to a parley, but only on the conditions that his men accompany him and that if talks were held at the meetinghouse, one side should be occupied by his people and the other by the English.

Taunton's first meetinghouse sat at the head of Spring Street, on or near the present site of the First Parish Church at Church Green. (Church Green was once known as "Meeting House Common."[18]) The exact date of its construction is unknown, although it is believed to have been erected before 1647.[19] Taunton historian Samuel Hopkins Emery writes:

> We have in our mind's eye a distinct image of the structure—a plain, unadorned barn-like building, without tower, turret, belfry, but in the sight of the fathers and mothers of the town, a holy place, consecrated,

set apart for good purposes. The inhabitants of the town were expected to be present every Lord's day, and provision was made for their accommodation.[20]

In 1689–1690 repairs and additions were made to the structure, including a spindle and vane, and the hanging of a bell.[21] Sometime around 1729, and after considerable debate, a second meetinghouse replaced the first. In 1789 a third was built on the same spot, and in 1829 the present structure was constructed.[22] A tablet placed near the west entrance of the church grounds at the time of the city's 250th anniversary celebration in 1889 to commemorate the first meetinghouse[23] can no longer be found.

The meeting between Philip and the commissioners has been described by countless historians, most with more imagination than fact, and many with a traditional Puritan bias, as this example from Taunton historian Francis Baylies indicates:

> There they conferred, and the old meetinghouse at Taunton exhibited a scene alike singular and interesting. On one side were arrayed the austere Puritan English with formal garb, close shorn hair and solemn countenances, looking hostility and defiance . . . On the other side appeared the tawny and ferocious countenances of the Indian warriors; their long, black hair hanging down their back; their small and sunken eyes, gleaming with serpent fires; their persons covered with belts of wampum and fantastic ornaments.[24]

This is one of many events presaging King Philip's War where the lack of a contemporary Wampanoag account makes interpretation difficult. The story is told that Philip was caught in a set of lies and acknowledged the truth of the charges against him, including securing ammunition from the Narragansett and planning an attack on Taunton and Old Rehoboth.[25] The less biased view of Samuel Drake suggests that Philip "was now completely in the power of his enemies, and that he could only extricate himself by assenting to their demands, however unreasonable they might be."[26] The so-called Taunton Agreement, which, Hubbard notes, required that Philip "resign up unto the Government of New Plimouth, all my English arms,"[27] was probably taken seriously by the sachem only long enough to remove his party safely from the meetinghouse and away from the hostile crowd.

At the outbreak of the war four years later, Taunton (whose population comprised ninety-six families[28]) became an active military center, serving as a gathering place for troops under Major Bradford in June 1675 and July 1676. The town was said to have eight garrison houses,[29] though today we know the locations of only three.[30] The first was erected in a prominent position at the northwest corner of Cohannet and High Streets,[31] on or near Plumbley Hill and the site of present-day Cohannet School. The second was built on the south side of Washington Street, opposite the northwest corner of Washington and Tremont Streets.[32] The third, referred to as the Old Samuel Leonard House, was erected in 1653 by James Leonard at the site of Taunton's Ancient Iron Works Company, now in Raynham.[33] A memorial plaque marking the spot is located seven-tenths of a mile east from Route 44 along the south side of Route 104. Leonard was a friend of Philip and often repaired the sachem's firearms as he passed by the Iron Works on his way to Fowling Pond. It is said that his friendship saved Taunton from a coordinated attack early in the war, and perhaps from destruction.[34] A story persists that after Philip's death, his head was deposited in the basement (or under the doorstep) of Leonard's house for safekeeping before being sent to Plymouth.[35] However, none of the early historians indicated anything but that the head was sent directly to Plymouth for display.

Philip's hunting lodge at Fowling Pond, also in present-day Raynham, was one mile north of the Ancient Iron Works on present-day King Philip's Street near the end of Mill Street. Fowling Pond was said to be two miles long and three-quarters of a mile wide in King Philip's time. Today the pond has disappeared. However, a topographic description of Raynham written in 1793 gives some indication of how things may have looked in King Philip's time:

> The place already mentioned, by the name of Fowling Pond, is itself a great curiosity. Before Philip's war, it seems to have been a large pond ... Since then, the water is almost gone, and the large tract it once covered, is grown up to a thick set swamp, of cedar and pine. That it, however, was once a large pond, haunted by fowls, and supplied with fish

in great plenty, is more than probable, for here is found, upon dry land, a large quantity of white floor sand; and a great number of that kind of smooth stones, which are never found, except on shores, or places long washed with water. There is also on the east side a bank of sand, which is called Beaver's Dam, against which the water must formerly have washed up; and if so, the pond must once have been of such amplitude as that above mentioned. Add to this, that a large number of Indian spears, tools, pots &c. are found near the sides of the pond. This indicates that the natives were once thick settled here. But what could be their object? What could induce Philip to build his house here? It was, undoubtedly, fishing and fowling, in this, then large pond. But more than all, there is yet living in this town a man of more than ninety years old, who can well remember, that when he was a boy, he had frequently gone off in a canoe, to fish in this pond; and says, many a fish had been catched, where the pines and cedars are now more than fifty feet high.[36]

While Taunton was attacked twice during the war, it never suffered the kind of destruction visited upon colonial towns. On June 27, 1675, Wampanoag burned the homes of James Walker and John Tisdale, killing Tisdale.[37] In April 1676, with Wampanoag military activity in Plymouth county once again on the rise, residents of Taunton were invited to abandon the town and seek safety among the people of Cape Cod.[38] The townsmen graciously declined this offer, in part because "we may here be more serviceable to ye country than elsewhere."[39] This turned out to be an ominous prophecy. In June 1676, the Wampanoag captured Jethro, a black servant of Captain Willett's household. Shortly thereafter Jethro was able to escape, carrying the warning of Philip's planned attack on Taunton. When Wampanoag attempted to assault the town on July 11, 1676, they were met squarely and withdrew after burning two houses.[40] For this, "Jethro, who saved Taunton," was released from servitude after a term of two years.[41] Had the residents of Taunton deserted the town it surely would have been destroyed. In all, William Hubbard reported that Taunton lost eleven men, two women, and two youths during the war, not including a resident slain in Northfield during the September 1675 ambush of Captain Richard Beers.[42]

On August 6, 1676, a party of twenty Tauntonians surprised and captured twenty-six natives, probably at Lockety Neck, between the Rumford and Wading Rivers, now in Norton.[43] An 1871 map of the city shows an "Indian Battle Ground" just to the west of the Rumford River; transposed to a modern map, the site is about one-half mile from Route 140 and one and a half miles south of Wheaton College.

Also in Norton (part of Old Taunton), a monument was placed in 1889 marking the site of the first home in that town. The marker reads:

THE SITE
OF THE FIRST HOUSE IN
NORTON
BUILT BY
WILLIAM WITHERELL
A.D. 1669
ERECTED BY ORDER OF THE TOWN
A.D. 1889

Witherell, who served as a sergeant with the Plymouth Colony militia, was wounded in the Great Swamp Fight in South Kingstown, Rhode Island.[44] (Witherell's wound was so serious that he could not be moved from Rhode Island until October 1676, ten months after the battle.[45]) The monument for his homesite is a gray stone marker, about four and a half feet tall, on the east side of Bay Street, two-tenths of a mile north from the Taunton-Norton line, tucked into the woods just off the side of the road. The "First Burying Ground," in which Witherell, his family, and those killed in the early Indian wars are buried, was said to be located 193 feet east of the "First House" on private land.[46] The land has since been plowed and no evidence of the gravesite exists.

The Bobet stone, displayed by the Old Colony Historical Society in Taunton, marked the spot in present-day Berkley (part of Old Taunton) where Edward Bobet (Babbitt) was killed by natives. Bobet, who died on

June 15, 1675, was believed to have been the first victim of King Philip's War in Taunton. Edward lived with his wife and nine children on a farm in the section of present-day Berkley once known as "The Farms," some distance from the protection of Taunton Green. On June 25, two days after the outbreak of war at Swansea, Edward and his family walked the old footpath, now Point Street, to the safety of Taunton. According to family tradition, Edward and the family dog returned to his farm to secure some necessary household article but discovered on the return trip to Taunton that they were being pursued by natives. Edward climbed a tree and was hidden until his dog barked and gave away his hiding place. The Wampanoag shot through the tree and killed Edward. He was buried soon after where he fell and the spot was marked by a crude headstone.[47]

This same headstone, which was moved to a stone wall near the grave for many years, has since been placed in the Old Colony Historical Society. In 1911, a bronze memorial tablet was purchased by Bobet's descendants and located near his grave. The tablet reads:

IN MEMORY OF EDWARD BOBET
SLAIN HERE BY INDIANS
JUNE 25, 1675
AND BURIED NEAR THIS SPOT

The new tablet can be found on Berkley Street, in the front yard of a private residence, by crossing the Berkley Bridge from Dighton, passing the Bristol County Agricultural School, and turning left onto Berkley Street. The stone is located one-and-one-tenth miles from the corner of Center Street and Somerset Avenue in Dighton.

Finally, Taunton was home for many years to King Philip's Oak, once located at the southeast corner of White Street and Somerset Avenue. Tradition held that this giant tree, measuring more than sixteen feet at its base, was a regular meeting spot for Philip and his council.[48] In 1926, the Daughters of the American Revolution placed a plaque on the tree which

read THIS MARKS THE KING PHILIP OAK, A SENTINEL OF NEARLY FOUR CEN-
TURIES. However, age caught up with the tree. In 1973 it dropped a
twenty-five-inch-diameter branch on its owner's automobile, parked in-
nocently in the nearby driveway.[49] Ten years later, Taunton's Parks and
Recreation Department, charged with pruning the oak, found its limbs
rotted away and its trunk infested with bees and squirrels. Nearly dead,
its heavy branches a menace to the public, the entire tree was taken down.
Many in Taunton mourned its passing; another connection to King Philip
and colonial history had been lost.

Less than a week later, a local resident reported what no one had expected: sometime in the 1950s he had taken an acorn from King Philip's
Oak and planted it in his yard. When the seed became a sapling, it was
transferred to the north lawn of the First Parish Church at Church Green,
opposite Taunton's City Hall.[50] Today, this "son" of King Philip's Oak
reaches well over thirty feet. Appropriately, it grows very near the spot
where Philip himself met with colonial authorities in 1671.

The story of King Philip's Oak is steeped in the mystique so often a part
of the sites associated with Philip. And, as is often the case, the mystique
dissolves under scrutiny: When the original King Philip's Oak was felled
and the rings counted, a member of Taunton's Parks and Recreation Department reported that the oak appeared to have been planted some hundred years after Philip's death.[51]

THE DEATH OF JOHN SASSAMON,
LAKEVILLE, MASSACHUSETTS

Like Archduke Ferdinand's murder before World War I, the death of John
Sassamon at Assawompsett Pond in present-day Lakeville, Massachusetts,
on January 29, 1674/75[52] was, in many ways, the spark from which the war
would inevitably catch fire. Hubbard reported that Sassamon's body was
discovered in the spring of 1675 by friends, "who finding his hat and his
gun, they were thereby led to the place, where his body was found under
the ice."[53] Sassamon was buried near where he was found. While his body
was laid to rest the rumors about his death were not. Upon finding the

This engraving shows one of the murderers of John Sassamon hiding his body under the ice. Note that the artist has included Patuckson viewing the event from King Philip's Lookout in the background. (Courtesy of the Haffenreffer Museum of Anthropology, Brown University)

body, one friend had noticed bruises around Sassamon's head and reported this to the English authorities at Taunton. When word of possible foul play reached the governor, Sassamon's body was disinterred. According to Puritan historians, it was "very apparent"[54] from the condition of the body that Sassamon had been murdered and not accidentally drowned. The case for his murder was sealed when "by a strange Providence an Indian was found, that by accident was standing unseen upon a hill, had seen them murther the said Sausaman."[55]

Patuckson, the Wampanoag who claimed to have witnessed the murder and whose testimony would send three Wampanoag to their deaths, was said to have viewed the murder from present-day King Philip's Lookout, a cone-shaped hill to the south of Heritage Hill Drive, just off Route 105. A picture of the hill taken at the turn of the century shows a grassy, treeless knoll; today, the site is covered by homes and woods, so that a view of Assawompsett Pond is made more difficult, especially when the trees have foliage. Local historians place the site of Sassamon's murder near the hill, though this is purely conjecture and assumes that a murder actually occurred, that Patuckson found himself a spectator to the murder, and that Patuckson was being truthful. Tradition holds that Sassamon's grave is in an old Indian burial ground on the southern shore of Assawompsett Pond.[56]

Lakeville is also home to the Wampanoag Royal Burying Ground, located on the west side of Route 105 (Bedford Street), eight-tenths of a mile south of Long Point Road between Little Quittacus Pond and Great Quittacus Pond. Interred here are the descendants of Massasoit through his daughter, Amie, and her husband, Tispaquin. Amie was Massasoit's only child known to survive King Philip's War. Her family and descendants lived on Betty's Neck, about a mile northeast of the burying ground. The last person buried in the cemetery, Lydia Tuspaquin, drowned in 1812.[57] Lydia was descended from Massasoit through Amie, her son Benjamin, and his son Benjamin.[58] Lydia's father, Benjamin, married Mary Felix, who may have been the granddaughter of John Sassamon.[59]

ATTACK ON SWANSEA, MASSACHUSETTS

By 1675 Swansea was comprised of thirty or forty houses widely scattered in several distinct groups. One community developed between One Hundred Acre Cove and the crossing of the Palmer River, near the Baptist meetinghouse and Miles (Myles) garrison. A second settlement lay to the east at Mattapoisett, now called Gardiner's Neck, where the Jared Bourne garrison was located. A third major settlement of about eighteen houses was located to the south on the neck of land leading to Mount Hope along the east side of the lower Kickamuit River. This last settlement lay closest to Philip and his Pokanoket, and would be the first to feel their wrath.

On the evening of June 19, 1675, Job Winslow's home was vandalized by Pokanoket warriors. Winslow's home is thought to have been located on the east side of the Kickamuit River, just south of present-day Route 103[60] on land subsequently owned by Edward Ennis.[61] The Winslows were unhurt, but the community was suddenly alert to the gravity of the situation. (Winslow's home was eventually destroyed, but after the war he built a second home on or near the original site.)

The next day, Sunday, June 20, a band of Pokanoket looted several homes at Kickamuit, setting two on fire. The frightened settlers quickly sought safety in the Bourne garrison, which soon held sixteen men and fifty-four women and children.[62] The Bourne garrison, built of stone and probably used as a warehouse before the war,[63] stood south of Route 103 overlooking Lee's River at the sharp turn west in Old Gardiner's Neck Road. A white rock in the corner of the lot near the driveway to a modern home marks the likely location of the garrison.[64] Tradition holds that the garrison spring was in the meadow nearby,[65] though today it can only be discovered (if at all) by crossing private property.

It must have been disturbing to the settlers crowded into the Bourne garrison that Hugh Cole, their most affluent neighbor and leader of the local militia, was nowhere to be found. Cole had already fled with his family down the present-day Cole River to Mount Hope Bay and the safety of Portsmouth, Rhode Island. Today, the house at "Riverby" stands on the spot where Hugh Cole's home once stood, said to be the first house burned by the Wampanoag in King Philip's War. The Riverby house is located on Pearse Road slightly north of Dyer Street on the west side of Cole River not far from Warren. Legend has it that Cole's home was built on the site of a Wampanoag cemetery, which had incensed the Pokanoket. Only King Philip's friendship with Cole saved the family, which was warned in time to flee as their house burst into flames.[66]

Cole's neighbors lived on the western side of Touisset Point. Had they chosen to flee by water, as Cole did, they would have had to float past Philip's camp at present-day Bristol Narrows, a foolhardy risk at best. In any event they did not receive warning of trouble early enough and were forced to travel over land to the Bourne garrison.

While today only an empty field, the Miles garrison, shown here in an early twentieth-century photo, was located on Old Providence Road near its intersection with Barneyville Road in Swansea, Massachusetts. The Reverend John Miles was compensated by the Massachusetts Bay colony government for quartering twelve soldiers and supplying General Cudworth's and Captain Bradford's companies with bread, peas, tobacco, and liquor from July 17 to 19, 1675. (From King Philip's War, *George W. Ellis and John E. Morris, 1906)*

After the war, Cole returned with his family but did not rebuild on Cole River. Instead, he chose a new location on the Kickamuit River. The well of Cole's second house still sits on the east side of the Kickamuit River, south of Route 103 and west of present-day Warren High School. In the past the site was well marked, but the markers were stolen on at least two occasions and the dirt road that once led to the well is entirely overgrown and must be traveled by foot. The path begins across from the Warren Recreational Park.

As news of the attack spread, a messenger was immediately dispatched to Governor Winslow at Marshfield, who on June 21 and 22 sent orders to

Bridgewater and Taunton to raise a force of about two hundred men. Aid began arriving as early as the afternoon of the 21st, but events were spiraling out of control. On the morning of June 23, additional homes were ransacked and burned by the Pokanoket. Worse yet, Philip's men began shooting at the garrison sentries. On that day, however, the English drew first blood when John Salisbury shot and wounded a Pokanoket. On the following day, perhaps in direct retaliation, seven English settlers (including Salisbury) were killed when they left the Bourne garrison to gather corn at a deserted home about a quarter of a mile away.[67] Their ambush may have taken place in the vicinity of Swazey Corner[68] at the present-day intersection of Milford Road and Hortonville Road, just a short distance north of the Bourne garrison. Two other settlers were ambushed and killed when they rode in search of a surgeon.

The severed heads and hands of several of the men killed at Swazey Corner were discovered June 30 hanging from poles along the bank of the Kickamuit River. This location was pinpointed by Hubbard, who placed it about four miles from the Miles garrison,[69] and by Benjamin Church, who wrote that "they marched until they came to the narrow of the neck, at a place called Keekamuit, where they took down the head of eight Englishmen that were killed at the head of Matapoiset neck, and set upon poles."[70] From these descriptions historians George Ellis and John Morris, and other antiquarians, have placed the scene just above the ancient wading place, on the west side of the Kickamuit, directly east of Belcher's Cove in Warren.[71] This same wading place was used to describe the location of Job Winslow's property in the Swansea proprietors records. Consequently, we can conclude that the present-day location of this gruesome sight—"heads, scalps and hands cut off from the bodies of some of the English, and stuck upon poles near the highway, in the barbarous and inhuman manner bidding us defiance"[72]—would be on the west side of the Kickamuit River, just north of the crossing of Route 103.

The Kickamuit Cemetery on Serpentine Road is said to contain the graves of King Philip's War veterans,[73] though inscriptions in the cemetery are often difficult to read.

Once English troops had gathered at Swansea the desire to take the offensive grew. The Miles River Bridge, an important crossing into Pokanoket country, was the site of one of the war's first ambushes. The Pokanoket, who had ventured close enough to the Miles garrison to shoot two of its sentries, waited patiently as Benjamin Church and members of Captain Prentice's troops, led by Joseph Belcher and Corporal John Gill, made an ill-advised charge across the bridge into the woods on the other side. One man was killed and several wounded as the troops fell into disarray and retreated. The following morning found the Pokanoket still sniping at the garrison, so a larger body of soldiers charged back across the bridge and drove Philip's men from the area. The Miles River Bridge today crosses the Palmer River on Old Providence Road.

Nearby is the garrison site of John Miles, a Baptist clergyman born in Wales who settled in Swansea in 1662. During the July 1675 campaign, the Miles garrison served as general headquarters for the officers at Swansea. A tablet marks its approximate location on the north side of Old Providence Road at the intersection of Barneyville Road. The tablet reads:

MILES GARRISON HOUSE
SITE

NEAR THIS SPOT STOOD
THE JOHN MILES GARRISON HOUSE
THE PLACE OF MEETING OF THE TROOPS OF
MASSACHUSETTS BAY AND PLYMOUTH COLONIES
COMMANDED BY
MAJORS THOMAS SAVAGE AND JAMES CUDWORTH
WHO MARCHED TO THE RELIEF OF SWANSEA
AT THE OPENING OF KING PHILIP'S WAR
A.D. 1675

THESE FELL IN SWANSEA, SLAIN BY THE INDIANS
NEHEMIAH ALLIN   WILLIAM HAMMOND
WILLIAM CAHOONE   JOHN JONES
GERSOM COBB   ROBERT JONES

> JOHN DRUDGE   JOSEPH LEWIS
> JOHN FALL   JOHN SALISBURY
> WILLIAM SALISBURY
> TO MARK THIS HISTORIC SITE, THIS MONUMENT
> WAS ERECTED BY THE
> COMMONWEALTH OF MASSACHUSETTS
> A.D. 1912

Old photographs of the garrison indicate that it was probably west of the tablet and closer to the intersection of Barneyville Road.

A second marker on George Street, near the Swansea line, designates the location of the church established by John Miles in 1663 and burned to the ground in King Philip's War. After the war a new church was erected for Miles at Tyler's Point. Nearby, at the confluence of the Barrington and Warren Rivers, is Tyler's Point Cemetery where Miles in buried. His grave is marked by a large stone set under a pine tree near the middle of the cemetery. Hugh Cole is also said to be buried here, though no marker can be found.[74]

A tablet commemorating Swansea's veterans, from King Philip's War to the American Civil War, is prominently displayed in the Swansea Town Hall. Prepared by Job Gardner of South Swansea, the tablet reads, in part:

> KING PHILIP'S WAR 1675.
> TO THE MEMORY OF THE BRAVE MEN WHO FELL
> IN THE WAR WITH KING PHILIP.
> THEIR NAMES ARE UNKNOWN,[75] BUT THEIR DEEDS
> ARE
> NOT FORGOTTEN
> ERECTED BY
> THE TOWN OF SWANSEA
> A.D. 1896

BOSTON, MASSACHUSETTS, DURING KING PHILIP'S WAR

Boston was never attacked during King Philip's War,[76] though panic spread on September 23, 1675, and again on September 28 when a guard some thirty miles away at Mendon, Massachusetts, got drunk and accidentally fired his gun, alarming nearby towns.[77] Boston was spared destruction during the war because of its distance from the frontier and the natural defense afforded by its topography. Indeed, colonial Boston looked much different from what we know today; the town was set on a peninsula surrounded by tidewaters and flats, connected to the mainland by a narrow strip of land to Roxbury. The bounds of the peninsula were approximately present-day Charles, Brighton, Leverett, Causeway, Commercial, North, Merchants Row, Kilby, Batterymarch, Purchase, Essex, and Washington Streets.[78] The first bridge connecting Boston to the mainland (Charlestown) was not built until 1785,[79] more than a century after King Philip's War.

In addition, there is little evidence of a significant Native American presence in the Boston area after the early seventeenth century.[80] When a party led by Miles Standish scouted the peninsula in 1621 it did not see a single native.[81] John Thomas, an Indian purported to be over one hundred years old before his death in 1730, recalled that his father, while still young (circa 1600?), left Boston when a great sickness had wiped out most of his people. Thomas noted that "in both Dorchester and in Boston the dead were so many that they never were buried."[82]

That natives once frequented the area is clear, however. One of the most famous native fish weirs known, called the Boylston Street Fish Weir, was located in Boston. Now destroyed, the weir was discovered by workers excavating the foundation of a new building. The weir consisted of hundreds of wooden stakes planted in the floor of the bay over a two-acre area. At high tide, fish would swim into this enclosure, becoming trapped when the tide went out. Perhaps forty-five hundred years old, the weir may have been in use up to the time of English settlement.[83]

Cotton Mather claimed that three hundred Indian skulls were uncovered on Cotton Hill, perhaps indicating a burial site. In March 1731, workmen digging on Cotton Hill found the bones of a human they thought to be

The Granary Burying Ground is one of several cemeteries in Boston to hold the remains of the veterans and leaders of King Philip's War. (Eric Schultz)

an Indian.[84] Cotton Hill was leveled in 1838 and is the site of present-day Pemberton Square.

A second important peak in colonial Boston was Sentry Hill, rising 185 feet above sea level. The order to place a beacon on its summit in times of danger eventually gave it a new name, Beacon Hill. At the time of King Philip's War, notes Boston chronicler Annie Haven Thwing, Beacon Hill was "a grassy hemisphere so steep that one could with difficulty mount its sides."[85] Beacon Hill began to tumble in 1807, when the Mill Pond Corporation began using its soil to fill in Mill Pond.

A third peak, West Hill, together with Sentry and Cotton Hills, made up Boston's Trimount, a topographical feature captured in the modern-day name, Tremont Street.

Much of Governor Leverett's Boston was destroyed by two great fires, unrelated to King Philip's War, in November 1676 and August 1679. The former destroyed the North Meeting House, Increase Mather's house, and others around North Square.[86] The latter fire demolished eighty dwellings and seventy warehouses[87] and obliterated so many landmarks that the fixing of the estate boundaries was made difficult. Other fires throughout the years—in 1691, 1702, 1711, 1760 (when 349 buildings were consumed), and 1872—left little of colonial Boston standing. Today, it is believed that no building erected prior to 1676 survives.[88]

Leverett's house stood at the south corner of Court and Washington Streets. A portrait of the governor is held by the American Antiquarian Society in Worcester. In 1681 Increase Mather bought a house on the west side of Hanover Street, between Tilesston and North Bennet Streets.[89]

According to the *Memorial History of Boston*, the first town house was erected in Boston in 1657, "a very substantial and comely building, sixty-six feet in length, and thirty-six feet in breadth, set upon twenty-one pillars ten feet in height between the pedestal and capital.[90] This building was located in the market place at the head of State Street.[91] It was in these chambers that Governor Leverett and officials from Connecticut and Plymouth Colonies met to issue orders during King Philip's War. The town house was lost in the fire of 1711. The present "town house" was built in 1713, partially consumed by fire in 1767, and used as the State House until 1798, when it was replaced by the new one on Beacon Street.[92]

Boston is the final resting place for many important participants in King Philip's War. Major Thomas Savage is buried in the King's Chapel yard. He was a tailor by trade and lived near the northerly corner of North and Fleet Streets. Also buried in the King's Chapel yard are John Winthrop, the governor of Connecticut during the war and the eldest son of the former Massachusetts governor, and Lady Andros, wife of Sir Edmund. John Hull, Massachusetts Bay's treasurer during the war, is buried at "The Granary," known in colonial times as the South Burial Ground. The bodies of Captain Thomas Lake (killed by Abenaki at his trading post in present-day Maine) and Major Richard Waldron (killed by Indians in New Hampshire in 1689) are interred at Copp's Hill Burying Ground.

Captain Cyprian Southack, who fought alongside Benjamin Church, lived at the northern base of Cotton Hill; present-day Howard Street was originally named Southack's Court after him. Captain Samuel Moseley was born at Braintree but lived with his family on the corner of present-day Union and Hanover Streets.[93] Captain Daniel Henchman, severely criticized for his performance in fighting Philip at the Nipsachuck Swamp, lived and taught school in Boston prior to King Philip's War. His residence was located just north of Copp's Hill Cemetery, between Commercial Street and Charter Street. In 1674/75 he laid out a cart way ten feet wide, later called Declintion Alley, and today known as Henchman Street.

On the evening of October 30, 1675, a large body of Christian Indians, under suspicion by the English and forced to leave their homes against their will, were met on the Charles River by three vessels and transported to Deer Island in Boston Harbor. At the time of the war, the island—named for the many deer that used it as an escape from wolves on the mainland—was covered by forest and used for the grazing of sheep. The conditions under which these Indians prisoners lived during the war were wretched, and one report indicates that from five hundred to three thousand may have died in captivity.[94] The subsequent history of Deer Island is no less glamorous. The island was farmed until 1847, when it was turned into a quarantine station to treat some of the twenty-five thousand newly arrived Irish immigrants. During the nineteenth century it was also used by a dozen city institutions—including a truant school, two "houses of reformation," and a city almshouse—serving more than three thousand indigent people. In 1896 the Suffolk Country House of Correction was opened on the island, joined in the twentieth century by a piggery whose odor sometimes drifted over Boston proper. Structures on the island were finally razed in 1992 to make way for the Massachusetts Water Resource Authority's sewage treatment plant. No longer an island, Deer Island's 138 acres are connected by a landfill and road to Winthrop, Massachusetts.

Records indicate that on October 18, 1662, both Canonchet[95] and Philip visited Boston Common. *The Memorial History of Boston* describes the Common in colonial times as an area of "uninclosed waste, the stubbly cow-pasture, the bleak hill-side . . . when the wild roses bloomed upon its summit and the frogs croaked in the marshes at its base."[96] The earliest map of the Common shows only a handful of trees, one being "the Old

Elm,"which was thought to be growing before the first English settlement. This elm fell in 1876 and a sprout known as "the old elm's descendant"[97] grew near the same spot. Markers at the base of this second tree once commemorated both:

THE OLD ELM

THIS TREE HAS BEEN STANDING
HERE FOR AN UNKNOWN PERIOD.
IT IS BELIEVED TO HAVE EXISTED
BEFORE THE SETTLEMENT OF BOSTON,
BEING FULL GROWN IN 1722, EXHIBITED
MARKS OF OLD AGE IN 1792,
WAS NEARLY DESTROYED BY A STORM
IN 1832. PROTECTED BY AN IRON
ENCLOSURE IN 1854

J.V.C SMITH, MAYOR

THE OLD ELM
DESTROYED BY A
GALE FEB. 15, 1876

THIS ELM
PLANTED A.D. 1876

Today, neither elm nor any marker indicates the spot of these old trees, though a kiosk map at the Common indicates the location where they once stood.

Monoco was executed on September 26, 1676,[98] upon the gallows at "the town's end," not beyond the present Boylston Street.[99] But most of the early executions in Boston took place on "one of the knolls" of the Common,[100] possibly near "the Old Elm," and the burials were nearby. During King Philip's War the Common became the site of numerous Indian executions. In July 1676, Matoonas was tied to a tree (the Old Elm?) on the

Common and shot for committing the first murder of the war. (Ironically, in June 1656 Matoonas' father had also been shot on Boston Common.[101]) About thirty Indian war prisoners were hung there in August 1676. At least fifteen natives were shot or hung on the Common in September 1676 by Chief Marshall Edward Michelson.[102]

Finally, Boston served as the mustering place for Massachusetts troops in their expedition against the Narragansett in December 1675. About six hundred men were gathered on Dedham Plain, a piece of land abutting the Neponset River that subsequently became Hyde Park and was annexed to Boston. This spot, now covered with homes, was also a mustering place during the Civil War.

WOODCOCK'S GARRISON, NORTH ATTLEBORO, MASSACHUSETTS

John Woodcock's garrison was situated at an important location on the old colonial road from Boston to Providence. It was used by Captain Samuel Moseley's troops in June 1675, by Massachusetts Bay troops prior to the Great Swamp Fight in December 1675, by the survivors of Pierce's Fight in March 1676, and by other troops throughout King Philip's War. The garrison site today is occupied by a building called the Woodcock Garrison House, located on Route 1A, about four-tenths of a mile south of the North Attleboro–Plainville line. (The building is open one day in May and November and by appointment.) While some local residents believe that the existing structure is Woodcock's original structure built in 1669 (and it is so marked above the door), records and architectural evidence indicate that the present structure was built around 1720 by John Daggett. The old garrison and Daggett's newer building may have been attached by a two-story addition and operated as an inn by Daggett.[103]

In 1806 the Steamboat Hotel was constructed by Israel Hatch next to Daggett's structure directly on the site of the original garrison. In 1894, Attleboro's Bi-Centennial Anniversary program noted that "the garrison stood one hundred and thirty-six years, and at the end of that time its timber was sound, save where it had been pierced by bullets during King

Across Washington Street from Woodcock's garrison in North Attleboro, Massachusetts, sits a well-preserved colonial graveyard, resting place for some of the English victims of King Philip's War. (Eric Schultz)

Philip's War."[104] Local historian John Daggett reported that a relic of the original garrison was preserved by the Massachusetts Historical Society.[105] The Old Hatch House burned in 1893 and was itself eventually torn down.[106] Ellis and Morris noted that the foundation stones and cellar holes of the original garrison could still be seen in 1906.[107]

The present-day Woodcock Garrison House, while not a part of King Philip's War, is significant architecturally as the only known variant of a Rhode Island stone-ender—a frame house with one of the gable ends built mostly of stone or brick—in Massachusetts.[108]

Across Washington Street from the garrison, at the intersection of Routes 1 and 1A, is the Woodcock Historic Burial Ground (also called the Old North Burying Ground, 1776), the oldest burying spot in town. John Woodcock's son, Nathaniel, was shot by Indians here in April 1676 and was buried where he fell. A 1694 deed to the Woodcock property mentions this spot: "Except a small parcel of at least six rods square or the contents thereof, for a burying place, in which my wife and several of my children and neighbors are interred."[109] These graves are said to be situated in the center of the present cemetery in an area unmarked by any stones. In all, there are 112 stones in the cemetery.

John Woodcock, an "implacable enemy of the Indians," was sentenced on March 6, 1654/5, to sit in the stocks and fined forty shillings for going into an Indian's house and stealing some property and kidnapping a child as payment for a debt he believed the native owed him.[110] When Woodcock died in October 1701, it was reported that he had the scars of seven bullet holes on his body.[111]

ATTACK ON MIDDLEBORO, MASSACHUSETTS

At the time of King's Philip's War, Native Americans had been living on the land around Middleboro for perhaps twelve thousand years.[112] The Wampanoag village settled at the time of the war was known as Nemasket, located about one-and-one half miles southeast of the present-day center of Middleboro.[113] Not far away, on present-day Main Street at the Nemasket River, the so-called Wading Place is commemorated by a state marker that reads:

THE WADING PLACE
SITE OF THE FORD OF WADING
PLACE WHERE THE INDIAN TRAIL
FROM PLYMOUTH TO "MIDDLEBERRY"
(MIDDLEBOROUGH) CROSSED THE
NEMASKET RIVER. WHEN THE
TOWN WAS ESTABLISHED IN 1669, ITS
SOUTHERN BOUNDARY WAS
DESCRIBED AS EXTENDING "SIX MILES
FROM THE WADING PLACE."

"Hand Rock," located on Barden Hill in Middleboro, Massachusetts, is the stuff of legend: The hand print on the rock is said to be that of the Wampanoag who fell victim to John Thomson's long gun in June 1675. (Eric Schultz)

The sachem of the Nemasket, Tispaquin (the "Black Sachem"), was Philip's brother-in-law and trusted friend who led attacks throughout the war on Bridgewater, Plymouth, and Scituate. Tispaquin's wife and children were captured and taken to Plymouth by Benjamin Church in September 1676. Church, who referred to the sachem as "a great Captain,"[114] left word that if Tispaquin would surrender, he and his men would be enlisted to fight with Church in the continuing war in Maine. A few days later Tispaquin surrendered in Church's absence. He was immediately sent to Plymouth and shot. William Hubbard refers to this episode as a trap set by Church whereby Tispaquin "received the just reward of his former wickedness."[115] Other historians believed Church was sincere, and Plymouth authorities either acted without knowledge of Church's promise, or more likely, acted in bad faith.[116] Church himself wrote that when he "returned from Boston, he found, to his grief, the heads of Annawon, Tispaquin, etc., cut off where were the last of Philip's friends."[117] The nineteenth-century antiquarian Samuel Drake, who did extensive research on King Philip's War, called the act "barbarous."[118] Middleboro historian Thomas Weston felt that "this action on the part of the governor and council has led to perhaps more severe criticism than any portion of the public administration at New Plymouth."[119]

The authorities at Plymouth had first purchased land at Nemasket from the Wampanoag in 1661[120] and granted the new area township status in 1669, when it changed its name from Namassakett to Middleberry. Over the next six years Middleboro grew to about seventy-five residents[121] scattered across a sprawling settlement bounded by Plymouth, Taunton, and Bridgewater.[122] Because of the close proximity of Wampanoag and English, and the nearness of both to Plymouth and Mount Hope, each sensed trouble brewing long before the outbreak of violence in Swansea.

Shortly after incorporation of the town in 1669 Middleboro inhabitants built a fort on the western bank of the Nemasket River near the Wading Place. The Old Fort is commemorated by a state marker on Route 105, nine-tenths of a mile north from the intersection of Route 28, in front of the Middleboro Memorial Junior High School. The marker reads:

OLD FORT
FIFTY RODS EAST IS THE SITE
OF THE OLD FORT, BUILT ABOUT 1670
AS A PLACE OF DEFENSE AND REFUGE
IN TIME OF NEED. DURING KING
PHILIP'S WAR, AN INDIAN MAKING
INSULTING GESTURES ON INDIAN ROCK,
ACROSS THE NEMASKET RIVER, WAS
SHOT FROM THE FORT.

The fort is thought to have been on or near the baseball field behind the junior high school; a rock near the field is used as a landmark. From here, one stands on a bluff that commands a view of the Nemasket River and the Wading Place trail. While no description of the fort remains, it was large enough to accommodate all seventy-four residents of Middleboro for six weeks.[123] The fort was never attacked but was burned to the ground by Wampanoag after the abandonment of Middleboro.

The first attack on Middleboro was on July 9, 1675. John Thomson[124] (sometimes spelled Tomson, later Thompson), commander of the Middleboro fort and its sixteen militiamen, wrote to Governor Winslow afterward that his men were not strong enough to take the raiders head on, and had to watch as the town was set on fire. Thomson reported that "towards night they [the Wampanoag] returned to the top of Tispaquin's Hill with great triumph and rejoicing, with a shout. But we firing our long gun at them, they speedily went away."[125]

The long gun used to frighten the Wampanoag from Tispaquin's Hill is today known as the Thomson Gun and resides in the collection of the Old Colony Historical Society in Taunton, Massachusetts. The story that brought the gun its fame has more than one version. In 1675, when Thomson was made commander of the Middleboro fort, he required that each of his militiamen bring an ordinary gun for defense. In addition, Thomson bought his long gun, weighing twenty pounds, twelve ounces, and measuring a full seven feet, four-and-one-half inches long.[126]

In early June 1675 a band of warriors appeared on the opposite site of the Nemasket River, on a hillside (Barden Hill) near the so-called hand rock, notable for its impression of a man's hand. For several days the Wampanoag flung insults across the water until finally the English decided to respond. Isaac Howland, known for his marksmanship, was selected to fire the long gun. Some versions of the story say that he was to scare the warriors, and others claim that he was to kill one as a warning to the other Wampanoag.[127] In any event, no one expected much more than a startled reaction from the warriors since the distance from the fort to the Wampanoag was 155 rods, or about half a mile.[128] Much to everyone's surprise, one of the natives fell mortally wounded.[129] (Legend says it is his handprint on the rock.) He was carried about three miles distant and buried by his comrades. In 1821, according to tradition, a Major Thomas Bennett was ploughing his land and accidentally unearthed the bones, pipe, stone jug, and knife of the Wampanoag killed by the Thomson gun.[130]

The "hand rock" can still be seen today,[131] its handprint clearly visible despite vandalism.

John Thomson's home (in present-day Halifax, Massachusetts) was destroyed during the attack on Middleboro. The site is marked by a plaque set on an original hearthstone from the house. The plaque is located on Route 105 (Thompson Street) about one mile north of the Middleboro line and fifty yards east of the road.

Thomson is buried in the Nemasket Hill Cemetery; his original gravestone has been replaced by a granite marker. Isaac Howland is buried in the Middleboro Church of the Green Cemetery on Route 105.

The night that John Thomson's house was burned, Thomson stopped to warn George Danson of the attack. Danson either waited until the next morning[132] or proceeded to safety that night with something less than due haste. When he stopped to let his horse drink at a brook, tradition indicates that Danson was shot by a Wampanoag.[133] The site of his alleged death is at present-day Thompson Street in Middleboro, near the Halifax line, at a brook now bearing his name.

ATTACK ON OLD DARTMOUTH, MASSACHUSETTS

Old Dartmouth included New Bedford, which was established in 1787, and Fairhaven, established from New Bedford in 1812. Nearly all the dwellings of the English at Old Dartmouth were reduced to ashes in the July 1675 attack. Those garrisons that survived were occupied only long enough to allow the settlers to escape to safer communities. Once abandoned, the remaining settlement was completely destroyed by the Wampanoag.

Totoson was sachem of the Mattapoisett and one of Philip's principal lieutenants during the war. He led the July 1675 attack on Old Dartmouth (that allowed Philip to flee the Mount Hope peninsula) as well as the devastating raid on Clark's garrison in Plymouth later, in 1676. Historians believe that Totoson's main camp was located in present-day Mattapoisett, as described by Samuel Drake in 1829, on the left of the main road as you pass from the village of Rochester to Mattapoisett, and about two miles from the latter. It was a piece of high ground in a large swamp, connected to the high land by a narrow neck, over which, all had to pass to visit him. The road passes near where this neck joins the high ground.[134]

Today, this main road is no longer used, having given way to the higher ground along where present-day North Street runs. However, Totoson and his camp are not forgotten. His name was corrupted by the English to Tousand, and eventually Towser,[135] and thus he is the namesake for Towser's Neck Road. This overgrown trail cuts between Haskell Swamp and Towsers Swamp, east of North Street and north of Tinkham Hill, and represents the remnants of the former main road. Towser's Neck Road, which runs on private property and is difficult to reach, eventually passes the highland location of Totoson's camp.

Totoson was never captured by the English, escaping several times from Benjamin Church and once nearly killing him. Shortly before the death of Philip, Church captured most of Totoson's remaining company. Totoson and his young son escaped and made their way to present-day Wareham,[136] where the son fell ill and died. Totoson died soon after, possibly succumbing to the same sickness as his son, though Church ascribes his death to a broken heart:

> The wretch reflecting upon the miserable condition he had brought himself into, his heart became a stone within him, and [he] died. The old squaw flung a few leaves and brush over him, came into Sandwich, and gave this account of his death; and offered to show them where she left the body; but never had the opportunity, for she immediately fell sick and died also.[137]

John Cooke's garrison stood several miles from Totoson's camp in present-day Fairhaven.[138] The site is marked by a bronze tablet set into stone that stands on the north side of Coggeshall Street, just west of Garrison Street. The marker reads:

THIS BOULDER
MARKS THE SPOT WHERE BARRACKS
WERE PLACED FOR THE PURPOSE OF
PROTECTING THE EARLY INHABITANTS
DURING THE INDIAN WARS
THESE BARRACKS WERE ERECTED BY
JOHN COOKE
THE LAST SURVIVING PILGRIM OF THOSE
WHO CAME OVER IN THE MAYFLOWER
AND THE FIRST WHITE MAN TO SETTLE
IN THIS TOWN.

An 1899 history of Bristol County noted that the Cooke garrison walls "were in good preservation until recent times,"[139] though nothing remains today. A 1904 paper written for the Old Dartmouth Historical Society noted that "among the relics preserved in the rooms of our society are various arrowheads, spoons and cooking utensils dug up on the site of Cooke's garrison."[140] John Cooke's burial spot is marked not far away, on Pilgrim Avenue, west of Main Street in a small park overlooking the Achusnet River and New Bedford Harbor.

Jacob Mitchell and his wife, who resided in present-day Fairhaven south of Spring Street near the current Boys' Club, were killed as they fled to the Cooke garrison.[141] Thomas Pope and his wife, also fleeing to the Cooke garrison from their house and mill on Sconicut Neck, were killed at a location west of present-day Walnut Street on the south side of Spring Street.[142]

In 1907 Franklyn Howland recorded that the Wampanoag remaining in Fairhaven after King Philip's War were confined to a reservation "of about one acre located on the west side of the road on Sconicut neck, Fairhaven, about a quarter mile south of the present chapel."[143] The burying ground of these Wampanoag was located on the east side of Sconicut Road, about one-and-one-quarter miles south of Route 6, close to the shore. "At one time beneath a solitary clump of oaks, which had been sa-credly preserved, were a number of headstones," according to Howland. "But the oaks have been cut down; the stone have been removed; the mounds have been leveled, and all traces of this hallowed spot have disappeared."[144]

An Old Dartmouth garrison owned by John Russell was situated in the Apponogansett area of present-day South Dartmouth. The foundation of the Russell garrison is still visible, though briars and bramble have grown around the site. A tablet nearby reads:

THE RUSSELL GARRISON
A PLACE OF REFUGE FOR THE
EARLY SETTLERS OF DARTMOUTH DURING
KING PHILIP'S WAR
1675–1676
FOUNDATION REGISTERED BY THE
OLD DARTMOUTH HISTORICAL SOCIETY
1951

The Russell Garrison can be reached on Apponogansett Bay in South Dartmouth by taking Elm Street to Lucy Street to Fort Street. Directly across the bay from the Russell garrison was a Wampanoag village called Indian Town, from which the natives

> used to show themselves, and act all manner of mockery, to aggravate the English; they being at more than a common gunshot off. At one time one made his appearance, and turned his backside in defiance, as usual; but some one having an uncommonly long gun fired upon him and put an end to his mimickry.[145]

A garrison was also situated on Palmer's Island on the Achusnet River, though no remains are evident on this heavily built land now connected by bridges along Route 6.

Benjamin Church conducted many of his field operations in and around Old Dartmouth and the adjacent towns comprising Old Rochester. Undoubtedly one of Church's more pleasant wartime experiences occurred in the summer of 1676, after he had convinced Awashonks and her Sakonnet to join the side of the English. Returning from Plymouth with a new commission to lead the Sakonnet, Church was supposed to meet the natives at Sandwich, Massachusetts. When he arrived he found that the Wampanoag had already departed. Church caught a quick night's sleep and left the following morning with sixteen or eighteen men in search of his new troops. Church described his movements as follows:

> he proceeded as far as Agawom, where they had great expectation of meeting the Indians, but met them not. His men being discouraged, about half of them returned . . . . When they came to the Sippican river, Mr. Howland began to tire, upon which Mr. Church left him and two more, for a reserve, at the river . . . Proceeding in their march, they crossed another river, and opened a great bay, where they might see many miles along shore, where were sand and flats; and hearing a great noise below them, towards the sea, they dismounted their horses; left them, and creeped among the bushes, until they came near the bank, and saw a vast company of Indians, of all ages and sexes; some on horseback running races; some at football; some catching eels and flat fish in the water; some clamming, etc.[146]

Discovering this group to be Awashonks and her Sakonnet, Church soon joined them, feasting on "a curious young bass in one dish; eels and flat fish in a second; and shell fish in a third."[147] After dinner, a huge bonfire of pine was lit, and the mixed group danced around as a sign that "now they were all engaged to fight for the English."[148]

Historians do not know the precise location of this colorful affair. Henry Martyn Dexter suggests that the second river Church crossed was Mill Creek, flowing into Aucoot Cove. Church's report of a "wide view of the bay" might indicate that the location of Awashonks' celebration was between Angelica and Ned Points, or between Aucoot Cove and Angelica Point in present-day Mattapoisett.[149]

In 1984, Maurice Robbins of the Massachusetts Archaeological Society published *The Sandwich Path: Church Searches for Awashonks*, in which he attempted to recreate the likely path taken by Church. Robbins noted that the construction of the Cape Cod Canal in 1914 had eliminated the Scusset and Monomet Rivers, destroyed a large Wampanoag village near the Herring River, wiped away the nearby system of roads and paths,[150] and made the precise re-creation of the first segment of Church's journey impossible. However, once away from the canal, Robbins picked up the chase along Bournedale Road to the Head of Bay Road, into Wareham on Red Brook Road, passing along Route 6 to Elm Street. From there, Church may have followed Main Street to Fearing Hill Road and crossed the Weweantic River just north of Horseshoe Pond. Following Mary's Pond Road into Rochester, Church detoured south just past Mary's Pond itself to escape the wetlands where the current road ends, picking up Mary's Pond Road again near the southern tip of Leonard's Pond. From there, the path passed the Rochester Common, heading west on New Bedford Road, crossing into Acushnet on Perry Hill Road, and fording the Sippican River on the Hiller Farm. Church continued through Acushnet west across the Mattapoisett River to Mendall Road, south on Hathaway Road to South Main Street, and into Fairhaven, where Alden Street leads most directly to Pope Beach. It is here, after a march of about twenty-six miles from Sandwich, that Robbins believes Church found Awashonks and her Sakonnet.[151] This site is considerably farther west than Dexter's location, and given the century of archaeological discovery between Dexter and Robbins, probably more plausible.

THE POCASSET SWAMP FIGHT, TIVERTON, RHODE ISLAND, AND FALL RIVER, MASSACHUSETTS

Benjamin Church's adventure in July 1675 on Punkatees Neck convinced the English that Philip had escaped the Mount Hope peninsula and was coordinating battle plans from the Pocasset side of Mount Hope Bay (now Tiverton, Rhode Island, and Fall River, Massachusetts). With that in mind officials ordered Massachusetts Bay troops returning from Narragansett country to march to Taunton, where on July 18, 1675, they were joined by Plymouth forces under Major James Cudworth. From there, the combined

*While no one can be sure of the precise location of the Pocasset Swamp Fight,
this early twentieth-century photograph of Pocasset country gives a better sense
of the area's terrain than the well-developed business and residential neighbor-
hoods of today's Fall River, Massachusetts, and Tiverton, Rhode Island. (From*
King Philip's War, *George W. Ellis and John E. Morris, 1906)*

army marched eighteen miles to the "great swamp on Pocaseset,"[152]
thought by contemporaries to be a single swamp seven miles in length. On
July 19 Massachusetts and Plymouth forces entered this thick bramble and
engaged Philip's band. Five English were killed and seven wounded, several
mortally. All day the English advanced and the Wampanoag fought a spirited rear-guard action. When darkness approached the exhausted English
retreated from the thick undergrowth. Captain James Cudworth wrote the
following account to Governor Winslow on July 20 from the garrison on
Mount Hope:

On Monday [July 19] following we went to see if we could discover Philip, the Bay forces being now with us; and in our march, two miles before we came to the place of rendezvous, the captain of the Forlorn was shot down dead; three more were then killed or died that night, and five or six more dangerously wounded. The place we found was a hideous dismal swamp [Pocasset Cedar Swamp]; the house or shelter, they had to lodge in, contained, in space, the quantity of four acres of ground, standing thick together; but all women and children fled, only one old man, that we took there, who said, Wittoma was there that day, and that Philip had been there the day before, and that Philip's place of residence was about half a mile off; which we could made no discovery of, because the day was spent, and we having dead men and wounded men to draw off.[153]

In all, seven or eight English lay dead with little to show for their efforts, prompting the Reverend William Hubbard to conclude that "it is ill fighting with a wild beast in his den."[154] Cudworth concurred, writing:

Now so it is, that we judge it now our work to assault him at such disadvantages; for the issue of such a design will be to pick off our men, and we shall never be able to obtain our end in this way, for they fly before us, from one swamp to another.[155]

The exact site of the Pocasset Swamp Fight is unknown and subject to much conjecture. Historians believe Philip probably joined with Weetamoe and her Pocasset at or near the squaw sachem's camp, which historian Henry Martyn Dexter thought to be on the southern side of the present-day Pocasset Cedar Swamp, between South Watuppa Pond and "heights which look down on Mount-Hope Bay."[156] Writing a decade after Dexter, Ebenezer Peirce described the camp as being farther south on Nannaquaket Neck[157] "on a hill not far from the shore."[158] Peirce added that in 1878 he

rode to the stone Bridge in Tiverton, where I made inquiries of the oldest inhabitants, who agree with me that the place seems most probable to have been occupied by King Philip and his followers is the low grounds next to the Taunton River, about a quarter of a mile from the present line that divides Fall River, Mass., from Tiverton, R.I., and on the Tiverton side of that line. The railroad from Fall River to Newport runs directly through this tract, as does also a turn-pike road that used to connect Fall River with the settlement at Howlands' Ferry Bridge in Tiverton.[159]

In a history of Tiverton published in 1976, the author placed Philip and Weetamoe's initial hiding spot "in the woods between the Sucker Brook and what is known as the Bear's Den, east of the present Fish Road."[160]

Some of the difference in opinion regarding the location of Philip and Weetamoe's rendezvous point is undoubtedly due to the fact that they were in constant motion from the moment Philip bolted from the Pocasset peninsula. The two may well have occupied several sites on their journey from Tiverton to the Taunton River. Most of their march would today be obscured by the asphalt and concrete that make up urban sections of North Tiverton and Fall River. That leaves historians to speculate based on the historical record, which in itself poses problems. The area known today as the Pocasset Cedar Swamp is perhaps three-quarters of a mile long at its greatest span. This is far less than the seven miles reported by contemporary historians. Several miles of unconnected swampland run south from the Pocasset Cedar Swamp through Tiverton, though most historians place Philip and Weetamoe farther north at the time of the battle, with little inclination to march south.

Consequently, more modern writers such as George Ellis and John Morris conclude that the seven-mile swamp where the battle was said to occur "was rather a thick growth of woods and tangled underbrush than a wet and miry lowland"[161] stretching north from Pocasset Cedar Swamp into Fall River and then along the Taunton River. In *Fall River in History*, published in 1930, the Tercentenary Committee of Fall River located the Pocasset Swamp Fight "in the southeastern part of our city, the Peasefield district, probably Maplewood."[162] Ellis and Morris, writing in 1906, determined a location for the fight farther north:

There is evidence that the encounter was a point on the eastern shore of the Taunton River directly opposite the present village of Somerset, between the Assonet River and the railroad track leading to Middleboro, and hemmed in on the east by the highway from Fall River to Assonet village. This section of country is rolling, watered by several streams, with occasional marshes.[163]

This location, about two miles north of the Pocasset Cedar Swamp, would put Philip and his followers near a convenient fording spot across the Taunton River. This location corresponds with Peirce's findings and with Hubbard's assertion that "the swamp where they would lodge begins not far from the arm of the sea, coming up to Taunton, they taking the advantage of a low tide, either waded over one night in the end of July, or else wafted themselves over upon small rafts."[164] However, Ellis and Morris do not present any additional evidence used to determine this location. Samuel Drake, careful about pinpointing locations associated with the war, wrote only that the swamp fight's "exact locality is not pointed out."[165]

In summary, we are left to speculate on Philip and Weetamoe's exact route. We know that they fled north in hope of crossing the Taunton River, and that the English ended the chase still in unfriendly terrain they referred to as swamp. We also know that, whatever their route, the Wampanoag used the natural terrain of Tiverton and Fall River to their best advantage, inflicting real and psychological wounds on the English. This second escape from the colonial noose meant that the war would expand to all of New England and that all thoughts of a quick capture of Philip were ended.

RAID ON CLARK'S GARRISON, PLYMOUTH, MASSACHUSETTS

The William Clark garrison was located on the Eel River, three miles southeast of Plymouth.[166] On March 12, 1676, the house was attacked while many of the men were at a meeting in Plymouth. Eleven women and children from two families were killed and the garrison burned to the ground. Totoson led this lightening attack.[167] One of the Clark sons was wounded by a tomahawk during the fight, but recovered and had a silver plate fastened to his head to protect the wound. He was called "Silverheaded Tom" for the rest of his life.[168]

Henry Martyn Dexter described the Clark garrison as being situated about three miles southeast from the village of Plymouth, on the west bank of the Eel River, almost against the point of junction of Plymouth Beach with the mainland and perhaps three-quarters of a mile inland from the junction; the nineteenth-century home of the Reverend Benjamin Whitmore was said to be very near the former garrison site.[169] George Ellis and John Morris described the garrison in the same location, being "half a mile to the eastward of the village of Chiltonville on a site occupied by [the Whitmore house]," built about 1826.[170] This is, however, another case of past antiquarians being more assured than modern historians and archaeologists. The staff at Plimouth Plantation will explain that the precise site of the Clark garrison is unknown; no remains have ever been located. Some believe that the garrison may have been located near what is now the parking area for the Wampanoag Summer Campsite at Plimouth Plantation (see below).[171]

There are several other sites in Plymouth related to activities during King Philip's War. The town's famous Burial Hill was first called Fort Hill, the site of Plymouth's Fort Meeting House during the war. The location of the fort is marked by a sign that reads:

SITE OF THE
FIRST FORT
BUILT IN 1621
LOWER PART USED FOR CHURCH
ALSO SITE OF THE FORT
BUILT IN 1675
WHICH WAS 100 FT SQ SIDES 10 1/2 FT HIGH

On February 19, 1675, the town voted to fortify this structure by building a square palisade, ten feet high and one hundred feet on each side. Each man in town was required to build a three-foot section of it.[172] It was on this palisade that Philip's head was set after his death.[173] The fort on Burial Hill was abandoned as a defense in 1677. A visitor in 1807 discovered the remains of the ditch that surrounded the fortification,[174] though nothing of the fort can be seen today.

Material from the fort was sold to William Harlow for a house now known as the Harlow Old Fort House. Built in 1677, the Harlow House is a working museum that offers a glimpse of colonial life around the time of King Philip's War through daily demonstrations of household arts. The Harlow House is located on Sandwich Street across from the fire station.

The Jabez Howland House, built in 1666, is reported to be "the last house left in Plymouth whose walls have heard the voices of Mayflower Pilgrims." The house is located on the corner of Sandwich and Water Streets. Jabez Howland, son of John and Elizabeth (Tilley) Howland, fought under Benjamin Church and is mentioned often in Church's narrative of King Philip's War.

Among the antiquities preserved at the Pilgrim Hall Museum at 75 Court Street is the gun barrel with which Philip was killed; a leather pocketbook, a pair of spectacles, and a brick from the house of Benjamin Church; and many Winslow artifacts, including Josiah's portrait, baby shoes, and various household items. There are many Wampanoag artifacts in the museum as well. These items are often in storage, so special plans must be made to view them.

The Wampanoag Summer Campsite, off Route 3 at Plimouth Plantation, re-creates Hobbamock's Homesite, the village of a Pokanoket Indian who provided counsel to the Pilgrims. In 1995, an exhibit at Plimouth Plantation called "Irreconcilable Differences: 1620–1692" painted the tense, often violent world of the Wampanoag and Pilgrim, including the attack on Clark's garrison.

ATTACK ON BRIDGEWATER, MASSACHUSETTS

Tispaquin and a small party of Wampanoag attacked the old settlement of Bridgewater, present-day West Bridgewater, on April 9, 1676, burning a house and a barn in the east end of town. The town's minister, the Reverend

Dating to 1662 and shown here circa 1906, the home of Reverend James Keith, Bridgewater, Massachusetts' first minister, is still standing on River Street in West Bridgewater. A court case in 1818 proved conclusively that Keith lived and died in this house, which is today owned by the Old Bridgewater Historical Society. (From King Philip's War, *George W. Ellis and John E. Morris, 1906)*

James Keith, described the assault in a letter to the assistant governor of Plymouth, ending with the fears of the townsmen: "We are in expectation every day of an assault here. The Lord prepare us for our trial."[175]

On Monday, May 8, that assault came when Tispaquin led about three hundred natives in an attack on the settlement. Tradition holds that the warriors set fire to some buildings on "the east side of the village on the south side of the river,"[176] but a torrential downpour extinguished the flames. When Tispaquin and his men renewed their assault on the north side of the river, the residents were able to drive them away without loss.[177] In fact, during all of King Philip's War, not one of the inhabitants of Bridgewater was killed.[178]

The house of the Reverend James Keith, a Scottish immigrant and the first minister of Bridgewater, is still standing on River Street in West Bridgewater. The house dates to 1662, having undergone enlargements in 1678 and again in 1837. William Latham's *Epitaphs in Old Bridgewater* presents pictures of the house in each of its three stages, and relates a court case tried in 1818–1819 in which it was necessary to prove conclusively that Keith lived and died in this house.[179] Today, Keith's house is owned by the Old Bridgewater Historical Society, which opens it to the general public occasionally and also by appointment.[180]

Keith played a small but important part in King Philip's War. In September 1676, after Philip's death, colonial officials debated what sentence should be handed down to Philip's wife and nine-year-old son. The question of whether Philip's son should be put to death was especially troublesome, and so was turned over to the clergy. The ministers Samuel Arnold and John Cotton looked to Deuteronomy 24:16 for guidance—"Fathers shall not be put to death for their children, nor children put to death for their fathers; each is to die for his own sin"—but decided that Scripture did not apply if the crime was committed by "notorious traitors, rebels, and murderers, especially of such as have bin principal leaders and actors in such horrid villainies."[181] Bending Scripture to their purpose, Arnold and Cotton voted for death. Increase Mather concurred when he compared Philip's son to Hadad, who lived after his father's death and proved to be a "scourge to the next generation."[182]

Keith took an opposite view and wrote persuasively that, despite Psalms 137:8–9 ("happy is he who repays you for what you have done to us—he who seizes your infants and dashes them against the rocks"), Deuteronomy 24:16 should be a guide. His opinion evidently carried great weight, for the last we hear of Philip's son is on March 20, 1677, when John Cotton wrote to his brother, "Philip's boy goes now to be sold."[183]

Keith and his wife are buried in the Old Graveyard at West Bridgewater on the east side of South Street. Their gravestone reads:

| HERE LIES THE | HERE LIES THE |
| BODY OF THE REV. | BODY OF MRS. |

MR. JAMES KEITH,	SUSANNA KEITH,
DIED JULY 23, 1719	DIED OCT. 16, 1705
AGED 67 YEARS.	AGED 65.

MR. JAMES KEITH
FIRST MINISTER IN BRIDGEWATER
AND EDUCATED IN ABERDEEN,
SCOTLAND, AND LABORED
IN THE MINISTRY IN THIS TOWN 56 YEARS.

WEETAMOE'S DROWNING, SWANSEA, MASSACHUSETTS

In early August 1676, Weetamoe, accompanied by about twenty-six warriors—from a number that had once been as high as three hundred[184]—took refuge in a dense swamp near Taunton, Massachusetts. Perhaps she was attempting to reach Philip, or seeking safety in Narragansett country, or was simply unsure what her next move should be.

On August 6, a party of twenty men from Taunton, led by an Indian who had crossed over to the English side,[185] surprised and captured the band. Weetamoe escaped and attempted to cross the Taunton River; in Hubbard's words, "upon a raft or some pieces of broken Wood; but whether tired or spent with swimming, or starved with cold and hunger, she was found stark naked in Metapoiset, not far from the waterside."[186]

Weetamoe's corpse was mutilated and her decapitated head sent to Taunton, where it was placed on a pole, paraded through the streets of Taunton, and left on public display at the Taunton Green. Increase Mather described the scene: "The Indians who were prisoners there knew it presently, and made a most horrid and diabolical lamentation, crying out that it was their Queen's head."[187]

Both Hubbard and Mather state that Weetamoe's body was discovered at Metapoiset,[188] then a part of Swansea and now Somerset, Massachusetts. Recent tradition holds that her body was discovered near the present-day

129

Samuel Drake visited Anawan Rock, making (in his own words) "a rude sketch of the place, which was engraved upon a copper plate for my edition of Church's History." (Courtesy of the Haffenreffer Museum of Anthropology, Brown University)

Weetamoo Street, north of the Brightman Street Bridge in Fall River, Massachusetts.[189] Ebenezer Peirce reported in 1878 that

> in the city of Fall River, near the shore of Taunton River in which Weetamoo perished, stands a large cotton factory, named in honor of this unfortunate American queen. It was near the site of the Weetamoo Mill that her dead body was washed ashore, and mutilated by professed Christians in brutal triumph.[190]

One modern author even fixes her point of departure near the Slades Ferry Bridge in Somerset.[191] None of these latter reports are reliable; the early records indicate that Weetamoe's body was discovered on the west side of the Taunton River. By standing at Slades Ferry and looking north along the river to the Brightman Street Bridge, however, one still has a sense of just how long and treacherous this quarter-mile swim would have been.

ANAWAN'S CAPTURE, REHOBOTH, MASSACHUSETTS

Perhaps no site related to King Philip's War has been visited by as many people as Anawan Rock, located about a hundred yards south of Route 44 at Rehoboth, six-tenths of a mile west from the intersection of New Street. A small dirt parking lot leads to a footpath by which the rock is found. A sign in the lot reads:

ANAWAN ROCK
1676
SITE OF THE CAPTURE OF WAMPANOAG
INDIAN CHIEF ANAWAN BY CAPTAIN
BENJAMIN CHURCH ON AUG. 28, 1676
THUS ENDING KING PHILIP'S WAR.

The story of Anawan Rock begins with Philip's death on August 12, 1676, after which colonial troops began relentlessly hunting down the remaining bands of Algonquian hidden in the woods of Plymouth and Massachusetts Bay colonies. One of the most sought-after native leaders was Anawan, described by Church as a "great soldier . . . a valiant Captain under Asuhmequin [Massasoit] . . . and Philip's chieftain all this war."[192] Anawan was said to be quite old at the time of King Philip's War, though his spirit and vigor remained unquestioned. When Philip's camp was attacked in Bristol, Anawan "hallooed with a loud voice, and often called out, 'Iootash, Iootash,'"[193] according to the church, which meant to "stand to it, and fight stoutly."[194] Anawan was shrewd enough to escape the scene of Philip's death, and made his way with the remnants of Philip's people—perhaps fifty or sixty in all[195]—to a camp in the southeasterly part of present-day Rehoboth. This site, protected on three sides by the Squannakonk Swamp,[196] had as its northern boundary an imposing rock, down which any intruder would have to scale to gain surprise entry to the camp.

Captain Benjamin Church had returned to Plymouth after the death of Philip, but was summoned to Rehoboth when news was received that Anawan and his company had been spotted "ranging about their woods."[198] After capturing a number of Wampanoag, Church eventually learned the exact whereabouts of Anawan. Led by one of Anawan's own men, Church moved quickly on Monday, August 28, to capture the chief who "never roosted twice in a place,"[199] Church believed, and who "often said, that he would never be taken alive by the English."[200] Church, through his son Thomas, wrote a firsthand account of Anawan's capture destined to immortalize not only Church, but Anawan Rock as well:

> The old man had given Captain Church a description of the place where Annawon now lay, and of the difficulty of getting at him. Being sensible that they were pretty near to them, with two of his Indians he creeps to the edge of the rocks, from whence he could see their camps. He saw three companies of Indians at a little distance from each other; being easy to be discovered by the light of their fires. He saw also the great ANNAWON and his company, who had formed his camp or kenneling place by falling a tree under the site of the great cliffs of rocks, and setting a row of birch bushes up against it; where he himself, his son, and some of his chiefs had taken up their lodgings . . .
>
> The rocks were so steep that it was impossible to get down, [only] as they lowered themselves by the boughs, and the bushes that grew in the cracks of the rocks. Captain Church creeping back again to the old man, asked him, if there were no possibility of getting at them some other way? He answered, "No." That he and all that belonged to Annawon, were ordered to come that way, and none could come any other way without difficulty, or danger of being shot.
>
> Captain Church then ordered the old man and his daughter to go down foremost with their baskets at their backs, that when Annawon saw them with their baskets he should not mistrust the intrigue. Cap-

tain Church and his handful of soldiers crept down also, under the shadow of those two and their baskets.[201]

Church captured Anawan and his band, secured their weapons, and then shared a meal with the aged chief. In William Hubbard's version of events, published in 1677, Anawan confessed to a number of crimes against the English, which would help to justify his execution a short time later in Plymouth. However, Church's firsthand account fails to mention any confession, showing instead the respect and admiration each man had for the other.

The nineteenth-century antiquarian Samuel Drake visited the site of Anawan's capture in 1826,[202] the same year that the Taunton-Providence turnpike (now Route 44) was begun. (In Church's time, the path closest to Anawan Rock would have been a trail near the east flank of Great Meadow Hill, half a mile north of the rock, and a difficult march through unbroken woods.[203]) Drake described the rock in some detail, noting that the road passed within about forty yards of the rock, which extended northeast and southwest seventy or eighty feet. The rock's "southwest side hangs over a little, and the other, on the northeast part, seems in no very distant period, to have tumbled down in large clefts." He also remarked that "the northwest side of the rock is easily ascended, as it gradually slopes away from its summit to its base, and at an angle, perhaps, not exceeding 35 degrees." Drake also found, near the rock's south*west* extremity, "an opening of an angular form, in which, it is said, Annawon and the other chiefs were encamped."[204]

Ten years later Leonard Bliss Jr., in *History of Rehoboth*, described Anawan Rock in a way that so closely resembled Drake's description that it seems evident he was quoting from Drake's work.[205] Anawan Rock, Bliss wrote, was "a few rods south of the new turnpike from Taunton to Providence . . . on the northern border of a great swamp . . . this side can be seen from the turnpike, and is easily ascended." Bliss, however, placed the "opening of an angular form," Anawan's camping spot, on the rock's south*east* extremity. "In one of the perpendicular sides of this opening is an excavation or fissure, narrow at the bottom and widening gradually upwards, and commencing so near the ground as to make a very convenient seat. This is called 'Anawan's chair'; for it is said that in this is where Anawan used to sit." Within this angular opening there once stood a tree, blown down in the "September gale" of 1815, that "was covered for several feet from the ground with the names of many whom had visited the rock."[206]

Both Drake and Bliss agreed on the site, placement, and general description of Anawan Rock. Their disagreement over the position of the fissure seems odd, since Drake described it correctly as being on the southwest side of the rock, and Bliss seemed to be working from Drake's description. It is clear, however, that they were both describing the same rock, one generally held by their counterparts to be Anawan Rock.

Henry Martyn Dexter visited Anawan Rock some thirty years after Bliss, around 1865, and his description noted how the construction of present-day Route 44 "through the northern end of the swamp, with the natural change of years, has made the position more accessible than of old." Dexter reported the existence of a tree, "larger than any near it, which bears the marks of being often used as a hitching-post," a bit northwest of the rock. He relied on "a continuous tradition," a deep recess along the rock's southern face, "which answers well to Church's description of the spot in which Annawon was . . . encamped," and the site's protected nature to conclude that this was, indeed, the site of Anawan's camp.[207]

Another local historian, Ebenezer Peirce, visited Anawan Rock about 1858, and again in 1878 when he wrote his Indian *History, Biography and Genealogy*. He described the rock in the same terms as Drake, Bliss, and Dexter, probably referring to the writings of one or more of them. However, after comparing Anawan Rock to Church's writings, Peirce expresses considerable disappointment "to find so few evidences of the natural difficulties complained of by Capt. Church in getting from its top to the camping place of Annawon."[208] Peirce wrote:

> I am nineteen years older than Capt. Church was when he performed his feat that has been wondered at and applauded for more than two hundred years, and in that nineteen years I have grown, as Church would express it, "ancient and heavy" as well as clumsy; he had two

strong arms and two very active hands, which I have but one arm, and one hand and that an awkward left one; and yet I passed down the rock and passed up again without the aid of boughs or bushes, and in fact experienced less difficulty in doing so than in getting over many an ordinary stone wall.[209]

Most recently, local historian Bob Sharples has taken the accounts of Drake, Bliss, and Peirce to question whether the rock they described in the nineteenth century is the same one known today as Anawan Rock, and if that rock is the same one described by Church more than three hundred years ago. On all accounts there appear to be small discrepancies. Sharples notes, for example, that Anawan Rock is over twice as far from Route 44, and nearly twice as long as the seventy or eighty feet described by the three historians; in addition, Sharples adds, it "displays no evidence to support an 1836 account telling about pieces of the rock breaking away and tumbling down the northeast side."[210]

As for Church's description, Sharples finds, like Peirce, that Anawan Rock is less difficult to ascend or descend than he had envisioned. In addition, Sharples writes, "Standing on the great rock I could not imagine 70 or 80 Indian Braves camping and cooking as mentioned in Benjamin Church's account. I couldn't imagine them in that wet, mosquito infested swamp, the terrain I encountered when I viewed the site."[211]

With these issues in mind, Sharples investigated the area around the place known as Anawan Rock, along both sides of Route 44, in hopes of finding a site that better fit the evidence provided by historians. (Several rocks in the area are of comparable size and type to Anawan Rock.) Sharples settled on an imposing rock located two-tenths of a mile west of Anawan Rock on Route 44, 150 feet north of the highway:

> From the peak, there is a clear panorama of a wide flat and dry area, now dotted with young trees, forming a more logical Indian campsite. [So called] Sharples Rock is also more difficult to climb; footing is risky on the northeast side where loose pieces of the large rock have broken away.[212]

In addition, Sharples notes the existence of a cave located about five hundred feet away on the south side of Winthrop Avenue, now in a private yard and bricked up as a fireplace. This cave, in which several Indian artifacts were said to have been found, once extended about twenty feet inside a long rock mound. Sharples hypothesizes that Anawan may have hidden the tribe's wampum belts here, the same belts presented to Church by Anawan on the night of his capture.[213]

The true location of Anawan Rock, like many of the sites related to King Philip's War, cannot be proven conclusively. However, most local historians disagree with Sharples' conclusion, and suggest that the evidence supporting the existing rock is too powerful to be dismissed.[214] Besides tradition, which dates back to at least 1815 (when a tree already covered with the carved initials of the rock's many visitors blew down[215]), Anawan Rock also appeared in one of Rehoboth's proprietor's deeds as early as 1763.[216] This documentation was brought to light by E. Otis Dyer Sr., and his son, E. Otis Dyer Jr., both intimately familiar with Rehoboth's early history, and both land surveyors with over forty years experience in the town.

On September 19, 1763, Rehoboth granted Jonathan Bliss the land on which Anawan Rock sat; the rock was specifically named in the deed, the first time Anawan Rock had ever been privately owned. Signing on behalf of the town was Ephraim Bliss, a friend and business partner of Charles Church, grandson of Benjamin. It seems probable that Ephraim, through Charles, would have been familiar with Anawan Rock and been a reliable authority for its location. (It is interesting to wonder if Benjamin Church took his children and grandchildren on visits to the scenes of his various exploits, like Anawan Rock.) In any event, there was no confusion in the minds of the town's fathers about the location of Anawan Rock in 1763, a time when many who knew Benjamin Church personally would still have been alive.

Jonathan Bliss died in the late 1700s and granted the land on which Anawan Rock sat to his son, Asahel Bliss. This is the "Mr. A. Bliss" whom Samuel Drake visited on this trip to the rock in 1826, and the same man to whom Leonard Bliss referred in 1836 when he wrote his history of the

Anawan's capture, which occurred about a month after Philip's death, ended forever the era in New England when English and Algonquian would live peacefully side-by-side. (Courtesy of the Haffenreffer Museum of Anthropology, Brown University)

town. Asahel Bliss bequeathed the land around Anawan Rock to his daughter, Lydia Pratt, who in 1890 sold it to the Rehoboth Antiquarian Society.

This clear succession of Anawan Rock, which passed from the Rehoboth proprietors to the town's antiquarian society in 127 years through just three owners, all in the same family, would seem to lay to rest the "other rock" theory. To be sure, Anawan Rock does not match precisely with the exploits of Benjamin Church, though Church was nearly eighty when he dictated his account of the war, and prone to the exaggeration and lapses of any old soldier. Besides, few local historians have attempted to descend the rock in the dark of night, after a difficult march through uncut trails, with deadly enemies waiting below. In addition, the nature of the terrain directly adjacent to the rock may have been quite different three hundred years ago, making it nearly impossible to assess the true difficulty of descending Anawan Rock. As for the site's fitness as an enemy camp, it is important to recognize that Anawan and his people were running for their lives, probably did not intend to stay in any one location for more than a night, and would have willingly traded mosquitoes and dampness for disguise and security.

The rock designated by Bob Sharples is situated north of Route 44 and, therefore, unquestionably different from the sites described by Drake, Bliss, Dexter, and Peirce. Indeed, it more closely matches the sort of rock we would expect to find after reading about Church's exploits. However, the flat, dry ground around the rock is (on a current topographic map) badly exposed to the east, and to a lesser extent south, giving Church much easier entrance to Anawan's hideaway than down the sheer face of a rock. The existence of a nearby cave is interesting but speculative only; there is no mention of any such place by any of the contemporary historians (including Church). The distance from the current Route 44 to Anawan Rock is almost irrelevant, as we do not know if the course of the original turnpike traveled by nineteenth-century historians is identical to the current Route 44.

Taken as a whole, the small discrepancies between Church's account of Anawan Rock and two centuries of historical description should not dissuade us from the obvious: When we stand today atop Anawan Rock, we are as close to experiencing King Philip's War as the changes of over three centuries allows.

The capture of Anawan left one more titillating mystery for future generations: What became of Philip's intricately woven wampum belts, which told the history and traditions of the Pokanoket people? When Benjamin Church captured Anawan, the aged Pokanoket presented Church with

> Philip's belt, curiously wrought with wompom, being nine inches broad, wrought with black and white wompom, in various figures, and flowers and pictures of many birds and beasts. This, when hanged upon Captain Church's shoulders reached his ankles; and another belt of wompom he presented him with, wrought after the former manner, which Philip was wont to put on his head. It had two flags on the back part, which hung down on his back, and another small belt with a star upon the end of it, which he used to hang on his breast, and they were all edged with red hair, which Annawon said they got in the Mohog's [Mohawk] country.[217]

While Church was generous with Philip's possessions, it seems fairly certain that he delivered these great treasures to the governor of Plymouth Colony, Josiah Winslow.[218] In 1677, Winslow sent a letter to King Charles II, detailing the end of the war and adding:

> Craves His Majesty's favourable acceptance of a few Indian rarities, the best of their spoils of the ornaments and treasure of Sachem Philip, the grand rebel, most of them taken by Captain Benjamin Church (a person of great loyalty and the most successful of their Commanders) when slain by him, being his Crown, gorge, and two belts of their own making of their gold and silver.[219]

The governor sent these items to England courtesy of his brother-in-law, Major Waldegrave Pelham.

It was with great distress, then, that Plymouth received a letter from the Crown in 1679, chastening the Colony for neglecting to communicate to them the conclusion of King Philip's War. Winslow relayed this to the General Court in July 1679, where a second letter was ordered written, and copies of the original documents attached. Winslow made no mention of his brother-in-law's responsibility for this embarrassing incident.

The king received this second correspondence in September 1679, remarking in a note to Winslow that "they were the first letters received from him and is very thankful for the presents he never received, nor the letters, the copies of which he has sent."[220] We know, therefore, that in September 1679 Philip's belts were still "at large," no longer in Winslow's hands but not yet in the hands of the Crown.

In May 1680 Winslow wrote again to the king, this time naming his brother-in-law specifically as the culprit in the 1677 misadventure:

> The letters were delivered to Mr. Ashurst of London, merchant, and by him delivered to Winslow's wife's brother, Major Waldegrave Pelham, an Essex gentleman, of Ferriers Hall in Bewers. Was very unwilling because of their relation to have named him, but has twice written to him very plainly and advised him to frame the best excuse he could for his neglect and yet to deliver them the presents, but he will not give a word in answer."[221]

Strangely enough, the letter of June 26, 1677, accompanying the belts that Josiah Winslow sent to the king, eventually made it into Whitehall's catalog of state papers, though it was inserted out of place, among the documents of 1680. Whether this was a duplicate copy of Winslow's letter, sent later, or proof that the original letter (and belts?) were finally delivered by Pelham to the king is unknown. Nothing more was heard from Pelham on the subject; he retreated to his family home called Ferriers, near Bures Town in Essex, and died in 1699. His manor became in modern times Ferrier's Barn/Farm, a self-help cultural cooperative for the elderly.

Where Philip's belts lie today remains a mystery. Perhaps they are hidden among the treasures of the British Crown, or locked away in some dusty storage area of the British Museum. (The museum had disclaimed any knowledge of Philip's belts,[222] and entreaties to the Crown go unanswered, as one might expect.[223]) Perhaps, too, they are buried in the ground near the old Pelham manor in Essex. Or maybe, as some historians hold, the belts never made it to England at all, but still reside somewhere in New England. One nineteenth-century antiquarian was told that a family in Swansea, Massachusetts, held Philip's belts.[224] Likewise, a bead belt held by the Rhode Island Historical Society was thought for many years to be that of King Philip, and went by the name King Philip's belt. Not long ago it was determined that the beads for the belt could not have been manufactured much before the 1790s, placing the age of King Philip's belt a century younger than Philip himself.[225]

One tantalizing clue as to the belts' whereabouts remains. In the 1980s, Maurice Robbins of the Massachusetts Archaeological Society, believing he may have located the belts, began negotiations with a small museum in Great Britain for their return. Several members of the society remembered discussion of a possible trade, as the corresponding museum was interested in a particular type of cannon to add to its collection. With Robbins' death in 1990, however, the negotiations broke off, and members of the society today have no written record of Robbins' work or remember the museum with which he was corresponding.[226]

This beautiful 1859 illustration by F. A. Chapman is titled "The Perils of our Fore-fathers" and shows the so-called "Angel of Hadley," long considered a myth of King Philip's War. It is now believed that the "angel," who appeared miraculously in the midst of an Indian attack on the town to help the English repel the invaders, was General William Goffe. The general stands at the doorway while his benefactor, the Reverend John Russell, gestures from the pulpit. (Courtesy of the Hadley Historical Society)

· Chapter 5 ·

King Philip's War in Central and Western Massachusetts

NIPMUC CAMPS: WACHUSETT, MENAMESET, QUABAUG OLD FORT, WEKABAUG

THE HISTORIANS OF KING PHILIP'S WAR often referred to three native camps located in Nipmuc country that were each used extensively throughout the war as places of shelter and defense. These sites, called Wachusett, Menameset, and Quabaug Old Fort, were strategically located between Narragansett and Wampanoag territory to the south, and the Connecticut River Valley Indians to the west. As such, they were centers of command that played host to an extraordinary mix of Native American peoples throughout King Philip's War.

The first and most vaguely defined site was described by William Hubbard when he reported that the Narragansett, after their defeat at the Great Swamp Fight, marched north into Nipmuc country "toward Watchuset Hills meeting with all the Indians that had harbored all winter in those woods about Nashaway."[1] This same camp at "Watchuset Hills" was nearly attacked by Major Thomas Savage in March 1676, but the assault was called off when Savage marched to the Connecticut River to counter threats of an attack there.[2] Mary Rowlandson was held captive at or near this same camp in April 1676; local historians place this site "on the western side of Wachusett, probably Princeton."[3] Despite these several references, the precise site of the Nipmuc's "Wachusett Hills" camp is today unknown, though hikers and skiers undoubtedly trace the same paths that Philip and his armies walked in 1675 and 1676.

Menameset (sometimes written as Wenimisset) was perhaps the most important Native American military site of the war, and the site to which the Nipmuc fled immediately after the outbreak of hostilities in 1675. Menameset comprised three villages, described in detail by J. H. Temple in his *History of Brookfield, Massachusetts*. All three villages were seated on the eastern bank of the Ware River, in the northern section of New Braintree and the southern section of Barre.

The most southern (or "lower") site of Menameset is marked by a small, inscribed stone situated on the north side of Hardwick Road just east of Wenimisset Brook. Behind the marker is a flat plain of perhaps five acres, bordered by the brook on one side. Historians George Ellis and John Morris believed that the encampment was about twenty rods from the Ware River,[4] but modern historians are less convinced that the correct site has been discovered.[5]

Menameset's "middle village" (heading upstream), thought to be another campsite that King Philip visited in 1675,[6] is located north of Hardwick Road about a mile northeast of the first site. It can be found by walking north through North Cemetery at the "bend" in Hardwick Road and continuing through a small pine grove behind the cemetery. There one finds a perfectly flat plain of about forty acres stretching back to the Ware River, large and ideally suited for a camp, where numerous native artifacts have been found.

The northernmost camp ("upper village") of Menameset is today a sand pit, located in the town of Barre just west of Airport Road, about seven-tenths of a mile from the New Braintree border. There, the Ware River forms a double oxbow, and it was in the lower bend of about nine acres that the camp probably sat.[7] Many historians think it was here that Mary Rowlandson was held captive from February 12 to February 28, her third remove,[8] and that this would be where she met Robert Pepper, who had been captured at Beers' Ambush. Any evidence of Native American activity has been generally destroyed by the work of backhoes.

Temple also discussed in detail the sites of several other important Nipmuc villages, including their stronghold known as Quabaug Old Fort. Also called Ashquoach, this village has traditionally been located on Indian Hill, north of Sherman's Pond ("Great Pond") in Brimfield, Massachusetts, a short distance from the Warren town line.[9] Levi Badger Chase, in his description of the Bay Path, noted the importance of Ashquoach's location:

Four paths are mentioned as diverging from this point. The western path from Quabaug "Old Fort" passed north of Steerage Rock to the bend in Quabaug River; parting there, one branch kept south of the river, to Springfield, the other crossed the river into Palmer and on to the Great Falls of the Connecticut, now Holyoke City. Another path ran to the falls of Ware River; and still another to the Indian village of Wickabaug, now West Brookfield.[10]

Temple noted that Ashquoach was distinguished for its great corn fields and strong defenses, situated as it was at the highest point of the hill with an open view in all directions.[11] It is thought that King Philip stopped here on August 5, 1675, on his flight from the Nipsachuck Swamp Fight, but finding the fort deserted, marched to Menameset where Nipmuc warriors were preparing for war.[12] Today, the traditional site of Ashquoach can be found on the southeastern knoll of Indian Hill, on a flat spot beside the steep eastern slope, north of the split between Marsh Hill Road and Brookfield Road. The site is on private land and partially fenced.

More recently, in *Wheeler's Surprise: The Lost Battlefield of King Philip's War*, author Jeffrey Fiske has reexamined historical records and concluded that Ashquoach was most likely located "on a hill northwest of Quaboag Pond" in present-day Brookfield. Fiske believes the confusion has come about from use of the term "Connecticut Path" to describe not one, but three ancient paths in Massachusetts.[13]

Wekabaug, not central to the war but the single largest Nipmuc camp in the area, was built on a bluff at the southerly end of Wekabaug (Wickaboag) Pond, adjacent to the pond,[14] in present-day West Brookfield. This camp was visited by Massasoit in 1657 and apparently pledged allegiance to him at the time. Related sites include a camp located about three-quarters of a mile southeast and just across the river, a burial spot on a bluff at the northeasterly end of Wickaboag Pond, and two camps on Quaboag Pond in Brookfield. One of these latter camps was located at the fork of the

Seven Mile Brook and Five Mile Brook, formerly a steep hill leveled during construction on the East Brookfield railroad station and freight yard.[15]

ATTACK ON MENDON, MASSACHUSETTS

Massachusetts Bay had been involved in King Philip's War from its outset, sending troops to assist Plymouth Colony at Swansea and to meet with the Narragansett in Rhode Island. On July 14, 1675, however, the war took on new meaning for officials in Boston when violence spread into Massachusetts Bay Colony itself. A Nipmuc band under Matoonas killed five or six residents of Mendon at work in the fields. The Nipmuc did not press their attack, fleeing instead into the surrounding woods. Hubbard noted that the settlement, "lying so in the Heart of the Enemies county, began to be discouraged," and shortly after was abandoned.[16]

That winter the Nipmuc returned and burned the deserted settlement to the ground. The Reverend Increase Mather, in a rare attempt at humor, spoke to the spiritual health of the colony when he wrote that in "Mendam, had we mended our ways as we should have done, this misery might have been prevented."[17] Very little is known about the actual assault, nor have all the names of the victims been identified. One frustrated Mendon historian complained that the town records do not furnish "a single item of intelligence"[18] concerning King Philip's War. Based on land records, antiquarians have suggested an approximate location of the attack, and a marker at Providence Road and Hartford Avenue that designates the site reads:

NEAR THIS SPOT
THE WIFE AND SON OF
MATTHIAS PUFFER
THE SON OF JOHN ROCKWOOD
AND OTHER INHABITANTS OF
MENDON
WERE KILLED BY NIMUCK INDIANS

In addition to this marker, the state of Massachusetts has designated the site of Mendon's First Meetinghouse on Route 16 at Main Street. This structure was built in 1668 and lost in the general destruction of 1676.

In 1967, the town celebrated its three hundredth anniversary by issuing a commemorative coin, the reverse side of which depicted the massacre.

WHEELER'S SURPRISE, NEW BRAINTREE, MASSACHUSETTS

On August 2, 1675, one of the war's best known and most devastating ambushes, Wheeler's Surprise, took place within the bounds of present-day New Braintree. The ambush occurred just as Philip was making his escape from English soldiers in the Nipsachuck Swamp and heading north to join his Nipmuc allies.

Captain Edward Hutchinson had been assigned the unenviable task of negotiating a treaty with the Nipmuc, in part because "he had a very considerable farm thereabouts, and had occasion to employ several of those sachems there, in tilling and plowing his ground, and thereby he was known by face to many of them."[19] Such a treaty, more threat than negotiation, was designed to keep the Nipmuc from joining Philip. In retrospect, the mission was doomed to failure: Mendon, Massachusetts, had already been destroyed by Nipmuc warriors, and Philip had just slipped past the English at Pocasset and was on the move. At the time, however, colonial officials still held that Wampanoag aggression could be contained in southern New England.

Hutchinson was experienced in this type of highly charged negotiation, having met with Narragansett leaders in June and July 1675 to force their signatures on a treaty of neutrality. He was accompanied in this new effort by three friendly Indians; three men from nearby Brookfield, including Sergeant John Ayres; Ephraim Curtis, an able and courageous scout who built the first home at Quinsigamond, or present-day Worcester; and Cap-

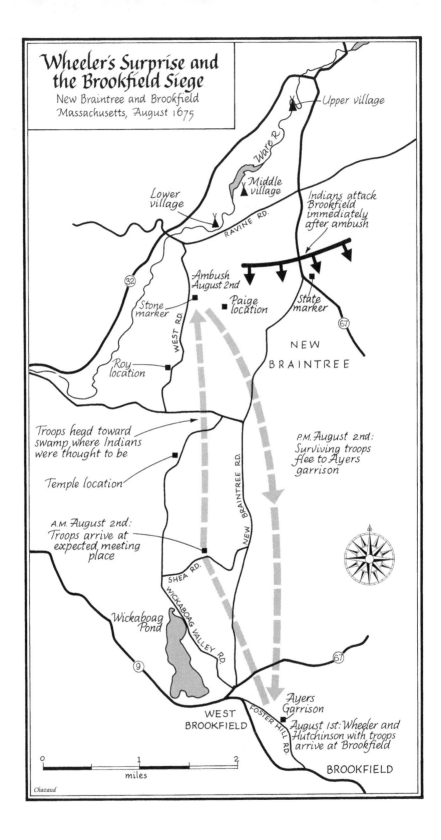

Wheeler's Surprise and the Brookfield Siege
New Braintree and Brookfield
Massachusetts, August 1675

Upper village

Ware R.

Middle village

Lower village

RAVINE RD.

Indians attack Brookfield immediately after ambush

32

Ambush August 2nd

Stone marker

Paige location

State marker

67

NEW BRAINTREE

WEST RD.

Roy location

Troops head toward swamp where Indians were thought to be

Temple location

A.M. August 2nd: Troops arrive at expected meeting place

P.M. August 2nd: Surviving troops flee to Ayers garrison

NEW BRAINTREE RD.

SHEA RD.

WICKABOAG VALLEY RD.

Wickaboag Pond

9

67

Ayers Garrison

WEST BROOKFIELD

FOSTER HILL RD.

August 1st: Wheeler and Hutchinson with troops arrive at Brookfield

BROOKFIELD

0   1   2
miles

Chazaud

tain Thomas Wheeler, whose mounted force consisted of twenty men.[20] Hutchinson, Wheeler and his troops had marched from Cambridge to Sudbury on July 28, 1675, and then west into Nipmuc territory. Most of the soldiers under Wheeler were from Billerica, Chelmsford, and Concord, and did not know the area into which they were riding.

When Wheeler and the party arrived at Brookfield (called Quaboag Plantation, now the Foster Hill section of West Brookfield) on Sunday, August 1, Curtis and three others were sent to arrange a meeting with the Nipmuc. Curtis discovered the Nipmuc at a camp about ten miles from Brookfield and drew from them a promise to meet with Hutchinson the following morning at 8 AM. The designated rendezvous spot was "upon a plain within three miles of Brookfield,"[21] often thought to be the small plain at the intersection of Shea and Madden Roads in West Brookfield.[22] When Hutchinson's party arrived at the appointed hour there were no Nipmuc to be found.

This location can be visited today, though there is little left resembling what Hutchinson and Wheeler might have seen. The site was examined as long ago as 1871 by historian Ebenezer Peirce, who wrote:

> the scene was almost entirely changed from that of one hundred and ninety-six years before. True, the pond [Wickaboag Pond] occupied the site it did then, and the soil of the plain was yet there, but all else, how completely changed! I suppose that I passed over the identical ground on which it was proposed to meet and make a new treaty with the Indians.[23]

Upon reaching this location, the men debated among themselves whether to proceed with the mission or return to Brookfield. Captain Wheeler, who would survive the ensuing ambush and write a firsthand account not many months later, noted:

> But the three men who belonged to Brookfield were so strongly persuaded of their freedom from any ill intentions toward us . . . that the said Captain Hutchinson, who was principally entrusted with the matter of Treaty with them, was thereby encouraged to proceed and march forward towards a Swamp where the Indians then were.[24] When we

came near the said Swamp, the way was so very bad that we could march only in a single file, there being a very rocky hill on the right hand, and a thick swamp on the left, in which were many of those cruel blood-thirsty heathen, who there way laid us, waiting an opportunity to cut us off; there being also much brush on the side of the said hill, where they lay in ambush to surprise us. When we had marched there about sixty or seventy rods, the said perfidious Indians sent out their shot upon us as a shower of hail, they being, (as we supposed,) about two hundred men or more.[25]

Eight English were killed immediately or wounded and left for dead, including all three men from Brookfield who had encouraged Hutchinson to push on. Five others were wounded but escaped, including Wheeler, Wheeler's son (who saved his father's life), and Hutchinson. Hutchinson died from his wounds soon after and was buried in Marlboro, Massachusetts.[26]

When the party attempted to retreat, the Indians prevented them from going back the way they came, forcing them instead to retreat by clambering up a "steep and rocky hill."[27] Wheeler added that "we returned to the town as fast as the badness of the way and the weakness of our wounded men would permit, we being then ten miles from it,"[28] and also noted that "none of us knew the way, those of the town being slain; and we avoiding any thick woods, and riding in open places to prevent the danger by the Indians."[29]

There are the essential facts of the ambush and retreat as they have been handed down through Wheeler's firsthand account. Ever since, historians and antiquarians have speculated as to the precise location of the attack. In a footnote to the 1843 publication of an oration he delivered in 1828, Joseph Foot suggested that the precise site would never be determined:

The spot where Captain Hutchinson and his company were attacked cannot be ascertained. There are two places, which tolerably answer the description given by historians. The one is near the line of Brookfield and New Braintree. The other is nearly two miles north of this line. Without records and with contradictory traditions it is probably impossible to determine with certainty at which place the onset was made.[30]

Foot's conclusion notwithstanding, speculation on the site of Wheeler's Surprise became something of a heated debate in the late nineteenth century, with so many papers being delivered on the subject that one historian felt a complete bibliography was needed.[31] However, all the debate focused around two particular locations—not necessarily consistent with Foot's theory—both of which can still be investigated by historical sleuths interested in determining for themselves the true location of Wheeler's Surprise.

In 1884, the Reverend Lucius R. Paige published a paper in the *New England Historic Genealogical Register* entitled "Wickaboag? Or Winimisset? Which Was the Place of Capt. Wheeler's Defeat in 1675?" In it, Paige made the case for Wheeler's Surprise having occurred in Winimisset Meadows, somewhere along a mile stretch east of the Winimisset Brook, just west of the steep hill rising toward Brookfield Road. Paige knew this area well "because his grandmother in her girlhood resided on the border of the Winimisset (or Meminimisset) Valley . . . and because he saw it so often when he was a boy."[32] Today that site is along Slein Road, perhaps near an A-frame house located about one-half mile north of the intersection of Wine Road. (This site is referred to by Paige as the Fay Farm or Brookside Farm.) A bird's-eye view of the area can be seen from a stone marker commemorating Wheeler's Surprise, located on West Road, three-tenths of a mile north of Unitas Road. The marker reads:

SOMEWHERE WITHIN 1/2 MILE
ALONG THE BASE OF THIS HILL
CAPT. EDWARD HUTCHINSON AND
HIS COMPANY WERE ATTACKED
BY INDIANS LYING IN AMBUSH
AUG. 2 1675 AND HE AND MORE
THAN ONE HALF HIS MEN SLAIN
OR WOUNDED.

The state of Massachusetts has indicated this same general area on a marker located on Route 67 (Barre Plains Road) near Thompson Road.

Paige's argument relied on an interpretation of Wheeler's report that his party was ambushed in the same swamp in which Curtis had met with the Nipmuc the prior day, "about ten miles north-west from us,"[33] according to Wheeler, or about "eight miles from Quabouge,"[34] according to Curtis. Winimisset (or Wenimisset) Meadows is eight to ten miles from Foster Hill, depending upon the route taken. This location was bolstered by William Hubbard's history, in which he reported that Wheeler's party was ambushed "four or five miles"[35] from the appointed rendezvous place; Winimisset Meadows is four of five miles from the plain at the head of Wickaboag Pond. In addition, local tradition had long indicated Winimisset Meadows as the site of Wheeler's Surprise.

In 1893, nine years after Paige made his case for Winimisset Meadows, a map entitled "A New Plan of Several Towns in the Country of Worcester," prepared by General Rufus Putnam and dated March 30, 1785, was discovered at the Massachusetts Historical Society. The map, which measured twenty by twenty-eight inches and covered an area of about 450 square miles, included the towns of Rutland, Oakham, Hardwick, New Braintree, Brookfield, and Warren, as well as parts of about thirteen other nearby towns. The map had been given to the historical society on April 9, 1791, and was accidentally bound into a folio volume entitled *Atlas Ameriquain Septentrional* and, hence, lost for over a century.[36] Designated on this map in the general vicinity of the site indicated by Paige was the note: "Hutchinson & Troop Ambushed between Swamp & Hill."[37] This map, prepared by an esteemed Revolutionary War soldier, a noted civil and military engineer, and a man who spent part of his childhood in New Braintree, seemed to prove Paige's conclusion. Paige "expressed his satisfaction in the discovery of the Putnam map, inasmuch as it so fully coincided with his own opinion . . . [and] if not full proof of the correctness of his own theory, [it was] at least a very respectable precedent."[38]

Several important issues remained, however, and these were tackled by J. H. Temple in his *History of North Brookfield, Massachusetts*, published in 1887 after Paige's publication but before the discovery of Putnam's map. Temple offered the opinion that Wheeler's Surprise occurred in a more southerly location, only a few miles north of Wickaboag Pond, between

Mill Brook and Whortleberry Hill. As part of his research, Temple "traversed the valley from Barre Plains to Wekabaug pond"[39] but could find no location in Winimisset Meadows matching Wheeler's description of a "narrow defile." Further, Temple did not believe that the Nipmuc would endanger their own camp by setting an ambush so close to it.

Temple then turned to the testimony of two Indian guides in Wheeler's party. One, James Quannapohit, said that Menemesseg (another name for Winimisset; neither term was ever used by Wheeler in his report) was "about eight miles north from where Capt. Hutchinson and Capt. Wheeler was wounded and several men with them slain."[40] George Memicho, who was taken captive in the ambush, said that he was taken to a camp "six miles from the swamp where they killed our men."[41] Temple believed that both descriptions pointed to a location south of Winimisset Meadows and not far from the head of Wickaboag Pond. In fact, Temple noted, if William Hubbard's estimate of Wheeler and his party riding four to five miles were applied to their starting location at Foster Hill, this would also point to his more southerly location.[42]

What sealed this new location (sometimes referred to as the Pepper farm) for Temple, however, was his identification of a spot in "very complete agreement of existing conditions with all the details given in Capt. Wheeler's Narrative."[43] That spot, which is nearly unchanged today from the engraving shown by Temple in his *History of North Brookfield*, is located on private land off Barr Bridge Road along Mill Brook. A walk along this hillside, which is no longer particularly rocky, gives one a good sense for how an ambush might develop, how difficult the defile between the hillside and swamp might have been to travel, and how impossible it would have been to escape on horseback in any direction but up and over the hill.

To the modern historian, both sites are interesting but neither conclusive. Paige's location carries the weight of tradition, made an even less reliable source than usual in New Braintree because nobody lived there at the time of the ambush. There is, however, a tantalizing note from Captain Samuel Moseley written to Governor Leverett from Lancaster on August 16, 1675, in which Moseley and about sixty men marched I(n) company with Capt. Beers & Capt. Lathrop to the Swamp where they left me & took their march to Springfield and as soon as they ware gone I took my march Into the woods about 8 miles beyond the Swamp where Capt. Hutchinson and the rest were that were wounded & killed.[44]

If Moseley knew the location of the ambush, then perhaps it was common knowledge to many soldiers stationed in the area. This would bolster tradition as a historical source despite New Braintree's lack of settlement in 1675. Paige also has General Putnam's map supporting him, but Putnam prepared the map more than a century after the event and himself relied on local tradition. Perhaps most damaging to Paige is that no location can be found which resembles even vaguely the one described by Wheeler. Modern historians believe that the swamp along Winimisset Brook was closer to the hillside in former times, but whether it ever matched Wheeler's description is unknown. In 1899, D. H. Chamberlain investigated Winimisset Meadows, taking six trips on foot, horseback, or wagon and making ten separate visits to particular points. He was, even a century ago, unable to find a location matching Wheeler's description.

Temple has in his favor the discovery of a location that very closely matches Wheeler's report. In addition, local tradition also sides with Temple; older citizens of New Braintree referred to the Pepper farm location as "Death Valley." The weaknesses in Temple's arguments are Hubbard's contention that Wheeler's party rode four to five miles from their first rendezvous point, near the head of Wickaboag Pond, which would place them eight to nine miles from Foster Hill.[45] Also, Wheeler says that his party retreated ten miles from the scene of the ambush back to Foster; even riding a circuitous route through North Brookfield to avoid ambush, it is difficult to find ten miles between Temple's ravine and Foster Hill.

George Bodge, writing in 1906, found merit in both arguments and noted that "both Paige and Temple are eminent authorities in antiquarian research; both reason from the same evidences in general . . . I am free to say that reading the arguments of both again and again, I am unable to decide which is the most probable site of the encounter."[46]

Some historians, including Chamberlain, have virtually dismissed the use of mileage, arguing that the distances given were estimates made under extreme duress. Others, like Louis Roy, have guessed at the best path between Brookfield and the Nipmuc camps at Winimisset and, by examining a topographic map, determined the location of the ambush. Roy believed that Wheeler's party traveled the Bay Path and that the ambush occurred on present-day Padre Road, about two-tenths of a mile south of the split from West Road.[47]

Of course, the real surprise in Wheeler's Surprise for modern historians may be that we have completely missed the route taken by Wheeler's party. It is possible that, having left the first rendezvous point, Wheeler and his men rode to the east of Whortlebury Hill, along the high land of West Brookfield Road. They may have taken this route specifically to avoid ambush along the more heavily traveled Bay Path, or because the distance was shorter, or because the terrain was better for a large group on horseback.[48]

Local historian Jeffrey Fiske, in his thoughtful and thorough *Wheeler's Surprise: The Lost Battlefield of King Philip's War*, has taken a careful look at the information and misinformation surrounding 1) the destination of Wheeler and Hutchinson; 2) their route of march; and 3) how their distance was calculated and reported. Fiske concludes that, "while the ambush sites suggested by Josiah Temple and Dr. Louis Roy are incorrect," and the general area suggested by Lucius Paige is a reasonable estimate for the location of Wheeler's Surprise, " I have not been able to absolutely identify the ambush site."[49]

Two rumors had surfaced in the distant past concerning Wheeler's Surprise. One concerned Wheeler's sword, which was said to have been discovered in Winimisset Meadows. The other had to do with a pile of horse bones uncovered in the same location. Both are unsubstantiated and add only color to our knowledge of Wheeler's Surprise, which remains nearly as much a mystery today as it was a century ago.

SIEGE OF BROOKFIELD,
WEST BROOKFIELD, MASSACHUSETTS

When Captain Thomas Wheeler and his remaining men fled the ambush at New Braintree, they sought safety at the English settlement of Quabaug,

The Nipmuc used this flaming cart, filled with birch bark, straw, and powder, in an unsuccessful attempt to dislodge the English from the Ayres garrison. (Courtesy of the Haffenreffer Museum of Anthropology, Brown University)

now the Foster Hill area of West Brookfield. Quabaug had been settled in 1660 by men from Ipswich, Massachusetts. At the time of King Philip's War, it was an isolated farming settlement of barely twenty homes.[50] Its closest neighbor was Springfield, a day's journey to the west. Douglas Leach suggests that "indeed, scarcely a town in all of Massachusetts could claim the dubious distinction of being more isolated than Brookfield."[51]

The surprise return of Wheeler and his exhausted troopers from their disastrous meeting with the Nipmuc alerted the settlers at Quabaug to danger. The frightened inhabitants abandoned their homes and fled to the house of Sergeant John Ayres. (Ayres had accompanied Wheeler and Hutchinson on their mission to parley with the Nipmuc, and for his efforts was lying dead at the New Braintree ambush site.) In all, eighty people gathered in this one home and prepared to defend themselves against the Nipmuc assault. Henry Young and Ephraim Curtis immediately set out on horseback for Marlboro but soon met hostile Nipmuc. They fled back to the garrison and shortly thereafter the assault began.

The August 1675 siege of Brookfield would last almost three days and become one of the most dramatic military engagements of the war. Upon their arrival at Quabaug, the Nipmuc warriors under Muttawmp immediately set fire to all of the structures except the fortified garrison. For forty-eight hours they surrounded the building and, in William Hubbard's account,

> assaulted the poor handful of helpless people, both night and day pouring in shot upon them incessantly with guns and also thrusting poles with fire-brands, and rags dipped in brimstone tied to the ends of them to fire the house; at last they used this devilish stratagem to fill a cart with hemp, flax and other combustible matter, and so thrust it back with poles together sliced a great length, after they had kindled it; But as soon as it had begun to take fire, a storm of rain unexpectedly falling, put out the fire, or else all the poor people, about seventy souls, would either have been consumed by merciless flames, or else have fallen into the hands of their cruel enemies, like wolves continually yelling and gaping for their prey.[52]

The English in the Ayres garrison responded as best they could, but the scene must have been chaotic and terrifying. Henry Young ventured too close to a window and was mortally wounded. A son of Sergeant William Pritchard attempted to secure desperately needed supplies from a nearby building, perhaps his own residence on the first lot east of Ayres' garrison, but was captured and killed. For intimidation, the Nipmuc mounted Pritchard's head on a pole. (Sergeant Pritchard himself had been killed at Wheeler's Surprise). Thomas Wilson, one of the earliest English settlers at Quabaug, was shot through the jaw while attempting to secure water from a well not far from the garrison. Amidst this death and destruction there was also life, however, as two sets of twins were reported born during the siege.[53]

The English were surrounded but not completely helpless. They returned fire and continually thwarted Nipmuc attempts to set the garrison aflame. Reports of eighty Nipmuc killed were undoubtedly inflated,[54] but Muttawmp and his warriors did not go without loss. Indeed, Ephraim Curtis was able to find enough weakness in the siege line to crawl past the Nipmuc on August 3 and make his way by foot the thirty miles to Marlboro.

Major Simon Willard and his forty-eight troopers[55] were conducting operations west of Lancaster and arrived first at Quabaug. Willard, who at seventy years of age was the chief military officer of Middlesex County, had heard reports of the Nipmuc attack from people traveling along the Bay Path. He and his men rode the thirty-five or forty miles to Brookfield and arrived after nightfall on August 3,[56] where they charged past the Nipmuc sentries, whose warning shots went unnoticed. Increase Mather wrote:

> the Indians were so busy and made such a noise about the house that they heard not the report of those guns; which if they had heard, in all probability not only the people then living at Quaboag, but those also that came to succor them had been cut off.[57]

Willard's party[58] rode almost to the door of the Ayres garrison before they were spotted. With their arrival, the Nipmuc fired the remaining buildings and broke off the siege. Soon after, colonial reinforcements arrived, swelling the ranks of men under Willard to 350 English plus the Mohegan that had pursued Philip so successfully at Nipsachuck. Willard would stay for several weeks to direct military activity in the area, but the residents had little reason and little hope of real security, so the settlement at Quabaug was abandoned.

The landmarks related to the original Quabaug Plantation settlement are well marked along the north side of Foster Hill Road in present-day West Brookfield. Much of the site today is a large, open field. Traveling west, the first marker (set in a stone wall near a more modern home) designates the Ayres garrison, followed by a more elaborate memorial to John Ayres and a small stone marking the well at which Major Wilson was shot.

Foster Hill Road in West Brookfield, Massachusetts, is the site of Quabaug Plantation, attacked and destroyed by the Nipmuc in August 1675. The large memorial on the right designates the site of the Ayres garrison. (Eric Schultz)

Further west, still on the north side of Foster Hill Road, is a stone indicating the location of the first meetinghouse, burned in 1675, and a second built in 1717. The plantation's burial ground, dated 1660–1780, is designated to the northeast of the meetinghouse location.

The precise site of the Ayres garrison was apparently in some dispute in the early nineteenth century. In 1843 Joseph Foot noted:

There has been of late years no small disagreement respecting the place, where the fortified house stood. Some have attempted to maintain that it was northeast of Foster's Hill. But as no satisfactory evidence in support of this opinion has been found, it is to be regarded as unworthy of credence. There are several weighty reasons for believing, that it stood on a hill. 1. The principal English settlement was there. 2.

This beautiful, detailed engraving shows the assault on the Ayres garrison, which lasted for three days and resulted in the abandonment of Brookfield. (Courtesy of the Haffenreffer Museum of Anthropology, Brown University)

The meeting-house which was burned by the Indians was there. 3. In the account of the attack on the fortification a well in the yard is mentioned, and a well has been discovered near the north west corner of Mr. Marsh's door yard, of which the oldest inhabitants can give no account except as they have been told, it belongs to the fortified house. 4. At a distance of a few feet north of the well the ground when cultivated as a garden was unproductive. As the soil appeared to be good, it was difficult to see any reason for the barrenness. On examination however it was found that a building had stood on the place. Several loads of stone, which had formed a cellar and chimney were removed, amongst which various instruments of iron and steel were found. 5. There is a hill directly west of this place, which corresponds sufficiently well with the descriptions of that, down which the Indians rolled the cart of kindled combustibles. There is then good reason to conclude that it stood between Mr. Marsh's house and barn.[59]

A state marker on Route 9 at the boundary of Brookfield and West Brookfield encapsulates the whole grim story of Brookfield's early years in a few short lines:

BROOKFIELD

SETTLED IN 1660 BY MEN FROM
IPSWICH ON INDIAN LANDS CALLED
QUABAUG. ATTACKED BY INDIANS
IN 1675. ONE GARRISON HOUSE
DEFENDED TO THE LAST. REOCCUPIED
TWELVE YEARS LATER.

BATTLE OF SOUTH DEERFIELD, WHATELY, MASSACHUSETTS

On August 24, 1675, just a few weeks after the siege of Brookfield, the English held a council of war at Hatfield to address the growing native presence at the Norwottock village, located on a bluff along the western bank of the Connecticut River above Northampton. A force of one hundred men commanded by Captains Thomas Lathrop and Richard Beers was ordered to surprise and disarm these natives, none of whom had committed any hostilities against the English. Divining English intent, the Norwottock fled the camp just before Lathrop and Beers arrived on the morning of August 25. Finding the native fires still smoldering, the English sent a portion of their troops to defend Hatfield while the remainder set off in pursuit of the natives.

A mile south of present-day South Deerfield, near the rise known as Wequomps (present-day Sugarloaf Mountain), colonial soldiers overtook the Norwottock, who dashed into present-day Hopewell Swamp. There they set an ambush for the English troops. Mather reported that

> on a sudden the Indians let fly about forty guns at them, and was soon
> answered by a volley from our men; about forty ran down into the
> swamp after them, poured in shot upon them, made them throw down
> much of their baggage, and after a while our men after the Indian

While the exact location of the battle is unknown, Hopewell Swamp in South Deerfield, Massachusetts, shown circa 1906, was the location of the so-called Battle of South Deerfield, a three-hour skirmish that Puritan commentators fashioned as a great victory for the English army. In reality, it turned the peaceful Norwottock against the colonists and cost the English nine soldiers. (From King Philip's War, *George W. Ellis and John E. Morris, 1906)*

manner got behind trees, and watched their opportunities to make shots at them.[60]

The fight lasted three hours. The English lost nine men and the natives were said to have lost twenty-six,[61] probably an exaggeration designed to turn the first military engagement in the Connecticut River valley into a desperately needed English victory. The real result of this Puritan-styled "Battle of South Deerfield" was to turn the neutral Norwottock into deadly enemies. Writing in 1872, J. H. Temple discovered a location that met all the particulars of the Battle of South Deerfield. The spot was located about a quarter-mile south of Sugarloaf Mountain where the old Deerfield trail skirted the edge of Hopewell Swamp. Here, Temple wrote, was a ravine that allowed the natives good cover, the ability to fire up both sides of the bluff, and an excellent retreat route. Temple even made an engraving of the location.

Today local tradition places the battle in Whately, Massachusetts, though there is no agreement as to the precise location. The swamp south of Sugarloaf Mountain is quite large and has been altered considerably over the years by drainage, industry, and the construction of homes. There are many spots that would seem to match Temple's description, and it seems unlikely that we will ever have more than a general sense as to where the battle took place.[62]

BEERS' AMBUSH, NORTHFIELD, MASSACHUSETTS

Squakeag, now Northfield, was located a few miles north of Deerfield near the present-day New Hampshire border. Barely three years old, Northfield, as described by Ellis and Morris, consisted of "some seventeen thatched cabins, a palisade of rough logs eight foot high set upright in the ground and pierced with loopholes, and a log fort and church."[63] The most far-flung of the Connecticut Valley settlements, Northfield was generally isolated from the violence that had occurred in Brookfield, Whately, and New Braintree, and in the Plymouth colony settlements farther south.

On September 1, 1675, sixty natives attacked and burned buildings and barns in Deerfield. When the inhabitants of Northfield awoke on Thursday, September 2, they were still unaware of this attack. Heading off in pursuit of their daily activities, the Northfield settlers were suddenly assaulted by a mixed band of Pocumtuck and Nashaway led by Monoco. Eight English were killed. The settlers rushed from their houses and fields to the stockade, watching as their homes went up in flames.

Massachusetts Bay authorities decided to evacuate Northfield immediately. On Friday, September 3, thirty-six mounted men and one ox team under the command of Captain Richard Beers of Watertown, Massachusetts, began the thirty-mile march from Hadley. Unable to reach Northfield

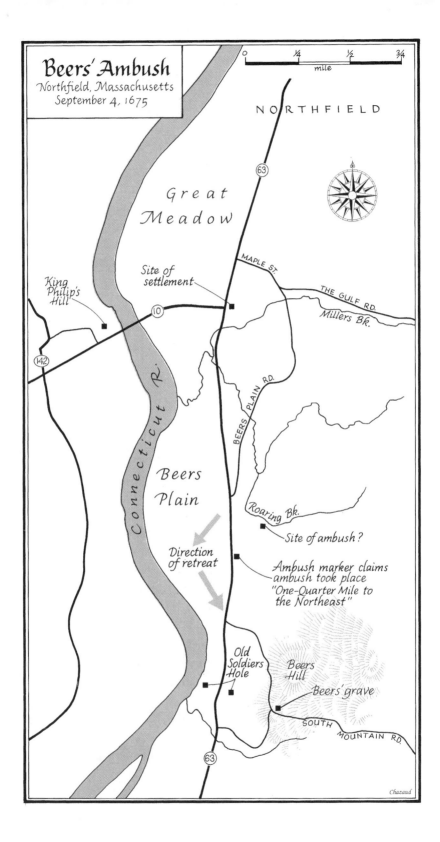

Beers' Ambush
Northfield, Massachusetts
September 4, 1675

NORTHFIELD

Great
Meadow

¼ ½ ¾
mile
0

63

Site of
settlement

MAPLE ST.

THE GULF RD.

Millers Bk.

King
Philip's
Hill

10

142

Connecticut R.

BEERS PLAIN RD.

Beers
Plain

Roaring Bk.

Site of ambush?

Direction
of retreat

Ambush marker claims
ambush took place
"One-Quarter Mile to
the Northeast"

Old
Soldiers
Hole

Beers
Hill

Beers' grave

SOUTH
MOUNTAIN RD.

63

Chazaud

before sundown, Beers and his men camped three miles south of the town, perhaps near Four-mile Brook.[64]

On Saturday morning, September 4, Beers left his horses under guard at the camp and began the short march to Northfield. His decision to approach the town by foot may have indicated that he expected to meet resistance, but Beers did not take the usual precaution of sending scouts and flankers to protect the main force. In addition, Beers made no attempt to alter his route from the usual approach to Northfield, along the high plain.

Marching north, the English troops kept to the high way[65] until they sighted Sawmill Brook, which flowed through a ravine still thick with summer growth. (This main path to the settlement was probably to the east of present-day Route 63, on slightly higher ground.)[66] They followed along the left bank of the brook and then

> attempted to cross it where a depression in the plain made a passable fordway, in order to reach the hard land south and west of dry swamp, and so come into the village near where is now the south road to Warwick.[67] This was the common route of travel at the time; and the Indians knew that, as matter of course, he would take it, and made their plans accordingly. Concealed in front, and behind the steep bank below the crossing-place, on his right, they fired upon the carelessly advancing column just as the head was passing the brook, when it would have been exposed for its entire length.[68]

The location of the ambush is marked on the east side of Route 63, just north of the Community Bible Church. The marker reads:

INDIAN COUNCIL FIRES

TWO HUNDRED AND FIFTY YARDS
EASTWARD ARE THE SITES OF THREE
LARGE INDIAN COUNCIL FIRES. THE
BEERS MASSACRE OF SEPTEMBER
4, 1676, TOOK PLACE IN A GORGE

165

ONE-QUARTER MILE TO THE
NORTHEAST

Sawmill Brook, shown on modern topographic maps as Roaring Brook, can be reached by a dirt road north of the marker. (The dirt road is on private property and sometimes blocked.) The precise location of Beers' crossing is conjecture only, though one or two places seem logical. The spot where the dirt road first skirts the brook also affords an excellent view of Beers Mountain and Beers Hill, the direction in which the captain retreated.

The English were thrown into confusion by the attack but, as J. H. Temple and George Sheldon describe the encounter, were able to fight their way out of the ravine and make a stand "towards the south end of the plain, where is a slight rise of land."[69] This plain, now called Beers Plain, is designated by a marker just a short distance north of the "Indian Council Fires" sign.[70] Beers Plain runs north from this spot and west toward the Connecticut River. Temple and Sheldon believe it to have once been the site of a Native American village, "as attested by the remains of their granaries, and their large burial places."[71]

As the English fell, Beers and a few survivors were able to retreat to a small ravine about three-quarters of a mile away on the southern spur of present-day Beers Mountain, sometimes called Beers Hill. Here Captain Beers was killed. Two days later his body was buried.

A marker on the east side of Route 63 near the Community Bible Church designates the general area of Beers' last stand. The site of Beers' grave can be found at the base of the main building of the Linden Hill School near the intersection of South Mountain Road and Lyman Hill Road. A modern stone marker indicates the burial spot. Temple and Sheldon, writing in 1875, provide a glimpse as to how the site was altered before the present stone marker was set.

The tradition which marks this as the spot where Capt. Beers was killed and buried, is of undoubted authenticity. The old men in each generation have told the same story, and identified the place. And the

This nineteenth-century engraving may represent the ambush of Captain Beers and his men in Northfield. The movement of goods from abandoned towns not only fed the English army, but also deprived the natives of the spoils of war. (Courtesy of the Haffenreffer Museum of Anthropology, Brown University)

existence here from time immemorial of two stones—like head and foot stones—set at the proper distance apart, certainly marks the place of a grave; and the care to erect stones indicates the grave of more than a common solider. The new house of Capt. Samuel Merriman, built about 50 years ago, was set directly across the ravine, which was made to answer for a cellar by filling in the space front and rear. Capt. Ira Coy informs the writer that, before any thing was disturbed, he and Capt. M. dug into the grave. They found the well defined sides and bottom, where the spade had left the clay solid; and at the depth of about twenty inches (the shallowness indicating haste) was a layer of dark colored mold, some of it in small lumps, like decayed bones. The grave was then filled up, a large flat stone laid over it, and the hollow graded up.[72]

The Linden Hill School building which now sits near the site is more recent than the one described by Temple. Beers' grave marker has been moved from its original site, farther along the lawn to a position closer to the street.[73]

Temple and Sheldon also note that iron from the teamsters' cart used by Beers was discovered in the early nineteenth century and worked up by a local blacksmith.[74] In addition, local histories relate that as late as 1824, "at a sandy knoll on the west side of the road, near the place where the attack commenced, the bones of the slain are still to be seen, in some instances, bleaching in the sun. Until lately the mail route from Montague to Northfield passed over this ground."[75]

The ambush was devastating to the English, who lost twenty-one men. Thirteen men, including the guard left with the horses, returned to Hadley that evening. Two more straggled in the following day, including one who had escaped from capture and reported, however accurately, the deaths of twenty-five natives during the attack.[76] One arrived confused and nearly starved six days later; he had escaped the ambush by hiding in a gully and covering himself with leaves. This gully is known as Old Soldiers Hole, a deep ravine leading from Beers Plain to the Connecticut River, one-quarter of a mile south of the lower point of Three-little Meadows.[77] It is today split by Route 63 and the railroad embankment, almost directly west of Beers Hill.

On September 6, Major Robert Treat and about one hundred men rescued the anxious settlers of Northfield, still stranded in their stockade. Along the way Treat and his men found the decapitated heads of some of those slain stuck on poles, and one, wrote Hubbard, was found "with a chain hooked into his under jaw, and so hung up on the bow of a tree."[78] Such sights completely demoralized the English, who buried the dead, evacuated the town, and left it to be destroyed.

Several other sites around Northfield are associated with King Philip's War. On Monday, March 6, 1676, Mary Rowlandson of Lancaster stayed with her Indian captors at a camp by the side of the Great Swamp described by Temple and Sheldon near "where the highway to Wendell crosses Keeup's Brook, to the east of Crag Mountain."[79] The historians add that Philip's Hill, "a projection of the plain which comes near to the river bank,"[80] is located on the west side of the Connecticut River north of Bennett's Meadow. This was said to be a fortified Indian site during the war and Philip's camp for part of the winter of 1675–1676. "This hill was defended by a ditch and bank on the westerly side, and otherwise by its steep ascent; but being only about sixty feet high, it was a position of no great strength."[81] In 1897, twenty-five years after postulating the existence of Philip's fort at this site, Sheldon reversed his position, writing, "What you see on Philip's Hill is the work of honest John Tomkins, and not that of a fort which King Philip never built." Tomkins, Sheldon continued, was a "hedger and a ditcher" who left a legacy of ditches around Northfield designed as the "the cheapest and most enduring fences" to hold livestock.[82]

BLOODY BROOK, SOUTH DEERFIELD, MASSACHUSETTS

On September 12, 1675, just a few days after the evacuation of Northfield, the settlement at Deerfield was assaulted for a second time by a small band of warriors who managed to burn two houses and steal several wagons full of food. Deerfield was a tempting target for the Indians because of its poor defenses and excellent fall harvest. Recognizing this, Massachusetts Bay leaders decided to evacuate Deerfield and sent troops under Captain Thomas Lathrop of Beverly, Massachusetts, to escort teamsters from Deerfield to Hadley. There, the foodstuffs could be distributed throughout the Connecticut River valley towns during the winter months.

On September 18, Lathrop led seventy-nine men[83] and a number of carts loaded with provisions on a slow march from Deerfield to Hadley. Several miles south of Deerfield near a shallow brook in present-day South Deerfield, the convoy's lead stopped to rest and allow the teamsters in the rear time to catch up. Like Increase Mather, who describes a scene in which many of the soldiers were "so foolish and secure as to put their arms in the carts, and step aside to gather grapes, which proved dear and deadly grapes to them,"[84] we can only wonder what Lathrop was thinking at the time, given the recent attacks on Deerfield and the fatal ambush of Captain Beers on a similar mission to Northfield two weeks before. Edward Everett suggested that nearby scouting activity by Captain Moseley and his troops,

This depiction of the massacre at Bloody Brook shows Captain Lathrop's men marching from Deerfield and illustrates how the distance between the teamster carts made a concentrated defense against the Nipmuc ambush nearly impossible. (Courtesy of the Haffenreffer Museum of Anthropology, Brown University)

and the sense that one of the more difficult legs of the journey had been completed, led to carelessness:

> Captain Moseley, who had arrived on Connecticut River three days before, was at this time stationed with his company at Deerfield, and proposed, while Captain Lothrop was on the march downward, to range the woods in search of the enemy . . . It is not improbable that Captain Lothrop and his men, relying too much on Moseley's cooperation, proceeded without due caution. Having passed with safety through a level and closely-wooded country, well calculated for a surprise, and deeming themselves in some degree sheltered by the nature of the ground

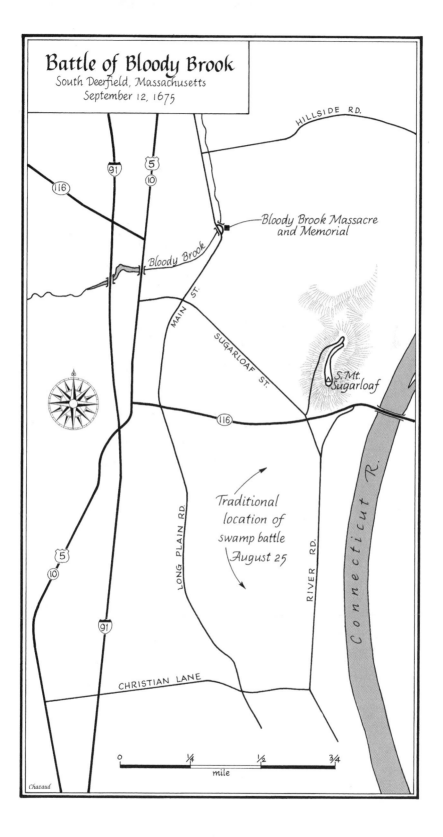

Battle of Bloody Brook
South Deerfield, Massachusetts
September 12, 1675

HILLSIDE RD.

91

5
10

116

Bloody Brook Massacre
and Memorial

Bloody Brook

MAIN ST.

SUGARLOAF ST.

S. Mt.
Sugarloaf

116

Traditional
location of
swamp battle
August 25

5
10

LONG PLAIN RD.

RIVER RD.

91

Connecticut R.

CHRISTIAN LANE

0   ¼   ½   ¾
mile

Chazaud

Not only did Deerfield suffer considerable destruction during King Philip's War, but the village would fall victim again in 1704 to a lightning raid by Indians migrating along the Connecticut River valley to Canada.

they had reached, the tradition is, that on their arrival at the spot near which we are now assembled, their vigilance relaxed. The forest that lines the narrow road, on which they were marching, was hung with clusters of grapes; and, as the wagons dragged through the heavy soil, it is not unlikely that the teamsters, and possibly part of the company, may have dispersed to gather them.[85]

Lathrop's lapse in judgment would prove fatal. Muttawmp and his "multitudes"[86] set upon the English in a "sudden and frightful assault,"[87] killing Lathrop almost immediately. More than forty soldiers and seventeen teamsters were killed.[88] Captain Samuel Moseley and his troops were patrolling nearby and dashed to the rescue, only to be drawn into the fight with taunts of "Come on, Moseley, come on. You want Indians. Here are enough Indians for you."[89] All afternoon Moseley and his men fought, losing eleven[90] and coming dangerously close to being completely surrounded and destroyed, until Major Robert Treat arrived around dusk with enough reinforcements to drive Muttawmp and his men from the field.

The brook at which Lathrop and his men paused, once called Muddy Brook, was said to have turned red with English blood and has ever since been known as Bloody Brook. Today, it crosses under Main Street in South Deerfield about one mile south from the intersection of Route 5; this is said to be precisely the spot at which Lathrop passed.[91]

Two memorials are maintained at the site. A white marble monument was erected in 1838 and stands just south of the brook at the bend in the road near Frontier High School. The cornerstone for the monument was laid in 1835 at an occasion that brought Edward Everett, General Epaphas Hoyt of Deerfield, and about six thousand people to the site. Everett delivered his keynote address under a walnut tree just east of the monument.

The second Bloody Brook memorial, and perhaps the oldest surviving monument to veterans in America, is found about one hundred yards south of the marble monument in the front yard of 286 North Main Street. This rectangular slab is set horizontally in the ground and marks the common grave of Lathrop and the men buried there by Treat and Moseley the day following the ambush.[92] This monument was moved so many times by owners of the property that in 1835 a committee of investigation was formed[93] to identify the precise location of the mass grave. Guided by "tradition and some aged people"[94] the committee located the spot. A contemporary account reported that the bones of about thirty men were found "in a state of tolerable preservation, but fell to pieces on exposure to the air";[95] these were all that remained of the "sixty persons buried in one dreadful grave"[96] described by Increase Mather. On the same day that the English

The Bloody Brook Memorial was dedicated in 1838 by the governor of Massachusetts, Edward Everett, and stands today as one of the most visible reminders of King Philip's War. (Eric Schultz)

The site of the Bloody Brook battle, captured in this early twentieth-century photograph, shows the crossing at North Main Street in South Deerfield, Massachusetts, and the marble monument placed in 1838. Bloody Brook is one of the most famous and best-visited sites of King Philip's War. (From King Philip's War, George W. Ellis and John E. Morris, 1906)

mass grave was rediscovered, the committee also reported finding a grave with the remains of ninety-six Native Americans, about a half mile distant, to the southwest of the grave of Lathrop.[97] Contemporaries assumed that these natives had been killed in the fight. Edward Everett supposed that the Indian warriors

> fled across the brook, about two miles to the westward, closely pursued by the American force, and here the action was probably suspended by the night. A quantity of bones, lately found in that quarter, is very probably the remains of the Indians who fell there at the close of the action.[98]

We will never know if Everett was correct in his assumption, but we can be sure that Moseley and Treat would have been surprised to discover that, in Everett's nineteenth-century terms, they had become the "American force" at Bloody Brook.

ATTACK ON SPRINGFIELD, MASSACHUSETTS

Springfield's location on the Connecticut River and at the junction of two important colonial trails made it second only to Hartford in importance among the Connecticut River Valley towns. On the eve of King Philip's War the settlement boasted a population of five hundred English settlers scattered about four distinct villages. These included the town center; a settlement opposite the center on the west bank of the Connecticut River; Longmeadow, located four miles south of the center; and Skepnuck, situated three miles northeast of the center.

About a mile south of the center, on a bluff along the east bank of the Connecticut River nearly opposite the Westfield River, sat a palisaded Agawam Indian village. The site is today referred to as Longhill, and the village itself, Fort Hill (which is designated by a marker at the intersection of Sumner Avenue and Longhill Street[99]). It was established as a native village about 1650 and made famous as the staging grounds for an Agawam-led assault on Springfield during King Philip's War.

Fort Hill's boundaries have never been precisely determined, but a Springfield historian's description of the site in 1886 noted the following:

> A little plateau on a prominent spur of a hill, with abrupt declination shaped liked a sharply truncated cone, afforded natural advantages for a fort. There is a deep ravine on the south side, which was probably the fortified approach to the fort. Many stone arrow-heads and hatchets have been found in this ravine . . . It has been assumed by some that only a part of the plateau was included in the fort . . . [but] it is fair to conclude that the whole brow of this hill was surrounded by a stockade.[100]

In 1895 local historian Harry Andrew Wright excavated Fort Hill. He discovered (among hundreds of artifacts) "the site of ten rows of lodges and two large council houses," as well as "a pattern of post molds uncovered along the western margin of the bluff,"[101] confirming that the village had been palisaded. A short distance south of the site, Wright uncovered thirteen burial sites.

More recently, William R. Young and John P. Pretola of the science museum in Springfield have studied Fort Hill.[102] The site has yielded artifacts (housed in collections at the Springfield Science Museum, the Skinner Museum at Mount Holyoke College, and the Peabody Museum at Harvard University) such as a German silver-plated spoon consistent with the mid-seventeenth-century occupation of Fort Hill; "Dutch fairy pipes" from Bristol, England; finished gunflints; three good examples of Native American ceramics; and even an oyster and quahog shell, indicating contact with coastal native groups.[103] More puzzling to Young and Pretola is the relative lack of structural features at the site, making it impossible to reconstruct the configuration of Fort Hill, and leaving the possibility that more of the site is still unexplored.[104]

Among Springfield's most influential residents was Major John Pynchon, son of Springfield's founder and a successful merchant who played an important role in the establishment of several Connecticut River Valley towns. Despite his business success, Pynchon was no soldier and had asked Massachusetts Bay officials on two occasions to be relieved of his post as commander of all colonial troops in the valley. Pynchon was especially at odds with the council's military strategy, which emphasized an offensive campaign where every soldier took to the field, often leaving Springfield and nearby towns undefended.

Pynchon watched with anguish as Captain Richard Beers was ambushed on September 4, Lathrop's troops were massacred at Bloody Brook on September 18, and Pynchon's own mill complex in present-day Suffield, Connecticut, was destroyed on September 26. With small bands of warriors roaming the woods throughout the valley, sniping at settlers and soldiers alike, and the council pushing him to act, Pynchon knew that he must locate and engage the main body of Indians.

Also troubling to Pynchon was the suspicion that the local Agawam might not remain loyal to the English, despite their neutrality thus far. To

A town constable of Springfield, Massachusetts, Lieutenant Cooper was convinced
that the Agawam would remain loyal to the English. This conviction cost Cooper
his life, and a marker on present-day Mill Street designates the spot of his ambush.
(Courtesy of the Haffenreffer Museum of Anthropology, Brown University)

head off any threat, Pynchon had requested that hostages be sent to the
English as a sign of good faith. The Agawam balked.

Pynchon's suspicions were well-founded but not strongly enough held.
On October 4, 1675, he led a large force from Springfield to join troops stationed at Hadley. On the morning of October 5 this combined force attacked a large Indian camp located about five miles to the north. Springfield
was left suddenly defenseless, a point not lost on the Agawam.

It would be revealed later that the Agawam had been sheltering within
Fort Hill, for some period before October 5, a body of hostile warriors. On
the night of October 4 as many as several hundred additional warriors had
been secretly admitted into the Agawam village. With their encouragement,
a plan was devised to attack Springfield the following morning, once Pynchon's troops were well clear of the town. This plot was revealed by Toto,
an Indian employed by an English family at Windsor, Connecticut. Messengers were sent to Springfield on October 5 and managed to awaken res-

idents and gather the population in three fortified houses. A messenger was sent to Hadley to recall the recently departed troops.

Among Springfield's three garrisons was the home of John Pynchon (once thought to be a brick house but now believed to be a wood-frame house built by his father near the corner of present-day Main and Fort Streets).[105] The second garrison belonged to Jonathan Burt and stood near the southwest corner of present-day Broad and Main Streets.[106] The third garrison, built in 1665, was the Ely Tavern, located on Main Street, a little south of present-day Bliss Street.[107] The Ely Tavern was moved about 1843 to Dwight Street, west of State Street, and was demolished in 1900. All signs of these early garrisons have been lost to the growth of Springfield's central business district.

When all remained quiet on the morning of October 5, Lieutenant Cooper and Thomas Miller, the town's constable, decided to ride to Fort Hill and investigate. Cooper in particular was convinced that the Agawam would remain loyal to the English despite hostilities throughout the valley. He was wrong; only a short distance from the garrisons the two were ambushed. Miller died instantly but Cooper kept his mount long enough to warn the nearest garrison, at which point he also died. A marker on present-day Mill Street designates the spot of the ambush.

A body of warriors estimated at between one hundred and three hundred[108] was hot on Cooper's heels and immediately attacked the garrisons. Meeting with resistance, they began to fire the unoccupied structures, burning thirty-two houses and twenty-five barns.[109] Had help not arrived at this point, the Reverend William Hubbard wrote, "The poor people having never an officer to lead them, being like sheep ready for the slaughter . . . no doubt the whole town [would have] been totally destroyed."[110] Major Robert Treat appeared on the west bank of the Connecticut River with troops but was unable to cross in the face of enemy fire. He still managed to distract enough of the warriors so that the destruction of the town was slowed. By the time Major Pynchon and his 190 men reached Springfield in the early afternoon, riding nonstop all day, the native forces had escaped to Indian Orchard on the Chicopee River six miles east of Springfield.[111]

The assault on Springfield was traumatic. Three English had been killed, great quantities of provisions were lost, Pynchon's remaining mills were destroyed, only thirteen houses were left standing in the town center, and any sense that Springfield might offer a safe haven from hostilities was shattered. Hubbard wrote, "Of all the mischiefs done by the said enemy before that day, the burning of this town of Springfield did more than any other, discovered the said actors to be the children of the devil, full of subtlety and malice, there having been from about forty years so good correspondence betwixt the English of that town and the neighbouring Indians."[112] For the third time Pynchon asked to be relieved of his command and would soon learn that orders had already been sent appointing Major Samuel Appleton to his post.

The center of Springfield was not attacked again during the war and the town was never abandoned. However, on March 26, 1676, a group of sixteen or eighteen settlers and soldiers under Captain Whipple, many "having most of the winter [been] kept from the public meeting on the Lords Days, for fear of the enemy,"[113] were ambushed by eight warriors[114] while walking to church from Longmeadow to Springfield. Two English were killed and four captured. Tradition locates the ambush in present-day Forest Park, at the southern end of Springfield, near the Pecowsic Brook.[115] The following day English troops caught up with the kidnappers, who killed both children and one of the women while severely wounding the other.

ATTACK ON HATFIELD, MASSACHUSETTS

Hatfield, located on the western bank of the Connecticut River opposite Hadley, had been the "west side" of the Hadley settlement until 1670, when the General Court granted its independence. Seventeenth-century Hadley

made a general picture not so different from today. The settlers viewed a wide valley, abounding in large meadows of lush native grass, good for mowing but devoid of timber except for tree clumps in swampy parts or along the river . . . The mighty Connecticut River flowed to the sea—the river bed narrower and its banks further from Main Street than they are today. The road to Northampton made the same big bend as it does today before turning up Main Street. Except that it was a narrow or path, Main Street in 1661 was, just as now, about a mile in length with a Common on the south end . . . The first houses were set back on either side and extended from the present Maple Street corner approximately to the present School Street.[116]

By the time of King Philip's War, there were about fifty houses and 300 or 350 settlers in Hatfield.[117]

By the middle of October 1675, the lower Connecticut River Valley was alive with the activity of native warriors encouraged by their victories at Brookfield, Deerfield, Northfield, and Springfield. Major Samuel Appleton had recently taken over command of the valley troops from John Pynchon, and hardly knowing from which direction the next assault might come, divided his army among three towns. In Northampton he placed a force under Lieutenant Nathaniel Sealy, supplemented by troops under Major Robert Treat of Connecticut. In Hatfield he stationed Captains Jonathan Poole and Samuel Moseley. Meanwhile, Appleton himself commanded a force stationed at Hadley.

At noontime on October 19 the anxious waiting was over. Several fires were spotted north of Hadley. Perhaps against his better judgment, Captain Moseley sent out a scouting party of ten men who marched two miles from the garrisons and were caught in an ambush. Six men were killed, three captured, and only one returned to Hatfield.

Fearing the worst, Moseley sent to both Hadley and Northampton for reinforcements. Appleton left twenty soldiers in Hadley and crossed the river with the remainder to join Moseley. At about 4 PM a large band of warriors[118] appeared at the edge of the meadows and rushed the settlement. William Hubbard, undoubtedly the recipient of a firsthand account of the battle from his neighbor, Samuel Appleton, recorded that "Major Appleton with great courage defending one end of the town and Capt. Moseley as stoutly maintaining the middle, and Capt. Poole the other end; that [the Indians] were by resolution of the English instantly beaten off, without doing much harm."[119] Appleton caught a bullet through his hat and another soldier was killed, but the force of the English volleys convinced the warriors that the town was too well fortified to defeat. After about two hours they retreated in some confusion, their first real setback in the war.

The battle at Hatfield was a turning point for the English, proving that native warriors could be repulsed if the military was prepared. In addition, Hubbard recorded, "This resolute and valiant repulse put such a check upon the pride of the enemy, that they made no further attempt upon any of those towns for the present,"[120] retiring for the winter to plan their spring campaign.

After this first attack on Hatfield the settlers copied Northampton's example and constructed a stockade, working throughout the fall and winter to encompass nearly half of the town's existing structures.[121] The wooden stockade stood ten to twelve feet high and ran four hundred feet. A 1910 history described it as follows:

> The house of Fellows, Cole, and Field at the south, and several at the north, were outside. The south line of the palisades was below the Godwin lot, occupied by Rev. Hope Atherton, and the Daniel Warner allotment on the opposite side of the street. The north line was between the houses of Daniel White, Jr. and John Allis, crossing the street to include the homestead of Samuel Dickinson.[122]

A successful attempt was made about 1839 to trace the line of the stockade, though it is unclear from the historical material what precisely was being "traced."[123] A more recent history reported that the "two lengthwise walls of the enclosure ran parallel to Main Street, thus closing in the houses and barns on either side."[124] The southern perimeter of the stockade wall crossed at present-day 12 Main Street and the northern perimeter at 49 Main Street.[125]

On May 30, 1676, "a great number"[126] of warriors appeared in Hatfield, burning twelve outlying structures and stealing cattle and sheep. Many of these warriors were thought to be survivors of the fight at Peskeompskut (Turner's Falls) earlier in the month. Twenty-five men rowed across from the Hadley side to offer reinforcement but were cut off from both the stockade and a retreat to the river. Five were killed before soldiers came rushing out of the Hatfield stockade to their defense. A short time later Captain Benjamin Newberry and his troops appeared on the opposite shore at Hadley. The Indians held off Newberry's men and continued their attack briefly but were unable to breach Hatfield's stockade and retreated at dusk. In all, seven English were killed and five wounded.

The most devastating assault on Hatfield occurred on September 19, 1677, more than a year after King Philip's death, when a party of forty to fifty natives attacked the town, catching the settlers completely off guard. Many of the town's men were working in the fields or helping to raise the frame of a house outside Hatfield's palisade, which likely was at the very end of the village street.[127] Several men were shot down from the top of a house they were raising while others were carried away captive. The warriors rushed through Middle Lane (present-day School Street) and set fire to several structures. A vicious battle took place at the intersection of Middle Lane and present-day North Main Street.[128] Twelve English were killed, four wounded, and seventeen kidnapped[129] by this band of Canadian-bound Indians, who never attempted to breach Hatfield's stockade. Breaking off the raid, they raced with their captives across the fields to the Pocumtuck Path. Heading north, the warriors took additional captives and caused more destruction at Deerfield.

MOHAWK AMBUSH OF PHILIP, SCHAGHTICOKE, NEW YORK

Contrary to the beliefs of the English settlers, who saw Philip's hand in every battle of the war, Philip played little part in the events in New England during the winter months of 1675 and 1676. While his precise movements are unknown, it appeared that shortly before the bloodiest day of the war, the Great Swamp Fight (at South Kingstown, Rhode Island, on December 19, 1675), expecting little assistance from the Narragansett, Philip and his men had headed northwest to seek other allies. By December 1675[130] the Pokanoket sachem had settled into winter quarters as a guest of the Mahicans in Schaghticoke, New York, north of Albany on the Hoosic River. Philip's plan, to acquire additional guns and encourage the Mahicans to take up arms against the English, apparently met with some success; a report delivered to New York Governor Edmund Andros in February 1676 indicated that Philip had gathered twenty-one hundred warriors.[131]

This was all the governor needed to hear. Fearing the war's spread into New York, Andros encouraged the Mohawk—already hated enemies of the

Algonquian—to attack Philip's army. In a ruthless surprise assault late in February, the Mohawk killed all but forty of about five hundred men with Philip. A second band of about four hundred scattered.[132] One historian wrote that "this was the blow that lost the war for Philip."[133] Philip hobbled back to New England, destined to spend the remainder of the war as a relatively minor figure, more hunted than hunter. Without this fresh source of ammunition and men, the native alliance began to crumble. Individual sachems, like Canonchet, would emerge as prominent military leaders, but a coordinated native war strategy would become increasingly difficult to prosecute.

Schagticoke is an ancient Indian habitat dating back many centuries before King Philip's War. The site of the Mahican settlement during the war is thought to be land at the crossroads of the Hoosic River and the Tomhannock Creek (the name Schagticoke might mean "comingling of waters"), and it is here that Philip may have quartered during the winter of 1675–1676. Local legend suggests several places in Schagticoke where an Indian battle occurred, though there is no conclusive evidence to indicate the location of the Mohawks' surprise attack on Philip and his army. The eighteenth-century Knickerbocker mansion, on Knickerbocker Road off Route 67, is the best landmark for this area as it sits in the center of Old Schagticoke and the ancient Indian settlements.[134] The nearby Knickerbocker Family Cemetery, site of the oldest marked graves in town, is said to contain both Indian and slave burials.

A field located just before the Tomhannock Creek on the north side of Route 67 is said to be an Indian burying ground.[135]

This part of the Hoosic River Valley has come to be known as the Vale of Peace. It was the site of an important meeting in late 1676 (or 1677), after Philip's death, in which Governor Andros of New York brought together English, Dutch, Mohawk, Mahican, and Algonquian refugees from New England, promising the latter a safe haven from the New England authorities demanding their return.[136] An oak tree, known as the Witenagamot Oak, was planted to mark the occasion. This tree survived until 1948.[137] A second oak was planted nearby in 1701. In this way Andros was able to turn enemies of New England into "New York's staunch supporters."[138]

RAID ON EAMES GARRISON, FRAMINGHAM, MASSACHUSETTS

Thomas Eames' farm was located within the bounds of the Plantation of Framingham, on the southern slope of Mount Wayte, about seven miles southwest of Old Sudbury. On February 1, 1676, while Eames was away, the house was assaulted by about a dozen Nipmuc under Netus.[139] Tradition holds that two of the children were captured at the well, and Eames' wife attempted to fight off the attack by pouring boiling liquid (from the manufacture of soap) on her assailants.[140] Netus and his men, according to Hubbard, "burned all the Dwellings that belonged to the Farm, Corn, Hay and Cattle, besides the Dwelling-house."[141] Eames' wife and three or possibly four of their children were killed, while the rest were carried off toward Lancaster. At least one son eventually made an escape, and others of the children were ransomed. Thomas Eames lived only a few years after the tragedy, dying in 1680, and Netus was killed at Marlboro on March 27, 1676.[142]

On Mount Wayte Avenue in present-day Framingham sits a marker designating the location of Thomas Eames' house. Town historian William Barry wrote in 1847 that "a partial depression of the surface, with the surrounding apple trees, still indicate[d] the spot,"[143] though nothing can be seen today.

ATTACK ON LANCASTER, MASSACHUSETTS

On the tenth of February, 1676, came the Indians in great numbers upon Lancaster. Their first coming was about sun-rising. Hearing the noise of some guns, we looked out: several houses were burning, and smoke ascending to heaven. There were five persons taken in one house: the father, the mother, and a sucking child they knocked on the head: the other two they took and carried away alive. There were two others, who being out of their garrison on some occasion, were set upon; one was knocked on the head, the other escaped. Another there was, who, running along, was shot and wounded, and fell down; he begged of them his life, promising them money, (as they told me,) but

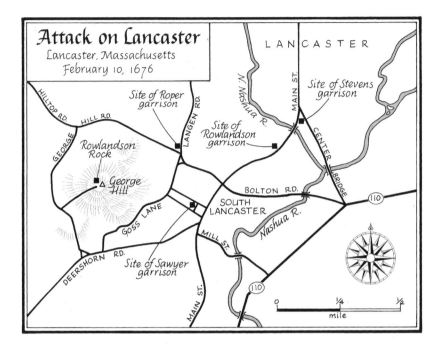

Attack on Lancaster
Lancaster, Massachusetts
February 10, 1676

LANCASTER

Site of Roper garrison

Site of Stevens garrison

Site of Rowlandson garrison

Rowlandson Rock

△ George Hill

BOLTON RD.

SOUTH LANCASTER

Nashua R.

110

Site of Sawyer garrison

110

0   ¼   ½
mile

they would not hearken to him but knocked him in the head, stripped him naked and split open his bowels. Another, seeing many of the Indians about his barn, ventured and went out, but was quickly shot down. There were three others belonging to the same garrison who were killed; the Indians getting up upon the roof of the barn, had advantage to shoot down upon them over their fortification. Thus these murderous wretches went on burning and destroying [all] before them.

At length they came and beset our own house, and quickly it was the dolefullest day that ever mine eyes saw.[144]

So began one of the great epics of colonial literature, *The Narrative of the Captivity and Restoration of Mrs. Mary Rowlandson,* written by the wife of Lancaster's first ordained minister. The book, published in 1682, chronicled Mary's ordeal as a captive of Quannopin, a sachem of the Narragansett who helped lead his people in the attack on Lancaster. Mary's captivity lasted al-

The native attack on Lancaster, shown here as it was being planned, devastated the town and led to, in Mary Rowlandson's words, "The dolefullest day that ever mine eyes saw." (Courtesy of the Haffenreffer Museum of Anthropology, Brown University)

most three months and took her on an arduous journey as far south as New Braintree, Massachusetts, and as far north as Chesterfield or Westmoreland, New Hampshire.[145] During her captivity she suffered hunger and exhaustion, watched her youngest child die in her arms of a wound received in the attack, but also lived and worked with Quannopin, Weetamoe, and Philip—giving us one of the few glimpses of the Algonquian at war.

187

This marker, moved often by road crews and for a time hidden behind a stone wall, commemorates the Rowlandson garrison in Lancaster, Massachusetts. Not far away, a tall pine tree designates the precise site of the garrison, destroyed in the war. (Michael Tougias)

At the time of the attack, Lancaster consisted of about fifty families organized around six garrisons. The defense of the town was placed in the hands of fifteen soldiers, detailed to the various garrisons. Conscious of Lancaster's exposed position and prompted by threats of impending attack, the Reverend Joseph Rowlandson had traveled to Boston to seek additional military assistance.

The assault on Lancaster came at dawn on February 10, 1675/76, and was led by Monoco. Five of the town's garrisons held, but the Rowlandson garrison had several disadvantages upon which the natives quickly seized. First, the garrison stood on the slope of a hill, so that the natives could lie along the crest and fire continuously with little fear of being hit by return fire. More devastating, however, was a mistake made by the settlers in piling winter firewood against the loopholes in the rear of the garrison. Seeing this, the natives seized a cart from the barn and, using the same strategy as that employed at Brookfield, set its cargo of hay, flax, and hemp on fire and launched it at the garrison. Soon after, the Rowlandson garrison was in flames and its occupants were racing for other garrisons. Of ten or twelve men within the garrison, only Ephraim Roper escaped. All of the women and children were captured, including Mary Rowlandson.

The site of the Rowlandson garrison is on the north side of Main Street, across from Whitcomb Drive, on land owned today by Atlantic Union College. A dirt road off Main Street leads past the location. A white pine was planted to mark the site of the garrison, and a cemetery sits on the south side of Main Street where the town's meetinghouse stood. No marker is evident near the pine, though just off Main Street, tucked directly behind the stone wall running along the road, is a stone marker. This marker once sat near the road, but was moved several times and eventually ended up in a spot that can only be seen by climbing on top of the wall itself. The marker reads:

IN THE FIELD NEARBY WAS
SITUATED THE GARRISON HOUSE
OF THE REV. JOSEPH ROWLANDSON
FIRST ORDAINED MINISTER OF
LANCASTER.
DURING HIS ABSENCE ON
FEBRUARY 10, 1675–76 THIS
GARRISON HOUSE WAS ATTACKED
AND DESTROYED BY INDIANS.

THE INHABITANTS WERE
MASSACRED OR CARRIED INTO
CAPTIVITY. LATER MOST OF THEM
WERE REDEEMED.
THE MINISTER'S WIFE
IMMORTALIZED HER EXPERIENCE
IN "THE NARRATIVE OF THE
CAPTIVITY AND RESTORATION OF
MARY ROWLANDSON"
PRINTED IN CAMBRIDGE,
MASSACHUSETTS, 1682.

The Algonquian were said to attack from the west of the fir tree marker, where a pond has since been dug.[146]

Meanwhile, the arrival of Captain Samuel Wadsworth and forty soldiers from the east spurred the natives to retreat, but not without first firing most of the outlying buildings, gathering up great stores of food and livestock, and then forcing twenty-four English captives to march with them. Total casualties for the town probably exceeded fifty.[147] The survivors, under the protection of colonial troops, buried their dead, probably near where they fell. A few headed east to be with relatives, while others took refuge in the garrisons of Cyprian Stevens and Thomas Sawyer. The Stevens garrison is marked on Center Bridge Road, near Neck Road, on the south side of the North Nashua River. The marker reads:

SITE OF THE HOME
OF CYPRIAN STEVENS
IN THE ASSAULT UPON THE
TOWN, FEB 10, 1675/6, A RELIEF
FORCE FROM MARLBORO
RECOVERING A GARRISON HOUSE
BELONGING TO CYPRIAN STEVENS
THROUGH GOD'S FAVOR

PREVENTED THE ENEMY FROM
CUTTING OFF THE GARRISON

Stevens' father-in-law was Major Simon Willard, who rode to the rescue of Brookfield and was active in a variety of military operations during King Philip's War.

The site of the Thomas Sawyer garrison is marked at the corner of Main and Prescott Streets. The marker reads:

SITE OF
THOMAS SAWYER'S
GARRISON HOUSE

BETWEEN THE MASSACRE OF
FEBRUARY 10, 1675–6,
AND THE
ABANDONMENT OF THE TOWN,
THE INHABITANTS TOOK REFUGE
IN THE STEVENS (WILLARD) AND
SAWYER GARRISONS

On March 26, Lancaster was abandoned, in the words of historian Robert Diebold, "more desolate than the rude wilderness from which it had been laboriously conquered."[148]

On her first night of captivity, Mary Rowlandson rested with her captors on George Hill, about a mile from the Rowlandson house. The location is marked by the so-called Rowlandson Rock, which can be found today in the woods at the end of Windsor Road, off George Hill Road, near the water tower. The rock is not immediately visible, but requires a hundred-yard hike northwest from the tower. (The state of Massachusetts has placed a commemorative marker at the junction of Main Street and Sterling Road, giving directions to the approximate location of Rowlandson Rock.) In her narrative of the captivity she describes the scene at this stopping place:

Oh the roaring, and singing, and dancing, and yelling of those black creatures in the night, which made the place a lively resemblance of hell . . . There remained nothing to me but one poor, wounded babe, and it seemed at present worse than death that it was in such a pitiful condition.[149]

A few days later her wounded daughter would die. The possible location of this death is marked in New Braintree on the north side of Thompson Road, a few hundred yards west of Hardwick Road. The marker reads:

SARAH P. ROWLANDSON
BORN SEPT. 15, 1669
SHOT BY INDIANS AT LANCASTER
FEB. 10, 1676
TAKEN TO WINNIMISSETT CAMP
DIED FEB. 18, 1676

Q. HIST. SOC.

Well treated throughout her captivity, Rowlandson nonetheless suffered the same deprivations as her captors, who were often without food and constantly forced to be on the move. In retrospect, it was a first glimpse of how desperate the Algonquian had become, despite the terror their victories in March and April 1676 would bring to the colonists.

On May 2, 1676, Mary was redeemed by John Hoar of Boston at a well-known gathering place of the Nipmuc since called Redemption Rock. It is located in Princeton, Massachusetts, along Route 140, .8 miles north of the Route 31 split. (This section of Route 140 is known as Redemption Rock Trail.) A small parking lot is adjacent to the rock. An inscription on the perpendicular face of the rock reads:

UPON THIS ROCK MAY 2ND 1676

Now a notable stop along the hiking trails of Mt. Wachusett in Princeton, Massachusetts, Redemption Rock marks the location of Mary Rowlandson's return from her native captors in 1676. (Michael Tougias)

WAS MADE THE AGREEMENT FOR THE RANSOM
OF MRS. MARY ROWLANDSON OF LANCASTER
BETWEEN THE INDIANS AND JOHN HOAR OF CONCORD
KING PHILP WAS WITH THE INDIANS
REFUSED HIS CONSENT

Shortly thereafter, Mary was reunited with her husband, sister, son, and daughter. In all, over twenty of the Lancaster captives were returned. The town was eventually resettled, but fell victim to assault once again on September 11, 1697, during King William's War. In one strange twist of fate, Ephraim Roper, who survived the attack at the Rowlandson garrison and survived the fight at Turner's Falls, would finally fall victim during the 1697 massacre.[150] Roper's garrison is marked on the north side of George Hill Road, just west of Langden Road in Lancaster.

The Rowlandsons Locker, a chest made of solid English oak, was thought for many years to have belonged to John White, Mary's father and one of the wealthiest early settlers of Lancaster. (White's home was located on the west side of Neck Road, near the road's only sharp bend.[151] The site is not marked.) The story was told that Mary had inherited the locker, that it had been rescued from her burning garrison, and that it was recovered by the family when they moved to Wethersfield, Connecticut, after the war. The town library purchased the piece in 1876 and placed it on display. More recently, evidence has been found to suggest that the locker, now preserved in Lancaster's historical collections, was purchased by the Rowlandsons after their move to Connecticut.[152]

ATTACK ON MEDFIELD, MASSACHUSETTS

When the natives attacked and destroyed Lancaster on February 10, the town had been ill-prepared and desperately seeking reinforcements. No such situation existed in Medfield, where eighty infantry under Captain John Jacob and twenty troopers under Captain Edward Oaks had been sent by Massachusetts Bay to bolster the town's militia of about one hundred men.[153] Together, these two hundred soldiers seemed capable of preventing the kind of destruction visited upon their western neighbor. Nonetheless, eleven days after the destruction of Lancaster, Monoco and perhaps three hundred warriors[154] infiltrated Medfield and attacked at daybreak on February 21. The colonial soldiers, scattered throughout the town and completely unsuspecting of an assault so early in the day,[155] watched half of Medfield burn to the ground before they could fire a warning cannon and chase the intruders from the settlement.

Medfield was located about twenty-two miles[156] from Boston and ten miles southeast of Dedham, the town from which Medfield split off in 1651. Medfield was created, at least in part, to buffer its more established parent from the Indian-infested wilderness.[157] However, the greed of Medfield's settlers, who, the historian Hubbard criticizes, were "every where apt to engross more Land into their Hands than they were able to subdue,"[158] left the town "over run with young Wood and seated amidst of a Heap of

Bushes,"[159] perfect conditions for a surreptitious attack by Monoco's men. This exposed condition was not lost upon the residents of Medfield, who, in petitioning the governor and council for aid on February 14, wrote: "Our Towne is a frontier Towne . . . what will become of the city if the hands of the country grow feeble."[160]

While tradition says that natives were spotted on Noon Hill (south of Noon Hill Street) and Mount Nebo (north of Philip Street) after Sunday services[161] on February 20, Hubbard and other historians generally believed that the Algonquian did not actually begin their quiet invasion of the settlement until that evening, from the west,

> some getting under the Sides of the Barns and Fences of their Orchards, as is supposed, where they lay hid under that Covert, till break of Day, when they suddenly set upon sundry Houses, especially those Houses where the Inhabitants were repaired to Garrisons [and] were fit for the Purpose: some were killed as they attempted to fly to their Neighbors for Shelter: some were only wounded, and some taken alive and carried Captive.[162]

The first house burned was that of Samuel Morse, at the east end of Medfield, thought to be a general signal for the attack to begin. Morse had gone out to his barn early in the morning to feed his cattle, and was surprised to see a native hiding in the hay. Morse, so tradition says, feigned ignorance, left the barn immediately to gather up his family, and watched his dwelling burst into flames as he and his family fled for a garrison. It was this early warning that saved the entire town from being destroyed.

The Morse residence, no longer standing, was located nearly directly across from Peak House on the south side of present-day Main Street (Route 109).[163] It was at this point that Main Street turned to the southeast, and instead of following the present Route 109 (which did not exist until the nineteenth century), crossed to the north and east of Mount Nebo and picked up present-day Foundry Street.

Peak House, undoubtedly the best known historic structure in Medfield, was the site of the Benjamin Clark house, destroyed during the attack on February 21.

Peak House in Medfield, Massachusetts, was the site of the Benjamin Clark house, destroyed during the February 21, 1676, attack on the town. In 1677 Clark rebuilt the present structure, which is considered typical of seventeenth-century cottages, with the exception of the steeply pitched roof. (From Historical Collections, *John Warner Barber, 1848.)*

Benjamin rebuilt the house in 1677 and petitioned the General Court of the Colony for relief from taxes while he recovered from his losses. This replacement house built in 1677 is the present "Peak House." It is a typical 17th century cottage of one-room plan, one and one-half stories in height. Its most unusual feature is its exceptionally steep pitched roof, the highest pitch on record in the Commonwealth of Massachusetts for a 17th century house.[164]

Peak House was restored to its assumed seventeenth-century appearance in 1924 and donated to the Medfield Historical Society, which owns it today. The ancient structure is located at 347 Main Street (Route 109), about a mile from the Dover town line.[165]

There were several garrisons located in Medfield at the time of King Philip's War. That of Isaac Chenery was located east of Mount Nebo; in 1876, its remains were still visible:

> It is situated upon a knoll or rise or land, upon the borders of a large swamp. To be seen at the present time are the remains of the stockade, in almost the exact form of a horseshoe, and in nearly the middle the almost perfectly square cellar of the old house. The corners are as plainly to be discerned as any portion.[166]

The tradition is that Chenery spotted natives lurking around his home the evening before the assault, but unable to warn the town, he spirited his family to a cranberry meadow, where they spent the night safely under the protection of a great rock.[167] The location of Chenery's garrison was at the end of present-day Foundry Street, in Walpole; the vague shape of a fort can still be seen, though the land is now occupied by a private residence and permission to view the remains must be sought.[168]

A second garrison was located at the northwest corner of Main and Brook Streets, the present site of a red saltbox.[169] Another garrison was situated in front of the present home at 72 Harding Street; some of the old timbers from the garrison were said to be used in the present structure.[170] A fourth garrison was thought to be located on present-day North Street, opposite the head of Dale Street, where apartments now sit. In the western part of Medfield, now Millis and Sherborn, settlers gathered for protection in the "Stone House," located near the Millis-Sherborn line near Route 115.[171] Constructed entirely of stone, this structure, according to local historian Richard Desorgher, was larger and better fortified than "any similar structure on the then frontier."[172]

Deaths in the Medfield attack totaled seventeen or eighteen.[173] One woman, Elizabeth Smith, was killed near the junction of South and Pound Streets while fleeing with her infant; her baby was left for dead by the natives but survived.[174] The wife of Lieutenant Henry Adams, Elizabeth Paine Adams, survived the attack but was shot to death that night in the home of the minister when a firearm accidentally discharged from the floor below, of which Increase Mather wrote, "It is a sign God is angry, when he turns our Weapons against ourselves."[175]

The total number of houses and barns destroyed in Medfield was forty or fifty.[176] Two mills were reported burned; one, that of Henry Adams, was located near Mill Brook, close to the present-day Elm Street.[177] The home of John Partridge, located near the corner of North and Harding Streets, was burned.[178] Several houses in the Castle Hill area near North Street were destroyed, says Desorgher, going on to catalog still more devastation:

> The Bridge Street section was totally destroyed . . . Also to go up in flames at about the same time was the Gershom Wheelock home, located near the corner of Main and Causeway St., and the Joseph Bullard house, located off West Main Street . . . On the west bank of the Charles River, the Indians set fire to the Jonathan Adams house and John Russell, then nearly 100 years old, was burnt alive inside it.[179]

Despite these losses, William Hubbard reported that all of Medfield's garrison houses and "the chiefest and best of their Building escaped the Fury of the Enemy."[180]

Loaded with plunder, some natives withdrew across a bridge over the Charles River leading to Sherborn. Another group of natives crossed the "Great Bridge," thought to be located southeast of the present Brastow Bridge (also called "the Poor-farm Bridge," at the crossing at West Street–Dover Road), about halfway between the bridge and Route 109.[181] Its crossing is marked by large rocks on either shore[182] that can still be seen from Brastow Bridge. It was on this bridge[183]—no longer standing—that a letter was posted, probably written by a young Indian who had formerly operated a printing business in Boston, known as James the Printer. The letter was designed to strike fear in a badly shaken English populace:

> Know by this Paper, that the Indians that thou has provoked to Wrath and Anger will war this twenty-one Years, if you will. There are many Indians yet. We come 300 at this Time. You must consider that the Indians lose nothing but their Life. You must lose your fair Houses and Cattle.[184]

Before the English could rally, the natives fired both bridges, making pursuit impossible. Then, upon a hill in full sight of the smoking ruins, Monoco and his men roasted an ox. The site of this victory celebration is marked by a clump of tupelo trees, which have been called "King Philip's Trees" for almost three centuries. (Whether Philip actually participated in the attack is subject to disagreement, though it appears certain that Monoco was the chief military commander.) King Philip's Trees can be found in present-day Millis, on private land off Dover Road, a short distance west of the bridge.

On February 22 the natives returned to their camp at Menameset. Mary Rowlandson reported:

> But before they came to us, oh the outrageous roaring and hooping that there was! They began their din about a mile before they came to us. By their noise and hooping they signified how many they had destroyed (which was at that time twenty three). Those that were with us at home were gathered together as soon as they heard the hooping, and every time that the other went over their number, those at home gave a shout, that the very earth rang again.[185]

Not far to the southwest of Medfield is the present-day town of Franklin, Massachusetts, once a part of Wrentham, Massachusetts. Wrentham was abandoned before March 30, 1676, in the wake of the destruction at Lancaster and Medfield, and burned shortly after by the natives. However, prior to its destruction (the exact date is unknown) a man by the name of Rocket, while searching for a lost horse, stumbled upon the camp of forty-two warriors. Returning to Wrentham, he recruited a dozen men who crept back to the camp and attacked shortly after daylight. A nineteenth-century Franklin historian named Mortimer Blake told the story:

> The suddenness of the attack so confused the Indians who escaped the first shot that they rushed and leaped down a steep precipice of the rock; where they, maimed and lamed by the fall, became speedily victims to the quick and steady aims of the whites. One or two only escaped to tell the fate of their comrades.[186]

This location, today known as Indian Rock, is located off Jordan Road (which runs off Route 140) in Franklin. In 1823, the town celebrated the Fourth of July with an oration at the rock. In 1976, Franklin's Historical Commission rededicated Indian Rock.

ATTACK ON GROTON, MASSACHUSETTS

Settled in 1655, Groton was home to about sixty families on the eve of King Philip's War.[187] In August 1675, residents had complained to Governor Leverett that they were lacking both guns and ammunition to defend themselves.[188] By February 1676, the town was in a miserable state, feeling itself encircled by the enemy, its livestock unprotected, its food supply disappearing, with the soldiers sent to protect the town fast contributing to its poverty.

Five garrisons had been established to protect Groton's residents in the event of an attack. Four were set along Main Street, "so near together," says Hubbard, "as to be able to command from one to the other."[189] An 1848 description by local historian Caleb Butler placed one at Captain James Parker's house lot,

> now owned by Dr. A. Bancroft and his son, on both sides of the great road, and his house probably stood as near the brook as was convenient. John Nutting's house lot joined Parker's on the north side of the brook, and his house might be within "eight or nine poles" of Parker's, at or near the house of Aaron Perkins. Mr. Willard, the minister, owned the house lot south of Parker's, and tradition places his garrison on the land of Jonathan Loring, partly between his house and the road.[190]

Today, a Massachusetts commemorative maker located on Main Street between the town hall and Court Street designates the location of Parker's garrison. Nutting's garrison was located on the north corner of Court and Main Streets, home to Sergeant's Drugstore in the 1990s.[191] The Willard garrison, thought to have been destroyed many years ago, was rediscovered in the late 1960s when residents undertaking renovations on a home off Main Street found evidence of seventeenth-century construction. The home was investigated by the Massachusetts Historical Commission and is now believed to be that of the Reverend Samuel Willard. Willard's house is located on the west side of Main Street, four houses away from the town hall near the junior high; it is the second house behind a small gift shop.[192] Groton's fifth garrison was about a mile away, and several sites have been identified as possibilities, though the precise location is unknown.

On March 2, a small band of warriors raided eight or nine houses and made off with some cattle. The following day, Major Simon Willard and Captain Joseph Sill combed the area but could find no trace of the enemy.

On March 9, several warriors, who had spent two days rifling through some of Groton's abandoned homes, ambushed a cart sent from one of the town's garrisons to gather hay. One man was killed and one taken captive. Hubbard recorded that the latter was "sentenced to Death, but the Enemy not concurring in the manner of it, execution was deferred, and he by the Providence of God escaped by a bold Attempt the Night before he was designed to Slaughter, and fled to the Garrison of Lancaster."[193]

The first two Indian assaults on Groton were frightening but relatively harmless. On March 13, however, Monoco led perhaps four hundred warriors[194] in a major assault on the town, which succeeded in destroying the town's meetinghouse and a large number of dwellings. The attack unfolded like so many others: Monoco and his forces infiltrated the town during the evening and early morning hours. When morning came, most residents went about their business as usual until two warriors were spotted along the top of one of the town's nearby hills. An alarm was given and soldiers serving under Captain Parker rushed after the pair, leaving one garrison entirely unprotected. When the soldiers reached the brow of the hill, however, they suddenly found themselves in an ambush. (Butler believed this hill was on Dr. Bancroft's land, nearer to Nutting's garrison than Parker's;[195] today, this hill can be seen from Main Street, rising behind the First Baptist Church.) One man was killed, three wounded, and the rest fled in disarray.

Meanwhile, a second band of warriors had reached the unprotected garrison and pulled down its palisade. (Butler conjectured that this was the Nutting garrison.)[196] The women and children, Hubbard wrote, "by the Goodness of God made a safe Escape to the other fortified House without

Harm, leaving their Substance to the Enemy, who made a Prey of it, and spent the Residue of the Day in removing Corn and House-hold stuff (in which Loss five Families were impoverished)."[197] Among the warriors in this second party was Monoco.

Soon, all over town, homes and barns were set on fire. The settlers did well to protect their remaining garrisons, but could do little to stop the destruction. That night many of the warriors retreated to an "adjacent Valley,"[198] while others felt secure enough to sleep in the town, some in the garrison itself.

There is a story, passed down by Hubbard, that Monoco kept up a dialogue all night long with "his old neighbor,"[199] Captain Parker, the garrisons being close enough that conversation was possible. (Monoco resided near Lancaster before the war; Parker had lived in Groton for many years.) If Hubbard was correct, Monoco discussed the causes of the war, how to bring about peace, and boasted that he had burned Medfield and Lancaster, that he would now burn Groton, and that he would soon burn Chelmsford, Concord, Watertown, Cambridge, Charlestown, Roxbury, and Boston. Monoco ended this dialogue with the words, "What Me will, Me do."[200] (Monoco was hung in Boston on September 26, 1676, having carried out only part of his threat.)

In all, forty houses and a number of other buildings were destroyed in Groton.[201]

Soon after the March 13 attack, Groton's residents abandoned the town and took refuge in Concord. The evacuation had great similarities to that of Bloody Brook, and could have easily turned into a massacre of the English had luck not been on their side. Hubbard recorded that Captain Sill was sent

> with a small Party of Dragoons of eight Files to fetch off the Inhabitants of Groton, and what was left from the Spoil of the Enemy, having under his conduct about sixty Carts, being in Depth from Front to Rear about two Miles: when a Party of Indians lying in Ambush at a Place of eminent Advantage, fired upon the Front, and mortally wounded two of the vaunt Carriers, who died both the next Night;

and might (had God permitted) had done eminent Damage to the whole Body, it being a Full Hour before the whole Body could be drawn up . . . but the Indians after a few more Shots made, without doing Harm, retired and made no further Assault.[202]

The place of the ambush, where the natives had "eminent Advantage," was thought by Caleb Butler to be the "ridges." After the war, travelers making their way across the ridges at night were said to hear the screams of women and children, ghostly echoes of the ambush. One night, Colonel James Prescott was returning from Boston when he passed through the ridges, and knowing the story, he stopped to listen. Sure enough, he soon heard an un-usual noise, but instead of fleeing in terror, decided to investigate. He tied his horse and began walking toward the sound, coming to the pond (prob-ably Knopps Pond) on the north side of the ridge road, and proceeding to the north side of the pond. There he discovered the source of the noise: not ghosts of Groton's past, but a litter of young minks.[203]

The ridges can be found at what today is Route 119 south of the vil-lage, just north of Four Corners and east of Knopps Pond. The ridges them-selves are a series of steep, curving slopes that one Groton historian described as "looking quite like a railroad embankment"[204] and left by glacier activity; Route 119 itself is constructed on a ridge. Before the forest was allowed to grow in this area, the ridges were plainly visible.[205]

ATTACK ON NORTHAMPTON, MASSACHUSETTS

By mid-March 1676 Northampton was as well secured as its frontier location would allow. The town, formed in 1653 and home to about five-hundred people,[206] had been fortified over the winter months by a long, wooden palisade that enclosed the structures around its central meeting-house. In addition, the settlement was host to one company of soldiers under Captain William Turner and two under Major Robert Treat of Con-necticut, or about three hundred soldiers in all. Turner had arrived on March 8 and Treat on the 13;[207] had the river Indians realized this they might never have attacked.

On the morning of March 14 a sizable force[208] of local warriors, perhaps aided by Narragansett and Nipmuc,[209] assaulted Northampton, breaking through the palisade in three places. Nine houses were set on fire outside the palisade, and one within,[210] before the soldiers could respond, but once the natives recognized the huge force present, they turned and fled. The palisade designed to keep them out now, in Hubbard's words, boxed them in, "like Wolves in a Pound, that . . . could not fly away at their pleasure."[211] Eleven or twelve were killed, while five English lost their lives and five others were wounded.[212] The remaining warriors retreated into the forest. In the process, they made off with a few horses and sheep, but it was hardly the victory for which they had hoped. For the first time in many months, the English were able to celebrate.

Part of the reason for Northampton's readiness was its several prior encounters with native warriors. The first had occurred on August 20, 1675, when Samuel Mason was killed.[213] A month later, on September 28, 1675, Praisever Turner and Uzacaby Shakspeare were murdered and scalped while cutting wood, probably on Turner's lot in the area east of Elm Street and present-day Paradise Road.[214] Most of the houses standing in this area now were built in the period between 1870 and 1890, and are within the Smith College campus.[215]

On October 28 of that same year, seven or eight of Northampton's settlers, harvesting crops in Pynchon Meadow, were surprised by a band of warriors but managed to elude their attackers, who, according to local historian James Russell Trumbell, burned four or five houses and several barns "that stood some distance from the principal settlement."[216] Pynchon's Meadow comprised 120 acres at the most northerly turn of the "Ox Bow," bounded by present-day Pynchon Meadow Road, Curtis Nook Road, and Old Springfield Road.[217] The settlers fled along present-day South Street.[218]

The current locations of the structures destroyed in the October 28 attack are more difficult to pinpoint, since they were said to be located on South Street,[219] which in colonial times was south of Mill River. The course of Mill River has changed significantly over three hundred years: It now flows south from Paradise Pond, but it once flowed west, more parallel with

Main and Pleasant Streets. Local historian James Trumbell placed the destroyed homes near the Starkweather estate,[220] found on an 1873 map to be in the area east of present-day Old South Street, near Dewey Court. This area, once south of Mill River, is now considerably east.

On October 29 the same group surprised and killed two men and a boy in the meadows opposite the town mill, at the upper end of present-day Paradise Pond,[221] but were unable to destroy the mill. The Northampton Town Mill was built in 1671 at "Red Rocks," near the bend in the Mill River between present-day College Lane and Paradise Road, upon the land of Praisever Turner.[222]

These two attacks prompted Northampton to construct its wooden palisade, which Hubbard describes as "a Kind of Barricado . . . of cleftwood about eight Foot long,"[223] never thought to be sturdy enough to withstand an attack, but strong enough to "break the force of any sudden assault."[224] The location of the palisade constructed as a result of King Philip's War has never been precisely determined. However, it was known to have been north of Mill River, and to have enclosed the meetinghouse (located where the Hampshire County Courthouse now stands, on the corner of Main and King Streets[225]) and the structures closest to it. Trumbell used the boundaries of a second palisade, constructed in Northampton a decade after the close of King Philip's, to hypothesize where a portion of the first may have been built: The eastern bound of the 1675 palisade may have been along Hawley Street, beginning at Bridge Street. From there the palisade would have run west along the bank of the old course of the Mill River, approximately where the New York, New Haven, and Hartford railroad tracks now run. From there, the palisade crossed West Street, and jogged north, following the banks of the Mill River.[226]

The palisade was breached in three places[227] during the March 14 attack, each of which give us additional clues as to its boundaries. One breach was on the east side of Round Hill, south of Summer Street and west of Prospect Street. A second was west of King Street, just north of Myrtle Street. The third was on the west side of Pleasant Street, across from the junction of Holyoke Street, perhaps the southeast corner of the palisade. Trumbell wrote that this last was the "most serious demonstration; here the defenses were quickly broken through, and a desperate conflict ensued."[228]

Northampton was threatened again shortly after the March 14, 1676, attack,[229] but was spared another assault during the remainder of the war.[230] Like many colonial towns, Northampton was not spared other tragedy, however. At the fight at Turner's Falls in May 1676, twelve of thirty-one Northampton soldiers were killed.[231]

ATTACK ON MARLBORO, MASSACHUSETTS

In 1675, Marlboro was a frontier town of about 225 people[232] situated over a wide territory along the Connecticut Road between Boston and the Connecticut River Valley settlements. Comprising perhaps thirty homes,[233] Marlboro was also the site of the Praying Indian community of Okamakemest, which had been in conflict with the English settlers since the building of the town's first meetinghouse in the 1660s. It seems that Marlboro's minister, the Reverend William Brimsmead (also written Brinsmead), had located the meetinghouse upon an old Indian planting field, in a position that essentially blocked access from the Praying Village to Marlboro's main thoroughfare. It was, as one modern-day historian has noted, the single location most likely to cause bitterness among the Praying Indians.[234] (Indeed, one story related that the natives, prior to the war, would hide in a swamp east of the meetinghouse on Sunday and fire their guns in the direction of the structure to harass the English.[235])

The meetinghouse, says Marlboro historian Ella A. Bigelow, was a "small, one-storied building with oil paper in the windows for light and thatched with straw and a kind of tall grass taken from the meadow."[236] It was located on the north side of the present-day Main Street, on the hill at the intersection of Rawlins Avenue, immediately in front of Marlboro's former high school (now the Walker Building).[237] This hill is thought to have been more elevated than at present.[238]

Because of Marlboro's strategic position, it played an important role in King Philip's War, being garrisoned for military operations in February 1676. The settlement was attacked and partially destroyed on March 16, 1676, and assaulted again on April 17, when many of the town's remaining struc-

The Reverend William Brimsmead, who lost his home in the March 1676 attack on Marlboro, is interred in the town's oldest burying ground, Spring-Hill Cemetery, located at Brown Street and High Street. (Eric Schultz)

tures were burned.[239] Even after the second assault and subsequent abandonment by its residents, Marlboro continued to be maintained by the military as a supply depot. Because of this, a few of Marlboro's structures survived the war, and some survive to this day.

On Sunday, March 26, the colonists were assembled in their meetinghouse, with the Reverend Mr. Brimsmead about to begin his sermon, when the cry went up, "The Indians are upon us."[240] (One version of the story says that a Mr. Thomas Graves, suffering from a toothache, had stepped outside for a moment during the sermon and spotted the natives beginning their assault.)[241] The attack proceeded quickly, as the settlement was widely scattered and the garrisons could offer little resistance; "thirteen of their dwellings, and eleven barns, were laid in ashes; their fences thrown down; their fruit-trees hacked and peeled; the cattle killed or maimed; so that their ravages were visible for many years," wrote Charles Hudson in his 1862 history of Marlboro.[242] Since many of the attacking natives had converted to Christianity, there is a tradition that says they were unwilling to set fire directly to the meetinghouse, but set fire instead to Brimsmead's nearby house, situated to the southwest; from there, the flames leapt to the meetinghouse. Both structures were destroyed. Several accounts suggest that all but one of the congregation safely escaped to the Deacon Ward garrison, located about a quarter-mile away, though if even half the town were attending the meeting the garrison would have been overflowing. The Ward garrison, located on present-day Hayden Street at a location since called the "Daniel Hayden farm," survived the war but did not survive two subsequent fires.[243]

William's Tavern, destroyed by natives and "promptly rebuilt," was located on the south side of West Main Street and Gleason Street, at the sharp turn to Lakeside Avenue. A small strip mall now occupies the spot. A state marker designating the location has been removed, though the town plans to reerect it. The marker reads:

WILLIAMS TAVERN

THE FIRST TAVERN WAS ERECTED ON
THIS SITE BY LIEUTENANT ABRAHAM
WILLIAMS IN 1665. DESTROYED BY
INDIANS IN 1676. IT WAS PROMPTLY
REBUILT AND MANAGED BY THE
WILLIAMS FAMILY UNTIL 1829. HERE
THE EARLY CIRCUIT COURTS CONVENED,
STAGE COACHES CHANGED HORSES,
AND HISTORIC PERSONAGES TARRIED.

(One of these historic personages was said to be George Washington.) A photograph of the rebuilt William's Tavern is hanging at the Marlboro City Hall.

Another of Marlboro's garrisons was located in the northern part of town, on land flooded in the nineteenth century to create the Fort Meadow Reservoir.[244] Based on old maps, the garrison may have been located at the far eastern end of the reservoir, near present-day Hosmer Street.

The Brigham house, said to be a garrison during the war and still standing (though greatly changed), is located in the southern part of Marlboro on Brigham Street at the corner of LaRose Drive. Some of the natives who returned to Marlboro after the war lived near here, on the Brigham farm.[245]

William Brimsmead, who outlived the assault on Marlboro by a quarter-century, is interred at the town's oldest burying ground, Spring-Hill Cemetery, located at Brown Street and High Street. His marker placed near the site of his grave reads:

WILLIAM BRINSMEAD
FIRST PASTOR OF
MARLBOROUGH
1660 1701

PLACED BY
THE GEN. JOSEPH BADGER CHAPTER D.A.R.
1912

Spring-Hill Cemetery's first burial was that of Captain Edward Hutchinson of Boston, ambushed in Wheeler's Surprise at the present-day New Braintree, Massachusetts. Mortally wounded, he rode for home but died at Marlboro on August 19 in the public house operated by John Howe. Hutchinson's inscription reads:

CAPTAIN
EDWARD HUTCHINSON
AGED 62 YEARS
WAS SHOT BY
TREACHEROUS INDIANS
AUGUST 2 1675

ERECTED BY
THE GEN. JOS. BADGER
CHAPTER OF THE
DAUGHTERS OF THE
AMERICAN
REVOLUTION
OCT. 27,
1921

The Howe Tavern, where Hutchinson was said to have died, is still standing (as a private residence) at the end of Fowler Street, off Stevens Street.[246]

One of the few natives to participate in the war and return to live in an English community was David Munnanow. Hudson says his "wigwam was on the borders of the pond near the public house long known as William's Tavern, where he lived with his family many years, and died in extreme old age."[247] Munnanow admitted to having assisted in the destruction of Medfield, but for whatever reason, was allowed to live his life peacefully.

Elizabeth Howe, seventeen years old and a resident of Marlboro, was visiting her sister, Ann (Howe) Joslin, at Lancaster on the day that that town was attacked. She was captured and later released. Tradition says that she lived to an old age but, according to Ella Bigelow, "never quite overcame the shaking and trembling which the fright brought upon her."[248]

THE SUDBURY FIGHT, SUDBURY, MASSACHUSETTS

With the abandonment of Lancaster and Groton, and the partial evacuation of Marlboro, the settlement at Sudbury had become even more exposed to the danger of attack. Much of Sudbury's old settlement was located east of the Sudbury River, in present-day Wayland, though several garrisons and the town's first gristmill (called Noyes' Mill or Hop Brook Mill) were situated to the west of the river. A wooden bridge crossed Hop

Brook near this mill, connecting Sudbury to the Marlboro Road. A second bridge, known as Town Bridge, crossed the Sudbury River, connecting the west bank settlers with the town's meetinghouse and central settlement. The Old Lancaster Road ran east into town, splitting two prominent rises of land, Goodman's Hill and Green Hill.

By early April colonial authorities were aware that a sizable body of natives had gathered at a camp near Mount Wachusett. Under orders from the colonial Council of War, Captain Samuel Wadsworth marched about seventy men to the garrison at Marlboro, passing through Sudbury on the evening of April 20, 1676. Even as Wadsworth and his troops marched westward through the settlement along the Marlboro Road, as many as five hundred warriors from the Wachusett camp—Philip probably among them—had begun infiltrating Sudbury. In the early morning of April 21, 1676, they sprang their attack, focusing first on the well-fortified but poorly situated[249] Deacon Haynes garrison, built about 1646[250] on the western bank of the Sudbury River. John C. Powers, in *We Shall Not Tamely Give It Up*, writes:

> Clouds of smoke spurted upwards from the stonewalls and woods surrounding the Haynes garrison house. Musket shot rattled like hail against the stout planking . . . Added to the din came the sounds of heavy fighting from the east side of the river where a determined force of settlers made heavy resistance to another strong raiding party in the center of town, and a desperate hand to hand, house to house battle ensued.[251]

The Haynes garrison drew fire all morning, though George Ellis and John Morris say the attack "was not vigorously pressed, being probably in the nature of a feint."[252] The barn to the west of the house was set on fire but collapsed without harming the garrison. To the rear of the garrison a slight rise provided cover to a group of natives busily loading one of Haynes' wagons with combustible material; however, when the flaming cart was pushed down the hill its wheel hit a rock, harmlessly spilling its fiery contents.[253] In the end, the Haynes garrison would hold, even as destruction raged around it.

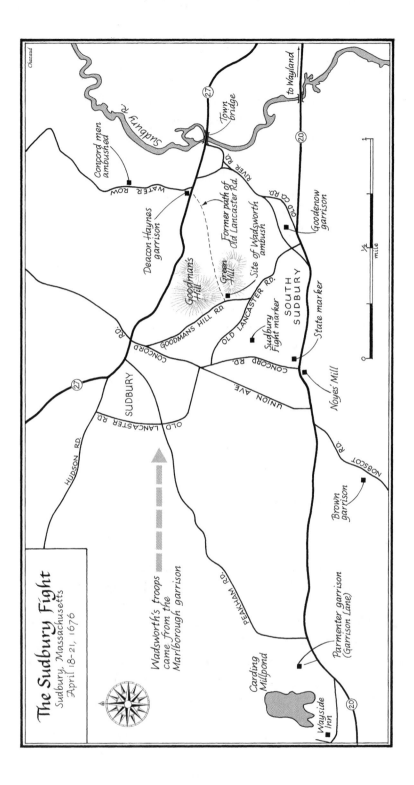

The Sudbury Fight
Sudbury, Massachusetts
April 18–21, 1676

Wadsworth's troops
came from the
Marlborough garrison

Today, the site of the Deacon Haynes garrison is marked on Water-Row Road, about two-tenths of a mile north of Old Sudbury Road (Route 27). The house was situated about fifteen yards from the road, facing south.[254] It survived the Sudbury Fight, only to be demolished sometime after 1876.[255] The cellar hole of the garrison is still visible. A marker on the site reads:

SITE OF THE
HAYNES GARRISON HOUSE
HOME OF DEACON JOHN HAYNES
HERE THE SETTLERS
BY THEIR BRAVE DEFENSE
HELPED SAVE THE TOWN
WHEN THE INDIANS TRIED
TO DESTROY SUDBURY
18–21 APRIL 1676[256]
ERECTED BY
WAYSIDE INN CHAPTER D.A.R.
OCT. 1922

John J. McCann, a Sudbury resident who was born in the Haynes garrison in 1860, remembered that "the rooms on the second floor toward the hill were bricked about four feet high, between the outer and inner walls"[257] to keep the Indians from shooting those sleeping.

When news of the attack on Sudbury reached Concord, eleven brave but foolhardy men of that town marched along the west bank of the Sudbury River. There, in full view of the settlers at the Haynes garrison, they were ambushed and virtually wiped out, with only one man escaping.[258]

Sometime in the early afternoon, troops under Captain Hugh Mason of Watertown drove the natives from the central settlement and crossed the Town Bridge to the western bank of the Sudbury River. By now, the heaviest action was occurring on Green Hill, which Mason and his troops tried repeatedly and unsuccessfully to reach. At risk of being surrounded and cut off, they eventually retreated to the garrison of Captain Goodenow (or Goodnow), Sudbury's second important fortification on the western side of the Sudbury River.

A state marker at the intersection of Old County Road and the Boston Post Road (Route 20) designates the site of the Goodenow garrison. The marker reads:

THE GOODENOW GARRISON HOUSE
PORTION OF THE GOODENOW GARRISON
HOUSE IN WHICH SETTLERS
TOOK REFUGE FROM KING PHILIP'S
INDIANS DURING THE BATTLE OF
APRIL 18–21, 1676.

Despite the sign, no remains of the Goodenow garrison remain. The house was standing as late as about 1815, but was moved or destroyed shortly thereafter.[259]

Captain Wadsworth had learned of the attack on Sudbury soon after his arrival at Marlboro. Gathering together most of his exhausted troops, including those under Captain Samuel Brocklebank already stationed in Marlboro, Wadsworth rapidly retraced his march from Sudbury. As the combined force crossed the bridge at Noyes' Mill and marched to a point just south of Green Hill, they spotted a few warriors fleeing northward in the large field at the base of the hill. Thinking they had surprised Philip's rear guard, Wadsworth and Brocklebank's fifty men left the road and set off in hot pursuit along the west side of Green Hill. (Local historian Alfred Hudson believed there was a path already here that connected Hop Brook Mill with the Old Lancaster Road.)[260] When they reached the pass between Green Hill and Goodman's Hill, however, a deadly ambush was sprung; shots rang out from both hillsides as bodies of warriors—perhaps five hundred in all[261]—rushed to block the northern and southern retreats.

Wadsworth's men, thrown momentarily into a panic, were able to form a

The Sudbury Fight, a brilliant victory for the native alliance, is marked in several locations throughout the town of Sudbury, Massachusetts. This grave marker, at Wadsworth Cemetery off Concord Road, commemorates the deaths of Captains Samuel Wadsworth and Samuel Brocklebank and twenty-seven of their men, and is near the spot where many of them fell. (From King Philip's War, *George W. Ellis and John E. Morris, 1906)*

square, repulsing several native charges. As the afternoon wore on and relief—such as Captain Mason and his troops, Corporal Solomon Phipps and his troopers from Charlestown, Captain Edward Cowell (on the march from Brookfield to Boston), and Captain John Cutler—was effectively blocked from reaching Green Hill, Wadsworth and his troops made their way up its side. By late afternoon the English had reached the top, losing only five men in about four hours of fighting, and for the first time found their position defensible. Nearby to the south sat the Goodenow garrison and the Noyes' Mill, the latter uninhabited but able to be fortified. Darkness might bring hope of escape.

It was then that the natives lit the dry brush of Green Hill on fire, forcing Wadsworth and his men to flee from the choking smoke and chaos. As they retreated to the south, in the direction of Noyes' Mill and the Goodenow garrison, most of the English, including Wadsworth and Brocklebank, were cut down; *The Old Indian Chronicle* records that "the Indians . . . came upon them like so many Tigers, and dulling their active Swords with excessive Numbers, obtained the Dishonor of a Victory."[262] As night fell the natives, having completed their rout, retreated to the west, leaving the frightened settlers scattered throughout Sudbury's garrisons to wonder what fate would bring them in the morning.

The site of Noyes' Mill is marked on Route 20, west of Concord Road, near the present-day Mill Village shopping center. The marker reads:

HOPBROOK MILL
TO THE LEFT IS THE SITE OF
HOPBROOK MILL, ERECTED IN 1659
BY VIRTUE OF A TOWN GRANT TO
THOMAS AND PETER NOYES, "TO
BUILD AND MAINTAIN A MILL TO
GRIND THE CORN OF THE SETTLERS."
IT IS NOW THE PROPERTY OF
HENRY FORD.

While the distance to the summit of Green Hill is not great, it is far enough away to understand how so many of Wadsworth's men were lost. With most of the English driven into garrisons, the area between the hill and the mill must have been alive with warriors.

The day after the battle Captain Samuel Hunting and his native troops, who had arrived on foot from Charlestown late the prior day, searched the area for the English dead, gathering the bodies of five of the Concord militia. These were buried in a common grave at the east end of Town Bridge.[263] Also, early that morning, the garrison at Marlboro watched silently as the victorious natives shouted seventy-four times to indicate the number of English they believed were lying dead in Sudbury.[264]

Wadsworth, Brocklebank, and about twenty-seven of their men were buried in a mass grave described by Alfred Serend Hudson as about six feet square "in which bodies were placed in tiers at right angles to each other."[265] The spot was marked by a heap of stones, in part to deter wolves. In 1852 the remains of these men were excavated and moved fifty feet north to the site of a new monument. A state marker at Boston Post Road (Route 20) and Concord Road designates this memorial, which is four-tenths of a mile north on Concord Road at the Wadsworth Cemetery. The marker reads:

SUDBURY FIGHT
ONE-QUARTER MILE NORTH
TOOK PLACE THE SUDBURY FIGHT
WITH KING PHILIP'S INDIANS ON
APRIL 21, 1676. CAPTAIN SAMUEL
WADSWORTH FELL WITH TWENTY-
EIGHT OF HIS MEN. THEIR MONUMENT
STANDS IN THE BURYING GROUND.

The monument itself sits toward the back of the cemetery and reads:

THIS MONUMENT IS ERECTED BY THE COMMONWEALTH OF
MASSACHUSETTS AND THE TOWN OF SUDBURY IN GRATEFUL
REMEMBRANCE OF THE SERVICE AND SUFFERINGS OF THE
FOUNDERS OF THE STATE AND ESPECIALLY IN HONOR OF
CAPT. S. WADSWORTH OF MILTON
CAPT. BROCKLEBANK OF ROWLEY
LIEUT. SHARP OF BROOKLINE
AND TWENTY SIX OTHERS, MEN OF THEIR COMMAND, WHO FELL
NEAR THIS SPOT ON THE 18 OF APRIL 1676 WHILE DEFENDING
THE FRONTIER SETTLEMENTS AGAINST THE ALLIED INDIAN FORCE

Samuel Wadsworth's stone, set in 1730 by his son, Benjamin (then president of Harvard College), was moved with the bodies to the base of the new monument. It reads:

CAPT. SAMUEL WADSWORTH OF
MILTON, HIS LIEU. SHARP OF
BROOKLINE, CAPT. BROCKLEBANK
OF ROWLEY, WITH ABOUT
TWENTY-SIX OTHER SOLDIERS
FIGHTING FOR YE DEFENSE OF
THEIR COUNTRY WERE SLAIN
BY YE INDIAN ENEMY, APRIL 18TH
1676, & LYE BURIED IN THIS PLACE.

Several other garrisons not known to be actively involved in the battle on April 21 are designated in Sudbury. The Parmenter garrison is commemorated by a stone marker on Garrison House Lane, a dirt road on the north side of Boston Post Road (Route 20), about six hundred feet east of the entrance to the Wayside Inn. The marker reads:

NEARBY IS THE SITE OF
THE PARMENTER GARRISON,
A STONE HOUSE BUILT
PREVIOUS TO 1686 AND
USED AS A PLACE OF REFUGE
FROM THE INDIANS.
RAZED IN 1858.
ERECTED BY
WAYSIDE INN CHAPTER D.A.R

The Parmenter garrison was a two-room, one-story structure.[266] Tradition holds that workmen building the Wayside Inn retreated to this garrison at night for safety.[267]

The Brown garrison was probably built about 1660 by Major Thomas Brown[268] and stood at the intersection of Nobscot and Dudley Roads. The structure, made of wood and lined with brick, was demolished in about 1855[269] and no sign of it remains.

Other houses in Sudbury were thought to be used as garrisons, though none remain. One of these, a blockhouse torn down in the early nineteenth century, was said by one observer to have bullet marks on it.[270]

The Sudbury Fight should have been one of the natives' finest hours. The feint at the Haynes garrison, the ambush of the Concord men, the ambush of Wadsworth's troops, the ability to seal off Green Hill from reinforcements, and the firing of Green Hill were as fine a display of military tactics as occurred during King Philip's War. (If it could be proved that Philip had masterminded this battle—which it cannot—then it would lay to rest the question of his military prowess.) A victory this close to Boston, inside the Marlboro defense and standing toe-to-toe with English soldiers, should have given the Wampanoag, Nipmuc, and Narragansett warriors a tremendous lift. However, such was not the case.

Perhaps the natives took unacceptable losses. Perhaps the fact that Sudbury still stood, and English reinforcements continued to pour in from all directions, was disheartening. Perhaps the fact that the natives still found the garrisons to be nearly impossible to crack made the victory hollow. In any event, when the war party returned to its camp at Wachusett, Mary Rowlandson wrote:

> To my thinking, they went without any scruple but that they should prosper and gain the victory. And they went out not so rejoicing, but they came home with as great a victory. For they said they had killed two captains and almost an hundred men. One Englishman they

brought alive with them, and he said it was too true, for they had made sad work at Sudbury, as indeed it proved. Yet they came home without that rejoicing and triumphing over their victory which they were wont to show at other times, but rather like dogs (as they say) which have lost their ears. Yet I could not perceive that it was for their own loss of men; they said they had not lost but above five or six; and I missed none, except in one wigwam. When they went, they acted as if the Devil had told them that they should gain the victory; and now they acted as if the Devil had told them that they should have a fall.[271]

Shortly after the Sudbury Fight the native alliances would splinter, with Philip returning to his homeland and native warriors concentrating their efforts not so much on war, but on feeding their people.

BATTLE OF TURNER'S FALLS, MONTAGUE, MASSACHUSETTS

By early May 1676, negotiations for the release of English hostages had stalled any coordinated offensive campaign by the colonial troops in the Connecticut River Valley. Meanwhile, settlers along the valley were growing restless and frustrated, as small bands of natives from the upper valley made repeated incursions, stealing livestock and making planting impossible. Public pressure for a renewed offensive grew.

The prospects for an aggressive campaign looked bleak. Captain William Turner, a tailor in Boston prior to the war, was stationed in Hadley with fifty-one men, many of them young, inexperienced, and, in George Madison Bodge's estimation, "in great distress for want of clothing both Linen and Woolen."[272] An additional fifty-five men and boys, also poorly armed and supplied, were garrisoned in Springfield and Northampton.[273] Turner himself was weak from sickness (perhaps the "epidemic distemper or malignant cold" spreading throughout the colonies,[274] or residue from his long imprisonment as a Baptist at the hands of Massachusetts Bay authorities), and had asked to be relieved of his commission some time before.

What was most aggravating to many of the valley's settlers was that a large native encampment was known to exist at Peskeompskut, present-day

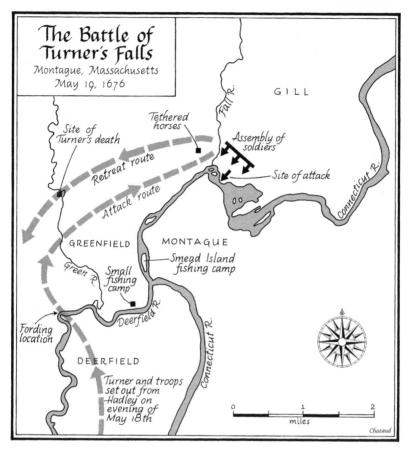

The Battle of
Turner's Falls
Montague, Massachusetts
May 19, 1676

GILL

Fall R.

Tethered
horses

Site of
Turner's death

Assembly of
soldiers

Retreat route

Attack route

Site of attack

Connecticut R.

GREENFIELD

MONTAGUE

Smead Island
fishing camp

Green R.

Small
fishing
camp

Deerfield R.

Fording
location

DEERFIELD

Connecticut R.

Turner and troops
set out from
Hadley on
evening of
May 18th

0   1   2
miles

Chazaud

Turner's Falls in the town of Montague. Turner coauthored a letter to the General Court on April 19, reporting that "it is strange to see how much spirit (more than formerly) appears in our men to be out against the enemy . . . [who] now come so near us, that we count we might go forth in the evening, and come upon them in the darkness of the same night."[275] The close encampment of which Turner wrote comprised three sites near the "upper falls" of the Connecticut. George Ellis and John Morris place one of these sites on "high ground on the right bank at the head of the falls, another on the opposite bank (possibly present-day Great Island),[276] and the third on Smead's Island, a mile [farther down the river]."[277] The Indians living there, themselves short of food, were going about the business of fishing and planting, largely unmolested. Many were women, children, and the aged. If their activity were allowed to continue, the Nipmuc and river Indians would be refortified for an aggressive summer campaign.

Three events spurred the English to action. The first was the escape of John Gilbert, who had been taken prisoner in Springfield a month before. Gilbert was able to brief Turner on the size and makeup of the Peskeompskut camps and alert him to the natives' slackened preparedness. Then, on May 12, warriors from Peskeompskut swept down into the valley, across the Hatfield meadow, and made off with a herd of seventy horses and cattle. This was a great loss to the English that turned frustration into anger. Three days later, Thomas Reed, a soldier captured near Hadley on April 1 and held at Peskeompskut, appeared in Hatfield to confirm Gilbert's information. He added that the natives were also planting as far south as Deerfield, and that the huge camps included no more than "sixty or seventy fighting men . . . [who] were secure and scornful, boasting of great things they have done and will do."[278] The Connecticut Council of War nonetheless continued to balk at taking action, in part because the camp at Peskeompskut still held a large number of English hostages.

Despite the lack of support from Hartford, the ill-preparedness of the English troops, and his own sickness, Turner decided that the time to strike had come. Calling for volunteers from Hatfield, Northampton, and Hadley, he assembled more than 150 mounted men at Hatfield. The group waited for several days in anticipation of additional reinforcements from Connecticut, but finally giving up hope, they began their twenty-mile march to Peskeompskut near sundown on May 18.

Turner's men marched past the scene of the Hopewell Swamp fight, across Bloody Brook, along the same path that Beers had traveled, and through ravaged Deerfield, which they reached around midnight.[279] An approaching thunderstorm, memories of the disasters that had occurred along their path of march, and fatigue must have taken some of the early excitement out of the expedition. Ellis and Morris relate, however, that they pressed on, crossing the Deerfield River at the "northerly end of the meadows, near the mouth of Sheldon's Brook," where they were almost discov-

William Turner's surprise attack on the Native American camp at Peskeompskut, or present-day Turner's Falls, Massachusetts, turned to near disaster for the English. Turner himself died in the helter-skelter retreat, and the spot of his death is marked today in Greenfield, Massachusetts. (Eric Schultz)

ered by a native fishing camp at present-day Cheapside.[280] The Indians appeared with torches to investigate the disturbance, but determined that a herd of moose must have crossed the river and returned to sleep.

As the rain began falling and lightening lit up the sky, the troops crossed the Green River, passing the great ash swamp to the east, and reached the high ground just under Mount Adams at daybreak.[281] Leaving their horses about a half-mile from the falls, they crossed the shallow Fall River just above the site of the Old Stone Mill,[282] near the Connecticut River,[283] and marched up a steep hill above the upper Peskeompskut encampment.

All was quiet in the camp below: Hubbard says the natives "were almost in a dead Sleep, without any Scouts abroad, or watching about their Wigwams at Home; for in the Evening they had made themselves merry with new Milk and roast Beef."[284] Turner's men rushed the sleeping camp, firing into the wigwams so quickly that the Indians had little time to respond. Some natives were shot and others were drowned while trying to escape across the river. Captain Samuel Holyoke, grandson of William Pynchon, discovered five Indians cowering in the rocks by the shore and killed them with his sword. As the warriors fled, more of the aged and young were indiscriminately massacred. Meanwhile, the camp was set on fire, food stores destroyed, and two forges used for the repair of guns hurled into the river.

To this point, the English had lost only one man. However, once the initial blow fell, the battle quickly began to turn. Turner had failed to station men at the crossing from Smead's Island, where warriors were now springing into action directly in the path of the English retreat. Turner's men had lingered too long in their destruction, and were now set upon by the same warriors they had chased from the camp. As the Indians pressed their attack, the inexperienced English panicked; their horses were almost stolen, their rear guard cut off and left to escape on its own, with the rest fleeing in disarray. A rumor that Philip had appeared with one thousand warriors quickly spread, adding to the frenzy.

Turner tried to lead a coordinated retreat, while Holyoke held the rear. At the Green River, near the mouth of Ash Swamp Brook, Turner was fatally shot at the river's edge,[285] near the site where Nash's Mill was later built.[286] This spot was commemorated in "Turner Square," located at the upper end of Conway Street, at the junction of Silver Street in present-day Greenfield. A stone marker was erected there in 1905. When Interstate 91 was constructed, Fall Brook, a western spur of Fall River, was routed underground and the Turner monument removed to the town swimming pool near the Green River, thought to be a more accurate indication of where Turner fell. In the late 1980s a second, more detailed marker was erected near the first.[287]

About 1874, at a place described in Lucy Cutler Kellogg's *History of*

Greenfield as being "on the Lucius Nims farm near the Meadow road just south of the road to Nash's Mills," Judge Thompson uncovered human bones that he believed were those of Captain Turner. The bones had been buried on higher ground, away from the river. Judge Thompson stored them in a box in a nearby mill in the Nash's Mills neighborhood; this mill eventually burned down, taking the bones with it.[288]

With Captain Turner fallen, the retreat continued, passing through Deerfield to Deerfield South Meadows and a place known as the "Bars."[289] All the while the natives kept pace, harassing and killing the terrified troops. Eventually, Captain Holyoke was able to reestablish some sense of order, and, says Hubbard, had he "not played the Man at a more than ordinary rate, sometimes in the Front, sometimes in the Flank and Rear, at all Times encouraging the Soldiers, it might have proved a fatal Business to the Assailants."[290]

When the English troops reached Hatfield late in the morning, forty-five were missing. Six would straggle in over the next few days. Shortly thereafter Connecticut sent a company of eighty men under Captain Benjamin Newbury to bolster the Connecticut Valley towns.

Estimates regarding native losses ranged as high as three to four hundred,[291] but the best guess might be one or two hundred, many being women, children, and old people.[292] (Even Increase Mather admitted, "victory was not so great as when first apprehended.")[293] However, worse than these losses, the fight at Turner's Falls broke the back of native resistance in the Connecticut River Valley. Most of the Indians' hard-earned supplies were lost. Their hope for a stable food source was gone. And their strategy of negotiating with the English to buy time had failed. There would be other attacks as King Philip's War wound down, but military activities in the valley would become an entirely one-sided affair in the aftermath of the fight at Turner's Falls.

The battle site at Turner's Falls has changed dramatically since the days of King Philip's War. Before the construction of dams, the water around the falls was one of the chief spawning grounds for shad and salmon. In *History of the Town of Gill*, Ralph Stoughton notes that Great Island, situated in the Connecticut River near the falls, "originally towered high above the normal water level, a rugged pinnacle of rock with a sheer drop on its west-

ern side to a lower expanse containing some three acres of fertile soil."[294]
From Great Island to the Gill shore, a four-hundred-yard long flume sped
the river along; from Great Island to the Montague shore there formed a
natural waterfall.

Today, Great Island is but a shadow of its former self, connected by
steel and asphalt to the shore, sitting low to the water which quietly passes
by on either side. Smead's Island, located farther south, is today sometimes
submerged underwater.

A monument at the intersection of Montague City Road and French
King Highway looks down upon the scene of the fight and across to the village of Turner's Falls. The rise of land behind the monument is the slope
down which Turner's men marched to attack the camp.

THE ATTACK ON HADLEY, MASSACHUSETTS, AND THE "ANGEL OF GOD"

In August 1675, the military designated Hadley as headquarters for operations along the Connecticut River Valley. The town was fortified by troops,
supplies, and a stockade that stretched from riverbank to riverbank, taking
advantage of Hadley's position along a bend in the Connecticut River.
In "Seventeenth-Century Military Defenses Uncovered," Rita Reinke
recorded that in 1990 a team from the University of Massachusetts at
Amherst, working with town records and deeds, discovered a small segment of this palisade when they uncovered "a ditch, at least one-and-one
half feet deep, and three feet wide . . . and running parallel to it, was a shal-
lower trench for the palisade's posts." (Evidence of the palisade had been
first uncovered about 1905, when a local farmer was plowing on the east
side of West Street Common.) Archaeologists noted that floods, construction, and farming would have obliterated much of this old fortification, but
to have discovered a segment of it meant, according to Reinke, that
"Hadley is now one of the few places in New England where the evidence
of 17th century military defenses has been seen."[295]

It was from this relatively secure position that the ill-fated troops under Captain Richard Beers would leave to evacuate Northfield, and those

under Captain Thomas Lathrop would depart to evacuate Deerfield.

On June 12, 1676, Hadley was subject to a vigorous assault that quickly melted away when native warriors discovered—so most histories record—three hundred English soldiers and two hundred English-allied Indians on hand to meet them. The battle began in the early morning as three soldiers, unwisely leaving the settlement without their arms, came charging back toward the fortification pursued by twenty natives. Two of the soldiers were killed and the third mortally wounded. Soon a band of warriors was being engaged and driven back on the south side of the settlement, while at the north end of town, according to Increase Mather's account, "a great Swarm of Indians issued out of the bushes, and made their main assault."[296] Some of the natives attacked a house where the inhabitants fired what Mather describes as a "great gun,"[297] causing them to flee in panic. Finally, concludes Hubbard's version of the event, the natives felt "such a smart Repulse, that they found the Place too hot for them to abide it."[298]

When the Indians retreated en masse, they were pursued only a short distance. Both Hubbard and Mather, usually reticent in their criticism, questioned this lack of pursuit, and the loss of an opportunity to destroy so large a force.

The English reported that as many as seven hundred natives had attacked the settlement,[299] but could find only three dead. Later reports, not necessarily reliable, indicated that the Mohawk may have fallen upon the warriors' women and children while this attack was going on.[300]

While there is little disagreement among historians that Hadley was assaulted on June 12, 1676, there has been a great deal of controversy throughout the years as to whether Hadley also suffered an earlier attack, on September 1, 1675. Some notable historians were convinced that the September 1 attack occurred, and that colonial authorities participated in one of America's first military cover-ups. Other historians, including most modern writers, claim that the attack on September 1 was a fanciful creation based on tradition and legend.

At the root of the controversy lies the presence in Hadley of Major-General William Goffe, a member of the High Court of Justice that sentenced King Charles I to death in 1649. (Russell Bourne notes that, for

To add to the scene's drama in this depiction of the Angel of Hadley, Chapman shows the natives inside Hadley's palisade, even though all the destruction occurred outside the fortification. (Courtesy of the Hadley Historical Society)

Puritans, Goffe "was as close as a man could come to being a saint.")[301] In May 1660, when the exiled King Charles II was restored to the throne, Goffe fled to Boston, arriving there in July.[302] The following February he moved to New Haven, Connecticut, accompanied by his father-in-law (and fellow regicide judge) Lieutenant-General Edward Whalley. These two lived as fugitives in New Haven until October 1663, when they moved to the home of the Reverend John Russell at Hadley.[303]

According to tradition, few in Hadley knew that Goffe and Whalley were residents at the town's parsonage for nearly ten years. In fact, Goffe would be successful in eluding the king's agents, said to be searching the colonies for his presence, and die of natural causes many years after the end of King Philip's War.

The only contemporary account of an extraordinary event occurring at Hadley on September 1, 1675 was written in 1677 by Increase Mather. The minister noted that the residents of the town "were driven from the Holy Service they were attending by a most sudden and violent Alarm, which routed them the whole day after."[304] Mather said nothing more about the event. William Hubbard, generally more detailed in his description of the war than Mather, failed to mention the alarm entirely. Increase Mather's son, Cotton, who later wrote his own history of King Philip's War, was as silent as Hubbard. Indeed, nothing more was heard on the subject—not from the minister Russell, Springfield's John Pynchon, or in any records of the time—until 1764, nearly a century after the war, when Governor Thomas Hutchinson published his history of Massachusetts.

Hutchinson was in possession of Goffe's diary, in which the general described his years of concealment as a fugitive. As Hutchinson described Goffe's adventures, he added to his history what was described by George Sheldon as an "anecdote handed down through Gov. Leverett's family."[305] It seems that when the alarm was sounded in Hadley on September 1, 1675, the frightened residents were thrown into confusion. Hutchinson wrote:

> Suddenly a grave, elderly person appeared in the midst of them. In his mien and dress he differed from the rest of the people. He not only encouraged them to defend themselves, but put himself at their head, rallied, instructed and led them on to encounter the enemy, who by this means were repulsed. As suddenly the deliverer of Hadley disappeared. The people were left in consternation, utterly unable to account for this strange phenomenon. It is not probable that they were ever able to explain it. If Goffe had been then discovered, it must have come to the knowledge of those persons, who declare by their letters that they never knew what became of him.[306]

In his 1794 history, *The Judges of Charles I*, Ezra Stiles, the president of Yale College, embellished Hutchinson's account, repeating the basic story but adding that the residents of Hadley felt they had been delivered by an "Angel of God."[307] Stiles' account most certainly came directly from Hutchinson; the language seems too similar, and the story too consistent:

Suddenly, and in the midst of the people, there appeared a man of very
venerable aspect, and different from the inhabitants in his apparel,
who took the command, arrayed and ordered them in the best military
manner, and, under his direction, they repelled and routed the Indians,
and the town was saved. He immediately vanished, and the inhabitants
could not account for the phenomenon, but by considering that person
was an angel sent of God upon that special occasion for their deliverance; and for some time after, said and believed that they had been delivered and saved by an angel.[308]

With impeccable sources like Hutchinson and Stiles as their bedrock, historians repeated Goffe's valiant rescue of Hadley for a century. With each
retelling the assault grew more threatening, more detailed, and often more
confusing. By 1824, one respected local historian had muddled the alleged
attack of September 1 with the real attack on June 12 the following year.[309]
By 1859 another historian had decided that the attack took place on the east
side of the village, since "an aged woman, in a remote part of town, says she
had heard that Goffe saw the Indians entering the town from the mountains
in the distance."[310] Later, it was revealed that Goffe had observed the Indians from his chamber, which had a window toward the east, and that the attack was "undoubtedly upon the outskirts of town."[311]

While history was being adorned, some explanation for Mather and
Hubbard's silence had to be given. The theory of a colonial cover-up designed to protect Goffe and Whalley from the king's agents was well suited
to the task. Under this interpretation, Mather's reference to an "alarm" was
nothing less than a cryptic reference to the assault. The complete silence of
Hubbard, so thorough in other respects, was proof positive of a colonial
plot. Local historian Sylvester Judd believed Hutchinson's account of the
September 1 attack and concluded that "it was necessary at the time, and
long after, to throw a veil over the transaction of that day."[312]

In 1874, George Sheldon wrote a stinging critique of the attack on
Hadley for *The New England Historic Genealogical Register*, tracing every
known historical account back to Hutchinson. Why, Sheldon asked, would a
cover-up need to include the attack itself, not simple silence on Goffe's role?

Why, if the appearance of Goffe had been so unique, would the tradition of the attack have been handed down only in Governor Leverett's family? Indeed, Sheldon noted, Hutchinson had access to the personal papers of both Increase and Cotton Mather, and to Goffe's personal diary, and yet he still had to rely on a Leverett family tradition as a source for his story. Sheldon concluded his detailed argument by writing that "there was no attack on Hadley Sept. 1st, 1675 . . . [and] that the story of General Goffe's appearance either as man or angel, at any attack on the town is pure romance."[313]

Most twentieth-century historians, no doubt reading Sheldon, have likewise been skeptical about a September 1675 attack. George Ellis and John Morris wrote that "the alleged furious attack on Hadley, which made it necessary for Goffe to take command of the panic-stricken settlers, never occurred."[314] Douglas Edward Leach noted that "the episode is legendary rather than historical."[315] Russell Bourne referred to the story as "the best example of Puritan writers' creative efforts."[316] It would seem that the matter had been laid to rest, once and for all.

In 1987, however, Douglas C. Wilson published an article in the *New England Quarterly* casting doubt on Sheldon's analysis and opening the door again to the conspiracy theory. First, Wilson noted, Goffe and Whalley had a wide and intricate network of connections within the colonies. Their friends included Daniel Gookin (who had crossed the Atlantic with them and harbored the two when they first reached New England), Governor John Leverett (who had fought under Whalley in England's Civil War), Increase Mather, and a number of other important colonial leaders. These colonial leaders were ready and capable of hiding their guests from the king's agents.

Second, Wilson concurs with Sheldon that an attack on Hadley on September 1 probably never occurred. However, by drawing on a letter from Hadley's pastor, John Russell, written in 1677, Wilson conjectured that Goffe may have played a vital role in the real attack on Hadley in June 1676.

Sheldon had dismissed the need for Goffe's assistance on June 12 because Hadley was alive with soldiers—some five hundred Connecticut men under Major Talcott. The truth, however, is that Talcott and his men were probably stationed across the river in Northampton.[317] In addition,

Mather's description of the event is unclear, and several of his lines can be taken to imply that Hadley's settlers were involved in repulsing the first wave of warriors. Unquestionably, Talcott himself was across the river in Northampton,[318] which would help to explain why there was no order given to pursue the fleeing Indians.

Goffe's role in the battle would have been protected by Mather and Hubbard, and also by the official military correspondence of Major Talcott (who was the brother-in-law of Goffe's host, the minister John Russell). A few months after the battle, Goffe left for Hartford, a sign that his secret of twelve years might have been compromised.

Like many mysteries in King Philip's War, the arguments concerning the "angel of Hadley" weigh heavily on both sides, yet neither is entirely convincing. Conspiracy or legend, Goffe's role in the attack on Hadley is another indication that historians of King Philip's War often wrote more than history; it is only through the careful efforts of people like George Sheldon and Douglas Wilson that the rest of us know the difference.

THE TALCOTT MASSACRE, GREAT BARRINGTON, MASSACHUSETTS

On August 11, 1676, between 200 and 250 natives, intent on fleeing the war and seeking refuge with the Indians of New York, crossed the Chicopee River on rafts and headed for Westfield, Massachusetts. Major John Talcott and his Connecticut forces, which had been engaged in operations shortly before near Taunton, Massachusetts, were alerted by the settlers at Westfield to the native presence. Talcott followed in hot pursuit, eventually overtaking the refugees on August 15 at their camp on the western bank of the Housatonic River. Talcott divided his troopers, sending half to cross the river below the camp and approach from the west, while the remainder would attack from the east. This first band was spotted by a native fishing in the river; the Indian was killed immediately, but the shot cost the English an element of surprise. Despite this, at least thirty-five natives were killed and twenty captured.[319] Hubbard wrote that others must have been wounded given the "dabbling of the Bushes with Blood, as was observed by them that followed them a little further."[320] Talcott, short of supplies, was forced to break off the chase.

Hubbard placed this massacre at the "Ausotunnoog River (in the middle Way betwixt Westfield and the Dutch River, and Fort-Albany) . . ."[321] This area was wilderness in 1676, and would be for another fifty years. The town historian of Great Barrington, Charles Taylor, wrote in 1882 that "Talcot's fight with the Indians is, we believe, the earliest occurrence connecting this section of country with history."[322] Therefore, determining the present-day location of the massacre is left to tradition and conjecture.

Taylor wrote of traditions that placed the massacre in Stockbridge, and in the "northeast part of Salisbury, at the locality now called Dutcher's Bridge."[323] However, the most logical route that a large group of natives would take, proceeding in great haste west from Westfield toward the Hudson River, would cross the Housatonic River at the fordway by the so-called "Great Wigwam" in present-day Great Barrington. The precise location of the Great Wigwam, a ceremonial meeting place of the natives, is unknown, but thought to be near the site (in the 1990s) of the Congregational Church between Pleasant and Church Streets.[324] The site of the massacre itself is designated on the west bank of the Housatonic River, near Bridge Street, by a large granite marker.

This image of Philip's death—while dramatic—shows the sachem dressed to conform to nineteenth-century sensibilities, not to Benjamin Church's more accurate but less modest description. (Courtesy of the Haffenreffer Museum of Anthropology, Brown University)

· Chapter 6 ·

King Philip's War in Rhode Island and Connecticut

POKANOKET HOMELAND,
WARREN AND BRISTOL, RHODE ISLAND

The site of Massasoit's Spring is designated by a bronze tablet at the west end of Baker Street in Warren, Rhode Island, near the banks of the Warren River.[1] This was thought to be the location of Sowams, the Wampanoag sachem's principle village. The marker reads:

THIS TABLET
PLACED BESIDE THE GUSHING WATER
KNOWN FOR MANY GENERATIONS AS
MASSASOITS'S SPRING
COMMEMORATING THE GREAT
INDIAN SACHEM MASSASOIT
"FRIEND OF THE WHITE MAN"
RULER OF THE REGION WHEN THE
PILGRIMS OF THE MAYFLOWER
LANDED AT PLYMOUTH
IN THE YEAR OF OUR LORD 1620
ERECTED BY THE STATE OF RHODE ISLAND
1907

There is no spring readily apparent at this location, as a wooden fence and the surrounding buildings sit virtually on the street. Several theories have been advanced throughout the years that Sowams was actually located across the Warren River in Barrington, Rhode Island, or farther south in Bristol, Rhode Island, but tradition favors this site in Warren.[2]

It is believed that Philip's primary village was located south of Sowams on the eastern side of the Mount Hope peninsula in present-day Bristol, Rhode Island. This location sat on the western edge of present-day Bristol Narrows and looked directly across at Touisset Point in Swansea, just south of the English settlement. (Some writers refer to this site as Mount Hope, although it is about one-and-one-half miles north of Mount Hope itself.) Early in the war the colonial army built a fort on or near this site to hold the peninsula after Philip had abandoned it. Writing in 1845, local historian Guy Fessenden claimed that after a careful search he had located the remains of this fort

> situated on the top of the most south-western of several hills on the north side of a cove. They consist now chiefly of the remains of the fire-place in the fort. This fire-place was made by preparing a suitable excavation and laying low stone walls at the sides and the end for which flat stones were used, evidently brought from the adjoining beach. The remains of these ruins are low beneath the surface of the ground, which at this place is depressed several inches below the average surface of the ground in the immediate vicinity. The hill is fast wearing away by the action of the water which washes its base. The wearing away has already reached the fire-place from which the charcoal and burnt stones are often falling down the steeply inclined plane beneath.[3]

By 1906 the sea had eroded the site completely.[4]

Burr's Hill Park is located northwest of Philip's village on present-day Water Street in Warren. The park is built on the remains of a natural gravel bank that overlooked the Warren River. In the mid-nineteenth century, workers mining gravel in the area discovered human remains and a vast array of European and Wampanoag artifacts.[5] In the spring of 1913, archaeologists working under local resident and town librarian Charles Read Carr excavated forty-two Wampanoag graves.[6]

Despite Carr's careful work and the obvious importance of the site, the destructive gravel mining went on and numerous private individuals un-

This image of Philip appears to use Revere's engraving as its model, right down to the designs on the sachem's belt and crown. (Courtesy of the Collections of the Library of Congress)

earthed and made off with important artifacts. Carr eventually struck a deal with the New York, New Haven, and Hartford Railroad, which owned the gravel bank (and whose abandoned track still lies nearby), to ensure that all artifacts would become the property of Warren's George Hail Free Library. Over time, pilfered artifacts were repurchased from individuals and the collection eventually came to be held at three primary locations: at the Warren library, at the Haffenreffer Museum of Anthropology in Bristol, Rhode Island, and at the Museum of the American Indian Heye Foundation in New York.

The graves at Burr's Hill were notable for the wealth of material goods they contained, most of which dated to the seventeenth century, and more particularly to the period of Philip's sachemship.[7] The cemetery's proximity to Sowams also has led to speculation, usually downplayed by the archaeologists and historians, that Massasoit, Alexander, or both may have been buried there. One of the graves unearthed was particularly rich in artifacts and contained a copper necklace thought to have been presented by Edward Winslow to Massasoit. Materials detailing the excavation of this grave are held by the Haffenreffer Museum.

Burr's Hill was purchased by Warren in 1921 and made into a public park. Today, Burr's Hill Park includes a baseball field, a playground, and parking for Warren residents interested in sunbathing along the river.

THE BATTLE OF ALMY'S PEASE FIELD, TIVERTON, RHODE ISLAND

In July 1675, as Massachusetts forces were engaged in negotiations in Narragansett country and Plymouth's troops were building a fort on the Mount Hope peninsula, Captain Matthew Fuller, Benjamin Church, and three dozen men crossed the Sakonnet river into Pocasset territory in present-day Tiverton, Rhode Island. There they hoped to meet with Weetamoe, and perhaps Awashonks to the south, to head off any agreement they might make to join Philip.

After a fruitless night spent attempting to trap unsuspecting Wampanoag, the band split into two groups of about twenty each under the commands of Fuller and Church. Fuller's group quickly met up with Wampanoag warriors, retreated, and was ferried back to Aquidneck Island. Church's troops marched south, probably along a Wampanoag trail east of Nannaquaket Pond where Main Road now runs.[8] There they found tracks that turned inland.[9] The small group followed these until they met with a rattlesnake (which were common in New England at the time), probably near Wildcat Rock.[10] More afraid of snakes than Wampanoag, the men abandoned the tracks and returned to the main trail, heading south once again. Church later wrote, "Had they kept the track to the pine swamp, they had been certain of meeting Indians enough, but not so certain that any of them should have returned to give [an] account [of] how many."[11]

After crossing onto Punkatees Neck (also called Pocasset Neck), probably west along the present-day Neck Road from Tiverton Four Corners,[12] they proceeded south along the neck. Soon, they discovered more tracks heading up a hillside near an abandoned field of peas on land owned by John Almy. Shortly thereafter they spotted a pair of Wampanoag warriors, but when they attempted to follow, the English were caught in a thunderous volley "of fifty or sixty guns"[13] from the hillside above. Church and his men, surprised and outgunned but unhurt, retreated "immediately into the pease field . . . But casting his eyes to the side of the hill above them, the hill seemed to move, being covered over with Indians, with their bright guns glittering in the sun, and running in a circumference with a design to surround them."[14] On the precise location of the peas field, James E. Holland, a lawyer whose longtime practice had its offices at the Old Grist Mill at Tiverton Four Corners, observed in a 1995 issue of *Old Rhode Island* that

> the exact location of the peasefield on the Neck is the subject of speculation especially among those now living in its purported vicinity vying to attach some historical significance to their land holdings. However it appears from Church's account that the field was somewhere on the hillside between the present Neck Road and the River, a short distance north of the road leading to Fogland Point.[15]

This nineteenth-century illustration recreates Benjamin Church's defense along the shore of Fogland Point in Tiverton, Rhode Island. (From Indian History for Young Folks, *Francis S. Drake, 1885)*

Church's men retreated to the beach on the neck of land between Punkatees and Fogland Point, where they hastily constructed a barricade of rocks. Here they fought throughout the afternoon, holding off their attackers as a rescue attempt launched by men from present-day McCurry Point[16] failed. Finally, Captain Roger Goulding, whose sloop was anchored at present-day Gould Island,[17] spotted the battle and sailed south. Finding the sloop too large to beach, Goulding anchored so close that the ship's "sails, colours and stern were full of bullet holes."[18] He then let a canoe over the slide, allowing the tide to wash it onto the beach. There, two of Church's men grabbed on and were pulled back to the sloop by rope. This rescue went on—two by two—until Church and his entire band were safely on board.

A check at day's end revealed that two of Captain Fuller's men had been wounded but—miraculously—not a single man under Church was hurt.

The precise location where Church and his troops mounted their defense was lost for some years by an error in a 1772 edition of Church's *History*. When Church originally described the scene of the battle, he noted that "the Indians also possessed themselves of the ruins of a stone-house that over look'd them, and of the black rocks to the southward of them."[19] For some unknown reason, reference to these black rocks was omitted from the 1772 edition, and all subsequent editions. While editing an 1865 edition of Church's *History*, Henry Martyn Dexter discovered the error, and armed with this new information, visited Punkatees Neck. Dexter wrote:

I found on the edge of the shore the remains of an outcropping ledge of soft black slaty rock, which differs so decidedly from any other rocks in the vicinity, and which—making allowance for the wear of the waves for near 200 years—answers so well to the demand of the text, as to incline me to the judgment that they may identify the spot. If this be so, the peasefield must have been on the western shore of Punkatees neck, a little north of the juncture of Fogland Point with the main promontory, and almost due east of the northern extremity of Fogland Point.[20]

Dexter also discovered the spring at which Church's men quenched their thirst, "a spring stoned round like a well, and sending a tiny rivulet down to the sea, a few rods south of these remains of what were once 'black rocks.'"[21] In 1906, Ellis and Morris noted that "the spring at which Church records himself as quenching his thirst, has disappeared, and it is most probable the shore on which Church's force actually stood has been encroached upon and swallowed up by the sea."[22]

NIPSACHUCK SWAMP FIGHT, SMITHFIELD, RHODE ISLAND

The Pocasset Swamp Fight was frustrating for the English, but the battle at Nipsachuck was disheartening. As Philip and Weetamoe crossed Seekonk Plain (the land around modern-day Route 1 in East Providence) they were pursued by men from Old Rehoboth, who chased them across the Paw-tucket River into the town of Providence. From there the chase headed north, and at dawn on August 1, 1675, a battle was fought at a place called Nipsachuck, located in present-day Smithfield, Rhode Island. Philip's men fought 130 English and fifty Mohegans, taking heavy losses in the ex-change. Several of his chief captains were lost, and in all twenty-three Wampanoag died.[23]

By 9 AM the sides had disengaged, with Philip and his men fleeing into the nearby Nipsachuck Swamp. At 10 AM Captain Daniel Henchman ar-rived to take command with an additional sixty-eight English and seventeen friendly Indians, making the combined force 265 men. Philip cowered some three-quarters of a mile away, outnumbered three or four to one, low on am-munition, and prepared to surrender.[24] Inexplicably, Henchman rested until the following day, allowing Philip to slip away into Nipmuc country and Weetamoe to advance south into the open arms of the Narragansett.

It is easy to criticize many of the actions of colonial military comman-ders in King Philip's War. It is also generally unfair, since such criticism is the result of far greater information than the commander had and is made from the security of three centuries' distance. However, in the case of Henchman at Nipsachuck, both modern historians and Henchman's contemporaries agree on his poor judgment. The captain was immediately and roundly crit-icized by his own troops anxious to pursue Philip. William Hubbard, whose work had to pass muster with Massachusetts Bay censors, noted: "But what the reason and why Philip was followed no further, it is better to suspend, than to critically enquire."[25] Later in the year the General Court reappointed Henchman to lead one hundred men gathered at Roxbury but the men re-fused to serve under him. He was eventually assigned command of the gar-rison at Chelmsford and served ably in military activities throughout Nipmuc country. The episode at Nipsachuck, however, would dog Hench-man throughout the remainder of his military service.

The precise location of the Battle of Nipsachuck is unknown. The Nip-sachuck Swamp runs north to south across the border of North Smithfield and Smithfield, about ten miles north of Providence.[26] Nipsachuck Hill, ris-ing over five hundred feet, sits to the northeast of the Swamp. Captain

Nathaniel Thomas, who was present with Henchman, wrote an account of the battle on August 10, 1675. Thomas described a party of English and Mohegan scouting on the evening of July 31

> who made some discovery of the enemy, by hearing them cut wood, and we left our horses there upon the plain, with some to keep them, and in the night marched on foot about 3 miles to an Indian field belonging to Philip's men, called Nipsachuck, and at dawning of the day marched forward, about 40 rods, making a stand to consult in what form to surprise the enemy, without danger to one another, and in the interim, while it was so dark as we could not see a man 50 rods, within 30 rods of us, there came up towards us five Indians from Witamoes camp, (we supposed to fetch beans, &c. from the said field) perceiving nothing of us, at whom we were constrained to fire, slew two of them, the others fled, whereby Wittamas and Philip's Camp were alarmed. Wittama's camp then being within about an 100 rod of us, whom we had undoubtedly surprised, while they were most of them asleep and secure, had it not been for the said alarm; who immediately fled and dispersed, whom we pursued, slew some of them, but while we were in pursuit of them, Philip's fighting men showed themselves upon a hill unto us, who were retreated from their camp near half a mile to fight us. Philip's camp was pitched about 3 quarters of a mile beyond Witamas. Philip's men upon our running towards them dispersed themselves for shelter in fighting, and so in like manner did we, the ground being a hilly plain, with some small swamps between us, as advantageous for us, as for them, where we fought until about 9 of the clock.[27]

Assuming that the hill upon which Philip's men showed themselves was Nipsachuck Hill, Thomas' description would place Weetamoe's camp and the scene of the battle about one-quarter mile from the hill (i.e., Philip's men camped three-quarters of a mile from Weetamoe, came one-half mile toward the English, and showed themselves upon a hill). The direction is less clear, though the English were pursuing Philip from the south and probably caught Weetamoe south or southeast of Nipsachuck Hill.

Henchman took up pursuit of Philip the following day, trailing him "till they had spent all their provision, and tired themselves, yet never coming within sight of Philip."[28]

After a month of travel and three dramatic escapes from Mount Hope, Pocasset, and Nipsachuck, the sachem had successfully rendezvoused with his Nipmuc allies at Menameset in present-day New Braintree and Barre, Massachusetts.

THE GREAT SWAMP FIGHT,
SOUTH KINGSTOWN, RHODE ISLAND

The single bloodiest day of King Philip's War was Sunday, December 19, 1675, when more than 1,150 English and Mohegan soldiers attacked the fortified camp of the Narragansett, sometimes called Canonchet's Fort, located in the Great Swamp in present-day South Kingstown, Rhode Island. Tales of the attack would become the stuff of New England folklore, and the site of the fort itself a mystery that remains unsolved to this day.

The Narragansett campaign was set in motion on November 2 when the commissioners of the United Colonies assembled in Boston and accused the Narragansett, officially neutral to that point in the war, of being

> deeply accessory in the present bloody outrages of the Barbarous Natives; That are in open hostilities with the English. This appearing by their harboring the actors thereof; Relieving and succoring their women and children and wounded men; and detaining them in their custody Notwithstanding a Covenant made by their Sachems to deliver them to the English; and as is credibly Reported they have killed and taken away many Cattle; from the English their Neighbors; and did for some days seize and keep under a strong Guard Mr. Smith's house and family;[29] and at the News of the sad and lamentable Mischief that the Indians did unto the English at or Near Hadley; did in a very Reproachful and blasphemous manor triumph and Rejoice thereat; The Commissioners doe agree and determine that besides the Number of soldiers formerly agreed upon to be Raised and to be in constant Readiness for the use of the Country; there shall be one thousand more Raised and furnished;

with their armies and provisions of all sorts to be at one hour's warning, for the public service the said Soldiers to be raised in like proportions in each Colony as the former were.[30]

The covenant referenced by the commissioners took the form of two agreements signed between the English and the Narragansett in July and October 1675. Both documents promised that the Narragansett would deliver

to the English all Wampanoag in their midst, with the October agreement specifically obligating the Narragansett "at or before the 28th day of this Instant month of October to deliver . . . every one of the said Indians; whether belonging unto Philip; the Pocasset Squaw or the Saconet Indians Quabaug Hadley or any other Sachems; or people that have bin or are in hostility with the English."[31] The Narragansett were disdainful of both documents, which carried as little weight as Philip's agreement at Taunton four years earlier.

Resistance by the Narragansett to English demands and the increasingly volatile state of affairs in Rhode Island was reported by Richard Smith Jr. in a series of letters to his friend, Governor John Winthrop Jr. of Connecticut. Smith operated the oldest and most active English trading post in Narragansett country and had as much at stake as any colonist in preserving peace with his Indian neighbors. In an August 5 letter, Smith noted that the Narragansett had brought in seven heads of the Wampanoag. More ominously, he added, "Many straggling Indians are abroad for mischief, some Nip Nap Indians joined with Philip, some Indians in Plymouth Patan are come into the English, about 120 in all as I here."[32] On September 3 he explained the source of the seven heads and his unease with the Narragansett, which was

> that we are in jealousy whether the Narragansett will prove loyal to the English; if they pretend favor and hath lately brought in to me seven of the enemies heads, they being surprised by the Nipnaps first and delivered up to the Narragansett Sachem Conanicus. Here are very many inland Indians lately come in hither, and some of the enemy amongst them, which they, I judge, will not deliver. I believe yt Conanicus of him self & some others inclines to peace rather then war, but have many unruly men which cares not what becomes of them. These Indians hath killed several cattle very lately . . . It will be good to be moderate as regards the Narragansett at present I humbly conceive, for that a great body of people of them are here gathered together, may doe much mischief, and it if not brought into better decorum, here will be no living for English.[33]

Nine days later he sent another mixed message to Winthrop, who had now traveled to Boston to confer with commissioners of the United Colonies. Smith accused the Narragansett of hiding Philip's people—"which these doe obscure all they can, and will not confess how many"[34]—but of also bringing in additional heads. Again Smith pled for moderation:

> Cononocous hath brought in to me in all 14 heads, seven of which was lately, & some of them Phillips chief men. These being a great number it will be good to be moderate with them as it; for should we have war with them they would doe great damage . . . I should be sad if I could not be active in any respect whereby I might promote any thing that would tend to the peace & welfare of the Country.[35]

Finally, on October 27, just a day before the Narragansett deadline to deliver Wampanoag to the English, Smith wrote to Winthrop in Boston explaining that the Narragansett were "forward and willing to doe it, but say it is not feasible for them to doe at present, many of them being out a hunting, and their owne men being not so subordinate to their commands in respect of affinity, being allies to them, so that if by force they go about to seize them, many will escape."[36] Smith also reported that most of the English inhabitants in the area had fled, "the report common amongst Indians and English is at present of an army coming up. I request your favor to given me timely notice if any expedition be higherward."[37]

This last point is remarkable in several respects. Smith and his fellow colonists—far from the flow of Boston politics—appeared to anticipate the Narragansett campaign several days before it was officially announced and nearly two months before the actual Great Swamp Fight. The same rumors had undoubtedly reached the Narragansett, who may have been well along in fortifying their Great Swamp village (about seventeen miles from Smith's garrison), protecting their food stores, and readying their arms. If so, Canonchet would have had almost two full months to prepare his defensive strategy against the English prior to the December battle. However, if the Narragansett were steeling themselves for an English assault, Smith apparently did not learn of it and failed to report the existence of any kind of fort construction to the commissioners. The chance of hiding such a concentration of people and activity from English eyes might seem unlikely, until we recognize that neither Smith nor any of his countrymen ever discovered the Queen's Fort (see below), a Narragansett installation located less than four miles from Smith's trading post.

By the first week of December 1675, rumor became fact when troops from all over New England began to assemble. The Massachusetts militia, 527 men led by Major Samuel Appleton, gathered at Dedham, Massachusetts, on December 8. Many of the officers from earlier campaigns—Samuel Moseley, Benjamin Church, and Thomas Prentice, who headed seventy-five troopers—were pressed back into service. Plymouth assembled 159 men at Taunton under William Bradford. Major Robert Treat advanced three hundred Connecticut soldiers, supplemented by 150 Mohegan, northward from New London, Connecticut. Governor Josiah Winslow was named general in chief and would soon assume command of the combined armies.

It seems unlikely that even now colonial officials suspected the existence of the Narragansett fort. Smith had still made no mention of such an installation. On November 19 the commissioners ordered that "provisions of all sorts and Ammunition shall be provided and sent to the place of their Rendezvous sufficient for two months,"[38] a clear indication that they anticipated a campaign of skirmishes similar to what Major Samuel Appleton had conducted in the Connecticut River Valley the previous fall.

On November 2 when the commissioners had officially instructed the army to "compel . . . [the Narragansett] thereunto by the best means they may" to honor the terms of their agreements, colonial policy appeared somewhat equivocal in its goal for the Narragansett campaign. However, the commission to the commander in chief, written about the same time, was direct in its message:

> You are accordingly to Instruct command & order all your inferior officers & soldiers in all respects with full power for the treating surprising fighting killing & effectual subduing & destroying of the Narrowganset Enemy & all their accomplices & Assistants as well the former open enemy or any others that you shall meet with in hostility against the English.[39]

On November 28, still several weeks before the army would march, the Council at Hartford reported their appointment of Major Treat to lead Connecticut forces, "desiring of them to engage the Pequot and Moheags to destroy the enemy, what they could."[40] With military leaders receiving orders like these, there could have been little doubt in any soldier's mind as he assembled with his comrades in December that the army's mission was to engage and destroy the Narragansett.

William Harris, a long-time foe of both Roger Williams and moderation with the Narragansett, perhaps best summed up the official colonial position regarding the campaign when he wrote to Sir Joseph Williamson:

> The war was also just with the Narragansetts, many of whom were with Philip in the first fight about Mounthope, and on Philip's flight thence were received back with a great woman of Philip's party [probably Weetamoe] and her men; the Narragansetts, at the demand of the English, entered into articles to deliver them but did not, making large pretenses of peace so as to delay the war until after the harvest, and receiving rewards from the English for the heads of persons said to be of Philip's party, but all in deceit, the heads being those of men killed by the English or of Narragansett deserters, or of certain of Philip's men against whom they had a grudge ... The Narragansetts had then many of Philip's men whom they did not deliver up, and all about Hadley and Deerfield they aided Philip's men against the English.[41]

With such strong sentiments commonly held against the Narragansett, the Massachusetts Bay and Plymouth troops marched south. Along the way, General Winslow ordered his men to kill or capture any Narragansett encountered, attempting to ensure that word of the march would not reach the main body of Indians. Winslow sought especially the capture of Pumham, a Narragansett sachem whose territory included much of present-day Warwick, Rhode Island. Pumham had declared his independence from the Narragansett in 1644, allying himself with Massachusetts Bay officials who helped the sachem construct a fort on the eastern shore of Warwick Cove. The fort protected the entrance to the cove and was itself protected by an impenetrable marshy thicket[42] to its rear. Pumham's fort, occupied for a time by English soldiers, secured the interests of both Pumham and Massachusetts Bay.

The site of Pumham's fort may still be viewed in Warwick on the north side of present-day Paine Street, at the bend in the road. The remains of the fort once formed a large and small oval in the earth but are now covered by brush and an accumulation of trash. The marshy thicket has been replaced by paved roads and graded home lots. The marker designating the site has been stolen, although its base is still standing.[43]

Despite his friendship with the English, Pumham allied himself with Philip once the war began and was now considered by the English to be a shrewd and dangerous opponent. Winslow's attempt at his capture proved fruitless; Pumham was far too resourceful to be taken by surprise in his own fort. Winslow and his troops settled for the capture of thirty-five prisoners[44] and continued their march.

Seven months later, on July 25, 1676, Pumham was attacked and killed at Dedham Woods.[45] Hubbard described Pumham as

> one of the stoutest and most valiant sachems that belonged to the Narragansett; whose courage and strength was so great, that after he had been mortally wounded in the fight, so as himself could not stand: yet catching hold of an English man that by accident came near him, had done him a mischief, if he had not been presently rescued by one of his fellows.[46]

Mather is more direct when he says that Pumham, mortally wounded, would still have killed an English soldier had the soldier not been rescued by his comrades.[47]

Richard Smith Jr.'s garrison and trading post at Wickford, Rhode Island, sometimes called Smith's Castle, was chosen as the base of operations for the United Colonies' combined troops. The location was ideal from the standpoint of being the center of political, social, and religious activity in the developing Narragansett area,[48] having excellent access by water, and having a proprietor whose knowledge of the territory and enemy had been gathered through years of close contact with the Narragansett. In September 1684, nine years after the Great Swamp Fight, Richard Smith Jr. petitioned the commissioners of the United Colonies for compensation for the use of his trading post during the Narragansett campaign. His letter illustrates the activity that went on at his Wickford garrison in its role as headquarters for a poorly provisioned thousand-man army:

> The humble petition of Richard Smith of Wickford, in the Narragansett, showeth, that your petitioner in the time of the late troubles and ware with the Indians here at Narragansett did suffer much in his estate by entertaining the many companies of soldiers, at his cost and charge, sent up by the Colonies; for which no recompense has yet been done to your petitioner.
>
> 1st. Major Savage and companies, with about 6 hundred, and Connecticut forces with him under command of Capt. Winthrop, they had horse shoes and nails to value 3lb 12sh, besides their entertainment 8 or 10 days, never pd. one farthing. After which, the entertainment of the whole army, myself and six of my servants being one service, one of which was slain at the swamp fight, had no allowance for our service. Also 26 head of cattle killed and eaten by the soldiers, with 100 goats at least, and at least 30 fat hogs; all the copper, brass and wooden vessels for the army used spoiled, stole and lost, to the value of near 100li sterling; great part of my post and rail fences being fetched and burnt for the soldiers; my oxen and cart and utensils being all lost, after the garrison went away; and lastly my housing burnt, being of great value. All which is too much for one particular man to bare; I having been to my utmost power ready to serve the Country always in what I could, nor even had anything allowed me for all above expressed, only for what the commissaries kept an account of, which was most salt provisions kept by me by order, for use of the army. Other men have had satisfaction in some measure; and when I last petitioned your Honors at Boston, I had a promise of consideration; wherefore this 2d time I doe request your Honors to take the premises into your judicious and wise consideration, to allow me in your wisdom what you shall think requisite, and your petitioner shall pray etc. and subscribe.[49]

Today, Smith's Castle is located on Richard Smith Drive off Route 1 (Post Road) in North Kingstown and is maintained as a museum and gift shop by the Cocumscossoc Association. The present structure has gone through substantial alterations over the years. Smith's original blockhouse, possibly set on the site of Roger Williams' first trading post or on an adjoining tract of land,[50] was burned to the ground by the Narragansett in 1676, as was every Rhode Island structure south of Warwick.[51] In 1678 Smith's son used some of the undamaged wood from the first house to build a three-room structure on the same site. Some of the 1678 building remains today, protected by an eighteenth-century expansion.[52] On the north lawn of the house a burial ground holds the remains of forty English soldiers killed in the Great Swamp Fight. A tablet marks the spot of burial. No remains have been discovered at the site, though this may be due to the shallowness of the graves and rapid decomposition. A second graveyard at Burying Point, a short walk northwest of the house, is the final resting place of Richard Smith Sr.

Samuel Moseley's troops, accompanied by Benjamin Church, had been sent ahead of the main army to secure Smith's garrison and begin scouting activities. As the troops assembled at Wickford, a number of natives were captured, including a Narragansett named Peter. Peter immediately proved his worth to the English, alerting Winslow to two nearby Narragansett villages, which the English attacked and burned. However, Peter's true value would come a few days later when he led the colonial army directly to the Narragansett's fortified village hidden in the Great Swamp.

One of the deserted villages destroyed by the English was probably that of Queen Magnus, also called Quaiapen, Natantuck, the Saunk Squaw, and the "Old Queen" of the Narragansett. Not far from this village, in present-day Exeter, Rhode Island, was Quaiapen's more famous "Queen's Fort," a natural stone fortification never discovered by the English during the war.

Signs of the Queen's Fort still exist today, as does a long-standing mystery surrounding the site. The fort is located about three and one-half miles northwest of the Smith garrison, west of Route 2 on the south side of Stony Lane in Exeter. A fire trail about two hundred yards west of a barn and stone wall owned by Stonehaven Farm leads to the site, which is perhaps

The Narragansett sachem Pumham had such courage and strength, according to William Hubbard, that he nearly killed an English soldier despite being fatally wounded and unable to stand. (Courtesy of the Haffenreffer Museum of Anthropology, Brown University)

best described as a "geological trash pit" of huge glacial rocks. These rocks were thought to have been connected in a defensive pattern by the erection of stone walls, said to be the work of Stonewall John, a skilled Narragansett mason employed for a time by Richard Smith. The fort also appears to have two structures, perhaps bastions or flankers, on the northeast corner and west side.

According to the legend, Quaiapen occupied an underground chamber situated about one hundred feet outside the western perimeter of the fort. This chamber was described by Elisha R. Potter in his 1835 *History of Narragansett*, and again in detail in 1904 by Sidney S. Rider in *The Lands of Rhode Island as They Were Known to Canounicus and Miantunnomu.* Rider reported that the chamber consists of an open space beneath an immense mass of boulder rocks; the tallest men can stand within it; the "floor" is fine white sand; the entrance is so hidden that six feet away it would never be suspected; the boulders piled about it represent a thickness of fifty or sixty feet.[53]

Despite these detailed descriptions and its appearance on several maps, the queen's chamber can no longer be visited because—careful searches notwithstanding—its precise location is no longer known.

Quaiapen and her people occupied the fort after the Great Swamp Fight. In June 1676, sensing the end of the war, Quaiapen's hungry band headed north, only to be attacked and massacred by forces under Connecticut's Major John Talcott on July 2 in a cedar swamp at Nipsachuck. Both Quaiapen and Stonewall John lost their lives in the attack. Talcott wrote:

These may acquaint you that we made Nipsaichooke on ye first of July and seized 4 of ye enemy, and on the 2d instant being ye Sabbath in ye morning about sun an hour high made ye enemies place of residence, and assaulted them who presently in swamped them selves in a great spruce swamp, we girt the said swamp and with English and Indian soldiers: dressed it, and within 3 hours slew and took prisoners 171.[54]

Ellis and Morris called the spot of the massacre "Nacheck" and wrote that "this was on the south bank of the Pawtucket River, below Natick. The exact place of the massacre is not known. It was seven miles from Providence."[55] However, the correct location was determined by members of the Society of Colonial Wars in the State of Rhode Island and Providence Plantations, who placed it "in Nipsachuck Swamp near Tarkin Station in North Smithfield."[56]

The Narragansett fort located in the Great Swamp, probably built under Canonchet's direction, was much different from the Queen's Fort. It consisted of a complete village situated on four to five acres of highland, surrounded by swamp and enclosed by a wall of thick wooden stakes driven into the ground, earth, and brush. This fort contained some five hundred wigwams and was undoubtedly overcrowded due to the Narragansett policy of accepting any and all Wampanoag and Nipmuc refugees from the war.[57] The English were not unaccustomed to seeing fort construction done by New England's Native Americans; in fact, certain features of this fort strongly suggested the influence of European engineering.[58] However, the Narragansett fort about to be assaulted was thought to be larger and more elaborate than anything in the colonists' experience.[59]

The intent of both English and Narragansett became clear on December 15. Stonewall John appeared at Wickford allegedly to sue for peace.[60] He was accompanied by a band of warriors hidden in the woods, suggesting that his real goal may have been to assess English military preparations. In any case, neither side proved flexible and Stonewall John was sent on his way. Shortly thereafter several English soldiers were attacked, including an assault on the hated Moseley, and the first English blood of the Narragansett campaign was spilled.

About this same time, nine miles south of Wickford, Jireh Bull's stone garrison on Tower Hill in present-day Narragansett was attacked and destroyed by the Narragansett, who killed fourteen or fifteen English.[61] While this assault is usually expressed as a tragedy for the English, Ebenezer Peirce wrote from the Narragansett perspective when he called it "a daring feat on the part of the Indians, with so large an [English] army not far distant and large reinforcements to that army daily and hourly expected."[62] What also made the feat daring was the apparent impregnability of the Bull garrison, described in a letter Captain Wait Winthrop wrote to his father, Governor John Winthrop Jr. of Connecticut, on July 9, 1675, as being a "convenient large stone house with a good stone wall yard before it which is a kind of small fortification to it."[63] Increase Mather would surmise that the structure was fortified well enough to withstand on outright attack, and must have been taken by stealth: "a body of the enemy did treacherously get into the house of Jerem. Bull (where was a garrison,) and slew about fourteen persons."[64]

In 1918 the site of the garrison was positively identified through archaeological work undertaken by the Society of Colonial Wars of Rhode Island:

Part way up the eastern slope of Tower Hill on that portion of the "Bull-Dyer farm," which is now owned by Mr. Samuel G. Peckham, here has been for many years a series of mounds, betrayed as stone heaps by the outcropping fragments, and marked, in part, as a rectangle by an old growth and buckthorns. The spot thus indicated has always been the traditional site of what is generally called Bull's Garrison or Block House.[65]

Excavations at this site uncovered a wealth of artifacts and the existence of a stone house measuring thirty feet wide by forty feet long, with two fireplaces at its western end and the remains of a paved court on its eastern side. (A silver bodkin marked MB, perhaps for Mary Bull, was discovered at the site along with fragments of glass and tinned brass and iron spoons.) When the workers began digging westward in search of the wall Wait Winthrop had described, they found instead, about ten feet away, the outer wall of an even larger building. This second structure was divided into two rectangles by a heavy partition wall; the western rectangle—at twenty-seven feet wide and sixty-five feet long—was itself larger than the first building uncovered in the excavation. Remains of a heavy central chimney were discovered near the south wall and, on the eastern side of the chimney, a hearth made from blue slate. Among the objects uncovered in this second building were a pair of cock's head hinges, a pair of H hinges, glass, part of a gun barrel, a flintlock, a dripping pan and bits of various tools.[66] About twenty feet south of this second structure workers discovered a third rectangular building that measured sixteen feet from north to south and showed evidence of a fireplace.

Historians believe that it was the second and largest of the structures that Wait Winthrop described and that fell to the Narragansett in December 1675. The first structure excavated was probably built by Jireh Bull or his son after King Philip's War ended, perhaps after 1684. The small, southern structure is perhaps the oldest building on the property, though a fourth structure may yet be uncovered. All of the buildings on the property undoubtedly served as a ready supply of stones for the building of walls and foundations at nearby farms; "the outer wall of which Winthrop speaks was probably the first to go. Then the stones from the others were taken till the masonry was cut down to the level of the ground where it was soon covered by earth and grass."[67]

In 1925 the Society of Colonial Wars published a further account of the objects discovered at the site. The account noted:

> It is possible that in all there may have been three homes in this small clearing . . . and it is therefore impossible now to determine in which of the ruins some of the objects were discovered, as the laborers were not careful in reporting the exact locations of their finds . . . Some of the objects are undoubtedly from the house that was burned in 1675, others are certainly of a later period and from the house that Bull built after the war. Some of the objects may be still later, as the ruins of the houses may have been occasionally used as dumps for refuse . . . It is understood that practical jokers have recently buried skulls, bones and bottles containing messages, in the ruins in the hope of deceiving future excavators.[68]

Two years later, in 1927, the Society of Colonial Wars published *A Plat of the Land of Capt. Henry Bull at Pettaquamscutt, Drawn by James Helme, Surveyor, January 8, 1729*. This plat was prepared for the grand-nephew of Jireh Bull by the grandson of Jireh's northern neighbor, Rouse Helme, giving the document a strong basis in tradition[69] and substantiating work done by archaeologists. The site of the Bull garrison, landlocked by private property, can be found today on the west side of Middle Bridge Road in Narragansett.[70]

Stonewall John's visit, the destruction of Jireh Bull's garrison, and the lack of adequate food supplies convinced Winslow that the war must be taken immediately to the Narragansett. On December 18, Massachusetts and Plymouth forces marched south to join Treat's Connecticut troops; the combined army spent a wretched winter's night camped around the darkened shell of the Bull garrison.[71] At about 5 AM on the morning of December 19, with Peter in the lead, the colonial army trudged stiffly through the cold and snow:

> What route they took to reach the fort—whether they went over Tower Hill, as some suppose, thence westerly by Dead Man's Pool of the Saugatucket, over Kingston Hill and across the plains of Queen's

River; or by the Pequot Path southerly from Wickford, along the ridge of Tower Hill through Wakefield to what is now Sugar Loaf Hill, and so northerly again to the Swamp fort—perhaps never may be accurately known. Not one of the present roads was then in use except the Pequot path. But tradition has it that the Indian Peter, who was forced to be their guide under penalty of being hanged, was taken prisoner near the smoking ruins of Jireh Bull's house on Tower Hill. If this may be accepted, the shortest path to the fort led across the Saugatucket, over Kingston Hill, and to it Canonchet's hiding-place, full seventeen miles from Wickford.[72]

Some mystery remains in the distance and direction of this morning march. The Jireh Bull garrison is between seven and eight miles (on a straight line) from Canonchet's fort. Joseph Dudley reported that the army's march was "without intermission" and that the time of arrival at the Swamp was "about two of the clock afternoon."[73] (Captain James Oliver placed the arrival time "between 12 and 1.")[74] If the army were able to march straight to the fort, that would assume a speed of one mile per hour or less. Compare this to their retreat march when, burdened by the dark of night, frozen limbs, the walking wounded, and conveyance of the dead, the army would cover seventeen to eighteen miles between the fort and Smith's Castle in ten hours between 4 PM and 2 AM, or nearly twice the speed of their first march. We are left to wonder what happened to so dramatically slow the march on the morning of December 19. Many historians exaggerate the mileage to rationalize the time, confusing the forward march with the retreat.[75] Hubbard wrote that "they marched from the break of the next Day, *December 19th*, till one of the Clock in the Afternoon . . . thus having waded fourteen or fifteen Mile."[76] Thomas Hutchinson (perhaps repeating Hubbard) stated that "at the break of day, the 19th, they marched through the snow fourteen or fifteen miles, until one o'clock afternoon, when they came to the edge of the swamp where the enemy lay."[77] Ellis and Morris allowed that the fort was "sixteen miles to the west, by a circuitous route."[78] George Bodge solved the problem by assuming that the colonial troops marched north along the high ground to McSparren Hill and then turned west, crossing the Chippuxet River between Larking Pond and Thirty Acre Pond.[79] It is only through this roundabout march via McSparren Hill that any distance close to the assumed fourteen to sixteen miles can be calculated, and even this assumes that the army would have marched almost as if it were lost, stumbling in a random pattern to the swamp. (Even if Peter were leading the troops so as to avoid a Narragansett ambush, the additional distance is still extraordinary.) It also assumes that Massachusetts Bay and Plymouth troops were required to march to the Jireh Bull garrison on the eighteenth—when word of its destruction had already reached them on December 16,[80]—only to retrace their steps the following morning. This would have added four difficult miles to their total march. It seems more probable that General Winslow chose the Bull garrison as a convenient rendezvous point with Connecticut troops and assumed that a direct westerly route to the fort could be taken from Pettaquamscut. How or why the army would take as much as nine hours to reach a fort seven miles away remains a question.

Sometime after noon the lead colonial troops reached a "position on rising land some two miles beyond the present village of West Kingston."[81] There, at the edge of the Great Swamp, they traded fire with an advance party of Narragansett. It was then that the English discovered that the swamp, which was impassable most of the year, had frozen solid and would allow their advance to the fort.[82] This factor, along with Peter's knowledge of the fort's weakness, would prove decisive for the English.

Benjamin Church, who would enter the fort only after the most intense fighting was over, reported that the English infiltrated the swamp "next the upland."[83] Writing in 1906, George Bodge interpreted this to mean "the rising land in front of the 'Judge Marchant' house," which lay north of the supposed battlefield.[84]

The entrance to the fort used by the Narragansett consisted of a long tree spanning a "place of water."[85] This spot was well protected and would have been almost impossible for the English to breach. However, one small area remained unfinished along the fort's lengthy stockade. This gap in the defense had been barricaded with a large tree trunk, about five feet off the ground. Most accounts record that Peter led the English directly to this spot, where the attack began. The fighting was vicious and went well at first for the Narragansett, who killed two English captains and drove the colonial force back into the swamp. Captain Moseley, near the front of the charge, drew particular interest from the Indians, who knew him well; he afterward told the general that he saw "50 aim at him."[86] The second wave ordered by Winslow breached the barricade, however, and the intense fighting moved in and around the tightly clustered wigwams. It was then that the order to set fire to the wigwams was given. As the afternoon wore on, many Narragansett men, women, and children were driven by flames and muskets to their deaths.

While Peter's ability to lead the English directly to Canonchet's Fort is unquestioned, the issue of the fort's unfinished section deserves scrutiny. Peter was captured by Moseley's men around December 16; this would have been the extent of preparations he would have witnessed at Canonchet's fort. If a large segment of the fortifications were undone on the sixteenth, Peter could hardly have known the precise location of the last "chink" in Narragansett armor three days later when the English attacked. Conversely, if he knew about this specific spot of weakness—a single large tree trunk—on the sixteenth, the Narragansett would have had two or three days to repair this relatively minor deficiency before the assault occurred. A more logical conclusion would be that this spot was intentionally planned by the Narragansett, as was Peter's capture, to ensure that the English would attack at a well-defended point and to discourage a search for other ways into the fort (which may have been plentiful, as they were intended as easy exits for Narragansett women and children). Perhaps this spot was intended to allow Narragansett reserves in if the English had attacked at another point in the palisade. Perhaps it served some other unknown military use. In any event, it presented a deadly passage for the English. Had the Narragansett not run out of gunpowder during the fight and instead pursued the decimated English troops, this contrived entrance might have been viewed not as a weakness but as a brilliant military tactic by Canonchet in a smashing Narragansett victory. The argument that it was the single unfinished and weakest point in the fortification either underestimates or misconstrues the Narragansett defensive strategy.

Other aspects of Canonchet's leadership in the Great Swamp Fight are less brilliant. One wonders why the English were not harassed by the Narragansett at the Bull garrison or along the route of their march to the fort. The English had overextended their supply lines, were marching on unfamiliar terrain, had undoubtedly lost all element of surprise, and were attacking a fortified defensive position with numbers that would have been held vastly inadequate by modern military thinking. The Narragansett had two months to prepare their defenses and held almost every advantage in the Great Swamp Fight. Yet, by allowing the English to reach the swamp essentially unmolested, and then relying entirely upon the fort's defenses, Canonchet committed perhaps the Indians' single worst military blunder of the war. In addition, he failed to mount a flanking attack against the English position from outside the fort or even send a small band to harass Winslow's position, which most certainly would have distracted the English from the fort. He also failed to place an ambush along the retreat route of the English, a tactic employed brilliantly by the Nipmuc at other battles in King Philip's War.[87] Such tactics might have saved the lives of countless Narragansett women and children, who should have been able and encouraged to flee the fort before the worst of the fighting began and long before the decision by the English to set fire to the village was made. Indeed, stronger leadership could well have saved hundreds of lives and turned the English victory into a Narragansett rout, perhaps changing the course of the entire war.

About a month after the Great Swamp Fight the Narragansett were camped in the Misnock Swamp at present-day Coventry, Rhode Island, where they continued to be plagued by a shortage of gunpowder. A frustrated Canonchet is alleged to have said that "had he known they were no better furnished, he would have been elsewhere this winter."[88] One wonders if this wasn't a more general self-assessment of his decision to defend the Great Swamp fort.

Joseph Dudley served as chaplain to the army (and later governor of Massachusetts) and provided one of the few firsthand accounts of the battle. In a letter written from Smith's garrison to Governor Leverett on December 21, just two days after the fight, Dudley gave the following details:

Saturday [December 18] we marched towards Petaquamscot, through the snow, and in conjunction about midnight or later, we advanced; Capt. Mosely led the van, after him Massachusetts, and Plimouth and Connecticut in the rear; in tedious march in the snow, without intermission, brought us about two of the clock afternoon, to the entrance of the swamp, by the help of Indian Peter, who dealt faithfully with us; our men, with great courage, entered the swamp about twenty rods [about 110 yards]; within the cedar swamp we found some hundreds of wigwams, forted in with a breastwork and flankered, and many small blockhouses up and down, round about; they entertained us with a fierce fight, and many thousands shot, for about an hour, when our men valiantly scaled the fort, beat them thence, and from the blockhouses. In which action we lost Capt. Johnson, Capt. Danforth, and Capt. Gardiner, and their lieutenants disabled, and many other of our officers, insomuch that, by a fresh assault and recruit of powder from their store, the Indians fell on again, recarried and beat us out of the fort, but by the great resolution and courage of the General and Major, we reinforced, and very hardily entered the fort again, and fired the wigwams, with many living and dead persons in them, great piles of meat and heaps of corn, the ground not admitting burial of their store, were consumed.[89]

Benjamin Church says he entered the fort "that the English were now possessed of" with about thirty men, only to watch Captain Gardiner stumble toward him and fall, mortally wounded. Church also discovered and reported back to General Winslow that "the best and forwardest of his army, that hazarded their lives to enter the fort upon the muzzle of the enemy's guns, were shot in their backs, and killed by them that lay behind." He and his men then left the fort, found "a broad and bloody track where the enemy had fled with their wounded men,"[90] and proceeded to skirmish with the retreating Narragansett. Church was wounded three times, once severely, and would retire soon after to Rhode Island to nurse his wounds during the winter months.

Indian losses in the Great Swamp Fight were thought to be significant but have never been accurately determined, in large part because contemporary English observers contradicted one another and had reason to inflate the figures, while later historians were careless in quoting these conflicting numbers. On December 21, 1675, just two days after the fight, the Reverend Joseph Dudley wrote that "we generally suppose the enemy lost at least two hundred men; Capt. Mosely counted in one corner of the fort sixty four men; Capt. Goram reckoned 150 at least."[91] Dudley was with General Winslow throughout the fight and spoke with many of the men in the days following the battle. He chose as his sources two soldiers, Captains Moseley and Goram, who were in the thick of the fight from the start. However, their assessment might have been influenced by several factors: Like all victors, the two men would have had reason to exaggerate the numbers of their enemy slain. In addition, both Moseley and Goram would have had to contend with the confusion and shock of the battle itself. Also, the English departed shortly after the fighting stopped and were never able to make a thorough accounting of casualties. However, less than a month later (January 14) Joshua Tefft[92] gave credence to Goram and Dudley's estimate of 150 to 200 Algonquian killed. Tefft, an Englishman, had been living in the fort with the Narragansett prior to the fight and fled with the sachems during the battle to a secure position away from the fort. After the English had retreated, the Narragansett returned to the fort to assess their losses. Tefft told Roger Williams that "they found 97 slain & 48 wounded."[93]

James Quanpohit, a Christian Indian who spied for the English during the war, visited with Nipmuc and Narragansett warriors at their camps at Menameset not long after the Great Swamp Fight. Quanpohit probably would have been killed by the Narragansett (for his suspected friendship with the English) had not his long time friend, Monoco, intervened; "he said he was glad to see me; I had been his friend many years, and had helped him kill Mohaugs; and said, nobody should meddle with me."[94] Despite being suspected as a spy, Quanpohit would hear and pass on to colonial authorities a wealth of accurate information concerning native plans to conduct the remainder of the war. In addition, Quanpohit would report that the Narragansett lost "but forty fighting men, and three hundred old men, women and children."[95] Among Tefft, Dudley, and the Narragansett themselves (through Quanpohit), the estimate of Indian dead ranged from 100 to 340 people.

Despite having listened to a month of wild speculation surrounding the fight, Captain James Oliver wrote on January 26 that the English had killed "300 fighting men."[96] This number of warriors killed is the upper limit of the estimates given by participants in the battle.

Nevertheless, contemporary reporters were either insistent on magnifying the English victory or simply willing believers of the many proud veterans returning from the fight. In 1676, merchant Nathaniel Saltonstall wrote to London that "our Men, as near as they can judge, may have killed about 600 *Indian* Men, besides Women and Children. Many more *Indians* were killed which we could have no account of, by reason that they would carry away as many dead *Indians* as they could."[97] Here Saltonstall introduces the idea, readily embraced by future historians, that whatever the number of Indian dead the English could confirm, there must be many more who were whisked away by the Narragansett in the heat of the battle. With this speculative start, another contemporary writer could report that "we have great reason to bless God we came off so well, our dead and wounded not a Mounting to above 220, and the enemies by their own Confession to no less than 600."[98]

By the time Mather and Hubbard published their official accounts of the event, the numbers had grown again and the Puritan victory was even more glorious. Mather not only inflated the number but misquoted Joshua Tefft:

> Concerning the number of Indians slain in this Battle, we are uncertain, only some Indians, which afterwards were taken prisoners (as also a wretched English man [Joshua Tefft] that apostatized to the Heathen, and fought with them against his own Country-men, but was at last taken and executed) confessed that the next day they found three hundred of their fighting men dead in this Fort, and that many men, women and children were burned in their Wigwams, but they neither knew, nor could they conjecture how many: it is supposed that not less then a thousand Indian Souls perished at that time. Ninigret whose men buried the slain, affirmeth that they found twenty & two Indian captains among the dead bodies.[99]

Hubbard, who was a more careful observer and accurate reporter than Mather, still chose his sources in a way that would glorify the English victory. Hubbard wrote:

> What Numbers of the Enemy were slain is uncertain; it was confessed by one Potock a great Councilor amongst them, afterwards taken at Road-Island, and put to Death at Boston, that the Indians lost seven hundred fighting Men that Day, besides three hundred that died of their Wounds the most of them; the Number of old Men, Women and Children, that perished either by Fire, or that were starved with Hunger and Cold, None of them could tell.[100]

Benjamin Church is silent on the number of dead at the Great Swamp Fight. Hence, later historians who tended to rely on some combination of Church, Hubbard, and Mather for their information could easily establish that as many as seven hundred warriors perished in the Great Swamp Fight, and more than one thousand Indians in total lost their lives. Neither number squares with the few firsthand accounts remaining to us nor with the smaller numbers typical in New England colonial warfare.

It has generally been assumed that the English, by setting fire to the Narragansett wigwams, destroyed the better part of the Narragansett winter food stores. This rests on reports from Dudley, who noted that the fire consumed "great piles of meat and heaps of corn, the ground not admitting burial of the store";[101] from Captain James Oliver, who wrote that "we burnt above 500 houses, left but 9, burnt all their corn, that was in baskets, great store";[102] and from Church, who recorded that "the wigwams were musket proof; being all lined with baskets and tubs of grain and other provisions, sufficient to supply the whole army."[103] The extent of the damage to the Narragansett has been called into question by modern ethnohistorians, however. The Narragansett traditionally dried and stored their corn in the ground before an expected war,[104] and there is no reason to expect that corn stored above ground and burned at the Great Swamp Fight was more than a fraction of their total supply. The English did not dig for corn after the fight and, as far as we know, did not return to investigate the fort after the battle.[105] We know from Joshua Tefft, however, that the Narragansett visited the fort a short time after the English departed; they may have un-covered and removed great stores of food.[106]

The same food and shelter destroyed by the English were also lost to the English, forcing them to return to Wickford in a march that began about 4 PM and did not end at Smith's garrison until 2 AM the following morning. (One contemporary reported that "they marched above three miles from the fort by the light of the fires.")[107] General Winslow and a small group of men were separated and lost on the return march, traveling some thirty miles and not arriving at Smith's garrison until 7 AM.

English losses at the Great Swamp Fight are well-known. Captain James Oliver reported that

> we lost, that are now dead, about 68, and had 150 wounded, many of which are recovered. That long snowy cold night we had about 18 miles to our quarters, with about 210 dead and wounded. We left 8 dead in the fort. We had but 12 dead when we came from the swamp, besides the 8 we left. Many died by the way, and as soon as they were brought in, so that Dec. 20th were buried in a grave 34, next day 4, next day 2, and none since here. Eight died at Rhode Island, 1 at Petaquamscot, 2 lost in the woods and killed, Dec. 20, as we heard since, some say two more died.[108]

With some revision, modern historians have confirmed these numbers.[109] Major Treat's Connecticut soldiers took such severe losses that he deemed it necessary to return home immediately. Half of the combined officer corps had fallen, and four hundred soldiers who escaped wounds were so in-capacitated by exposure and lack of proper care that Winslow's army was incapable of continuing the winter campaign.[110] Only the lack of gun-powder—"which Captain Oliver estimated at "but 10 pounds left"[111]—kept the Narragansett from pursuing the English and, despite their tactical errors during the battle, changing the outcome of the Great Swamp cam-paign completely.

With one notable exception, firsthand and other contemporary ac-counts are unusually silent on the role Connecticut's Mohegan contingent played in the Great Swamp Fight. Numbering between 150 and 200 warriors, these allies of the English represented a fighting force equal in size to the Plymouth Colony regiment. If they had rushed the fort with the other Connecticut soldiers, they would have played a greater role in the battle than the Plymouth troops—who were held back as reserves by General Winslow—and taken even greater losses. Indeed, Connecticut historian Henry Trumbull believed the Mohegan suffered fifty-one dead and eighty-two wounded.[112] The Mohegan under Oneko had already distinguished themselves in the war, having trapped and nearly annihilated Philip and his men at Nipsachuck in the previous summer campaign. Yet when Captain Oliver recounted the fight in January, he reported that the "Monhegins and Pequods proved very false, fired into the air, and sent word before they came they would so, but got much plunder, guns and kettles."[113] In this claim Oliver reflected not only the institutional bias of Massachusetts Bay and Plymouth Colonies against the use of friendly Indians in warfare, but appeared to simply repeat the testimony of Joshua Tefft, who might have his own reasons for discounting Mohegan contributions to the fight. Tefft, soon to be executed as a traitor, told Roger Williams in January 1675/6 that "if the Monhiggins & Pequts had been true, they might have destroyed most of the Nihaggonsiks; but the Nahigonskis parleyed with them in the beginning of the fight, so that they promised to shoot high, which they did, & killed not one Nahigonsik man, except against their wills."[114] Old feuds between the Mohegan and Narragansett, the prior record of the Mohegan in King Philip's War, their losses suffered at the Great Swamp Fight, and the assumed biases of Oliver and Tefft notwithstanding, the story that the Mohegan deceived the English at the Great Swamp Fight was picked up by Samuel Drake in the *Old Indian Chronicle* and has been repeated without further substantiation by historians throughout the years.

The Great Swamp Fight ensured that the roused Narragansett would now prosecute the war against the English with great vengeance. A series of peace talks was held throughout the end of December and on into early 1676, but it seems in retrospect that both sides were stalling for time to recoup and plan their next moves. It is also possible that the Narragansett were paying for their neutrality with the Nipmuc and Wampanoag. James Quanpohit reported that "the Narragansett sent up one English head to them by two of their men; and they shot at the Narragansett, told them they had been friends to the English, and that head was nothing. Afterwards they sent up two men more, with twelve scalps; they received them, and hung the scalps on trees."[115] The delaying tactics used by the Narragansett may well have been an indication that they were, at least temporarily, caught between sides of the conflict. The English themselves were trying to deal with desertions brought about by the harsh weather and poor care following the battle. Authorities in Massachusetts Bay were forced to pass a law making it illegal for a man "to conceal or hide himself or armes from the country service."[116] A new request for the raising of one thousand men went out to the colonies while Winslow tried desperately to prepare his remaining army for a new campaign. Only in late January did the situation brighten for colonial troops when fresh English and friendly Indian recruits arrived at Wickford.

For the last century the site of the Great Swamp Fight has been subject to great debate. Nineteenth-century antiquarians wrote with confidence about its precise location. The *Memorial History of Boston*, published in 1882, claimed that the fort was near "Kingston hill, by which the Stonington railroad closely passes; the only vestiges to be found to-day are here and there a grain of Indian corn burned black in the destruction."[117] In 1885, J. R. Cole noted that "the Great Swamp above referred to is situated on a farm now owned by John G. Clarke . . . Mr. Clarke, who has given the subject much consideration, has, he says, plowed up charred corn, the relics of the battle."[118] George Madison Bodge noted in 1886 that the scene of the battle was well identified:

It is situated in West Kingston, R.I., and belongs to the estate of the late J. G. Clark, whose residence was about one mile north-easterly from the old battlefield. Many relics of the battle are in possession of Mr. Clarke's family. Saving changes incident upon the clearing and cultivation of contiguous land, the place could be easily identified as the battlefield, even if its location were not put beyond question by traditions and also by relics found from time to time upon the place. It is now, as then, an "island of four or five acres." Surrounded by swampy land, overflowed except in the driest part of the year. The island was cleared and plowed about 1775, and at that time many bullets were found deeply bedded in the large trees; quantities of charred corn were plowed up in different places, and it is said that Dutch spoons and Indian arrowheads, etc. have been found there at different times.[119]

In 1906 Ellis and Morris located the fort at the same site as Bodge, on an island "between the Usquapaug River and Shickasheen Brook."[120]

The site described by Ellis and Morris, by Bodge, and in the *Memorial History of Boston* represents the present-day location of the Great Swamp Fight Monument, placed in 1906 at a ceremony sponsored by the Societies of Colonial Wars of Rhode Island and Massachusetts. A roadside marker located one and one-third miles south of the intersection of Route 2 and Kingstown Road (Route 138) points to the location of the monument, which is found by walking or driving about one mile south from the marker along an unpaved road. The Great Swamp Fight Monument is made of solid granite, weighs eleven tons, and sits twenty-six feet high in the center of an upland "island."[121] Surrounding the shaft are four large boulders bearing the names of the three United Colonies and Rhode Island. The inscription at the base of the monument is badly damaged and, in any case, inaccurate when it suggests that the NARRAGANSETT INDIANS MADE THEIR LAST STAND in the Great Swamp Fight. The monument draws a large number of tourists and is an important site for descendants of both the English and Narragansett, who meet there annually to commemorate the battle.

Despite the certainty of nineteenth-century antiquarians, most modern historians and archaeologists disagree that the correct site of the Great Swamp Fight has been identified. Firsthand descriptions were vague and inconclusive. Benjamin Church said simply that the army marched "to a swamp which the Indians had fortified with a fort."[122] Another contemporary account noted that "our whole Army . . . went to seek out the enemy, whom we found (there then happening a great fall of Snow) securing themselves in a dismal swamp, so hard of access that there was but one way for entrance."[123] A third contemporary account described the following: "In the midst . . . [of the swamp] was a piece of firm land, of about three or four acres of ground, whereon the Indians had built a kind of fort, being palisado'd round, and within that a clay wall, as also felled down and abundance of trees to lay quite round the said fort."[124] Joshua Tefft reported that once the battle began he "stayed 2 volleys of shot, & then they fled with his master, & passed through a plaine, & rested by the side of a spruce swamp."[125] Such descriptions are remarkable for the paucity of detail they leave for modern historians and archaeologists.

An eighteenth-century diary entry and sketch by the Reverend Ezra Stiles, president of Yale University, is the slim piece of evidence most often used to bridge the gap between firsthand accounts and the site of the twentieth-century monument. Stiles visited the Great Swamp on May 28, 1782, and wrote:

> The swamp Islet is surrounded every way with a hideous Swamp 40 Rds to one mile wide, & inaccessible but at a SW Entrance & there a deep Brook or Rivulet must be passed. All the Narrag. Indian Tribe with the Indians of Mt. Haup or Bristol were assembled there in the Winter of 1675, when they were attacked by our Army of about a thousand men, who rushed over the narrow passage of Entrance & set fire to the Wigwams—a great Slaughter!
>
> The burnt Corn remains to this day, & some of the Bones are yet above ground, as I saw at this time. The owner of the Land Mr. Clark is now clearing up the Land, has cut down the Timber & Brush, and will plow it up this Summer.[126]

Stiles also sketched and measured the area on which he believed the fort was located. His map shows a kidney-shaped area of upland some four acres in size consistent with firsthand accounts. Stiles also noted two Narragansett burying places and two oak trees, cut down the same year of his visit, 1782. One of the oaks was found to have a bullet lodged near its center, which was surrounded by one hundred rings (presumed to indicate the correct period between Stiles' visit and the Great Swamp Fight).

Stiles' account, so detailed in some respects, fails on three counts. First, we are unable to place his location precisely within the Great Swamp. Second, Joseph Granger has pointed out that "it is unlikely that such trees [as the two oaks] would have been left standing in a village moved specifically for firewood availability as much as for protection."[127] None of the first-hand accounts mention trees within the fort, which might have been used as defensive positions by the Narragansett, or as badly needed material for the palisade, and in any case, would have been remarkable landmarks in an otherwise cleared village site. The third weakness in Stiles' description is what is left unsaid; the minister fails to mention the kind of substantial discovery of artifacts and "footprints" that would be left behind by a large, densely populated Narragansett village.

Since placement of the monument in 1906, historical and archaeological work has essentially confirmed skeptics' beliefs that the fort is mismarked. In the 1930s and 1940s, the memorial site itself was pockmarked with random holes left by visitors, many of whom paid local owners twenty-five cents a day to dig for artifacts. By the mid-1940s one local resident digging at the memorial site found nothing but sand.[128]

A promising start in identifying the fort was made in 1959 when professional anthropologists from the University of Rhode Island, Columbia, and Yale excavated a site on the southern end of Great Neck, about two miles from the monument. (Great Neck is one of the pieces of high ground within the swamp that some think may have been the site of the fight.) A newspaper account reported that

> in two weeks of painstaking digging and sifting, reaching about two feet under the surface of a rock shelter that served as an Indian home for centuries, the scientists have found nearly 2,000 pieces of bone, pottery, sea shells, ornaments and stones . . . Erwin H. Johnson, assistant professor of sociology at the University of Rhode Island . . . said some of the relics and artifacts "almost certainly" go back to the post-glacial period . . . Professor Johnson cautiously avoided appearing too confident that the search would definitely establish the site of the Great Swamp Fight. "It will take more studying and we'll have to do some digging at the place where the fight is supposed to have taken place" . . . Thomas J. Wright, chief of the Rhode Island division of fish and game and a student of Indian lore, suggested the site to Professor Johnson on the basis of his studies . . . He said that a number of persons

have had doubts over the years that the Swamp Fight was fought where some historians say it was . . . Professor Johnson does not discount the fact that the rock shelter where he and his associates are digging might have served as an ideal fort. It stands on high ground, backed up by more rocks, and overlooking a valley.[129]

Sometime after this activity, Johnson wrote in the URI *Alumni Bulletin*:

Old writings specify an island as the site of the fort and a first trip over the swamp in a helicopter this fall showed an island now filled in on one side and a line of differentiation in the foliage which could indicate a ditch or fortification. This possible location is one and a half or two miles from the monument. Any disturbance of the earth such as an old foundation is much more readily visible from the air. We plan to take aerial photographs of the area, because these often show a perceptible change in the type and shade of foliage where there were habitations and burial areas even centuries ago. The next step will be to reach the spot on foot and then dig test trenches to look for evidence of palisades of the old fort and charcoal left from its burning.[130]

One of the students working with Johnson, Joseph Granger, conducted additional archaeological work around the site in 1960. Digging several test pits within 150 feet of the monument, Granger found the pits sterile and concluded that "no case may now be made for the Monument Site as the location of the Great Swamp Site of the Narragansett village of 1675."[131] Additional test area sites throughout the Great Swamp yielded intriguing but inconclusive evidence as to where the fort might have been located. Granger did conclude, however, that there were "traditional selective forces which governed [the fort's] placement . . . [and that] topographic and environmental factors once isolated and combined with ethnohistoric data may show that, far from being a defensive reaction to Colonial encroachment, the 1675 winter village was merely a typical seasonal settlement in a consistently used refuge area."[132]

Like Johnson and Granger, both professional and avocational archaeologists believe that there are pieces of high ground in the swamp away

The Great Swamp Fight Memorial is designated by a state marker along South County Road in South Kingstown, Rhode Island. Many colonial Rhode Islanders, whose homes would later be destroyed by the Narragansett, might well have questioned the "decisive" nature of the Narragansett's defeat. (Eric Schultz)

from the memorial site and not detailed on topographic maps that may indicate alternative sites for the fort.[133] Many of these sites, suitable for traditional woodlands camps, are located on the northern perimeter of the swamp, around which bullets and burned corn have been found.[134] It is also likely, according to historian William Simmons, that the Great Swamp has dried up since the seventeenth century so that "the fort site may be not in the present-day swamp but somewhere outside it, under plowed fields."[135]

The most recent and thorough archaeological study of the Great Swamp was completed in 1993 for the town of South Kingstown by the Public Archaeology Survey Team sponsored by the town and the Rhode Island Historic Preservation Commission. A reconnaissance-level archaeological survey (background research, surficial walkover, and subsurface testing) was conducted, including a study of Native American settlement patterns and resource procurement strategies.[136] Archaeological teams inspected all of the plowed fields within the Great Swamp Wildlife Reservation, nineteen in total, and discovered probable prehistoric artifacts in sixteen of those fields. In addition, the team located nine archaeological sites through subsurface testing, two of which included historic period components.[137] Many of the sites yielded valuable information about settlement patterns within the Great Swamp, but one in particular yielded artifacts that might finally indicate the location of the Great Swamp Fight:[138]

> These artifacts include 62 fragments of green bottle glass, four carbonized corn fragments, one calcined European gunflint fragment, one graphite stone, and charcoal fragments of varying size. The bottle glass fragments have been mended and crossmended and include base, body, neck and mouth fragments including a string type rim. It is not conclusive, but the bottle fragments reflect the bottle morphology of the period of the fort's occupation (Noel Hume 1991: 60–71). The carbonized corn fragments correlated with the primary accounts describing the Narragansetts' wigwams being "all lined with baskets and tubs of grain and other provisions sufficient to supply the whole army until the spring of the year . . ." (Hubbard 1971: 151; Church 1975: 100). The presence of charred or parched corn revealed by plowing at the fort site has been noted by 19th-century historians, including Elisha Potter in 1835 and Samuel Drake in 1841. One calcine gunflint fragment has been recovered and demonstrates wear patterns on the blade's edge reflective of firing use.[139]

The authors of the report concluded that the find, while intriguing, would require additional archaeological research to substantiate. If it were to prove conclusive, however, then one of the premier colonial historical mysteries will be solved, and the real work of interpreting the site and adding to our knowledge of the Great Swamp Fight and King Philip's War will begin.

DESTRUCTION OF SIMSBURY, CONNECTICUT

At the time of King Philip's War, Simsbury was a scattered settlement of about forty homes, stretching seven miles along both sides of the Farmington River.[140] Connecticut officials were keenly aware of the settlement's exposed position, and in October 1675 ordered its inhabitants to evacuate the town within one week.[141] Taking whatever crops and personal possessions they could gather, residents left for Windsor or Hartford, probably with thoughts of never seeing their homes again. However, when the expected attack did not materialize over the fall and winter, most returned to begin life anew.

By March 1676 the Narragansett had entered the war, Lancaster, Medfield, and Groton had all been recently attacked, and the threat of assault on Simsbury was more acute than ever. On March 3, the settlers at Simsbury were ordered to evacuate forthwith.[142] With little time, poor travel conditions, and the need to herd livestock before them, residents could take few personal possessions. When warriors struck on March 26, they

> destroyed by fire nearly every building in the town, as well as every thing else left by the English, which could be found, and which the invaders could not appropriate to their own use. The ruin was complete—nothing but utter desolation remained.[143]

Simsbury lay deserted for almost a year before residents began straggling back. After two evacuations and the settlement's complete destruction, many had no reason to return, and never did.[144]

Simsbury's destruction was barely touched upon by the Puritan historians of Massachusetts; Hubbard fails to mention it at all, and Mather notes that Connecticut "hath been in a manner untouched, saving that one small deserted plantation therein was burnt by the Indians."[145]

According to tradition, when the settlers at Simsbury evacuated the town, they hid many of their personal possessions by burying them in swamps, or placing them in wells that were then covered over. When the town was reoccupied, so the story goes, its residents were unable to find these possessions because the landmarks of the town had been so completely obliterated. Local historian Noah Phelps, writing in 1845, dismissed this tradition, saying that it would have been impossible for every landmark to have been lost, and noting that it is more likely the warriors discovered the goods and destroyed them.[146]

PIERCE'S FIGHT, CENTRAL FALLS, RHODE ISLAND

The ambush of Captain Michael Pierce and his Plymouth Colony soldiers occurred on Sunday, March 26, 1676, in the present-day city of Central Falls, Rhode Island. Sometimes attributed to the Narragansett sachem Canonchet,[147] this ambush was in many respects a textbook military operation. Several friendly natives escaped the engagement, but only nine English survived, and these nine men were later discovered dead several miles north of Central Falls in present-day Cumberland, Rhode Island, a site now known as Nine Men's Misery. Not only was the ambush deadly for Pierce and his men, but it was devastating to the morale of the colonies which, on the very same day, witnessed the murder of settlers in Longmeadow, Massachusetts, the burning of Marlboro, Massachusetts, and the destruction of Simsbury, Connecticut.

Pierce, a resident of Scituate, Massachusetts, had gathered in Plymouth a force of Englishmen from Scituate, Marshfield, Duxbury, Eastham, and Yarmouth, supported by twenty friendly natives from Cape Cod. Together, this band marched to Taunton, then along the Old Seacuncke Road (Tremont Street) to Rehoboth[148] (now East Providence, Rhode Island). There, they were joined by several men from Rehoboth, expanding their total number to sixty-three English and twenty friendly natives.

Reports indicated that a large group of the enemy had gathered in the area of Pawtucket Falls, an ideal location from which to catch alewives, salmon, and shad, and a natural fording spot in the river.[149] Pierce and his men set out in pursuit. On Saturday, March 25, they skirmished with the Narragansett, perhaps north of the falls,[150] where, historian Leonard Bliss concludes, Pierce "met with no loss, but judged he had occasioned considerable to the enemy."[151]

It is not unreasonable to think that Pierce had skirmished with a small patrol sent intentionally to meet and test the English—an exercise broken off by the natives once they had gathered information on the size and strength of their opponent. In any event, Pierce met no other natives and returned for the night to the garrison at Old Rehoboth. Meanwhile, armed with information from the skirmish, native leaders undoubtedly set to work devising a trap for the English troops.

On Sunday, March 26, Pierce and his troops returned to the field, probably marching from present-day East Providence, north along the Seekonk River (which becomes the Blackstone River), back toward Pawtucket Falls. It is said that as they marched, they were watched by Narragansett from Dexter's Ledge, now the site of Cogswell Tower in Jenks Park, Central Falls (rough distance and heavily wooded terrain made this questionable).[152] Somewhere close to the Blackstone, perhaps near a fording spot where Roosevelt Avenue now crosses the river,[153] in what Bliss describes as an "obscure woody place,"[154] they spotted four or five Narragansett fleeing as if wounded or hurt. Had a more experienced commander witnessed this show, he might have immediately fallen back. However, Pierce and his troops charged after the bait, suddenly finding themselves surrounded by "about 500 Indians, who, in very good order, furiously attacked them."[155]

Pierce apparently met the ambush on the eastern side of the Blackstone, but crossed to the western side, where the natives were engaged in force. A contemporary account of the battle by an anonymous Boston merchant, paraphrased by Bliss, made the English out to be as heroic as possible, but the devastation was complete:

> Our men had made the enemy retreat, but so slowly, that it scarce deserved the name; when a fresh company of about 400 Indians came in, so that the English and their few Indian friends, were quite surrounded and beset on every side. Yet they made a brave resistance for above two hours, during all which time they did great execution upon the enemy, whom they kept at a distance, and themselves in order. For Captain Pierce cast his 63 English and 20 Indians into a ring and fought back to back, and were double-double distance all in one ring, whilst the Indians were as thick as they could stand thirty deep: overpowered with whose numbers, the said captain, and 55 of his English, and 10 of their Indian friends were slain upon the place; which, in such cause, and upon such disadvantages, may certainly be styled the bed of honour."[156]

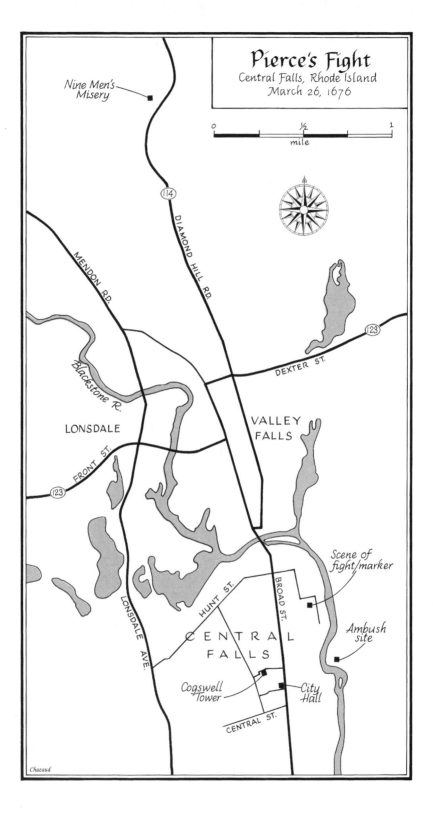

It is unlikely, of course, that nine hundred natives participated in the ambush. Nor does it seem logical that eighty-three men, disadvantaged by surprise, terrain, and numbers, would have much chance of forcing even four hundred warriors to retreat. (Contemporary writers reported that Pierce and his men killed 140 of their enemy,[157] a figure undoubtedly inflated.) However, if Pierce and his troops crossed the Blackstone near present-day Roosevelt Avenue, the battle may have moved northward along the river to a spot near present-day Macomber Field on High Street, where a commemorative marker was placed in 1907. The marker reads:

PIERCE'S FIGHT
NEAR THIS SPOT
CAPTAIN MICHAEL PIERCE
AND HIS COMPANY OF
PLYMOUTH COLONISTS
AMBUSHED AND OUTNUMBERED WERE
ALMOST ANNIHILATED
BY THE INDIANS
MARCH 26 1676

ERECTED BY THE STATE OF RHODE ISLAND
IN 1907

A visit to this site today places the traveler in a heavily industrialized area surrounded by factories and baseball fields. It is worth remembering, however, that Central Falls was once the "North Woods" of Providence and remained only sparsely settled throughout the eighteenth century.[158] Marching along, Pierce would have seen a wooded land of oak, walnut, chestnut, and birch trees with three falls (Pawtucket to the south, Valley to the north, and Central near the crossing at Roosevelt Avenue) supplying the Narragansett with rich fishing grounds.[159] By contrast, present-day Central Falls is so densely built that the Blackstone River is all but invisible from nearby Cogswell Tower.

Not far from the former Cistercian Monastery on Diamond Hill Road in Cumberland, Rhode Island, sits a stone memorial long-known to local residents as Nine Men's Misery. Dedicated in the early twentieth century, this cairn locates the gravesite of nine English soldiers under Captain Michael Pierce who were taken prisoner and executed by Narragansett in March 1676. (Eric Schultz)

Not all of Pierce's troops died in the ambush. Several of the friendly natives devised ingenious means of escape. One blackened his face with powder like the enemy and passed through their lines without incident.[160] Another pretended to chase his comrade with a tomahawk, the two running past their enemies and on to safety.[161] It appears also that nine English soldiers escaped death during the ambush, though the details of their story are conjecture only. One tradition holds that they had gone ahead of the main body of troops and were chased into present-day Cumberland, where they made their stand against a large rock and all perished.[162]

A more plausible explanation is that these nine survived the ambush, were taken prisoner, and were marched northward about three miles to a piece of upland surrounded by swamp known as Camp Swamp. Here, upon a large rock, they were executed. It was several weeks before their bodies were found, scalped and uncovered, on this rock. The men were buried some seventy yards northeast of the rock in a common grave. Above this grave a heap of small stones was used to construct a fourteen-foot-long stone wall, some three feet high and one foot wide at the base.[163] To this day, residents know this place as Nine Men's Misery.

In the early twentieth century a cairn of stones (since damaged) was placed over the spot, and in 1928 a granite marker was set by the Rhode Island Historical Society.[164] The marker reads:

NINE MEN'S MISERY
ON THIS SPOT
WHERE THEY WERE SLAIN BY
THE INDIANS
WERE BURIED THE NINE SOLDIERS
CAPTURED IN PIERCE'S FIGHT
MARCH 26, 1676

The cairn and marker can be found near the former Cistercian Monastery on Diamond Hill Road, about six-tenths of a mile south of Route 295 in Cumberland. (These grounds are now home to the Hayden Library, the Northern Rhode Island Collaborative School, the Cumberland Senior Citizens Department, and other city services.) A dirt road, heading north-northeast from the northeast corner of the grounds, leads directly to the site, which requires about a quarter-mile walk. (Many residents walk and jog in this area and are able to point a visitor in the right direction.)

Around the time of the American Revolution a physician dug up remains from the grave, identifying one skeleton as that of Benjamin Buckland of Rehoboth by its large frame and double set of teeth.[165] When the Catholic Order of Monks purchased the land, remains of the men killed at Nine Men's Misery were dug up and given to the Rhode Island Historical Society. During the 1976 bicentennial celebration, after the land had been turned over to the town of Cumberland for its use, the bones were reburied at their original site.[166]

ATTACK ON PROVIDENCE, RHODE ISLAND

In 1676 Providence, Rhode Island, was a small farming and fishing village set along the eastern shore of the Providence River and the Old Cove. The Old Cove (or Great Salt Cove) was an important feature of early Providence that occupied the present-day railroad terminal and municipal parking lot to its north. The Providence and Worcester Railroad renovated the area around the cove in the 1840s, building an eighty-foot walkway known as Cove Promenade around the basin; this lent its name to present-day Promenade Street.[167] By the early 1890s the cove was completely filled and converted to railroad yards.

Providence's main thoroughfare was Towne Street, a dirt road that followed present-day North and South Main Street (between Olney and Wickenden Streets). In 1650, fifty-two five-acre home lots had been laid out from Towne Street, across College Hill to Hope Street.[168] Houses were constructed at the front of the lots, with gardens and burial plots set in the rear. By 1659, Providence encompassed 380 square miles,[169] or most of the area in present-day Providence County west of the Blackstone River.[170] Providence could boast about five hundred residents prior to King Philip's War, though by early 1676 news of native victories had reduced the population to less than thirty men.[171] Among the town's remaining residents was seventy-seven-year-old Roger Williams, captain of the local militia and a long-time friend and trading partner of the Narragansett.

On March 26, 1676, Canonchet and his warriors appeared on the highlands north of the great Cove, where, tradition holds, Roger Williams took his staff and went out alone to try to pacify them. A traditional account of the exchange has been preserved by historian Samuel Greene Arnold:

"Massachusetts," said he, "can raise thousands of men at this moment, and if you kill them, the King of England will supply their place as fast as they fall."

"Well, let them come," was the reply, "we are ready for them. But as for you, brother Williams, you are a good man; you have been kind to us many years; not a hair of your head shall be touched."[172]

The location of this meeting was along the Old Cove near the present-day intersection of Canal and Smith Streets, looking west to the State Capitol from the Roger Williams National Memorial at North Main and Smith Streets.

In the subsequent attack, Providence lost fifty-four houses.[173] Others were destroyed after the town was abandoned. Many of the dwellings along Towne Street, including Williams' own, were lost.[174] The aging patriarch was forced to flee, and in a striking portent of the impact King Philip's War would have on old Puritan strictures, was given permission by Massachusetts Bay to seek safety in that colony. The house where Providence's town records were kept was plundered and the records thrown into the millpond, though some were recovered.[175]

Roger Williams' house was located near the northeast corner of North Main and Howland Streets;[176] across the street was the spring of fresh water used by the Williams family and now marked by the Hahn Memorial. Williams died in 1683 and was buried with martial honors in his family burying ground located to the rear of his home lot.

One of only two houses[177] in Providence to survive King Philip's War was the Roger Mowry House, built in the 1650s and located on the north side of Abbott Street near North Main Street. Built originally as a one-room structure, it was eventually expanded to two stories. It served as Providence's first inn and was used for town meetings. The Mowry House was destroyed by fire in 1900.[178] In the mid-eighteenth century foundation walls of several of the original buildings were still visible, but by the mid-nineteenth century these had disappeared.[179] No structures—or remains—from the time of King Philip's War now stand in Providence.

ATTACK ON OLD REHOBOTH,
EAST PROVIDENCE, RHODE ISLAND

The men of Rehoboth who pursued Philip before the Nipsachuck Swamp Fight in August 1675 were instigated by the Reverend Noah Newman, minister of Rehoboth, whom Hubbard viewed as deserving "not a little Commendation for exciting his Neighbors and Friends."[180] Newman's house, a new parsonage built for him just before the outbreak of hostilities, was used as a principal garrison by the English throughout the war. It stood on the north side of Newman Avenue between the Congregational Church and the Meeting House pond[181] in the present-day Rumford section of East Providence. This area, called Seacunke until 1645, was the Rehoboth of King Philip's time, and for several centuries would spin off new towns, like Attleboro, Massachusetts, and Cumberland, Rhode Island, from its initial grant. East Providence would finally become annexed to Rhode Island in 1862.

Old Rehoboth was parceled into six-, eight-, and twelve-acre lots according to the wealth of its proprietors. These lots, most long and narrow, all faced a two-hundred-acre town common known as the "Ring of the Greene" or the "Ring of the Towne." The exact shape of the Ring is unknown, but it probably coincided with present-day Greenwood Avenue, Elm Street, Bourne, Hoyt, Pawtucket, and Bishop Avenues, and Pleasant Street.[182] The town's principal garrison sat on the southeast side of the common,[183] though other garrison sites are also known.[184]

At the northeast corner of the Ring of the Greene, near the intersection of Route 114 (Pawtucket Avenue) and Route 1A (Newport Avenue), began a long, flat expanse of land known historically as the "great plaine," Seekonk Plain or Rehoboth Plain. It was over this terrain, running about four miles to the Attleboro, Massachusetts, line,[185] that Philip and his band were spotted after fleeing the Pocasset Swamp. (An old Indian path probably bisected the plain along where Route 1A now runs.)[186] Descriptions of the Seekonk Plain—prior to the construction of Route 1A and such landmarks as the Gansett Shopping Center, Narragansett Race Track, and Slater Memorial Park—indicate that it was an awe-inspiring topographic feature. In 1750 it was described as being "about 3 miles over without a scrub and quite level, surrounded with woods."[187] In 1833, local historian Ebenezer Peirce (then eleven years old) passed over the Seekonk Plain en route from Freetown to Pawtucket to see President Andrew Jackson and Vice President Martin Van Buren, who were both visiting Pawtucket. In 1878 Peirce wrote about the experience:

> The writer of this book has a very distinct recollection of the time that his eyes first beheld the great Seekonk Plain, and the wonder and astonishment with which he regarded the level unenclosed and barren-looking waste land. I have seen nothing like it since, save in some locations at the South where armies had long been quartered during the late war. Tradition says that a hot fire which consumed much of the wood and timber that formerly stood on Seekonk Plain, also burned the vegetable mould in the soil, thus rendering it unproductive. Large portions of this plain have within a few years been fenced in, so that its former novelty in appearance has in great measure ceased.[188]

On the morning of March 28, 1676, fifteen hundred natives[189] attacked Rehoboth, burning thirty barns and almost forty dwellings[190] around the common and in outlying areas. John Kingsley, an elderly resident of the town, wrote pathetically of the attack:

> They burnt our mills, brake the stones, ye, our grinding stones; and what was hid in the earth they found, corne & fowles, killed catel & took the hind quarters & left the rest . . . We are shut up in our garrisons & dare not go abroad far to our outlandes, without some strength. Some of our souldieres are removed, nobody comes to say, how doe ye.[191]

Other, smaller attacks followed, so that only two buildings in the old village of Rehoboth were said to survive King Philip's War. Today, no traces of any structure from the original settlement can be found.

The area we know today as Rehoboth was first settled by the English in the mid-1660s, about twenty years after the East Providence area of Old Rehoboth was established. By 1675, six or eight families occupied homes along the Palmer River, from present-day Summer Street to the current Swansea line.[192] Two garrisons were located within the bounds of this settlement, and both were documented by local resident Dr. William Blanding (1773–1857). Blanding prepared a notebook in which he sketched and wrote about many of the town structures standing when he was a boy. Among these was "Blockhouse #2," which even in 1782 was in "a decayed state and inhabited by some poor family or families."[193] This "simple thatched roof cottage . . . surrounded by a palisade-type fence"[194] was located on the southwest side of Providence Street, at the head of Reed Street. A visitor today will see only a small empty field.

A second garrison, known as "Blockhouse #1," was located "about a mile north of Blockhouse #2 between the Palmer River and Wheeler Street near where the present power line right of way is located."[195] This site, subsequently built on, is near present-day 144 Wheeler Street. In 1975 archaeologists dug at the site, discovering artifacts that suggested the presence of at least one earlier house dating from the seventeenth century.[196]

CANONCHET'S CAPTURE, CUMBERLAND, RHODE ISLAND

On April 3, 1676, Captain George Denison of Connecticut was heading a force of some forty-seven soldiers[197] accompanied by eighty friendly Niantic, Pequot, and Mohegan[198] through the Narragansett country around present-day Pawtucket, Rhode Island. There they captured a squaw who informed them that Canonchet's camp was not far away. Canonchet, with thirty men, had returned to his homeland from Nipmuc country to seek seed corn for the spring planting. He was also actively prosecuting the war, having ambushed Captain Michael Pierce and destroyed Providence on March 26 and 29 respectively.

The news of Canonchet's whereabouts, William Hubbard suggests, "put new Life into the wearied Soldiers, that had traveled hard many Days, and met with no Booty till now."[199] Pushing rapidly onward, Denison's force spotted two warriors on the crest of a hill; pursuing them, they came upon a small group of natives that fled in all directions. Canonchet, "having no Time to consult, and but little time to attempt an Escape, and no

Means to defend Himself,"[200] bolted to the back side of the hill, throwing off his blanket, his silver-trimmed coat, and his belt of wampum. This only encouraged his pursuers, who suddenly realized they were closing in on the Narragansett sachem himself.

Racing to the river, Canonchet waded in and slipped, falling into the water and soaking his gun. At this, his spirit seemed to dissolve—for, as Hubbard reported, "his Heart and his Bowels turned within him, so as he became like a rotten Stick,"[201] and he surrendered, upon which

> one of the first English that came up with him was Robert Stanton, a young man that scarce had reached the twenty second Year of his Age, yet adventuring to ask him a Question or two, to whom, this manly Sachem looking with a little Neglect upon his youthful Face, replied in broken English; you much Child; no understand Matters of War; let your Brother or your Chief come, him I will Answer.[202]

Canonchet was sent to Stonington, Connecticut, where he was offered his life in return for an end to hostilities. He refused, and when told he would die, Canonchet said "he liked it well, that he should dye before his Heart was soft, or had spoken any thing unworthy of himself."[203] The sachem was executed and his head carried to Hartford.

The site of Canonchet's capture is not known positively, though some historians conjecture that the hill where Denison spotted the sentinels was Study Hill, northeast of Pierce's Fight, along the Blackstone River.[204] Study Hill, located in the section of present-day Cumberland known as Lonsdale, was home to William Blackstone (the first settler of Boston, who left after a quarrel with later arrivals). The site can no longer even be investigated; the hill was leveled in the nineteenth century to fill and grade the nearby railroad yards.

PHILIP'S DEATH, BRISTOL, RHODE ISLAND

On August 6, 1676, Weetamoe died, and the following day troops under Benjamin Church captured a number of men in the camp of the Wampanoag sachem Totoson, driving Totoson to his death. Everywhere,

English soldiers and friendly Indians combed the countryside for Philip, thought to be fleeing southward toward Narragansett country.

On August 9, Church and his troops departed from Plymouth, searched the woods around Pocasset, and then crossed the narrows of the Sakonnet River to Aquidneck Island on August 11. There, Church received the information that would cost Philip his life. A Wampanoag had fled Philip's camp, telling the English that Philip had killed his brother for having suggested peace with the English.[205] This same native wanted to exact his revenge by leading Church and his men to the camp, which Church in his *History* says was located "upon a little spot of upland, that was in the south end of the miry swamp, just at the foot of the mount [Mount Hope], which was a spot of ground that Captain Church was well acquainted with."[206]

Church's force crossed the water at Tripp's Ferry (where the present-day Mount Hope Bridge crosses from Portsmouth to Bristol) and arrived "a little upland in the northern end of a miry swamp at the foot of Mount Hope."[207] At daybreak on August 12, Captain Roger Goulding—the same man who had rescued Church and his troops from Almy's "peasefield" the prior July—and a small group closed in silently on Philip's camp, hoping to surprise and drive the sachem into the ring of Church's men surrounding the camp. Goulding's men were told to shout once the battle began; anyone running silently from the camp would be shot.

The scheme was ruined when Goulding suddenly came face-to-face with one of Philip's men, at whom he fired. There followed immediately a volley by the English, but Philip's camp had barely enough time to respond to the first shot, so few were standing and few were hit. Confusion erupted. Benjamin Church wrote:

> They were soon in the swamp, and Philip the foremost, who starting
> at the first gun, threw his petunk and powderhorn over his head,
> catched up his gun, and ran as fast as he could scamper, without any
> more clothes than his small breeches and stockings; and ran directly on
> two of Captain Church's ambush. They let him come fair within shot,
> and the Englishman's gun missing fire, he bid the Indian fire away, and

Ironically, although thousands of English soldiers had been tracking him for months, King Philip, shown here fleeing from his camp, was fatally shot by Alderman, another Native American. (Courtesy of the Haffenreffer Museum of Anthropology, Brown University)

he did so to [the] purpose; sent one musket bullet through his heart, and another not above two inches from it. He fell upon his face in the mud and water, with his gun under him.[208]

The Englishman whose gun failed was thought to be Caleb Cook. The native who killed Philip was known as Alderman, a disenchanted Pocasset.[209] When news of Philip's death was reported to Church's men, "the whole army gave three loud huzzas."[210]

Five of Philip's men were killed, but most of the sachem's band, including Philip's war chief, Anawan, escaped. Church pulled Philip's body from the mud, describing him as "a doleful, great, naked, dirty beast."[211] Saying that Philip had caused many an Englishman's body to lie unburied, Church called upon a native to behead and quarter Philip. Each section of Philip's body was hung from a tree.

Historian Henry Dexter reminds us that some believed Philip was a traitor to King Charles II and that he should be treated as such under English law. This law, barbaric by modern standards, lasted in England until 1790.[212] It included being hung by the neck and cut down alive, having the entrails cut out and burned while still alive, being beheaded, and then having the body cut into four quarters. Dexter added that the colonies were simply part of the mother country, which had (less than twenty years before) disinterred Oliver Cromwell, hung his decayed remains, and stuck his head on a pole on the top of Westminister Hall fronting the palace yard.[213]

Philip's head was carried to Plymouth and set on a pole on August 17, where it remained for a generation. Philip's "one very remarkable hand, being much scarred, occasioned by the splitting of a pistol in it formerly,"[214] was given to Alderman, who kept it in a pail of rum and earned his livelihood by exhibiting it at taverns for a fee.[215] Church's troops returned to Plymouth, where each received four shillings and sixpence for their labors.[216]

The traditional site of Philip's death is located on the grounds of the Haffenreffer Museum of Anthropology in Bristol, Rhode Island. Also at this site is the Seat of Metacom, or King Philip's Chair, a natural rock de-

This photograph of King Philip's Chair in Bristol, Rhode Island suggests that the chair, while providing an impressive view of Narragansett Bay, was less a piece of outdoor furniture and more a creation of Anglo-America's imagination.
(Michael Tougias)

pression formed on the northeast slope of Mount Hope, where tradition says Philip met with his people. The site can be located on a map provided at the museum and is within easy walking distance of the main buildings.

The place of King Philip's death, also shown on the Haffenreffer map, is harder to reach. The spot is located on a private paved road that splits south from Tower Road at a sharp bend about two miles from the museum. From the split, a walk of about one hundred yards along an overgrown path and around a gate on land marked No TRESPASSING is necessary. There, the path forks to the west and a covered spring and block of granite can be seen about forty yards beyond, designating the site. The marker, referred to as the Cold Springs Monument, reads:

In The "Miery Swamp,"
166 Feet W.S.W. From This
Spring, According to Tradition,
King Philip Fell, August 12
1676, O.S.
This Stone Placed By
The R.I. Historical Society
December, 1877

Church described the location of Philip's camp as being "upon a little spot of upland, that was in the south end of the miry swamp, just at the foot of the mount [Mount Hope]." This site clearly matches Church's account. However, how the Rhode Island Historical Society could place the spot of Philip's death so accurately, two centuries after the event, is a tribute to power of tradition and a delight to skeptical historians.

One of the best known of King Philip's would-be artifacts, said to have been taken from Philip by Benjamin Church at the sachem's death, is a war club held by the Fruitlands Museum in Harvard, Massachusetts. Carved from maple, the club is twenty-two inches long and weighs one pound, twelve and a half ounces. Wielded with one hand, it must have been a formidable weapon, and brings into sharp relief what Mary Rowlandson meant when she said her Lancaster neighbors were "knocked on the head"[217] during the February 1676 attack on that settlement.

King Philip's war club was inlaid with fifty-eight white and twenty-eight violet beads, and two triangular-shaped pieces of purple shell.[218] Tradition holds that the beads represent the number of English and natives Philip killed, though this should be viewed skeptically: historians suggest that Philip was rarely in a position during King Philip's War to engage in direct combat with the English, and one has to wonder if the time or materials existed to continually update the club in the heat of war.

King Philip's war club was purchased for Clara Endicott Sears, founder of the Fruitlands Museums, in May 1930 by Warren K. Moorehead of

While inscribed with great precision by nineteenth-century antiquarians, this memorial to King Philip's death, set in the woods of Bristol, Rhode Island, marks at best the general location of Philip's death. (Michael Tougias)

Phillips Academy in Andover. Moorehead had first heard of the club in 1913 while investigating various archaeological sites in Maine, and had attempted unsuccessfully to purchase it for the Haffenreffer Museum in July 1929. When rumor circulated that it was about to be sold in New York, he again approached the club's owner, Laura Anne Daniels of Union, Maine, and this time managed to strike a deal.

The history of the club is recorded in the files of the Fruitlands Museums: The club was considered a precious family treasure and had been handed down to Mrs. Daniels through her great aunt, Angelica (Gilbert) James, originating with a distant ancestor, the Reverend John Checkley. Checkley was the rector of the Episcopal Church in Providence, Rhode Island, and family stories indicated that he had accompanied Benjamin Church on the expedition that would lead to Philip's death in the swamp at Bristol, Rhode Island. The club was said to have been taken from the body of Philip by Alderman, the Indian credited with shooting Philip. An 1842 newspaper report in the museum files says that Church had assisted Checkley with purchasing the club from Alderman, as well as a "large, heavy and handsomely wrought" pipe, and a belt "covered with various colored beads, made as in the Indian mode, of shells and bones."[219] All three objects, said to belong to Philip, were given in exchange for Checkley's gold watch.

In 1846, Angelica (Gilbert) James loaned the club, belt, and pipe, along with a boot that belonged to John Checkley, to the Historical Society of Connecticut in Hartford. The objects remained in the possession of the historical society for at least three decades,[220] and probably until the turn of the century,[221] when the club was eventually returned to James' family. The belt and pipe have since dropped from sight; whether they were returned from Hartford is unknown. To prove their existence, we have only the 1842 newspaper account describing them, and a receipt from a representative of the Historical Society of Connecticut who delivered them from Mrs. James' home in Utica, New York, to Hartford.

For forty years King Philip's war club was exhibited at Fruitlands until, on July 2, 1970, it was stolen in broad daylight during visiting hours. Two men driving a tan, 1963 Chevrolet parked directly in front of the door to the museum, allowed only because one pretended to be an invalid. A third man may have assisted in distracting the two attendants on duty, who shortly thereafter discovered the club missing from its Plexiglas case.[222] No significant clues or leads were ever discovered, and the trail grew cold until October 1994 when Ned Jalbert, an interior designer and collector of Native American artifacts, paid $125 for the club at a Worcester, Massachusetts, yard sale. The Fruitlands museum director Robert Farwell told the *Boston Globe* that serendipity played an important part in the war club's recovery:

> "We didn't know who he [Jalbert] was," Farwell said. "However, once we saw the club, there was no doubt it was King Philip's." . . . Over the years, Farwell said, tips about the club's fate come in periodically. None panned out. After Jalbert bought the club, he learned it was part of an estate sale held on behalf of a Worcester man whose wife had died recently. Jalbert called the seller back and came away convinced the man knew nothing of the club's value, historical or otherwise.[223]

On June 19, 1995, Jalbert, Farwell and members of several Wampanoag groups were on hand at a ceremony marking the return of the artifact to the museum.

Had the war club held by Fruitlands today really belonged to King Philip? A short time after the club was purchased, a descendant of John Checkley wrote to Clara Endicott Sears to correct the story regarding the purchase of the club. Checkley, it seems, was born in Boston in 1680, four years after Philip's death. He served as a missionary to the Indians of southeastern New England after his ordination in 1738, two generations after the end of King Philip's War, and almost twenty years after the death of Benjamin Church in 1717. Checkley's memoirs, published in 1897, stated that he spent time with Benjamin Church, though how much and under what conditions is unknown; he was most certainly not present when Alderman shot Philip. The *Memoirs* do mention that Checkley was "something of an archaeologist, and took a great interest in Indian implements and relics,"[224] but nowhere does it relate that Church was involved in any transaction for Philip's possessions. Checkley died at Providence in 1754, where his inventory of estate listed only "Indian toys."

Church is also quite clear in his *History* that Philip, startled in his camp by the English, "threw his petunk and powderhorn over his head, catched up his gun, and ran as fast as he could scamper, without any more clothes than his small breeches and stockings."[225] Nowhere is there mention of a war club, or the discovery of one after Philip's death.

Among the original papers said to accompany the club—all lost before its sale to Fruitlands—was a receipt from the Indian who sold the club, belt, and pipe to Checkley. (Whether this Indian was really Alderman or not is questionable.) Also lost was an affidavit from a number of prominent men, probably Checkley's neighbors in Providence, who knew and swore to the history of the club. Warren Moorehead attempted to locate these papers from Mrs. Daniels on several occasions after the sale but was unsuccessful.

Finally, the issue of the missing pipe and belt remains. In the early 1980s Fruitlands was offered for purchase an item purported to be "Philip's peace pipe," but rejected it as being probably nonauthentic. Whether this was the same pipe purchased by John Checkley that eventually made its way to another New England family, is unknown. As for the second item, it seems probable that whatever Checkley purchased, it was not Philip's belt. The Pokanoket belts were passed to Benjamin Church by Anawan a short time after Philip's death, and never fell into the hands of Alderman. The story of Philip's belts (detailed in chapter 4, "Anawan's Capture") would imply that whatever Checkley purchased, it could not have been the genuine article.

As much as romantics wish that King Philip's war club was actually owned and used by Philip, firm evidence is difficult to assemble. That John Checkley accumulated important and perhaps unique Native American artifacts is likely, that he bought them from Alderman with Benjamin Church's assistance unlikely, and that he traded for them at the time of Philip's death impossible. The loss of critical documents and the accumulation of hopeful family tradition obscure the war club's true story.

BENJAMIN CHURCH'S LITTLE COMPTON, RHODE ISLAND

At the start of his *Entertaining History of King Philip's War*, published in 1716, Benjamin Church writes through his son, Thomas:

> In the year 1674, Mr. Benjamin Church of Duxbury, being providentially at Plymouth in the time of court, fell into acquaintance with Captain John Almy of Rhode Island. Captain Almy with great importunity invited him to ride with him and view that part of Plymouth colony that lay next to Rhodeisland, known then by their Indian names Pocasset and Sogkonate. Among other arguments to persuade him, he told him the soil was very rich and the situation pleasant . . . He accepted his invitation, views the country and was pleased with it, makes a purchase, settled a farm . . . and being himself a person of uncommon activity and industry, he soon erected two buildings upon his farm, and gained a good acquaintance with the natives; got much into their favor, and was in a little time in great esteem among them.[226]

Church, nothing if not immodest, had high hopes of attracting others to the area, but when rumors of war arose the settlement's growth came to a halt.

Benjamin Church, shown here killing an Indian chief, gained fame as both a friend of New England's natives and as a relentless Indian fighter. (Courtesy of the Haffenreffer Museum of Anthropology, Brown University)

Not until 1682 was Little Compton formally established as a town.[227] In 1747, the town became part of Rhode Island. Due to Little Compton's relative isolation, no part of King Philip's War was fought there.

The natives to which Church referred were the Sakonnet, who lived on the present-day site of Little Compton, bordered to the north by the Pocasset of modern-day Tiverton, Rhode Island, and Fall River, Massachusetts. Punkatees was located on upland in Tompe Swamp, north of the present-day Swamp Road, in or near Wilbour Woods.[228] This site is the traditional burial site of Awashonks, the Sakonnet's squaw sachem, though this is purely speculation, as is her fate. Awashonks' camp at Tompe Swamp was sold before King Philip's War began, and the new reservation given her at the time, south of Taylor's Lane, "was lost, in ways unknown, by 1681," according to a 1988 report published by the Little Compton Historical Society. "She and her daughter Betty disappeared from history in 1683."[229]

Most of the area now called Sakonnet Point, at the southwest extremity of Little Compton overlooking the Sakonnet River and Rhode Island Sound, once belonged to Benjamin Church and his descendants.[230] It was here, in June 1676, near the war's end, while returning home from Plymouth, that Church happened upon several natives engaged in fishing. "They urged Mr. Church to come ashore, for they had a great desire to have some discourse with him."[231] In a short time Church had arranged a meeting with Awashonks, "two days after, at a rock at the lower end of Captain Richmond's farm, which was a very noted place."[232]

At the appointed time—much to the chagrin of his "tender and now almost broken hearted wife"[233]—Church met with Awashonks and her people. The meeting began poorly when Awashonks' men, dressed for battle, jumped from the grass and surrounded Church. After convincing them to lay down their guns "at some small distance, for formality's sake,"[234] Church offered Awashonks a rum drink; she would taste it only after Church drank first, for fear of poison. The icy meeting continued for a time, with Church slowly convincing the Sakonnet that peace with the English was a better course than maintaining their alliance with Philip. Eventually, perhaps realizing that an English victory was inevitable, the Sakonnet promised to fight Philip.

Treaty Rock, the site of this famous meeting, is on private property off Treaty Rock Road, near Treaty Rock Farmhouse. This structure, built around 1865, replaced a seventeenth-century house on the site destroyed by fire. John Richmond first settled the land surrounding this house, and his family lived there until the late twentieth century.[235] (The site is often referred to as the Richmond Farm.) Treaty Rock may only be accessed with permission.

The location of Benjamin Church's first home is unproved, though tradition indicates a site on the south slope of Windmill Hill, at the north end of Little Compton near the Tiverton line.[236] Several years after the end of King Philip's War, Church returned to Little Compton and built a home near the Sakonnet River. Markers along West Main Street, on the west side near the intersection of Swamp Meadow Lane, commemorate this site. The house of Church's son, Thomas, is located in the same area, closer to West

Benjamin Church, the founder and favorite son of Little Compton, Rhode Island, is commemorated by a memorial in the town's central graveyard. (Eric Schultz)

Main Road. Thomas Church's house is referred to as the Nelson or Wilbour house and is also known today as Blue Flag Farm.

Little Compton Commons, on Meeting House Lane, is the site of the United Congregational Church and its burial ground, laid out in 1675–1677. Benjamin Church, who died in November 1718, is buried here. Church's tombstone inscription reads:

> Here lyeth interred the [body]
> of the Honorable
> Col. Benjamin Church, Esq.,
> who departed this life, January 17, 1717–8 in
> the 78 yeare of his age.

Standing next to the tombstone is a tablet that reads:

THIS TABLET
ERECTED BY THE RHODE ISLAND SOCIETY
OF COLONIAL WARS
IN RECOGNITION OF THE EXCEPTIONAL
SERVICE RENDERED BY
COL. BENJAMIN CHURCH
HIS FEARLESS LEADERSHIP
AND EFFECTIVE COMMAND DURING
KING PHILIP'S WAR
1675–1677

Church's son, Thomas, who transcribed his father's book from dictation, is buried nearby.

Captain Frost narrowly escaped from his dwelling near Maine's Piscataqua River. His home was, in William Hubbard's words, "neither fortified, nor well manned, yet was far from Neighbors," a situation typical of many residences in this sparsely populated region of the Massachusetts Bay colony. (Courtesy of the Haffenreffer Museum of Anthropology, Brown University)

Chapter 7

King Philip's War in Maine and New Hampshire

ABENAKI ASSAULTS IN MAINE

THE FIRST SIGNS OF WAR in the region of the Massachusetts Bay Colony that became present-day Maine began about three months after the outbreak of war in Swansea, Massachusetts, and took the shape of marauding rather than violent assault. The home of Thomas Purchase, a man characterized by Hubbard as "an ancient planter about Pegypscot River, and a known trader with the Indians,"[1] was ransacked on September 5, 1675, the day after Richard Beers and his troops were ambushed in Northfield, Massachusetts. Hubbard says the Abenaki stole liquor and ammunition and killed livestock, but "offered no incivility to the mistress of the house."[2] They left, however, with the ominous warning that those coming after them "would deal far worse"[3] with the English. Purchase and his family took heed and moved to Lynn, Massachusetts, after the incident.

While several traditions exist, the precise location of Thomas Purchase's homestead can only be guessed. A history of Brunswick published in 1939 stated that Purchase may have lived on a knoll due east of the falls on the Androscoggin River once known as Fish House Hill.[4] Purchase may also have had a residence at the head of New Meadows River, near where the Androscoggin River and Merrymeeting Bay meet.[5]

If the attack on the Purchase home was restrained, then the assault a week later on the Wakely family home in the area of present-day Portland was a tragic sign that King Philip's War had come to Maine in all its fury. Thomas Wakely had been made a freeman of Massachusetts in 1636, so by the time of the war was undoubtedly an elderly man. Wakely and his family must have lived in an isolated location, for Increase Mather writes that they "lived many years in a plantation where there was no church at all,"[6] and, as Hubbard reported, it took a day before soldiers could arrive to investigate "the fire they discerned the day before."[7] Hubbard described the gruesome scene they found at Wakely's homestead:

> The house burned to ashes, the bodies of the old man and his wife half consumed with the fire, the young woman killed, and three of the grand children having their brains dashed out . . . one girl of about eleven years old, was carried captive by them.[8]

The captive, Elizabeth Wakely, was freed in June 1676 and was still living in 1723.[9]

The present-day location of Wakely's home is thought to be the east side of the Presumpscot River, three-quarters of a mile below the falls.[10]

Several other events associated with King Philip's War occurred in present-day Portland, though their locations have been covered by urban construction. On August 11, 1676, almost a year after the assault on Thomas Purchase's farm, the home of Anthony Brackett on the west side of the Back Cove was assaulted, with Brackett, his wife, and five children carried into captivity. A few days later his captors, who may have included Simon "the Yankee killer," heard about the destruction of an important English trading post on Arrowsic Island (see below). Eager to share in the booty, the Abenaki became lax, allowing Brackett and his family to escape in an old birch canoe that Mrs. Brackett mended with a needle and thread.

Brackett's home was located on Cleve's Neck, now the downtown area of Portland. In the early twentieth century, George Ellis and John Morris reported that the cellar hole of the house was still visible on Deering Avenue a "few rods beyond the railroad crossing just north of Deering's Oaks."[11] Today, however, this site is near the intersection of Routes 25 and 295, a completely developed area. No sign of the house exists.[12]

Likewise, the garrison of George Munjoy, used only briefly during the war, was located at the northwest corner of present-day Mountfort and Fore Streets.[13] Its foundation is now buried under the sidewalk.

Once called Munjoy's Island, present-day Peak's Island was the scene of an Abenaki ambush on September 3, 1676. A party of English attempt-

The Reverend William Hubbard referred to Pemaquid, Maine, as the "utmost boundary of New England." Today, Colonial Pemaquid retells the story of Pemaquid, in part, through the preservation of its archaeological sites. (Eric Schultz)

ing to secure sheep as food for their families were surprised and driven into the ruins of an old stone house on the southwest point of the island, four rods northeast of the Brackett family cemetery fence and a few rods from the channel separating Munjoy's from James Andrews' Island.[14] All seven men were killed—some by stoning and others shot.[15] Today, Peaks Island is reached by a twenty-minute ferry ride from Portland Harbor, and is Casco Bay's most heavily populated island.

Outside of Portland, attacks on English settlements continued in earnest throughout the fall of 1675 and into 1676. The house of Captain John Bonython, destroyed by Abenaki on September 18, 1675, was situated in present-day Saco along the Saco River. The site is shown on a 1901 map to be on the east side of present-day Hobson's Lane (the oldest road in Saco), just before where the road turns towards the wharf.[16] Today the site is covered by a landfill.

Bonython had abandoned his home prior to the attack, probably after being warned by a friendly Abenaki,[17] and taken up a defense across the Saco River at Major William Phillips' garrison, described in one Saco history as a "heavily timbered structure with an overhanging second story."[18] Within an hour of spotting the first smoke from the Bonython home, the fifty or so English huddled inside Phillips' garrison were assaulted. Hubbard writes that at the first report of Abenaki activity, Phillips rushed to the window, and

> another of his men, coming after, cryed "Master, What mean you, do you intend to be killed?" at which words he turned suddenly back from the window, out of which he was looking, when presently a bullet stuck him on the shoulder, grazing only upon it, without breaking the bone. The Indian upon the shot, thinking he had slain thereby (as they heard afterwards) gave a great shout, upon which they discerned that they were surrounded by them; whereupon they presently fired upon the enemy from all quarters, and from the flankers of the fortification, so as they wounded the captain of the Indians, who presently leaving the assault, retired three or four miles from the place.[19]

Hubbard continues, describing how the Abenaki spent the better part of the day destroying Phillips' sawmill and corn mill, and part of the night constructing a cart filled with combustible material to fire the garrison. The cart, apparently similar to the one used at the assault on Brookfield, was wheeled out by moonlight at four or five o'clock in the morning. Phillips' men

> were a little discouraged at the site of this engine; but he bid them be of good courage . . . the cart, when brought a little nearer, became unwieldy by reason of the barricado planted in it, and being to pass through a small gutter, one wheel stuck fast in the slough, which brought the cart suddenly to the left, whereby the drivers lay open to the right flanker.[20]

Six Abenaki were killed and fifteen wounded, and with their captain mortally wounded some distance away, the siege was ended. However, the exposed position of the Phillips' garrison also forced the English to abandon it. Soon after, the house was burned to the ground.[21]

The present-day site of the Phillips garrison is in Biddeford, Maine, on the west side of Pierson's Lane, about halfway up the hill from Water Street.[22] The neighborhood is now made up of two- and three-story apartment buildings.

The house of Richard Tozer at the old settlement of Newechewannick (present-day Berwick, Maine) was attacked on October 1, 1675, by two Abenaki, Andrew (of Saco) and Hope-Hood.[23] Fifteen women and children were trapped within the house, says Hubbard, and only through the courage of

> a young maid of about eighteen years of age. . . who being inbued with more courage than ordinarily the rest of her sex used to be . . . first shut the door, whereby they were denied entrance, till the rest within escaped to the next house, that was better fortified; that young Virago kept the door fast against them so long till the Indians had chop'd it in pieces with their hatchets; when entering the house, they knocked the poor maid down with their hatchets, and gave her many other wounds, leaving her for dead upon the place.[24]

After leaving the house, Andrew and Hope-Hood killed a three-year-old and captured an eleven-year-old. Miraculously, the "young maid" recovered from her wounds and was eventually "restored to perfect health again."[25]

Tozer's home was located about a mile from present-day Salmon Falls, New Hampshire, in present-day Berwick, Maine. This structure was known for years as the Old Garrison House and survived until the 1850s. Today, a nineteenth-century farmhouse sits on the exact location of the old cellar hole. The home can be seen on the west side of Route 236, at the top of the hill, about six-tenths of a mile north of the Boston and Maine Railroad tracks.[26]

On October 16, 1675, the Abenaki returned to Tozer's home, killing Richard Tozer and capturing his son. Lieutenant Roger Plaisted, in command of the nearby garrison, sent seven men to rescue Tozer and his family.

The party was ambushed, with two killed and the remainder barely able to reach the garrison. As Hubbard's account of the war in Maine continues, the following day Plaisted led a party of twenty men to locate and bury the dead:

> They were first to the furthest place, where they found Ro. Tozers body, and put it into their cart; but coming back to take up the other two bodies, which were fallen in a little swamp nearer to the garrison, they were set upon by an hundred and fifty of the enemy, that had hid themselves in the bushes, and under the stone-wall.[27]

Plaisted's band was forced to retreat, though Plaisted "disdaining either to fly from or yield himself,"[28] fought to the death. His eldest son and a third man were also killed, and another son mortally wounded.

The Plaisted garrison was situated near the Tozer home, on the same side of Route 236, about two-tenths of a mile from the railroad tracks. A new house today stands on the site of the old cellar hole. On the east side of Route 236 nearly three-tenths of a mile from the tracks is a nineteenth-century marker designating the spot where Roger Plaisted and his son were killed. This tombstone is just off the road, surrounded by a small iron-bar fence.[29] (This should not be confused with a small family burying ground just a few yards to the north.) The stone has fallen and is difficult to see without walking a short distance into the woods.

On August 13, 1676, the fortified house and trading post of Richard Hammond was attacked and destroyed by Abenaki warriors. Hammond and fourteen others lost their lives.[30] Only a young woman, either a servant or Hammond's daughter, fled in time to escape the assault. Hammond, described by Hubbard as "an ancient Inhabitant and Trader with the Indians up Kennibeck River"[31] was known for cheating his native customers, and the attack, says another historian, was marked by "particular ferocity."[32]

The precise location of Hammond's trading post was disputed for many years. The Reverend Henry O. Thayer finally established the location of Hammond's property through his research, writing that "it can be rebuilt in fancy upon the northeastern curve of Long Reach where are now grouped the village dwellings of Day's Ferry."[33] More precisely, Hammond's home and trading post were located on the east side of the Kennebec River, slightly northwest of the intersection of Route 128 and Old Stage Road in present-day Woolwich. Some excavation has been done, though the site is difficult to locate precisely without assistance and is now on private land.

ATTACK ON CLARKE AND LAKE TRADING POST, ARROWSIC, MAINE

The trading post of Thomas Clarke and Thomas Lake, two wealthy Boston merchants, was situated on the eastern edge of Arrowsic Island, along the Sasonoa River between present-day Mill Island and Spring Cove, near the town of Woolwich, Maine. Clarke and Lake had purchased the four-mile-long island in its entirety in 1657, building up a prosperous trade in lumber, fish, cattle, and furs along one of the Indians' well-traveled canoe routes. The trading post was large and in many ways self-sufficient. Hubbard described it as having

> convenient Buildings for several Offices, as well for Wares and Trading, as Habitation: six several Edifices are said to have been there erected. The Warehouse at that Time was well furnished with all Sorts of Goods; besides a Mill and other Accommodations, and Dwellings within a Mile of the Fort and Mansion House.[34]

The trading post was also well armed, though not to the extent of a true military fort.[35] Nonetheless, Hubbard conjectured that "had it been carefully defended it might have proved the Defense and Security of all that Side of the Country."[36]

In the early morning of August 14, 1676, fresh from their raid on the Hammond house, the Abenaki took advantage of a careless sentry to spring a lightening attack on the trading post. Hubbard reported, without explanation,[37] that the natives followed the sentry "in at the Fort-Gate,"[38] which must have been left open, "while others of them immediately seized the Port Holes thereof, and shot down all they saw passing up and down within the Walls, and so in a little Time became Masters of the Fort, and all that was within it."[39] Thomas Lake, sensing the futility of fighting, fled with his agent, Sylvanus Davis, and two other men "out at a back Door, whereby they escaped to the Water-side, where they found a Canoe, into which they all entered and made away toward another Island near by."[40] Their flight did not go unnoticed, however, as the natives launched a canoe in pursuit. Lake and his men reached the shore of Mill Island—about five-eighths of a mile distance—but not before Davis was wounded. Unable to run or fight, Davis hid in 'the Cleft of a Rock hard by the Place, where he first landed."[41] Two days later he emerged and escaped by canoe. Davis would survive the war, and it was likely his account from which Hubbard drew his description of the attack.[42] Hubbard records that the two other men with Lake safely escaped by foot, perhaps being younger than the sixty-one-year-old merchant. Lake, unable to elude his pursuers, was shot and killed near the spot where the canoe landed. Six months later, in February 1677, an expedition under Major Richard Walderne would discover Lake's body in almost perfect condition, "preserved entire and whole and free from Putrefaction by the Coldness of the long Winter,"[43] and transport it to Boston. There, it was interred at Copp's Hill Burying Ground, where Lake's gravesite is still visible today.

Having driven the English out of the fort, the natives stole or destroyed everything of value, including several structures outside of the fortification. Their victory was complete, having taken (possibly without loss) the best-fortified settlement in the region and gaining huge stores of food and supplies in the process. In addition, the victory took a huge psychological toll on the area; Hubbard reported that when news of the disaster at Arrowsic spread, "all the plantations of the English in those Parts were soon after left, and forsaken by Degrees."[44]

The location of the Clarke and Lake trading post was discovered in the 1890s by the minister Henry O. Thayer, who proceeded (in a not very scientific way) to excavate portions of the site. Thayer's announcement of his discovery also led to several generations of treasure hunters, who destroyed portions of the site for future archaeologists. Fortunately, professionals began excavating the site in 1967, and by 1970 Professor James Leamon and his students from Bates College were exploring the site on an annual basis as part of a six-week course in historical archaeology.[45] Today, the Clarke and Lake site is one of only a handful of English sites from the seventeenth century to have been extensively excavated in Maine.[46]

After excavating a portion of the site, Thayer wrote that "relics have been gathered, implements found, bones exhumed, flagstones of old pathways uncovered."[47] Thayer also discovered a brass sword hilt, since lost, and an unidentified iron artifact left in the possession of the Woolwich Historical Society.[48] Unfortunately, he left no plan of his work, and modern archaeologists are left to guess at the precise location where Thayer dug.

The best and most complete summary of the history and archaeology of the site is *The Clarke and Lake Company: The Historical Archaeology of a Seventeenth-Century Maine Settlement*, published by Emerson W. Baker in 1985. In it, Baker reviewed the discovery of six seventeenth-century structures, reported in detail on many of the artifacts found, and wove the findings into an historical interpretation of the site.

Among the discoveries was a large collection of prehistoric artifacts, indicating the presence of natives for thousands of years prior to the English settlement on Arrowsic. Historic artifacts included a brass "posey ring," common to colonial sites, mingled with calcified human hand bones; these bones, along with some nearby pieces of badly burned skull, were probably those of one of Clarke and Lake's employees killed in the August 1676 attack. These are the only human remains uncovered at the site (except for perhaps Thayer's report of "exhumed bones"), and the burial site of the settlers has never been located.[49]

More than seven thousand nails and nail fragments have been unearthed, and Baker conjectured that they may have been manufactured at the Saugus Iron Works in Massachusetts.[50] Clarke and Lake's two cannons were removed by Walderne's party in February 1677, when any working firearms overlooked by the Abenaki would also have been collected. However, evidence of the trading post's arsenal has surfaced in the form of a side plate to a snaphance pistol, a trigger guard from a musket, several musket balls, pieces of birdshot, and enough flint and chipping debris to indicate that flints may have been produced at Arrowsic.[51] Less exotic, but equally important, numerous artifacts related to daily living—buttons, buckles, pipes, stoneware, pewter, spoons, candleholders, clay marbles, a razor, a Jews' harp, spurs, and coins—have been uncovered at the site.

DESTRUCTION OF INDIAN FORT, OSSIPEE, NEW HAMPSHIRE

The first English expedition intended to destroy the Indian fort in the area of present-day Ossipee, New Hampshire was planned in December 1675, at about the same time as the Great Swamp Fight. The tactics were identical: Catch the Abenaki off guard, smash their winter quarters, and destroy their ability to wage war in the spring. However, the northern weather was uncooperative. Hubbard reported that the winter was so hard that "it was not possible to have marched a Days Journey into the Woods, without hazarding all their Lives that should venture up: The Snow being found generally in those Woods four foot thick on the tenth of December."[52]

The following year operations began a month earlier, so that by November 1, 1676, 130 English and forty Christian Indians under Captains Hawthorne and Sill began their difficult four-day march to Ossipee.[53] The fort they sought to attack had been built between 1650 and 1660[54] by some English tradesmen (possibly from Dover, New Hampshire, or Saco, Maine[55]), hired by the Indians to construct a defense against the Mohawk. Hubbard says the sturdy fort was built fourteen feet high with flankers at each corner.[56] When Hawthorne and Sill arrived, the fort was deserted; they proceeded to burn it, and sent a scouting party farther north to see if any natives could be found. Discovering none, the entire party headed home, "having run," concludes Hubbard, "more hazard of their limbs, by the sharpness of the frost, than of their lives by an assault from their enemies."[57]

This scene has changed dramatically in the last three hundred years. Today, where the fort once stood, is the second tee of the Indian Mound Golf Course in Ossipee.[58] It is the property of the Ossipee Historical Society. No recent archaeology has been conducted at the site, but work in the early nineteenth century concluded that the fort had included a palisade of about an acre in dimension.[59]

EVENTS AT BLACK POINT, SCARBOROUGH, MAINE

The fort at Black Point (present-day Scarborough, Maine) was the scene of one of Mugg Hegone's greatest military victories, and later, the scene of his death. Mugg, who styled himself "of Saco River," and was described variously as chief of the Androscoggins, principal minister of Madockawando, and Prime Minister of the Penobscot sachem,[60] was active as a military leader during King Philip's War. Mugg knew the English, having lived among English families for some years,[61] so that he also took on the role of diplomat, even traveling to Boston on a peace mission.

On October 12, 1676, between fifty and one hundred warriors attacked the garrison at Black Point, which was considered by the English, according to Hubbard, to be so strong that "a few Hands might have defended against all the Indians on that Side of the Country."[62] Captain Henry Jocelyn owned the garrison, and, in the absence of Captain Joshua Scottow, headed its defenses; like John Pynchon of Springfield, he was a successful merchant and influential man, but a poor soldier. (A letter from Jocelyn to Scottow in August 1676 reported "ye averseness of the generality of ye Inhabitants to obey military orders."[63]) When Mugg called Jocelyn out to discuss peace, the sachem offered to let all of the English leave with their possessions if the fort were surrendered peacefully. Jocelyn, who might have resisted the parley in the first place, retreated to the fort to present the offer. There, he discovered that all but his household servants had fled the garrison by boat. Unable to defend the fort, he surrendered. (Jocelyn was treated kindly and released the following spring.) Mugg Hegone and his force had taken Black Point without losing a man.

Having little use for the garrison, the natives deserted Black Point by November, and by early the following year the English had reoccupied it.[64] By May 1677, Lieutenant Bartholomew Tippen had command of the fort, and on May 14 Mugg Hegone and his forces again laid siege to it. This time the English resisted while the warriors mounted a fierce assault, killing three soldiers and capturing a fourth. The assault lasted three days until, on May 16, Lieutenant Tippen noticed the fatal wounding of a warrior observed to be "very busy and bold in the Assault," says Hubbard's account, "whom at the Time they deemed to be Simon, the arch Villain and Incendiary of all the Eastward Indians, but proved to be one almost as good as himself, who was called Mugg";[65] Mugg's death "damped the Courage of all of his Companions"[66] and the siege was lifted.

On June 22, 1677, Captain Benjamin Swett and Lieutenant James Richardson led a force of forty English—described by Hubbard as many "young, raw and inexperienced Soldiers, who were not able to look Danger, much less Death, in the Face"[67]—and two hundred friendly Indians (from the Natick, Massachusetts, area)[68] on an expedition to Piscataqua. Sailing to Black Point on June 28, they received intelligence that a large body of natives were nearby. The next morning Swett and Richardson led a force ashore and were joined there by men from the Jocelyn garrison.

The lessons of the war had unfortunately been lost on Swett, and the presence of friendly Indians was of no help. Swett's soldiers caught sight of some fleeing warriors, pursued them nearly two miles from the fort to a hill, and found themselves in the midst of a blistering ambush from swampland on either side of the hill. In Hubbard's account, the young soldiers panicked and scattered, while "a few resolute Men of Courage bore the Brunt of the Service till they were in a Manner all knocked down."[69] Richardson was killed and Swett, victim of twenty wounds, fought his way almost back to the garrison before falling. When it was over twenty friendly Indians and forty English lay dead,[70] including Swett and Richardson.

The scenes of these various encounters are today part of the Prouts Neck Wildlife Preserve and Bird Sanctuary in Scarborough. A marker for Jocelyn's garrison can be found one-tenth of a mile past the post office on the west side of the Route 207 extension. It reads:

GARRISON COVE
SITE OF THE
JOCELYN (OR SCOTTOW) FORT
HEADQUARTERS FOR DEFENSE
FIRST INDIAN WAR
CHIEF MOGG HEIGON

KILLED HERE IN AN ATTACK
MAY 1677

Also in the wildlife preserve is Massacre Pond, which commemorates Benjamin Swett's disastrous defeat. The ambush probably occurred some distance northeast of the pond near Moore's Brook. A common grave is said to lie at the southwest corner of Massacre Pond, though no marker commemorates the ambush, and signs discourage visiting this residential area.

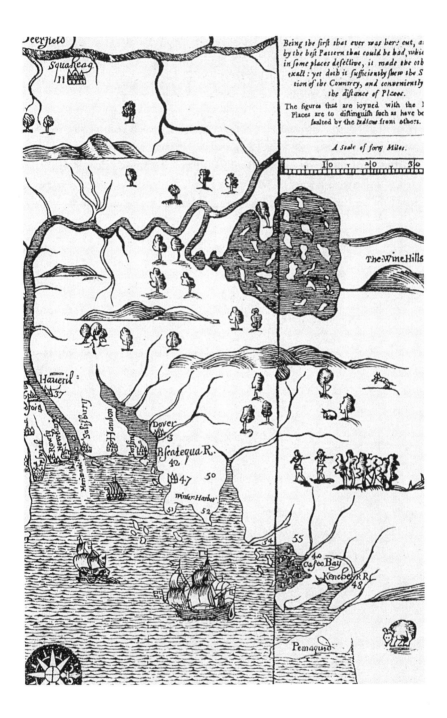

Being the first that ever was here cut, a[n]
by the best Pattern that could be had, whi[ch]
in some places defective, it made the oth[er]
exact: yet doth it sufficiently shew the S[ta-]
tion of the Country, and conveniently
the distance of Places.

The figures that are joyned with the [Names of]
Places are to distinguish such as have be[en as-]
saulted by the Indians from others.

A Scale of forty Miles.

10   20   30

Deerfield

Squakeag
11

The Wine Hills

Haueril
37

Salisbury

Hamton

Dover
3

Pscatequa R.
42

47   50

Winter Harbor
51   52

54   55

40
Caseo Bay
Keneber R.
48

Pemaquid

◆§ PART III ◈

THE DIARIES AND EYEWITNESS ACCOUNTS

This "Fac-simile of an original likeness of Col. Benjamin Church," probably bor-
rowed from Paul Revere's engraving, was used in Samuel Drake's 1827 edition of
Church's Entertaining History. (Courtesy of the Haffenreffer Museum of
Anthropology, Brown University)

· Chapter 8 ·

The Diary of Captain Benjamin Church

INTRODUCTION TO CAPTAIN BENJAMIN CHURCH

BENJAMIN CHURCH, of Little Compton, Rhode Island, was a brave man, a smart captain, and perhaps most important, a lucky soul. More than once fate smiled on him, saving him from what seemed to be certain death. With musket balls through his coat, wounds that were not disabling, and hatchets just missing his scalp, Church survived King Philip's War to be arguably the most effective leader in the colonial militias. While other military leaders stayed close to the garrisons, content to chase Indians *after* they attacked, Church took the battle to the natives, tracking them through swamps and forests, using friendly Indians as both scouts and fighters.

Prior to the war, Church was on friendly terms with many Indians, learning from them the ways of the forest and gaining insight into the Indian mind. He respected the Indians and enjoyed their company; ironically, it was this affinity that later made him such a devastating killer of natives.

Church was involved in the beginning, middle, and end of the war. He was at one of the first skirmishes of the war known as the Pease Field Fight (June 1675), followed by the massacre at the Great Swamp (December 1675), and finally, he led the expedition that resulted in King Philip's death (August 1676). Unlike so many of the writers of his day, Church's words have a balance that at least give the Indians credit for their courage and ingenuity on the battlefield. Church died at the age of 78 on January 17, 1717.

Church's son Thomas wrote his father's account of the war from dictation by using the captain's field notes or "minutes," and called the book *Entertaining Passages Relating to Philip's War Which Began in the Month of June 1675. As also of Expeditions more lately made against the Common Enemy, and Indian Rebels, in the Eastern Parts of New England: with some account of the Divine Providence Towards Benj. Church Esq.* While

319

the long-winded title might suggest an equally ponderous narrative, the writing for the most part is quite lively, and the reader, with just a little imagination, can travel with Church on his harrowing expeditions. The following excerpt is from Henry Martyn Dexter's edition (1865), re-issued by The Little Compton Historical Society in 1975. The first edition was published in 1716 and printed by B. Green in Boston.

EXCERPT FROM THE INTRODUCTION

It was ever my intent, having laid myself under a solemn promise, that the many and repeated favors of God to myself and those with me in the service might be published for generations to come. And now my great age requiring my dismission from service in the militia, and to put off my armor, I am willing that the great and glorious works of Almighty God to us children of men should appear to the world. And, having my minutes by me, my son has taken the care and pains to collect from them the ensuing narrative of many passages relating to the former and later wars, which I have had the perusal of, and find nothing amiss as to the truth of it, and with as little reflection upon any particular person as might be, either alive or dead.

And seeing every particle of historical truth is precious, I hope the reader will pass a favorable censure upon an old soldier telling of the many ran-counters he has had and yet is come off alive . . .

THE PEASE FIELD FIGHT

Now they passed down into Punkatees Neck, and in their march discovered a large wigwam full of Indian truck, which the soldiers were for loading themselves with until Mr. Church forbid it, telling them they might expect soon to have their hands full, and business without caring for plunder. Then, crossing the head of the creek into the neck, they again discovered fresh Indian tracks, very lately passed before them into the neck. They then got privately and undiscovered unto the fence of Captain Almy's pease field and divided into two parties. Mr. Church, keeping the one party with himself, sent the other with Lake, that was acquainted with the ground, on the other side. Two Indians were soon discovered coming out of the pease field towards them. When Mr. Church and those that were with him concealed themselves from them by falling flat on the ground; but the other division, not using the same caution, were seen by the enemy, which occasioned them to run; which, when Mr. Church perceived, he showed himself to them and called, telling them he desired but to speak with them and would not hurt them. But they ran, and Church pursued. The Indians climbed over a fence, and one of them, facing about, discharged his piece, but without effect on the English. One of the English soldiers ran up to the fence and fired upon him that had discharged his piece, and they concluded by the yelling they heard that the Indian was wounded; but the Indians soon got into the thickets, whence they saw them no more for the present.

Mr. Church, then marching over a plain piece of ground where the woods were very thick on one side, ordered his little company to march at double distance, to make as big a show (if they should be discovered) as might be. But, before they saw anybody, they were saluted with a volley of fifty or sixty guns. Some bullets came very surprisingly near Mr. Church, who, starting, looked behind him to see what was become of his men, expecting to have seen half of them dead, but, seeing them all upon their legs and briskly firing at the smokes of the enemy's guns (for that was all that was then to be seen), he blessed God and called to his men not to discharge all their guns at once, lest the enemy should take the advantage of such an opportunity to run upon them with their hatchets.

Their next motion was immediately into the pease field. When they came to the fence, Mr. Church bid as many as had not discharged their guns to clap under the fence and lie close, while the other, at some distance in the field, stood to charge, hoping that if the enemy should creep to the fence to gain a shot at those that were charging their guns, they might be surprised by those that lay under the fence. But casting his eyes to the side of the hill above them, the hill seemed to move, being covered over with Indians, with their bright guns glittering in the sun and running in a circumference with a design to surround them.

Seeing such multitudes surrounding him and his little company, it put him upon thinking what was become of the boats that were ordered to attend him. And, looking up, he spied them ashore at Sandy Point, on the Island side of the river, with a number of horse and foot by them, and wondered what should be the occasion, until he was afterwards informed that the boats had been over that morning from the Island and had landed a party of men at Fogland, that were designed in Punkatees Neck to fetch off some cattle and horses, but were ambuscadoed and many of them wounded by the enemy.

Now our gentlemen's courage and conduct were both put to the test; he encour-
ages his men and orders some to run and take a wall to shelter before the enemy
gained it. 'Twas time for them now to think of escaping if they knew which way.
Mr. Church orders his men to strip to their white shirts, that the Islanders might discover them to be Englishmen, and then orders three guns to be fired distinct, hoping
it might be observed by their friends on the opposite shore. The men that were ordered to take the wall, being very hungry, stopped a while among the pease to gather
a few, being about four rod from the wall. The enemy, from behind it, hailed them
with a shower of bullets, but soon all but one came tumbling over an old hedge
down the bank where Mr. Church and the rest were, and told him that his brother,
B. Southworth, who was the man that was missing, was killed, that they saw him
fall. And so they did indeed see him fall, but 'twas without a shot, and lay no longer
than till he had opportunity to clap a bullet into one of the enemy's forehead, and
then came running to his company.

The meanness of the English's powder was now their greatest misfortune when
they were immediately upon this beset with multitudes of Indians, who possessed
themselves of every rock, stump, tree, or fence that was in sight, firing upon them
without ceasing, while they had no other shelter but a small bank and a bit of a water fence. And yet, to add to the disadvantage of this little handful of distressed men,
the Indians also possessed themselves of the ruins of a stone house that overlooked
them, and of the black rocks to the southward of them, so that now they had no way
to prevent lying quite open to some or the other of the enemy but to heap up stones
before them, as they did, and still bravely and wonderfully defended themselves
against all the numbers of the enemy.

At length came over one of the boats from the Island shore, but the enemy plied
their shot so warmly to her as made her keep at some distance. Mr. Church desired
them to send their canoe ashore to fetch them on board, but no persuasions nor arguments could prevail with them to bring their canoe to shore. Which some of Mr.
Church's men perceiving, began to cry out, For God's sake to take them off, for their
ammunition was spent. Mr. Church, being sensible of the danger of the enemy's
hearing their complaints and being made acquainted with the weakness and scanti-
ness of their ammunition, fiercely called to the boat's master and bid either send his
canoe ashore or else begone presently or he would fire upon him.

Away goes the boat and leaves them still to shift for themselves. But then another

At Philip's death Benjamin Church's ambivalence was clear; he called the sachem both "a doleful, great, naked, dirty beast" and "a very great man [who] had made many a man afraid of him." (Courtesy of the Haffenreffer Museum of Anthropology, Brown University)

difficulty arose; the enemy, seeing the boat leave them, were reanimated and fired thicker and faster than ever. Upon which, some of the men that were lightest of foot began to talk of attempting an escape by flight, until Mr. Church solidly convinced them of the impracticableness of it, and encouraged them yet; told them that he had observed so much of the remarkable and wonderful Providence of God hitherto preserving them, that encouraged him to believe with much confidence that God would yet preserve them; that not a hair of their head should fall to the ground, bid them be patient, courageous, and prudently sparing of their ammunition, and he made no doubt but they should come well off yet, etc., until his little army again re-solve, one and all, to stay with and stick by him. One of them, by Mr. Church's order, was pitching a flat stone up on end before him in the sand when a bullet from the enemy, with a full force, struck the stone while he was pitching it on end, which put the poor fellow to a miserable start, till Mr. Church called upon him to observe how God directed the bullets that the enemy could not hit him when in the same place, yet could hit the stone as it was erected.

While they were thus making the best defense they could against their numer-ous enemies that made the woods ring with their constant yelling and shouting; and, night coming on, somebody told Mr. Church they spied a sloop up the river as far as Gold [Gould] Island that seemed to be coming down towards them. He looked up and told them succor was now coming, for he believed it was Captain Golding [Goulding] whom he knew to be a man for business and would certainly fetch them off if he came. The wind being fair, the vessel was soon with them; and Captain Golding it was. Mr. Church (as soon as they came to speak one with another) de-sired him to come to anchor at such a distance from the shore that he might veer out his cable and ride afloat, and let slip his canoe that it might drive ashore, which di-rections Captain Golding observed; but the enemy gave him such a warm salute that his sails, color, and stern were full of bullet holes.

The canoe came ashore but was so small that she would not bear above two men at a time, and when two were got aboard, they turned her loose to drive ashore for two more, and sloop's company kept the Indians in play the while. But when at last it came to Mr. Church's turn to go aboard, he had left his hat and cutlass at the well where he went to drink when he first came down. He told his company he would never go off and leave his hat and cutlass for the Indians; they should never have that to reflect upon him. Though he was much dissuaded from it, yet he would go fetch them. He put all the powder he had left into his gun (and a poor charge it was) and went presenting his gun at the enemy until he took up what he went for. At his re-turn he discharged his gun at the enemy to bid them farewell, for that time; but had not powder enough to carry the bullet halfway to them.

Two bullets from the enemy struck the canoe as he went on board; one grazed the hair of his head a little before; another struck in a small stake that stood right against the middle of his breast.

Now this gentleman with his army making in all 20 men, himself and his pilot being numbered with them, got all safe aboard after six hour's engagement with 300 Indians, whose number we were told afterwards by some of themselves. A deliverance which that good gentleman often mentions to the glory of God and His protecting providence.

THE GREAT SWAMP FIGHT

And now strong suspicions began to arise of the Narraganset Indians, that they were ill-affected and designed mischief; and so the event soon discovered. The next winter they began their hostilities upon the English. The United Colonies then agreed to send an army to suppress them. Governor Winslow to command the army. He, undertaking the expedition, invited Mr. Church to command a company in the expedition, which he declined. Craving excuse from taking commission, he promised to wait upon him as a reformado through the expedition. Having ridden with the General to Boston, and from thence to Rehoboth, upon the General's request he went thence the nearest way over the ferries with Major Smith to his garrison in the Narraganset country to prepare and provide for the coming of General Winslow; who marched round through the country with his army, proposing by night to surprise Pumham (a certain Naraganset sachem) and his town; but, being aware of the approach of our army, made their escape into the deserts.

But Mr. Church, meeting with fair winds, arrived safe at the Major's garrison in the evening. And soon began to enquire after the enemy's resorts, wigwams or sleeping places; and having gained some intelligence, he proposed to the Eldrigers and some other brisk hands that he met with, to attempt the surprising of some of the enemy to make a present of to the General, when he should arrive; which might advantage his design. Being brisk blades, they readily complied with the motion and were soon upon their march. The night was very cold but blessed with the moon. Before the day broke they effected their exploit and by the rising of the sun arrived at the Major's garrison, where they met the General and presented him with eighteen of the enemy they had captured. The General, pleased with the exploit, gave them thanks, particularly to Mr. Church, the mover and chief actor of the business. And sending two of them [as] a present to Boston, smiling on Mr. Church, told him that he made no doubt but his faculty would supply them with Indian boys enough before the war was ended.

Their next move was to a swamp which the Indians had fortified with a fort. Mr. Church rode in the General's guard when the bloody engagement began; but being impatient of being out of the heat of the action, importunately begged leave of the General that he might run down to the assistance of his friends. The General yielded to his request, provided he could rally some hands to go with him. Thirty men immediately drew out and followed him. They entered the swamp and passed over the log that was the passage into the fort, where they saw many men and several valiant captains lie slain. Mr. Church, spying Captain Gardner of Salem amidst the wigwams in the east end of the fort, made towards him, but on a sudden, while they were looking each other in the face, Captain Gardner settled down, Mr. Church stepped to him and, seeing the blood run down his cheek, lifted up his cap, and called him by his name. He looked up in his face, but spoke not a word, being mortally shot through the head. And, observing his wound, Mr. Church found the ball entered his head on the side that was next the upland where the English entered the swamp. Upon which, having ordered some care to be taken of the Captain, he dispatched information to the General that the best and forwardest of his army that hazarded their lives to enter the fort, upon the muzzle of the enemy's guns, were shot in their backs and killed by them that lay behind.

Mr. Church with his small company hastened out of the fort (that the English were now possessed of) to get a shot at the Indians that were in the swamp and kept firing upon them. He soon met with a broad bloody track, where the enemy had fled with their wounded men. Following hard in the track, he soon spied one of the enemy, who clapped his gun across his breast, made towards Mr. Church, and beckoned to him with his hand. Mr. Church immediately commanded no man to hurt him, hoping by him to have gained some intelligence of the enemy that might be of advantage, but it unhappily fell out that a fellow that had lagged behind coming up, shot down the Indian, to Mr. Church's great grief and disappointment. But immediately they heard a great shout of the enemy which seemed to be behind them, or between them and the fort; and discovered them running from tree to tree to gain advantages of firing upon the English that were in the fort. Mr. Church's great difficulty now was how to discover himself to his friends in the forts, using several inventions, till at length [he] gained an opportunity to call to and inform a sergeant in the fort that he was there and might be exposed to their shots unless they observed it.

By this time he discovered a number of the enemy almost within shot of him, making towards the fort. Mr. Church and his company were favored by a heap of brush that was between them and the enemy and prevented their being discovered to them. Mr. Church had given his men their particular orders for firing upon the enemy; and as they were rising up to make their shot, the aforementioned sergeant in the fort called out to them, for God's sake not to fire, for he believed they were some of their friend-Indians. They clapped down again but were soon sensible of the sergeant's mistake. The enemy got to the top of the tree, the body whereof the sergeant stood upon, and there clapped down out of sight of the fort, but, all this while, never discovered Mr. Church, who observed them to keep gathering unto that place, until there seemed to be a formidable black heap of them.

"Now, brave boys," said Mr. Church to his men, "if we mind our hits, we may have a brave shot, and let our sign for firing on them be their rising up to fire into the fort." It was not long before the Indians, rising up as one body, designed to pour a volley into the fort, when our Church nimbly started up and gave them such a round volley and unexpected clap on their backs, that they who escaped with their lives were so surprised that they scampered, they knew not whither themselves.

CHURCH WOUNDED

About a dozen of them ran right over the log into the fort and took into a sort of hovel that was built with poles, after the manner of a corn crib. Mr. Church's men having their cartridges fixed, were soon ready to obey his order, which was immediately to charge and run upon the hovel and over-set it, calling as he ran on to some that were in the fort to assist him in over-setting of it. They no sooner came to face the enemy's shelter, but Mr. Church discovered that one of them had found a hold to point his gun through, right at him; but, however, encouraged his company and ran right on till he was struck with three bullets, one in his thigh, which was near half of it cut off as it glanced on the joint of the hip bone; another through the gatherings of his breeches and draws, with a small flesh wound; a third pierced his pocket and wounded a pair of mittens that he had borrowed of Captain Prentice, [which] being wrapped up together, had the misfortune of having many holes cut through them with one bullet. But however, he made shift to keep on his legs and nimbly discharged his gun at them that wounded him.

Being disenabled now to go a step, his men would have carried him off, but he forbid their touching him until they had perfected their project of over-setting the enemy's shelter; bid them run, for now the Indians had no guns charged. While he was urging them to run on, the Indians began to shoot arrows, and with one pierced through the arm of an Englishman that had hold of Mr. Church's arm to support him.

The English, in short, were discouraged and drew back. And by this time the English people in the fort had begun to set fire to the wigwams and houses in the fort, which Mr. Church labored hard to prevent. They told him they had orders from the General to burn them; he begged them to forebear until he had discoursed [with] the General; and hastening to him, he begged [him] to spare the wigwams in the fort from fire, told him the wigwams were musketproof, being all lined with baskets and tubs of grain and other provisions sufficient to supply the whole army until the spring of the year, and every wounded man might have a good warm house to lodge in, which otherwise would necessarily perish with the storms and cold. And moreover, that the army had no other provision to trust unto or depend upon; that he knew that Plymouth forces had not so much as one biscuit left, for he had seen their last dealt out.

The General, advising a few words with the gentlemen that were about him, moved toward the fort, designing to ride in himself and bring in the whole army. But just as he was entering the swamp, one of his captains met him and asked him whither he was going? He told him into the fort. The Captain laid hold of his horse and told him his life was worth an hundred of theirs and he should not expose himself. The General told him that he supposed the brunt was over and that Mr. Church had informed him that the fort was taken. And, as the case was circumstanced, he was of the mind that it was most practicable for him and his army to shelter themselves in the fort. The Captain, in a great heat, replied that Church lied and told the General that if he moved another step towards the fort he would shoot his horse under him.

Then bustled up another gentleman, a certain doctor, and opposed Mr. Church's advice, and said, if it were complied with, it would kill more men than the enemy had killed. For, said he, "by tomorrow the wounded men will be so stiff that there will be no moving of them." And, looking upon Mr. Church and seeing the blood flowing apace from his wounds, told him that if he gave such advice as that was, he should bleed to death like a dog before they would endeavor to staunch his blood. Though after they had prevailed against his advice, they were sufficiently kind to him. And burning up all the houses and provisions in the fort, the army returned the same night in the storm and cold.

328

And I suppose everyone that is acquainted with the circumstances of that night's march deeply laments the miseries that attended them, especially the wounded and dying men. But it mercifully came to pass that Captain Andrew Belcher arrived at Mr. Smith's that very night from Boston with a vessel loaded with provisions for the army, who must otherwise have perished for want. Some of the enemy that were then in the fort have since informed us that nearly a third of the Indians belonging to all that Narraganset country were killed by the English and by the cold that night, that they fled out of their fort so hastily that they carried nothing with them, that if the English had kept in the fort, the Indians had certainly been necessitated either to surrender themselves to them or to have perished by hunger and the severity of the season.

Some time after this fort fight, a certain Sogkonate Indian, hearing Mr. Church relate the manner of his being wounded, told him that he did not know but he himself was the Indian that wounded him, for that he was one of that company of Indians that Mr. Church made a shot upon when they were rising up to make a shot into the fort; they were in number about 60 or 70, that just then came down from Pumham's town, and never before then fired a gun against the English; that when Mr. Church fired upon them, he killed 14 dead on the spot and wounded a greater number than he killed, many of which died afterwards with their wounds, in the cold and storm the following night.

Mr. Church was moved with other wounded men over to Rhode Island, where in about a month's time he was in some good measure recovered of his wounds and the fever that attended them. And then went over to the General to take his leave of him, with a design to return home.

TACTICS OF INDIAN WARFARE

He soon went out again, and this stroke he drove many weeks. And, when he took any number of prisoners, he would pick out some that he took a fancy to and would tell them, he took a particular fancy to them and had chose them for himself to make soldiers of; and, if any would behave themselves well, he would do well by them and they should be his men and not sold out of the country. If he perceived they looked surly, and his Indian soldiers called them "treacherous dogs," as some of them would sometimes do, all the notice he would take of it would only be to clap them on the back and tell them, "Come, come, you look wild and surly, and mutter, but that signifies nothing. These, my best soldiers were a little while ago as wild and surly as you are now. By that time you have been but one day along with me, you'll love me too, and be as brisk as any of them."

And it proved so. For there was none of them but, after they had been a little while with him, and seen his behavior, and how cheerful and successful his men were, would be as ready to pilot him to any place where the Indians dwelt or haunted (though their own fathers or nearest relations should be among them), or to fight for him, as any of his own men.

Captain Church was in two particulars much advantaged by the great English army that was now abroad. One was, that they drove the enemy down to that part of the country, viz., to the eastward of Taunton River, by which means his business was nearer home. The other was that whenever he fell on with a push upon any body of the enemy (were they never so many), they fled, expecting the great army. And his manner of marching through the woods was such, as if he were discovered, they appeared to be more than they were. For he always marched at a wide distance, one from another, partly for their safety; and this was an Indian custom, to march thin and scatter. Captain Church enquired of some of the Indians that were become his soldiers, how they got such advantage often of the English in their marches through the woods. They told him that the Indians gained great advantage of the English by two things: the Indians always took care in their marches and fights not to come too thick together. But the English always kept in a heap together; that it was as easy to hit them as to hit an house. The other was, that if any time they discovered a company of English soldiers in the woods they knew that there was all, for the English never scattered, but the Indians always divided and scattered.

Captain Church, now at Plymouth, something or other happened that kept him at home a few days, until a post came to Marshfield on the Lord's Day morning, informing the Governor that a great army of Indians were discovered, who, it was supposed, were designing to get over the river towards Taunton or Bridgewater to attack those towns that lay on that side the river. The Governor hastened to Plymouth, raised what men he could by the way, came to Plymouth in the beginning of the forenoon exercise, sent for Captain Church out of the meeting-house, gave him the news, and desired him immediately to rally what of his company he could; and what men he had raised should join them. The Captain bestirs himself, but found no bread in the storehouse and so was forced, to run from house to house to get household bread for their march. But this, nor anything else, prevented his marching by the beginning of the afternoon exercise. Marching with what men were ready, he took with him the post that came from Bridgewater to pilot him to the place where he thought he might meet with the enemy.

In the evening they heard a smart firing at a distance from them, but, it being near night, and the firing but of short continuance, they missed the place and went into Bridgewater town. It seems, the occasion of the firing was that Philip, finding that Captain Church made that side of the country too hot for him, designed to return to the other side of the country that he came last from. And, to Taunton River with his company, they felled a great tree across the river for a bridge to pass over on. And, just as Philip's old Uncle Akkompoin and some other of his chiefs were passing over the tree, some brisk Bridgewater lads had ambushed them, fired upon them, and killed the old man and several others, which put a stop to their coming over the river that night.

Next morning, Captain Church moved very early with his company which was increased by many of Bridgewater that listed under him for that expedition; and by their piloting, he soon came very still, to the top of the great tree which the enemy had fallen across the river. And the Captain spied an Indian sitting upon the stump of it on the other side of the river. And he clapped his gun up, and had doubtless dispatched him but that one of his own Indians called hastily to him, not to fire, for he believed it was one of his own men. Upon which, the Indian upon the stump looked about, and Captain Church's Indian, his face, perceived his mistake, for he knew him to be Philip; clapped up his gun and fired, but it was too late, for Philip immediately threw himself off the stump, leapt down a bank on the side of the river, and made his escape.

PHILIP KILLED

Then Captain Church offered Captain Golding that he should have the honor (if he would please accept of it) to beat up Philip's headquarters. He accepted the offer and had his allotted number drawn out to him, and the pilot. Captain Church's instructions to him were to be very careful in his approach to the enemy, and be sure not to show himself until by daylight they might see and discern their own men from the enemy. Told him also that his custom in the like cases was to creep with his company on their bellies, until they came as near as they could; and that as soon as the enemy discovered them, they would cry out; and that was the word for his men to fire and fall on. Directed him, when the enemy should start and take into the swamp, they should pursue with speed, every man shouting and making what noise they could; for he would give orders to his ambuscade to fire on any that should come silently.

Captain Church knowing it was Philip's custom to be foremost in flight, went down to the swamp and gave Captain William of Situate the command of the right wing of the ambush, and placed an Englishman and an Indian together behind such shelters of trees, that he could find and took care to place them at such distance as none might pass undiscovered between them; charged them to be careful of them-selves and of hurting their friends; and to fire at any that should come silently through the swamp.

But it being somewhat further through the swamp than he was aware of, he wanted men to make up his ambuscade. Having placed what men he had, he took Major Sanford by the hand, said, "Sir, I have so placed them that 'tis scarce possible Philip should escape them."

The same moment a shot whistled over their heads, and then the noise of a gun towards Philip's camp. Captain Church at first thought it might be some gun fired by accident, but, before he could speak, a whole volley followed, which was earlier than he expected. One of Philip's gang going forth to ease himself, when he had done, looked around him, and Captain Golding thought the Indian looked right at him (though probably 'twas but his conceit), so fired at him, and, upon his firing, the whole company that were with him fired upon the enemy's shelter before the In-dians had time to rise from their sleep, and so overshot them. But their shelter was open on that side next the swamp, built so on purpose for the convenience of flight on occasion. They were soon in the swamp, and Philip the foremost, who, starting at the first gun, threw his petunk and powder horn over his head, catched up his gun, and ran as fast as he could scamper, without any more clothes than his small breeches and stockings, and ran directly upon two of Captain Church's ambush.

They let him come fair within shot, and the Englishman's gun missing fire, he bid the Indian fire away. And he did so to purpose, sent one musket bullet through his heart, and another not above two inches from it. He fell upon his face in the mud and water, with his gun under him.

By the time, the enemy perceived they were waylaid on the east side of the swamp, tacked short about. One of the enemy who seemed to be a great surly old fellow, hallooed with a loud voice and often called out, "Iootash! Iootatash!"

Captain Church called to his Indian, Peter, and asked him, who that was that called so? He answered, it was old Annawon, Philip's great captain, calling on his soldiers to stand to it and fight stoutly.

Now the enemy, finding that place of the swamp which was not ambushed, many of them made their escape in the English tracks. The man that had shot down Philip ran with all speed to Captain Church and informed him of his exploit, who commanded him to be silent about it and let no man more know it until they had drove the swamp clean. But, when they had drove the swamp through and found the enemy had escaped, or at least the most of them, and the sun now up, and so the dew gone, that they could not so easily track them, the whole company met together at the place where the enemies' night shelter was. And then Captain Church gave them the news of Philip's death upon which the whole army gave three loud huzzas.

Captain Church ordered his body to be pulled out of the mire on to the upland, so some of Captain Church's Indians took hold of him by his stockings, and some, by his small breeches (being otherwise naked), and drew him through the mud unto the upland. And a doleful, great, naked, dirty beast he looked like.

Captain Church then said that, forasmuch as he had caused many an Englishman's body to lie unburied and rot above ground, that not one of his bones should be buried. And, calling his old Indian executioner bid him behead and quarter him.

Accordingly, he came with his hatchet and stood over him, but, before he struck, he made a small speech, directing it to Philip, and said, he had been a very great man, and had made many a man afraid of him, but so big as he was, he would now chop his ass for him. And so went to work and did as he was ordered.

Philip, having one very remarkable hand, being much scarred, occasioned by the splitting of a pistol in it formerly, Captain Church gave the head and that hand to Alderman, the Indian who shot him, to show to such gentleman as would bestow gratuities upon him. And accordingly, he got many a penny by it.

This being on the last day of the week, the Captain with his company returned to the Island, tarried there until Tuesday; and then went off and ranged through all the woods to Plymouth, and received their premium, which was thirty shillings per head for all the enemies which they had killed or taken, instead of all wages. And Philip's head went at the same price. Methinks it's scanty reward and poor encouragement; though it was better than what had been some time before. For this march they received four shillings and sixpence a man, which was all the reward they had, except the honor of killing Philip. This was in the latter end of August, 1676.

THE CAPTURE OF ANAWAN

◦§ After Philip's death, Church searched for Anawan, Philip's "chief captain," who "with his company was ranging about their woods and was very pernicious to Rehobeth and Swansey." Church's Indian scouts captured a small party of hostile Indians followed by the capture of an old warrior and young Indian woman whom Church interrogates in the following manner.

Captain Church immediately examined them apart, telling them what they must trust to if they told false stories. He asked the young woman, what company they came last from? She said, from Captain Annawon's. He asked her, how many were in company with him when she left him. She said, 50 or 60. He asked her, how any miles it was to the place where she left him? She said, she did not understand miles, but he was up in Squannaconk Swamp.

The old man, who had been one of Philip's Council upon examination, gave exactly the same account. Captain Church asked him, if they could get there that night? He said, if they went presently and traveled stoutly, they might get there by sunset. He asked, whither he was going? He answered, that Annawon had sent him down to look for some Indians that were gone into Mount-hope Neck to kill provisions. Captain Church let him know that those Indians were all his prisoners.

By this time came the Indian soldier and brought his father and one Indian more. The Captain was now in great straight of mind what to do next. He had a mind to give Annawon a visit, now knew where to find him, but his company was very small, but half-a-dozen men beside himself, and was under a necessity to send somebody back to acquaint his lieutenant and company with his proceedings. However, he asked his small company that were with him, whether they would willingly go with him and give Annawon a visit? They told him, they were always ready to obey his commands. But withal told him, that they knew this Captain Annawon was a great soldier, that he had been a valiant captain under Asuhmequn, Philip's father; and that he had been Philip's chieftain all this war, a very subtle man and of great resolution, and had often said that he would never be taken alive by the English. And, moreover, they knew that the men that were with him were resolute fellows, some of Philip's chief soldiers and therefore feared whether it was practicable to make an attempt upon him with so small a handful of assistants as now were with him. Told him further, that it would be a pity that, after all the great things he had done, he should throw away his life at last.

Upon which he replied, that he doubted not Annawon was subtle and valiant man, that he had a long time but in vain sought for him, and never till now could find his quarters; and he was very loath to miss of the opportunity and doubted not but that if they would cheerfully go with him, the same Almighty Providence that had hitherto protected and befriended them would do so still.

Upon this, with one consent they said they would go.

Captain Church then turned to one Cook, of Plymouth (the only Englishman then with him), and asked him, what he thought if it? Who replied, "Sir, I am never afraid of going anywhere when you are with me."

Then Captain Church asked the old Indian if he could carry his horse with him? (for he conveyed a horse thus far with him).

He replied that it was impossible for an horse to pass the swamps. Therefore, he sent away his new Indian soldier with his father and the Captain's horse to his lieutenant and orders for him to move to Taunton with the prisoners, to secure them there, and to come out in the morning in the Rehoboth Road, in which he might expect to meet him, if he were alive and had success.

The Captain then asked the old fellow, if he would pilot him unto Annawon? He answered that he, having given him his life, he was obliged to serve him. He bid him move on then; and they followed. The old man would out-travel them, so far sometimes that they were almost out of sight. Looking over his shoulder and seeing them behind, he would halt. Just as the sun was setting, the old man made a full stop and sat down, the company coming up also sat down, being all weary.

Captain Church asked, "What news?" He answered that about that time in the evening Captain Annawon sent out his scouts to see if the coast were clear, and, as soon as it began to grow dark, the scouts return. And then (said he), we may move again securely.

When it began to grow dark, the old man stood up again. Captain Church asked him if he would take a gun and fight for him? He bowed very low and prayed him not to impose such a thing upon him, as to fight against Captain Annawon, his old friend. "But," says he, "I will go along with you, and be helpful to you, and will lay hands on any man that shall offer to hurt you."

It being now pretty dark, they moved close together. Anon, they heard a noise; the Captain stayed the old man with his hand and asked his own men what noise they thought it might be? They concluded it to be the pounding of a mortar. The old man had given Captain Church a description of the place where Annawon now lay, and of the difficulty of getting at him. Being sensible that they were pretty near them, with two of his Indians he creeps to the edge of the rocks, from whence he could see their camp.

He saw three companies of Indians at a little distance from each other, being easy to be discovered by the light of their fires. He saw also the great Annawon and his company, who had formed his camp of kennelling-place by felling a tree under the side of the great clefts of rocks, and setting a row of birch bushes up against it, where he himself and his son and some of his chiefs had taken up their lodging, and made great fires without them, and had their pot and kettles boiling and spits roast- ing. Their arms also he discovered, all set together in a place fitted for the purpose, standing up on end against a stick lodged in two crotches, and a mat placed over them, to keep them from the wet or dew. The old Annawon's feet and his son's head were so near the arms as almost to touch them. But the rocks were so steep that it was impossible to get down but as they lowered themselves by the boughs and the bushes that grew in the cracks of the rock.

Captain Church, creeping back again to the old man, asked him if there was no possibility of getting at them some other way. He answered, no, that he and all that belonged to Annawon were ordered to come that way, and none could come any other way without difficulty or danger of being shot.

Captain Church then ordered the old man and his daughter to go down fore- most, with their baskets at their backs, so that, when Annawon saw them with their baskets, he should not mistrust the intrigue. Captain Church and his handful of soldiers crept down also under the shadows of these two and their baskets, and the Captain himself crept close behind the old man, with his hatchet in his hand, and stepped over the young man's head to the arms. The young Annawon, discovering of him, whipped his blanket over his head and shrunk up in a heap. The old Captain Annawon started up on his breech and cried out "Howoh!" and, despairing of escape, threw himself back again and lay silent until Captain Church had secured all the arms.

And, having secured that company, he sent his Indian soldiers to the other fires and companies, giving them instructions what to do and say. Accordingly, they went into the midst of them. When they discovered themselves who they were, told them that their Captain Annawon was taken, and it would be best for them quietly and peaceably to surrender themselves which would procure good quarter for them. Otherwise, if they should pretend to resist or make their escape, it would be in vain, and they could expect no other but that Captain Church with his great army, who had now entrapped them, would cut them to pieces. Told them also if they would submit themselves, and deliver up all their arms unto them, and keep every man his place until it was day, they would assure them that their Captain Church who had been so kind to themselves when they surrendered to him, should be as kind unto them.

Now, they being old acquaintance, and many of them relations, did much the readier give heed to what they said, and complied and surrendered up their arms unto them, both their guns and hatchets, and were forthwith carried to Captain Church.

Things being so far settled, Captain Church asked Annawon what he had for supper, for (said he), "I am come to sup with you."

"Taubut," said Annawon, with a big voice; and looking about upon his women, bid them hasten and get Captain Church and his company some supper; then turned to Captain Church and asked him whether he would eat cow-beef or horse-beef. The Captain told him cow-beef would be most acceptable. It was soon got ready, and, pulling his little bag of salt out of his pocket, which was all the provision he brought with him, this seasoned his cow-beef so that with it and the dried green corn, which the old squaw was pounding in the mortar, while they were sliding down the rocks, he made a very hearty supper. And this pounding in the mortar proved lucky for Captain Church's getting down the rocks, for when the old squaw pounded, they moved, and when she ceased to turn the corn, they ceased creeping. The noise of the mortar prevented the enemies' hearing their creeping; and the corn being now dressed, supplied the want of bread and gave a fine relish with the cow-beef.

Supper being over, Captain Church sent two of his men to inform the other companies that he had killed Philip, and had taken their friends in Mount-hope Neck, but had spared their lives, and that he had subdued now all the enemy (he supposed) expecting this company of Annawon's, and now, if they would be orderly and keep their places until morning, they should have good quarter, and that he would carry them to Taunton, where they might see their friends again. The messengers returned that the Indians yielded to his proposals.

Captain Church thought it was now time for him to take a nap, having had no sleep in two days and one night before. Told his men that, if they would let him sleep two hours, they should sleep all the rest of the night. He laid himself down and endeavored to sleep, but all disposition to sleep departed from him. After he had lain a little while, he looked up to see how his watch managed, but found them all fast asleep.

Now, Captain Church had told Captain Annawon's company, as he had ordered his Indians to tell the others, that their lives should all be spared, excepting Captain Annawon's, and it was not in his power to promise him his life, but he must carry him to his masters at Plymouth, and he would entreat them for his life.

Now, when Captain Church found not only his own men, but all the Indians fast asleep, Annawon only excepted, whom he perceived was as broad awake as himself; and so they lay looking one upon the other perhaps an hour. Captain Church said nothing to him, for he could not speak Indian, and thought Annawon could not speak English. At length, Annawon raised himself up, cast off his blanket and with no more clothes than his small breeches, walked a little way back from the company. Captain Church thought no other but that he had occasion to ease himself, and so walked to some distance rather than offend him with the stink. But, by and by, he was gone out of sight and hearing; and then Captain Church began to suspect some ill-design in him, and got all the guns close to him, and crowded himself close under young Annawon, that if he should anywhere get a gun, he should not make a shot at him without endangering his son. Lying very still awhile, waiting for the event, at length he heard somebody coming the same way that Annawon went. The moon now shining bright, he saw him at a distance coming with something in his hands, and, coming up to Captain Church, he fell upon his knees before him and offered him what he had brought. And speaking in plain English, said, "Great

Captain, you have killed Philip and conquered his country, for I believe that I and my company are the last that war against the English, so suppose the war is ended by your means; and therefore these things belong unto you."

PHILIP'S REGALIA

Then, opening his pack, he pulled out Philip's belt, curiously wrought with wompom, being nine inches broad, wrought with black and white wompom in various figures and flowers, and pictures of many birds and beasts. This, when hung upon Captain Church's shoulders, it reached his ankles. And another belt of wompom he presented him with, wrought after the former manner, which Philip was wont to put upon his head. It had two flags on the back part which hung down on his back, and another small belt with a star upon the end of it, which he used to hang on his breast. And they were all edged with red hair, which Annawon said they got in the Muh-hog's country. Then he pulled out two horns of glazed powder and a red cloth blanket. He told Captain Church, these were Philip's royalties which he was wont to adorn himself with when he sat in state. That he thought himself happy that he had an opportunity to present them to Captain Church, who had won them. Spent the remainder of the night in discourse, and gave an account of what mighty success he had formally in wars against many nations of Indians, when served Asuhmequin, Philip's father.

In the morning as soon as it was light, the Captain marched with his prisoners out of that swampy country towards Taunton, met his lieutenant and company about four miles out of town, who expressed a great deal of joy to see him again and said 'twas more than ever he expected. They went into Taunton, were civilly and kindly treated by the inhabitants, refreshed and rested themselves that night.

Early next morning, the Captain took old Annawon, and half-a-dozen Indian soldiers, and his own man, and went to Rhode Island, sending the rest of his company and his prisoners by his lieutenant to Plymouth. Tarrying two or three days upon the Island, he then went to Plymouth, and carried his wife and his two children with him.

◄§ The colonists showed no mercy to noble Anawon, beheading him a few days after his capture.

The attack on the Rowlandson garrison, pictured here, was reenacted dozens of times in garrisons around New England throughout 1675 and 1676. (Courtesy of the Haffenreffer Museum of Anthropology, Brown University)

· Chapter 9 ·
Excerpts from The Narrative of the Captivity and Restoration of Mrs. Mary Rowlandson

INTRODUCTION TO MARY ROWLANDSON

MARY ROWLANDSON, of Lancaster Massachusetts, was taken captive by the Indians and held for eleven weeks and five days. She was the wife of Lancaster's first ordained minister, the Reverend Joseph Rowlandson, and their home also served as one of the town's garrisons. While her husband was away in Boston, pleading for additional troops to protect Lancaster, the Indians struck the town at dawn on February 10, 1676. It is estimated that forty-eight English settlers were either killed or taken captive that day, Rowlandson being one of the lucky or unlucky (depending on your outlook) to be taken captive.

Rowlandson suffered incredible hardships (as did her captors) as they traveled across central Massachusetts and into southern Vermont and New Hampshire. While other captives complained, and were quickly killed with a "knock on the head," Rowlandson survived by making herself useful to her captors, knitting shirts, caps, and stockings. Her inner fortitude, her faith, and innate survival skills allowed her to endure the ordeal of marching through winter's snows with little food, clothing, or shelter.

Rowlandson's narrative, which was quite popular when it first appeared in 1682, refers to each movement on her journey as a "remove." She chronicles twenty removes before her eventual release at Redemption Rock, located in present-day Princeton, Massachusetts on Route 140.

Her account is important not only for what it says about her ingenuity and courage, but also because it provides an inside look at what the Native Americans were thinking and experiencing. While captive she comes to know Indian leaders such as Weetamoe, Quannopin, and even King Philip.

341

EXCERPTS FROM THE NARRATIVE OF THE CAPTIVITY AND
RESTORATION OF MRS. MARY ROWLANDSON

On the tenth of February, 1676, came the Indians in great numbers upon Lancaster. Their first coming was about sun-rising. Hearing the noise of some guns, we looked out: several houses were burning, and the smoke ascending to heaven. There were five persons taken in one house: the father, the mother, and a suckling child they knocked on the head: the other two they took and carried away alive. There were two others, who being out of their garrison on some occasion, were set upon; one was knocked on the head, the other escaped. Another there was, who, running along, was shot and wounded, and fell down; he begged of them his life, promising them money, (as they told me,) but they would not hearken to him but knocked him in head, and stripped him naked and split open his bowels. Another, seeing many of the Indians about his barn, ventured and went out, but was quickly shot down. There were three others belonging to the same garrison who were killed; the Indians getting up upon the roof of the barn, had advantage to shoot down upon them over their fortification. Thus these murderous wretches went on burning and destroying [all] before them.

At length they came and beset our own house, and quickly it was the dolefullest day that ever mine eyes saw. The house stood upon the edge of a hill. Some of the Indians got behind the hill, others into the barn, and others behind anything that would shelter them, from all which places they shot against the house, so that the bullets seemed to fly like hail. And quickly they wounded one man among us, then another, and then a third. About two hours (according to my observation in that amazing time) they had been about the house before they prevailed to fire it (which they did with flax and hemp which they brought out of the barn—and there being no defense about the house, only two flankers at the two opposite corners, and one of them not finished). They fired it once, and one ventured out and quenched it; but they quickly fired it again, and that took.

Now is that dreadful hour come that I have often heard of, but now mine eyes see it. Some in our house were fighting for their lives, others wallowing in their blood, the house on fire over our heads, and the bloodey heathen ready to knock us on the

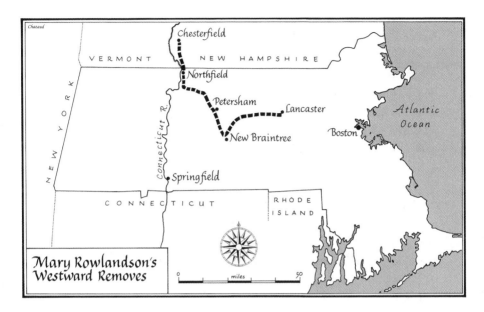

Mary Rowlandson's
Westward Removes

head if we stirred out. Now might we hear mothers and children crying out for themselves and one another, Lord, what shall we do?

Then I took my children (and one of my sisters her's) to go forth and leave the house. But as soon as we came to the door and appeared, the Indians shot so thick that the bullets rattled against the house as if one had taken an handful of stones and threw them, so that we were fain to give back. We had six stout dogs belonging to our garrison, but none of them would stir, though another time if an Indian had come to the door, they were ready to fly upon him and tear him down. The Lord hereby would make us the more to acknowledge his hand, and to see that our help is always in him. But out we must go, the fire increasing, and coming along behind us, roaring, and the Indians gaping before us with their guns, spears, and hatchets, to devour us. No sooner were we out of the house, but my brother-in-law (being before wounded, in defending the house, in or near the throat) fell down dead, whereat the Indians scornfully shouted, hallooed, and were presently upon him, stripping off his clothes. The bullets flying thick, one went through my side, and the same through the bowels and hand of my dear child in my arms. One of my elder sister's children, named William, had then his leg broken, which the Indians perceiving, they knocked him on the head. Thus were we butchered by those merciless heathens, standing amazed, with the blood running down to our heels. My eldest sister (Elizabeth) being yet in the house, and seeing those woeful sights, the infidels hauling mothers one way, and children another, and some wallowing in their blood, and her eldest son telling her that her son William was dead, and myself was wounded, she said, And, Lord let me die with them: which was no sooner said, but she was struck with a bullet, and fell down dead over the threshold. I hope she is reaping the fruit of her good labors, being faithful to the service of God in her place. In her younger years she lay under much trouble upon spiritual accounts, till it pleased God to make that precious scripture take hold of her heart, 2 Cor. xii. 9. And he said unto me, my grace is sufficient for thee. More than twenty years after, I have heard her tell how sweet and comfortable that place was to her. But to return: the Indians laid hold of us, pulling me one way, and the children another, and said, "Come, go along with us." I told them they would kill me. They answered, if I were willing to go along with them, they would not hurt me.

Oh! the doleful sight that now was to behold at this house! "Come, behold the works of the Lord, what desolation He has made in the earth." Of thirty-seven persons who were in this one house none escaped either present death or a bitter captivity save only one, who might say as he, Job 1:15, "And I only am escaped alone to tell the news." There were twelve killed, some shot, some stabbed with their spears, some knocked down with their hatchets. When we are in prosperity, oh, the little that we think of such dreadful sights, and to see our dear friends and relations lie bleeding out their heart-blood upon the ground! There was one who was chopped into the head with a hatchet and stripped naked, and yet was crawling up and down. It is a solemn sight to see so many Christians lying in their blood, some here and some there, like a company of sheep torn by wolves, all of them stripped naked by a company of hell-hounds, roaring, singing, ranting and insulting, as if they would have torn our very hearts out. Yet the Lord by his almighty power preserved a number of us from death, for there were twenty-four of us taken alive and carried captive.

I had often before this said that if the Indians should come I should choose rather to be killed by them than taken alive, but when it came to the trial, my mind changed; their glittering weapons so daunted my spirit that I chose rather to go along with those (as I may say) ravenous beasts than that moment to end my days. And that I may the better declare what happened to me during that grievous captivity, I shall particularly speak of the several removes we had up and down the wilderness.

◦§ Rowlandson's story now follows her days of captivity, most of which are in constant movement. The chapters in her book follow her "removes," or the different locations of her captivity, from her first remove to her twentieth and final remove. Her first night of captivity is spent on a hill overlooking the burning town of Lancaster. While the natives celebrate and feast upon captured farm animals, Rowlandson, stiff from her own wound, tries to comfort her wounded child through the night. The next morning they all trudge westward. Rowlandson, with her daughter in her arms, is allowed to ride on a horse part of the way, but falls over the horse's head because there is no saddle.

For the next three days they continue their trek, with no food and little water. Arriving at the Nipmuck village of Winimisset (along the Ware River in modern-day New Braintree), Rowlandson meets Robert Pepper, who was taken captive after being wounded during the ambush of Captain Beers' troops in Northfield in August 1675. Pepper tells Rowlandson how the Indians helped heal his wound by making a compact of oak leaves. Rowlandson decides to try the same technique and writes that "it cured me also."

On February 18 Rowlandson's wounded child dies, and the Indians bury her daughter on a hill. Also in the Winimisset Camp are two of Rowlandson's other children, and she is allowed briefly to see them. Rowlandson's "master" during captivity was Quannopin, a Narragansett sagamore married to Weetamoe (formerly the wife of King Philip's brother Wamsutta).

While still based at the Winimisset camp, warriors set out to attack Medfield, Massachusetts, on February 21, 1676. Rowlandson recounted the Indian's return from the attack.

◦§ ?◦

The next day, to this, the Indians returned from Medfield all the company, for those that belonged to the other small company came through the town that now we were at. But before they came to us, oh, the outrageous roaring and whooping that there was! They began their din about a mile before they came to us. By their noise and whooping they signified how many they had destroyed, which was at that time twenty-three. Those that were with us at home were gathered together as soon as they heard the whooping, and every time that the other went over their number, these at home gave (such) a shout that the very earth rung again. And thus they continued till those that had been upon the expedition were come up to the sagamore's wigwam. And then, oh, the hideous insulting and triumphing that there was over some Englishmen's scalps that they had taken (as their manner is) and brought with them! . . .

Now the Indians began to talk of removing from this place, some one way and some another. There were now besides myself nine English captives in this place, all of them children except one woman . . . The woman, Goodwife Joslin, told me she should never see me again and that she could find in her heart to run away; I wished her not to run away by any means, for we were near thirty miles from any English town and she very big with child and had but one week to reckon and another child in her arms, two years old, and bad rivers there were to go over, and we were feeble with our poor and coarse entertainment.

     This woman and her two-year-old child were later killed for complaining too much and begging to go home: They are tomahawked on the head and their bodies thrown into a fire; the Indians tell the other captive children that if they attempt to go home they "would serve them in a like manner."

     The next remove is to the Bacquag River (present-day Millers River in Orange, Massachusetts) and Rowlandson believes the reason for this "fifth remove" is because English soldiers are approaching. Rowlandson recounts how the soldiers stopped their approach when they reached a river, criticizing that "God did not give them courage or activity to go over after us."

     Food is scarce for both Rowlandson and her captives, and she writes how the Indians boiled an old horse's leg, "and we drank of the broth as soon as it was ready." The sixth remove finds her in Squakeag—present-day Northfield—at a huge camp where the "Indians were as thick as the trees." After the eighth remove, to the west side of the Connecticut River, Rowlandson comes face to face with King Philip. Curiously, her writing on the subject is as much about the evils of smoking as it is about King Philip.

     However, the reader sees an indication of King Philip's kindness toward Rowlandson, and his concern for his own son.

Mary Rowlandson's time with the Indians was marked by constant movement, a tactic they used throughout the war to avoid costly pitched battles with English colonial troops. (From History of King Philip, *John S.C. Abbott, 1899)*

❧

Then I went to see King Philip. He bade me come in and sit down and asked me whether I would smoke it (a usual compliment nowadays among saints and sinners), but this no way suited me. For though I had formerly used tobacco, yet I had left it ever since I was first taken. Its seems to be a bait the devil lays to make men lose their precious time. I remember with shame how formerly when I had taken two or three pipes I was presently ready for another, such a bewitching thing it is. But I thank God He has now given me power over it; surely there are many who may be better employed than to lie sucking a stinking tobacco pipe.

Now the Indians gather their forces to go against Northampton. Overnight one went about yelling and hooting to give notice of the design, whereupon they fell to boiling of groundnuts and parching of corn (as many as had it) for their provision, and in the morning away they went. During my abode in this place Philip spoke to me to make a shirt for his boy, which I did, for which he gave me a shilling. I offered the money to my master, but he bade me keep it, and with it I bought a piece of horseflesh. Afterwards he asked me to make a cap for his boy, for which he invited me to dinner. I went, and he gave me a pancake about as big as two fingers; it was made of parched wheat, beaten and fried in bear's grease, but I thought I never tasted pleasanter meat in my life. There was a squaw who spoke to me to make a shirt for her sannup [husband], for which she gave me a piece of bear. Another asked me to knit a pair of stockings, for which she gave me a quart of peas. I boiled the peas and bear together and invited my master and mistress to dinner, but the proud gossip [i.e. companion] because I served them both in one dish, would eat nothing except one bit that he gave her upon the point of his knife.

◦§ While Rowlandson's hardships were severe, she makes it clear she was never sexually molested by any Indian. Even while wandering about the camp or in the woods looking for her son, she "met with all sorts of Indians . . . and there being no Christian soul near me, yet not one of them offered the least imaginable miscarriage to me." (In fact, rape by Indians was almost unheard of.) After the ninth remove, farther up the Connecticut River, probably in modern-day New Hampshire, Rowlandson tells of her trials and tribulations trying to gain enough food to live on:

◦§ ℥◦

But I was fain to go and look after something to satisfy my hunger, and going among the wigwams I went into one and there found a squaw who showed herself very kind to me and gave me a piece of bear. I put it into my pocket and came home but could not find an opportunity to broil it for fear they would get it from me, and there it lay all that day and night in my stinking pocket. In the morning I went to the same squaw who had a kettle of groundnuts boiling; I asked her to let me boil my piece of bear in her kettle, which she did and gave me some groundnuts to eat with it, and I cannot but think how pleasant it was to me. I have sometime seen bear baked very handsomely among the English, and some like it, but the thoughts that it was bear made me tremble, but now that was savory to me that one would think was enough to turn the stomach of a brute creature.

Rowlandson's eleventh remove was still farther north up the Connecticut River. She notes how some Indians, while going to the French for powder, were ambushed by Mohawks, killing four of them, forcing the rest to turn back. Rowlandson believes this is a blessing, fearing her captive son might be sold to the French; "which might have been worse for him had he been sold to the French than it proved to be in remaining with the Indians." (This attack by the Mohawks illustrates that King Philip was unsuccessful in allying his Algonquian warriors with their long-time enemy. Had the Mohawks and the Mohegans joined King Philip, the result of the war might have been different.)

By Rowlandson's fifteenth remove, the Indians had once again reentered Massachusetts. She writes how the Indians suffered from lack of food and shelter, often sleeping in the rain, while she found a wigwam to share: "Thus the Lord dealt mercifully with me many times, and I fared better than many of them." But other times she was threatened with death for infractions such as violating Indian customs or begging. "Then I went home to my mistress' wigwam, and they told me I disgraced my master with begging, and if I did so anymore they would knock me in the head. I told them they had as good knock me in the head as starve to death."

Her first real glimmer of hope occurred while moving back toward modern-day Petersham, where she learns that "I must go to Wachusett to my master, for there was a letter come from the council to the sagamores about redeeming the captives and that there would be another in fourteen days and that I must be ready." During her trek to Wachusett (the nineteenth remove), she again has occasion to meet King Philip.

⁓ ⁓

They said when we went out that we must travel to Wachusett this day. But a bitter weary day I had of it, traveling now three days together without resting any day between. At last, after many weary steps, I saw Wachusett Hills but many miles off. Then we came to a great swamp through which we traveled up to the knees in mud and water, which was heavy going to one tired before. Being almost spent, I thought I should have sunk down at last and never got out, but I may say, as in Psal. 94:18, "When my foot slipped, Thy mercy, O Lord, held me up." Going along, having indeed my life but little spirit, Philip, who was in the company, came up and took me by the hand and said, "Two weeks more and you shall be mistress again." I asked him if he spake true. He answered, "Yes, and quickly you shall come to your master again who has been gone from us three weeks." After many weary steps we came to Wachusett where he was, and glad I was to see him. He asked me when I washed me. I told him not this month. Then he fetched me some water himself and bid me wash and gave me the glass to see how I looked and bid his squaw give me something to eat. So she gave me a mess of beans and meat and a little groundnut cake. I was wonderfully revived with this favor showed me, Psal. 106:46 "He made them also to be pitied, of all those that carried them captives."

My master had three squaws, living sometimes with one and sometimes with another one. This old squaw at whose wigwam [now] I was, my master had been [with] those three weeks. Another was Wettimore [Weetamoe], with whom I had lived and served all this while. A severe and proud dame she was, bestowing every day in dressing herself neat as much time as any of the gentry of the land, powdering her hair and painting her face, going with necklaces, with jewels in her ears, and bracelets upon her hands. When she had dressed herself, her work was to make girdles of wampum and beads. The third squaw was a younger one by whom he had two papooses. By that time I was refreshed by the old squaw with whom my master was. Wettimore's maid came to call me home, at which I fell a-weeping. Then the old squaw told me, to encourage me, that if I wanted victuals I should come to her, and that I should lie there in her wigwam. Then I went with the maid and quickly came again and lodged there. The squaw laid a mat under me and good rug over me; the first time I had any such kindness showed to me.

◦§ While at the Wachusett Camp, two Christian Indians bring news about a
possible redemption of captives. Rowlandson is asked her advice about redemption pay, and she is wise enough to give a figure high enough to make
the Indians want to complete the exchange, but still within her husband's financial means.

◦§ ℘◦

When the letter was come, the sagamores met to consult about the captives and called me to them to inquire how much my husband would give to redeem me. When I came, I sat down among them as I was wont to do as their manner is.

Then they bade me stand up and said they were the General Court. They bid me speak what I thought he would give. Now knowing that all we had was destroyed by the Indians, I was in a great strait. I thought if I should speak of but a little, it would be slighted and hinder the matter; if of a great sum, I knew not where it would be procured. Yet at a venture, I said twenty pounds yet desired them to take less, but they would not hear of that but sent that message to Boston that for twenty pounds I should be redeemed.

◄§ Shortly after this council, the Indians held a powwow to prepare themselves before attacking Sudbury, which they did on April 18. Rowlandson observes that the Indians came back victorious but without the usual rejoicing—perhaps the natives were beginning to realize that even with the victories, this war of attrition was wearing them down. Rowlandson described the aftermath of the Sudbury attack:

◄§ §►

And they went out not so rejoicing, but they came home with as great a victory, for they said they had killed two captains and almost an hundred men. One Englishman they brought along with them; and he said it was too true for they had made sad work at Sudbury, as indeed it proved. Yet they came home without that rejoicing and triumphing over their victory which they were wont to show at other times but rather like dogs (as they say) which have lost their ears. Yet I could not perceive that it was for their own loss of men. They said they had not lost but above five or six, and I missed none except in one wigwam. When they went, they acted as if the devil had told them that they should gain the victory, and now they acted as if the devil had told them that they should have a fall. Whither it were so or no, I cannot tell, but so it proved for quickly they began to fall and so held on that summer till they came to utter ruin.

They came home on a Sabbath day, and the powwow that kneeled upon the deerskin came home (I may say without abuse) as black as the devil. When my master came home, he came to me and bid me make a shirt for his papoose of a Holland lace pillowbeer. About that time there came an Indian to me and bid me come to his wigwam at night, and he would give me some pork, and groundnuts, which I did. And as I was eating, another Indian said to me, "He seems to be your good friend, but he killed two Englishmen at Sudbury, and there lie their clothes behind you." I looked behind me, and there I saw bloody clothes with bullet holes in them, yet the Lord suffered not this wretch to do me any hurt. Yea, instead of that, he many times refreshed me; five or six times did he and his squaw refresh my feeble carcass. If I went to their wigwam at any time, they would always give me something, and yet they were strangers that I never saw before. Another squaw gave me a piece of fresh pork and a little salt with it and lent me her pan to fry it in, and I cannot but re-member what a sweet, pleasant and delightful relish that bit had to me to this day. So little do we prize common mercies when we have them to the full.

➤ Rowlandson and the Indians then complete the twentieth remove, traveling just three or four miles, still within the vicinity of Mount Wachusett. Now, negotiations proceed in earnest, and an Englishman, John Hoar, arrives in camp accompanied by two Christian Indians.

➤ ➤

On Sabbath day, the sun being about an hour high in the afternoon, came Mr. John Hoar (the council permitting him and his own forward spirit inclining him) together with the two forementioned Indians, Tom and Peter, with their third letter from the council. When they came near, I was abroad; though I saw them not, they presently called me in and bade me sit down and not stir. Then they catched up their guns and away they ran as if an enemy had been at hand, and the guns went off apace. I manifested some great trouble, and they asked me what was the matter. I told them I thought they had killed the Englishman (for they had in the meantime in-formed me that an Englishman was come). They said, "No." They shot over his horse and under, and before his horse, and they pushed him this way and that way at their pleasure, showing what they could do. Then they let them come to their wig-wams. I begged of them to let me see the Englishman, but they would not; but there was I fain to sit their pleasure. When they had talked their fill with him, they suffered me to go to him. We asked each other of our welfare, and how my husband did and all my friends. He told me they were all well and would be glad to see me. Amongst other things which my husband sent me, there came a pound of tobacco which I sold for nine shillings in money, for many of the Indians for want of tobacco smoked hemlock and ground ivy. It was great mistake in any who thought I sent for tobacco, for through the favor of God that desire was overcome.

I now asked them whether I should go home with Mr. Hoar. They answered, "No," one and another of them. And it being night we lay down with that answer.

⊷§ The next morning Hoar invites the sachems to dine with him even though most of his provisions had been stolen in the night. No further decisions are made that day, as the Indians were "getting ready for their dance." That night, after the powwow, Hoar and Rowlandson meet with James the Printer, a Praying Indian who was taught to read and write by the Reverend John Eliot. Years earlier, Eliot had established the large Christian Indian community in South Natick.

⊷§ ৡ০

When we were laid down, my master went out of the wigwam, and by and by sent in an Indian called James the Printer who told Mr. Hoar that my master would let me go home tomorrow if he would let him have one pint of liquors. Then Mr. Hoar called his own Indians, Tom and Peter, and bid them go and see whether he would promise it before them three, and if he would, he should have it, which he did, and he had it. Then Philip, smelling the business, called me to him and asked me what I would give him to tell me some good news and speak a good word for me. I told him I could not tell what to give him. I would anything I had and asked him what he would have. He said two coats and twenty shillings in money and half a bushel of seed corn and some tobacco. I thanked him for his love, but I knew the good news as well as the crafty fox.

My master, after he had his drink, quickly came ranting into the wigwam again and called for Mr. Hoar, drinking to him and saying he was a good man. And then again he would say, "Hang (the) rogue." Being almost drunk, he would drink to him, and yet presently say he should be hanged. Then he called for me. I trembled to hear him, yet I was fain to go to him, and he drank to me, showing no incivility. He was the first Indian I saw drunk all the while that I was amongst them. At last his squaw ran out, and he after her round the wigwam with his money jingling at his knees, but she escaped him. But having an old squaw, he ran to her, and so through the Lord's mercy, we were no more troubled that night.

Yet I had not a comfortable night's rest, for I think I can say I did not sleep for three nights together. The night before the letter came from the council I could not rest, I was so full of fears and troubles, God many times leaving us most in the dark when deliverance is nearest. Yea, at this time I could not rest night nor day. The next night I was overjoyed, Mr. Hoar being come and that with such good tidings. The third night I was even swallowed up with the thoughts of things, that ever I should go home again and that I must go, leaving my children behind me in the wilderness so that sleep was now almost departed from mine eyes.

On Tuesday morning they called their General Court (as they call it) to consult and determine whether I should go home or no. And they all as one man did seemingly consent to it that I should go home except Philip who would not come among them . . .

. . . But to return again to my going home where we may see a remarkable change of providence. At first they were all against it except my husband would come for me, but afterwards they assented to it and seemed much to rejoice in it. Some asked me to send them some bread, others some tobacco, others shaking me by the hand, offering me a hood and scarf to ride in, not one moving hand or tongue against it. Thus hath the Lord answered my poor desire and the many earnest requests of others put up unto God for me.

◄§ Rowlandson, Hoar, and the two Christian Indians then leave the camp, traveling first to Lancaster. Because every building in the village has been destroyed they spend the night in an abandoned farmhouse just outside of town. The next morning they travel through Concord, where Rowlandson visited relatives and friends before pushing on to Boston to be reunited with her husband. (Months later she was reunited with a son and a daughter who were also released by the Indians.)

Mary Rowlandson ends her narrative with these final thoughts:

◄§ §►

I f trouble from smaller matters begin to arise in me, I have something at hand to check myself with and say, why am I troubled? It was but the other day that if I had had the world I would have given it for my freedom or to have been a servant to a Christian. I have learned to look beyond present and smaller troubles and to be quieted under them, as Moses said, Exod. 14:13, "Stand still and see the salvation of the Lord."

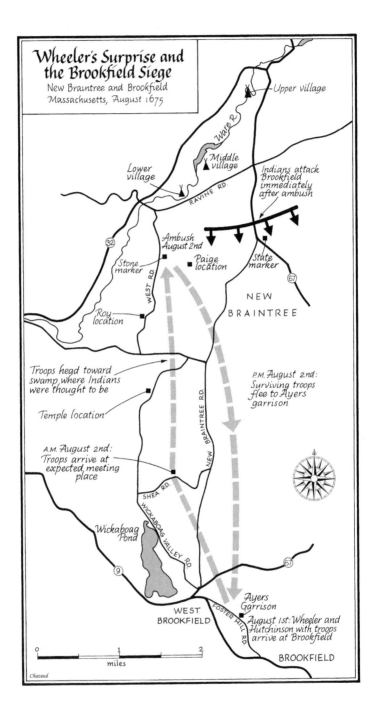

Wheeler's Surprise and the Brookfield Siege

New Braintree and Brookfield
Massachusetts, August 1675

Upper village

Water R.

Middle village

Lower village

RAVINE RD.

Indians attack Brookfield immediately after ambush

Ambush August 2nd

Paige location

Stone marker

State marker

WEST RD.

32

67

Roy location

NEW BRAINTREE

Troops head toward swamp, where Indians were thought to be

P.M. August 2nd: Surviving troops flee to Ayers garrison

Temple location

NEW BRAINTREE RD.

A.M. August 2nd: Troops arrive at expected meeting place

SHEA RD.

WICKABOAG VALLEY RD.

Wickaboag Pond

9

67

Ayers Garrison

WEST BROOKFIELD

FOSTER HILL RD.

August 1st: Wheeler and Hutchinson with troops arrive at Brookfield

BROOKFIELD

0   1   2
miles

Chazaud

· Chapter 10 ·

Captain Thomas Wheeler's Narrative

INTRODUCTION TO CAPTAIN THOMAS WHEELER AND THE "WHEELER'S SURPRISE" AMBUSH

IN THE SUMMER OF 1675 Captain Thomas Wheeler and Captain Edward Hutchinson marched into a deadly ambush in the present-day town of New Braintree, Massachusetts. Sent by the colonial authorities to ascertain the intentions of the Nipmuc (and demand their loyalty), the soldiers were well armed in case of trouble.

A meeting was arranged between the captains and the Nipmuc for eight o'clock on the morning of August 21, 1675, on a plain about three miles from Brookfield. But when the English arrived the Nipmuc were nowhere to be found. Instead of heading back to the safety of Brookfield the captains made a fateful decision to march farther into a swamp where the Nipmuc were located. When the soldiers reached a narrow passage on the trail, with swamp on one side and steep hill on the other, the Nipmuc ambushed them. The harrowing story of the ambush and the escape (by those soldiers who were not killed on the spot) is vividly told in the following excerpt from the narrative of Captain Wheeler.

A True Narrative Of the Lord's Providences in various dispensations towards Captain Edward Hutchinson of Boston and my self, and those that went with us into the Nipmuck Country, and also to Quabaug, alias Brookfield. The said Captain Hutchinson having a Commission from the Honoured Council of this Colony to Treat with several Sachems in those parts, in order to the publick peace and my self being also ordered by the said Council to accompany him with part of my Troop for Security from any danger that might be from the Indians: and to Assist him in the Transaction of matters committed to him.

The said Captain Hutchinson, and myself, with about twenty men or more marched from Cambridge to Sudbury, July 28, 1675; and from thence into the

Nipmuck Country, and finding that the Indians had deserted their towns, and we having gone until we came within two miles of New Norwich, on July 31, (only we saw two Indians having an horse with them, whom we would have spoke with, but they fled from us and left their horse, which we took,) we then thought it not expedient to march any further that way, but set our march for Brookfield, whither we came on the Lord's day about noon. From thence the same day, (being August 1,) we understanding that the Indians were about ten miles north west from us, we sent out four men to acquaint the Indians that we were not come to harm them, but our business was only to deliver a Message from our Honored Governor and Council to them, and to receive their answer, we desiring to come to a Treaty of Peace with them, (though they had for several days fled from us,) they having before professed friendship, and promised fidelity to the English. When the messengers came to them they made an alarm, and gathered together about an hundred and fifty fighting men as near as they could judge. The young men amongst them were stout in their speeches, and surly in their carriage. But at length some of the chief Sachems promised to meet us on the next morning about 8 of the clock upon a plain within three miles of Brookfield, with which answer the messengers returned to us. Whereupon, though their speeches and carriage did much discourage divers of our company, yet we conceived that we had a clear call to go to meet them at the place whither they had promised to come. Accordingly we with our men accompanied with three of the principal inhabitants of that town marched to the plain appointed; but the treacherous heathen intending mischief, (if they could have opportunity,) came not to the said place, and so failed our hopes of speaking with them there. Whereupon the said Captain Hutchinson and myself, with the rest of our Company, considered what was best to be done, whether we should go any further towards them or return, divers of us apprehending much danger in case we did proceed, because the Indians kept not promise there with us. But the three men who belonged to Brookfield were so strongly persuaded of their freedom from any ill intentions towards us, (as upon other grounds, so especially because the greatest part of those Indians belonged to David, one of their chief Sachems, who was taken to be a great friend to the English:) that the said Captain Hutchinson who was principally trusted with the matter of Treaty with them, was thereby encouraged to proceed and march forward towards a Swamp where the Indians then were. When we came near the said Swamp, the way was so very bad that we could march only in a single file, there being a very rocky hill on the right hand, and a thick swamp on the left, in which there were many of those cruel blood-thirsty heathen, who there way laid us, waiting an opportunity to cut us off; there being also much brush on the side of the said hill, where they lay in ambush to surprise us. When we had marched there about sixty or seventy rods, the said perfidious Indians went out their shot upon us as a shower of hail, they being (as was supposed,) about two hundred men or more. We seeing ourselves so beset, and not having room to fight, endeavored to fly for the safety of our lives. In which flight we were in no small danger to be all cut off, there being a very miry swamp before us, into which we could not enter with our horses to go forwards, and there being no safety in retreating the way we came, because many of their company, who lay behind the bushes, and had let us pass by them quietly; when others had shot, they came out, and stopt our way back, so that we were forced as we could to get up the steep and rocky hill; but the greater our danger was, the greater was God's mercy in the preservation of so many of us from sudden destruction. Myself being gone up part of the hill without any hurt, and perceiving some of my men to be fallen by the enemies' shot, I wheeled about upon the Indians, not calling on my men who were left to accompany me, which they in all probability would have done had they known of my return upon the enemy. They fired violently out of the swamp, and from behind the bushes on the hill side wounded me sorely, and shot my horse under me, so that he faultering and falling, I was forced to leave him, divers of the Indians being then but a few rods distant from me. My son Thomas Wheeler flying with the rest of the company missed me amongst them, and fearing that I was either slain or much endangered, returned towards the swamp again, though he had then received a dangerous wound in the reins, where he saw me in the danger aforesaid. Whereupon, he endeavored to rescue me, shewing himself therein a loving and dutiful son, he adventuring himself into great peril of his life to help me in that distress, there being many of the enemies about me, my son set me on his own horse, and so escaped a while on foot himself, until he caught an horse whose rider was slain, on which he mounted, and through God's great mercy we both escaped. But in this attempt for my deliverance he received another dangerous wound by their shot in his left arm. There were then slain to our great grief eight men, viz. — Zechariah Phillips of Boston, Timothy Farlow, of Billericay, Edward Coleborn, of Chelmsford, Samuel Smedly, of Concord, Sydrach Hapgood, of Sudbury, Serjeant Eyres, Serjeant Prichard, and Corporal Coy, the inhabitants of Brookfield, aforesaid. It being the good pleasure of god, that they should all there fall by their hands, of whose good intentions they were so confident, and whom they so little mistrusted. There were also then five persons wounded, viz. — Captain Hutchinson, myself, and my son Thomas, as aforesaid, Corporal French of Billericay, who having killed an Indian, was (as he was taking up his gun) shot, and part of one of his thumbs taken off, and also dangerously wounded through the body near the shoulder; the fifth was John Waldoe, of Chelmsford, who was not so dangerously wounded as the rest. They also then killed five of our horses, and wounded some more, which soon died after they came to Brookfield. Upon this sudden and unexpected blow given us, (wherein we desire to look higher than man the instrument,) we returned to the town as fast as the badness of the way, and the weakness of our wounded men would permit, we being then ten miles from it. All the while we were going, we durst not stay to stanch the bleeding of our wounded men, for fear the enemy should have surprised us again, which they attempted to do, and had in probability done, but that we perceiving which way they went, wheeled off to the other hand, and so by God's good providence towards us, they missed us, and we all came readily upon, and safely to the town, though none of us knew the way to it, those of the place being slain, as aforesaid, and we avoiding any thick woods and riding in open places to prevent danger by them. Being got to the town, we speedily betook ourselves to one of the largest and strongest houses therein, where we fortified ourselves in the best manner we could in such straits of time, and there resolved to keep garrison, though we were but few, and meanly fitted to make resistance against so furious enemies.

◄§ Brookfield settlers joined the ambushed soldiers in the garrison, and the Indians swept down upon the town two hours later. One of the war's most dramatic sieges ensued, with the Indians "sending in their shot amongst us like hail, through the walls, and shouting as if they would have swallowed us up alive." The English continued to take casualties; "a son of Serjeant Pritchard's adventuring out of the house wherein we were, to his father's house not far from it, to fetch more goods out of it, was caught by these cruel enemies as they were coming towards us, who cut off his head, kicking it about like foot-ball, and then putting it upon a pole, they set it up before the door of his father's house in our sight." The combatants were so close to each other, that the Indians, overhearing the soldiers saying, "God is with us and fights for us," responded by shouting, "Now see how your God delivers you!" Another time the Indians "went to the town's meeting house, (which was twenty rods of the house in which we were) who mocked saying, come and pray, and sing psalms, and in contempt made an hideous noise somewhat resembling singing."

On three different occasions Ephraim Curtis attempted to slip out of the garrison to run toward Marlboro for help, and on the third try, creeping on hands and knees just before dawn of the second day, Curtis made it past the attackers. Help, however, was already on the way, as travelers had seen the smoke and heard musket shots, and fled to Marlboro where word was sent to Major Willard, who led his men toward Brookfield.

Meanwhile the garrison held through the second night, even though the Indians shot burning arrows into its roof, which the settlers were able to extinguish by chopping holes in the roof and beating the fire out. Next, the Nipmuc set the side of the house on fire and the settlers "were forced to break down the wall of the house against the fire to put it out." On the third day (August 4) the Indians "took a cart, and filled it with flax, hay and candlewood, and other combustible matter, and set up planks, fastened to the cart, to save themselves from the danger of our shot." In addition, the Indians also made a kind of carriage attached to poles that they were going to push to the garrison after torching the carriage. But the plan was never carried out because a shower fell, making the firing of the combustible material difficult. Then, about an hour into the third night, Major Willard's soldiers arrived, and fought with those still alive in the garrison. On the morning of August 4, the Indians tired of the siege and withdrew. While the attack on Brookfield could be termed as a victory by the Indians (the town lay in ashes, and was later abandoned), it also revealed a weakness in the Indian strategy that would happen time and again. Too many braves were lost trying to take the garrison (a Nipmuc Indian later captured is reported to have said that eighty warriors were killed or wounded). A far better strategy would have been to hit and run, avoiding the cost of laying siege to a fortified garrison. In a war of attrition, such as this, where the English far outnumbered the natives, the storming of garrisons was a grave mistake.

INTRODUCTION

1. Douglas Edward Leach, *Flintlock and Tomahawk: New England in King Philip's War* (1958; reprint, New York: Norton, 1966), 166.

2. "Twelve Thousand Years of Maine," exhibit at the Maine State Museum, Augusta, Maine, 1991. "By the end of 1690, there were only four inhabited English communities, Wells, York, Kittery, and Appledore, left in Maine"(*Maine Catalog: Historic American Buildings Survey* [Lewiston, Maine: Maine State Museum, 1974], 1).

3. Samuel G. Drake reported about fifty towns partially or wholly destroyed. See Increase Mather, *The History of King Philip's War* (1676; reprint, edited by Samuel G. Drake, 1862; Bowie, Md.: Heritage Books, 1990), xxix.

4. Edward Everett, *Orations: Speeches on Various Occasions*, 7th ed., vol. 1 (Boston: Little, Brown, 1865), 657.

5. Edmund Randolph made this estimate in his report to the Crown; see Francis Jennings, *The Invasion of America: Indians, Colonialism, and the Cant of Conquest* (New York: Norton, 1975), 324.

6. The number of Algonquian-speaking peoples living in New England at the time of King Philip's War is purely conjecture. Leach suggests an Indian population in southern New England of around 20,000; see *Flintlock*, 1. Drake estimates a native population in New England of 30,000 to 40,000; see Mather, *History*, xxxix. Steven F. Johnson finds population estimates ranging from 21,500 to 60,600; see Johnson, *New England Indians* (sponsored by Pawtucket-Wamesit Historical Association, 1980). Perhaps the lowest estimate is that of Jennings, who derived a native population of 8,600 in 1674 based on the count of warriors by Daniel Gookin, superintendent of the Indians in Massachusetts prior to King Philip's War; see Jennings, *Invasion*, 26. This would

represent a decline of as much as 90 percent from Native American population levels in New England in 1600.

7. Benjamin Church, *Diary of King Philip's War, 1675–76* (1716; reprint, with an introduction by Alan and Mary Simpson, Tiverton, R.I.: Lockwood, 1975), 211. Accounts vary slightly as to the precise period of time the skull was exhibited. Cotton Mather, writing about twenty years after the first edition of his father's *History* appeared in 1676, noted that he "took off the jaw from the exposed skull. . ." (see Mather, *History*, 197).

8. William Hubbard, *The History of the Indian Wars in New England from the First Settlement to the Termination of the War with King Philip in 1677, from the Original Work by the Rev. William Hubbard* (1677), vol. 1 (reprint, edited by Samuel G. Drake, 1865; Bowie, Md.: Heritage Books, 1990), ix.

9. Robert M. Utley and Wilcomb E. Washburn, *Indian Wars* (Boston: Houghton Mifflin, 1977), 55.

10. Jill Lepore, *The Name of War: King Philip's War and the Origins of American Identity* (New York: Knopf, 1998), 191.

11. Everett, *Orations*, 669. Everett served as minister at Brattle Street, president of Harvard, governor of Massachusetts, and U.S. secretary of state. He was one of the intellectual giants of his day, and (after Webster, Clay, and Calhoun, who preceded him) its best known orator. It is a measure of the importance of Bloody Brook to nineteenth-century Americans that Everett would speak there, as he did at the dedication of the Lexington-Concord battle site and (with Abraham Lincoln) at Gettysburg.

CHAPTER 1: NEW ENGLAND BEFORE THE WAR

1. James Axtel indicates that on June 13, 1660, Wamsutta petitioned the Plymouth

authorities for a new name, "desiring that in regard his father [Massasoit] is lately deceased" (see Axtel, *The Invasion Within* [(New York: Oxford University Press, 1985], 168). There is some difference of opinion on the date of Massasoit's death (see William Hubbard, *The History of the Indian Wars in New England from the First Settlement to the Termination of the War with King Philip in 1677, from the Original Work by the Rev. William Hubbard* [1677], vol. 1 [reprint, edited by Samuel G. Drake, 1865; Bowie, Md.: Heritage Books, 1990], and George W. Ellis and John E. Morris, *King Philip's War* [New York: The Grafton Press, 1906], 36), but the 1660 date is generally accepted. Indeed, as Wampanoag tribal historian Russell Gardner notes, the Pokanoket signed an important deed in April 1660 that did not include Massasoit's sign, evidence that he was deceased by that time (personal communications with Russell Gardner, 1999).

2. Laurie Weinstein-Farson, *The Wampanoag* (New York: Chelsea House, 1989), 39. "In southern New England, at least in the first half of the seventeenth century, leadership among the Narragansett and neighboring groups. such as the Pokanoket (or Wampanoag), was invested in a hierarchy of sachems and under-sachems (Simmons 1978: 193). The sachems assigned lands, settled disputes, imposed judgments, presided at ceremonies, protected their followers. For these services they were entitled to tribute of corn, hides, and wampum . . . Although acknowledged as leaders, and enjoying the right to substantial tribute at specified times and on frequent occasions, the sachems' real power ultimately resided in their ability to persuade others" (William A. Turnbaugh, "Community, Commodities, and the Concept of Property in Seventeenth-Century Narragansett Society," in *Archaeology of Eastern North America: Papers in Honor of Stephen Williams*, Archaeological Report no. 25, edited by James B. Stoltman [Jackson, Miss.: Mississippi Department of Archives and History, 1993], 289–290).

3. Estimates of total Narragansett strength vary considerably. Daniel Gookin was told that the Narragansett had declined in strength from five thousand to one thousand before the start of King Philip's War; see Francis Jennings, *The Invasion of America: Indians, Colonialism, and the Cant of Conquest* (New York: Norton, 1975), 26. Ellis and Morris believed that the Narragansett had about twelve hundred warriors; see Ellis and Morris, *King Philip's War*, 56. Thomas Hutchinson estimated two thousand while Hubbard guessed four thousand; see Thomas Church, *The History of Philip's War, Commonly Called the Great Indian War of 1675 and 1676* (1717; reprint, edited by Samuel G. Drake, 1829; Bowie, Md.: Heritage Books, 1989), 20.

4. Samuel Drake noted that "when Commissioners attempted to establish the bounds between Massachusetts and Rhode Island in 1741, they were bewildered as to what was meant by 'the Country of the Nipmucs' and decided that it could not be ascertained" (see Drake, ed., *Old Indian Chronicle: Being a Collection of Exceeding Rare Tracts, Written and Published in the Time of King Philip's War* [Boston: Samuel G. Drake, 1867], 141).

5. Jennings, *Invasion*, 15.

6. Ibid., 29; Jennings derived these estimates from the writings of Daniel Gookin. William Turnbaugh elaborated: "The southern New England tribes generally suffered a rapid demographic decline in the first quarter of the seventeenth century as a result of several epidemics (Dobyns 1983; Ramenofsky 1987). It has been argued that some supposedly European-introduced infectious diseases actually may have been endemic to Native American populations even prior to European contact (Clark et. al. 1987). In this view, it was the cumulative consequences of cultural disruption during the early contact period that contributed to the particularly virulent seventeenth-century reactivation of diseases such as tuberculosis. Other infectious agents, such as smallpox, measles, influenza, and plague, were imported diseases that were equally deadly . . . New subsistence strategies, including greater reliance on imported European foods and drink, may have contributed to nutritional stress, which in turn led to a general decline in health and an increase in mortality. Contemporary notices suggest a pat-

terned change in the diet of local Indians, including a preference for sugar and sweet foods, alcohol, and greater proportions of starchy foods as consumption of animal protein decreased (Bartlett 1963: 19, 26, 301, 333; Williams 1936: 11)" (see Turnbaugh, "Assessing the Significance of European Goods in Seventeenth-Century Narragansett Society," *Ethnohistory and Archaeology: Approaches to Postcontact Change in the Americas*, edited by J. Daniel Rogers and Samuel M. Wilson [New York: Plenum, 1993], 145–146).

7. Steven F. Johnson, *New England Indians*, (sponsored by Pawtucket-Wamesit Historical Association, 1980), 13.

8. Harvey C. Jorgensen and Alexander G. Lawn, "The Development of the Narragansett Confederacy: An Economic Perspective," *Bulletin of the Massachusetts Archaeological Society* 44, no. 1 (April 1983), 3. "European goods rapidly attained importance in Narragansett society. They replaced most native objects in filling technical needs, stimulated new economic relationships, and, as we have shown, were quickly assimilated into Narragansett ritual and belief systems" (Turnbaugh, "European Goods," 154). Not all English goods were prized, however: "European clothing is one example. European coins provide another: The Indians drilled and suspended them as ornaments, later parting with them for items deemed of little value in European eyes (Gardener, 1901: 23)" (ibid., 143).

9. Jorgensen and Lawn, "Development," 3.

10. Ibid., 4. "The Narragansett played a pivotal role in the classic 'triangle' trade that developed by the second quarter of the seventeenth century (Ceci 1977:278–279). First, inexpensive goods from Europe were exchanged for wampum produced primarily by the Narragansett or obtained by them from their allies or neighbors; then, traders transported their wampum inland and exchanged it for furs which, finally, were returned to Europe to be sold at great profit. As the 'minters' (Wood 1977 [1634]: 81) of the wampum and as primary recipients of European goods, the Narragansett controlled two of the three classes of commodities."(Turnbaugh, "European Goods," 288).

11. Emerson W. Baker, *The Clarke and Lake Company: The Historic Archaeology of a Seventeenth-Century Maine Settlement*, occasional publications in Maine archaeology, no. 4 (Augusta, Maine: Maine Historic Preservation Commission, 1985), 14.

12. Patrick M. Malone, *The Skulking Way of War: Technology and Tactics Among the New England Indians* (Lanham, Md.: Madison Books, 1991), 42.

13. Ibid., 35. Even the "fog and dew of the morning" could be enough to extinguish a matchlock (Thomas Church, *History*, 116).

14. Malone, *The Skulking Way of War*, 58, 66.

15. Ibid., 66.

16. Douglas Edward Leach, *Flintlock and Tomahawk: New England in King Philip's War* (1958; reprint, New York: Norton, 1966), 7.

17. William Cronon, *Changes in the Land: Indians, Colonists, and the Ecology of New England* (New York: Hill and Wang, 1983), 25–26, 31, 33.

18. Ibid., 53.

19. Carolyn Merchant, *Ecological Revolutions: Nature, Gender, and Science in New England* (Chapel Hill: University of North Carolina Press, 1989), 70.

20. Eugene Aubrey Stratton, *Plymouth Colony: Its History and People, 1620–1691* (Salt Lake City, Utah: Ancestry Publishers, 1986), 169.

21. Jennings, *Invasion*, 181.

22. Stratton, *Plymouth Colony*, 169.

23. Leach, *Flintlock*, 15.

24. Hubbard, *History*, vol. 1, 57.

25. Stratton, *Plymouth Colony*, 107.

26. Jennings, *Invasion*, 144–145. If the deals were unfair, they were not always at the expense of the Indians. Roger Williams complained that the Narragansett sachem, Mixanno, and his sons "have long and most barbarously abused the [English] Inhabitants of Rode Iland, about the cutting of Grasse on Qunnunnagut, driving them (for their peace Sake) to hire and pay for, at extreame rates,

their owne Grasse" (quoted in Turnbaugh, "Community," 293).

27. Ibid., 135–136.

28. Mather, *History*, 46.

29. Ellis and Morris, *King Philip's War*, 293.

30. Hubbard, *History*, vol. 2, 71.

31. Ibid., 70.

32. John Raymond Hall, *In a Place Called Swansea* (Baltimore: Gateway Press, 1987), 62.

33. Ibid., 64. See also *Catalog of State Papers, Colonial Service, Whitehall, London, England for 1677–1680*, #1349, "Answer to the Inquiries of the Committee for Trade and Plantations about New Plymouth."

34. George Madison Bodge, *Soldiers in King Philip's War* (1906; reprint, Baltimore: Genealogical Publishing Co., 1991), 45.

35. Jennings, *Invasion*, 290.

36. There is evidence to suggest that Philip was not Massasoit's son, but his grandson. Treaties signed by Philip in 1662 refer to "this great Sachem Massasoiet, with Moanam his Son," and "Philip, the son of aforesaid Moanam." Copies of these treaties were included in accounts of King Philip's War published in London in 1676 and 1677. Original copies of the treaties have apparently been lost; see Betty Groff Schroeder, "The True Lineage of King Philip (Sachem Metacom)," *New England Historical and Genealogical Register* 144, no. 575 (July 1990), 211–214. However, Terence G. Byrne and Kathryn Fairbanks believe that Philip's relationship as grandson of Massasoit—first noted by seventeenth-century traveler and writer John Josselyn, and repeated by Boston merchant Nathaniel Saltonstall—reveals "a basic lack of common information and public record" (see Byrne and Fairbanks, "Sunconewhew: 'Philip's Brother'?" *Bulletin of the Massachusetts Archaeological Society* 57, no. 2 [fall 1996], 54). Wampanoag tribal historian Russell Gardner agrees, and argues that a careful reading of the records and understanding of Massasoit's genealogy indicates that Wamsutta—Philip's brother and Massasoit's son—himself had a son named Philip. Hence, Massasoit did, indeed, have a grandson Philip, but he should

not be confused with King Philip, Massasoit's son (Personal communications with Russell Gardner, 1999).

37. Hubbard, *History*, vol. 1, 50.

38. Ibid., 51.

39. Ibid., 51–52.

40. Tradition says that Philip was so angered by Winslow for the seizure and death of Alexander that eleven years later, in 1675, Winslow felt compelled to send his wife and children to Salem and placed his home in a complete state of defense throughout the entire war; see Lysander Salmon Richard, *History of Marshfield* (Plymouth, Mass.: Memorial Press, 1901), 60.

41. M. A. Dewolfe Howe, *Bristol, Rhode Island: A Town Biography* (Cambridge, Mass.: Harvard University Press, 1930), 28.

42. Maurice Robbins, *The Monponset Path*, Pathways of the Past, no. 4 (Attleboro, Mass.: Massachusetts Archaeological Society, 1984), 6.

43. No other sources place Bradford there.

44. Robbins, *The Monponset Path*, 5–6.

45. Jennings and others suggest that Wamsutta may have died in 1664; see Jennings, *Invasion*, 290.

46. Hubbard, *History*, vol. 1, 58–59.

47. John Easton, *A Relation of the Indyan Warr* (Albany, N.Y.: J. Munsell, 1858), 5–6.

48. Stratton, *Plymouth Colony*, 109.

49. Leach, *Flintlock and Tomahawk*, 30.

50. Ibid.

51. Increase Mather, *The History of King Philip's War* (1676)(reprint, edited by Samuel G. Drake, 1862; Bowie, Md.: Heritage Books, 1990), 48.

52. Jennings, *Invasion*, 296.

53. Ibid.

54. Mather, *History*, 48.

55. Ibid.

56. Ibid.

57. Ibid.

58. Hubbard, *History*, vol. 1, 63. Jennings

questions the timing of his death; see Jennings, *Invasion*, 296.

59. Wampapaquan may have been hanged again; versions of the story differ.

60. Easton, *Relation*, 12–15.

61. Ibid., 15.

62. Samuel Adams Drake, *Nooks and Corners of the New England Coast* (New York: Harper & Brothers, 1875), 265.

63. Russell Bourne, *The Red King's Rebellion: Racial Politics in New England, 1675–1678* (New York: Atheneum, 1990), 147.

64. Benjamin Church, *Diary of King Philip's War, 1675–76* (1716) (reprint, with an introduction by Alan Simpson and Mary Simpson, Tiverton, R.I.: Lockwood, 1975), 48.

65. Bradford F. Swan, *An Indian's an Indian* (Providence, R.I.: Roger Williams Press, 1959; unpaginated), second page.

66. Ibid., last page.

67. Ibid., second page.

68. Clifton Daniel, *Chronicle of America* (Mount Kisco, N.Y.: Chronicle Publishing, 1989), 134.

69. Swan, *An Indian's an Indian*, second page.

70. Ibid., first page.

71. Thomas Church, *History*, 125.

72. William S. Simmons, *The Narragansett* (New York: Chelsea House, 1989), 52.

73. Edward Wagenknect, *A Pictorial History of New England* (New York: Crown, 1976), 43.

74. Hubbard, *History*, vol. 2, 53.

75. Mather, *History*, 46.

76. Hubbard, *History*, vol. 1, 59.

77. Washington Irving, *Rip Van Winkle and Other Stories* (Garden City, N.Y.: Doubleday, 1955), 193.

78. Ibid.

79. Ibid, 211.

80. William Apes, *Eulogy on King Philip* (Boston: self-published by Apes, 1836), 26, 52.

81. Drake, *Nooks and Corners*, 415.

82. Bodge, *Soldiers*, 378.

83. Leach, *Flintlock and Tomahawk*, 241.

84. Bourne, *Red King's Rebellion*, 8.

CHAPTER 2: THE OUTBREAK OF WAR IN SOUTHEASTERN NEW ENGLAND

1. Thomas Church, *The History of Philip's War, Commonly Called the Great Indian War of 1675 and 1676* (1717) (reprint, edited by Samuel G. Drake, 1829; Bowie, Md.: Heritage Books, 1989), 25–27.

2. Ibid., 29.

3. William Hubbard, *The History of the Indian Wars in New England from the First Settlement to the Termination of the War with King Philip in 1677, from the Original Work by the Rev. William Hubbard* (1677), vol. 1 (reprint, edited by Samuel G. Drake, 1865; Bowie, Md.: Heritage Books, 1990), 59.

4. George W. Ellis and John E. Morris, *King Philip's War* (New York: Grafton Press, 1906), 45.

5. "In every frontier settlement there were more or less garrison houses, some with a flankart at two opposite angles, others at each corner of the house; some houses surrounded the palisadoes; others, which were smaller, built with square timber, one piece laid horizontally upon another, and loopholes at every side of the house; and besides these, generally in any more considerable plantation there was one garrison house capable of containing soldiers sent for defense of the plantation, and the families near, whose houses were not so fortified. It was thought justifiable and necessary, whatever the general rule of law might be, to erect such forts, castles, and bulwarks" (Thomas Hutchinson, *The History of Massachusetts from the First Settlement Thereof in 1628, Until the Year 1750*, 3rd ed., vol. 1 [Boston: Thomas Andrews, 1795], 67).

6. Douglas Edward Leach, *Flintlock and Tomahawk: New England in King Philip's War* (1958; reprint, New York: Norton, 1966), 109.

7. Ebenezer Peirce wrote that the Pokanoket had planted about one thousand acres of corn that spring. Had they anticipated war, or the threat of being driven from their peninsula, he does not believe the corn would have been planted. This is one argument to support the claim that Philip was not interested in starting a war, at least in June 1675; see Peirce, *Indian History, Biography and Genealogy* (North Abington, Mass.: Zerviah Gould Mitchell, 1878), 170.

8. Not only was Church dashing, he was also just plain lucky. He would survive an ambush in Swansea, retreat before meeting a superior force of Wampanoag in the Pocasset swamp (because his men were afraid of rattlesnakes), survive another ambush and siege at Tiverton, Rhode Island, and live through the Great Swamp Fight despite receiving three wounds.

9. Richard Slotkin and James K. Folsom, eds., *So Dreadful a Judgment: Puritan Responses to King Philip's War, 1676–1677* (Middletown, Ct.: Wesleyan University Press, 1978), 370.

10. Ibid., 377.

11. A note about dates: At the time of King Philip's War, England still used the Julian calendar, while other parts of Europe had switched to the Gregorian calendar, our modern method of keeping dates. In the Julian calendar, the year began on March 25 and ended on March 24. This confusion led the New England colonists to use a double-year dating system between January 1 and March 24. Hence, Benjamin Church's gravestone indicates that he died "January 17, 1717-18."

12. Leach, *Flintlock*, 42–43. Leach adds the traditional story that this idea may have been planted by the English to dissuade the Wampanoag from launching a war.

13. Easton, *A Relation of the Indyan War* (Albany, N.Y.: J. Monsell, 1858), quoted in Richard LeBaron Bowen, *Early Rehoboth*, vol. 3 (Rehoboth, Mass.: privately, printed, 1948), 10–11. Bowen concludes from this report and a second by a contemporary Boston merchant that William and John Salisbury, father and son, were responsible for the Pokanoket death on June 24.

14. George Madison Bodge, *Soldiers in King Philip's War* (1906; reprint, Baltimore: Genealogical Publishing Co., 1991), 59.

15. Moseley was not blind to his excesses. In October 1675 he wrote to Governor Leverett: "I desire to be Excuse if my tongue or pen has out run my witt being in a passion and seeing what mischief had beene done by the Indians which I have beene eye witness to, would make a wiser person than I am, willing to have revenge of aney of them" (ibid., xx).

16. Ibid., 73.

17. Wait Winthrop, "A Letter Written by Capt. Wait Winthrop from Mr. Smiths in Narragansett to Govr. John Winthrop of the Colony of Connecticut," issued at the General Court of the Society of Colonial Wars in the State of Rhode Island and the Providence Plantations by its governor, Henry Dexter Sharp, and the council of the society, August 8, 1919, Providence. Printed for the society by the Standard Printing Co., from the original manuscript in the Archives of the State of Connecticut, 21.

18. Bowen, *Early Rehoboth*, vol. 3, 65.

19. Hubbard, *History*, vol. 2, 41. Old Rehoboth refers to the present-day section of East Providence called Rumford.

20. Bowen concludes that the fort was located "between the southeastern side of this swamp and the shore of Mount Hope Bay on the west" (see Bowen, *Early Rehoboth*, vol. 3, 71). Modern archaeologists have never discovered the precise site.

21. Thomas Church, *History*, 36.

22. Eugene Aubrey Stratton, *Plymouth Colony: Its History and People, 1620–1691* (Salt Lake City, Utah: Ancestry Publishers, 1986), 112.

23. Bowen, *Early Rehoboth*, vol. 3, 101–102.

24. Hubbard, *History*, vol. 1, 91.

25. Stephen Saunders Webb, *1676: The End of American Independence* (New York: Knopf, 1984), 228. Anne Hutchinson was a leader in the Antinomian movement in Massachusetts Bay Colony. She was banned from the colony in November 1638 and, with William Coddington and John Coggeshall, founded a settlement at present-day Portsmouth, Rhode Island.

26. Ellis and Morris, *King Philip's War*, 229.

27. Ibid., 296.

28. William D. Williamson, *The History of the State of Maine: From Its First Discovery, A.D. 1602, to the Separation, A.D. 1820, Inclusive* (Hallowell, Maine: Glazier, Masters, 1832), 529.

29. Hubbard, *History*, vol. I, 13.

30. Ibid., 124.

31. Michael J. Puglisi, *Puritans Besieged: The Legacies of King Philip's War in the Massachusetts Bay Colony* (Lanham, Md.: University Press of America, 1991), 7.

32. Ellis and Morris, *King Philip's War*, 138.

33. A more detailed discussion of the timing of this event, and of Rhode Island's role, is given by Douglas Leach in "A New View of the Declaration of War Against the Narragansetts, November, 1675," *Rhode Island History* 15, no. 2 (April 1956), 33.

34. Many of those who survived carried reminders of the battle for the rest of their lives. It was reported, for example, that Major William Bradford, age seventy-three in 1697, "hath worn a bullet in his flesh about 20 of them" (see Increase Mather, *The History of King Philip's War* (1676) reprint, edited by Samuel G. Drake (1862; Bowie, Md.: Heritage Books, 1990), 109.

35. Ellis and Morris, *King Philip's War*, 138.

36. Ibid., 302.

37. Ibid., 163.

38. Francis Jennings, *The Invasion of America: Indians, Colonialism, and the Cant of Conquest* (New York: Norton, 1975), 313.

39. Mather, *History*, 126.

CHAPTER 3:
SPRING 1676: THE TIDE TURNS

1. George W. Ellis and John E. Morris, *King Philip's War* (New York: Grafton Press, 1906), 245.

2. Stephen Saunders Webb, *1676: The End of American Independence* (New York: Knopf, 1984), 238–239.

3. Ibid., 239.

4. Ibid., 241.

5. Russell Bourne, *The Red King's Rebellion: Racial Politics in New England, 1675–1678* (New York: Atheneum, 1990), 194–195.

6. Ellis and Morris, *King Philip's War*, 245.

7. Some believe this was at Nipsachuck, in Smithfield, Rhode Island.

8. Ebenezer W. Peirce, *Indian History, Biography and Genealogy* (North Abington, Mass.: Zerviah Gould Mitchell, 1878), 196.

9. Albert Edward Van Dusen, *Connecticut* (New York: Random House, 1961), 81.

10. Increase Mather, *The History of King Philip's War, 1676* (reprint, edited by Samuel G. Drake, 1862; Bowie, Md.: Heritage Books 1990), 196.

11. Benjamin Church, *Diary of King Philip's War, 1675–76,* 1716 (reprint, with an introduction by Alan Simpson and Mary Simpson, Tiverton, R.I.: Lockwood Publications, 1975), 110.

12. William Hubbard, *The History of the Indian Wars in New England from the First Settlement to the Termination of the War with King Philip in 1677, from the Original Work by the Rev. William Hubbard* (1677), vol. 1 (reprint, edited by Samuel G. Drake, 1865; Bowie, Md.: Heritage Books, 1990), 53.

13. Gerald E. Morris, ed., *Maine Bicentennial Atlas: An Historical Survey* (Portland: Maine Historical Society, 1976), 6.

14. Ellis, *History*, 306. Williamson dates this event September 23; see William D. Williamson, *The History of the State of Maine: From Its First Discovery, A.D. 1602, to the Separation, A.D. 1820, Inclusive* (Hallowell, Maine: Glazier, Masters, & Co., 1832), 540.

15. Ibid., 537.

16. Ibid., 539. Also see Bourne, *Red King's Rebellion*, 231–232.

17. Williamson, *Maine*, 539.

18. Ibid., 542.

19. Ibid.

20. Williamson, *Maine*, 543.

21. Ibid., 552.

22. Ibid.

23. Williamson, *Maine*, 553.

24. George Madison Bodge, *Soldiers in King Philip's War* (1906; Baltimore: Genealogical Publishing Co., 1991), 126.

25. Ibid., 262.

26. Ibid., 406.

27. Massachusetts Bay's quota for the Great Swamp Fight had been 527, though 538 were mustered at Dedham Plain. Plymouth's quota was 158. Together, 696 veterans (or their heirs) from the combined colonies would have been eligible for land grants. According to Bodge (p. 412), in April 1733 Massachusetts (combined Massachusetts Bay and Plymouth as of 1686) accepted 840 grantees.

28. Bodge, *Soldiers*, 441–442.

29. *Mattapoisett and Old Rochester, Massachusetts*, 3rd ed., 1907; (produced by the Mattapoisett [Mass.] Improvement Association, 1950), 16.

30. Michael J. Puglisi, *Puritans Besieged: The Legacies of King Philip's War in the Massachusetts Bay Colony* (Lanham, Md.: University Press of America, 1991), 46.

31. Ibid., 47, and Eugene Aubrey Stratton, *Plymouth Colony: Its History and People, 1620–1691* (Salt Lake City, Utah: Ancestry Publishers, 1986), 118.

32. Stratton, *Plymouth Colony*, 189.

33. William S. Simmons, *The Narragansett* (New York: Chelsea House, 1989), 51.

34. Ibid., 54.

35. Van Dusen, *Connecticut*, 82.

36. *Indians of Little Compton*, an interim report by members of the Little Compton Historical Society, 1988, 5.

37. George Howe, *Mount Hope: A New England Chronicle* (New York: Viking, 1959), 59.

38. Ibid., 61.

39. *Indians of Little Compton*, 6.

40. Laurie Weinstein-Farson, *The Wampanoag* (New York: Chelsea House, 1989), 35, 58.

41. Daniel R. Mandell, *Behind the Frontier: Indians in Eighteenth-Century Eastern Massachusetts* (Lincoln: University of Nebraska Press 1996), 2–3.

42. Colin G. Calloway, *The Abenakis* (New York: Chelsea House, 1989), 73.

43. Ibid., 76.

44. Bodge, *Soldiers*, 405.

45. Webb, *1676*, 221.

46. Ibid., 235–236.

47. Ibid., 236.

48. Puglisi, *Puritans Besieged*, 143.

49. Ibid., 144.

50. James Deetz, *In Small Things Forgotten: The Archaeology of Early American Life* (New York: Anchor Books/Doubleday, 1977), 38.

CHAPTER 4: KING PHILIP'S WAR IN SOUTHEASTERN MASSACHUSETTS

1. William Hubbard, *The History of the Indian Wars in New England from the First Settlement to the Termination of the War with King Philip in 1677, from the Original Work by the Rev. William Hubbard* (1677) (vol. 1 reprint, edited by Samuel G. Drake, 1865; Bowie, Md.: Heritage Books, 1990), 50.

2. Ibid., 40.

3. Ibid., 50.

4. Maurice Robbins, *The Monponset Path*, Pathways of the Past, no. 4 (Attleboro, Mass.: Massachusetts Historical Society, 1984), 3.

5. Robbins, *The Monponset Path*, 6.

6. Cynthia Hagar Krusell and Betty Magoun Bates, *Marshfield: A Town of Villages, 1640–1990* (Marshfield Mills, Mass.: Historical Research Associates, 1990), 10.

7. James Deetz, *In Small Things Forgotten: The Archaeology of Early American Life* (New York: Anchor Books/Doubleday, 1977), 94–95.

8. Francis Baylies, *An Historical Memoir of the Colony of New Plymouth*, part 3 (Boston: Hilliard, Gray, Little, and Wilkins, 1830), 18, quoted in Samuel Drake, ed., *Old Indian Chronicle: Being a Collection of Exceeding*

Rare Tracts, Written and Published in the Time of King Philip's War (Boston: Samuel G. Drake, 1867), 69.

9. The woods on the west side of Dighton Avenue and south of Baker Road were once known as "Trotter's Woods." Tradition held that if a person placed his ear to the ground he could hear the sounds of Indian mounts trotting along their old hunting trails; see Joseph Everett Warner, *Spirit of Liberty and Union, 1637–1939* (Taunton, Mass.: Joseph Everett Warner, 1947), 102.

10. Baylies, *New Plymouth,* quoted in Drake, ed., *Old Indian Chronicle,* 69.

11. Ibid. James Brown was a Swansea resident and friend of Philip. Mr. Williams was undoubtedly Roger Williams.

12. Correspondence with Lisa Compton, director, Old Colony Historical Society. Local historian Charles Crowley notes that there were no streets north of Main Street until the Revolution because this land was part of Taunton's Training Field, and that there may have been more than one training field since Cohannet Street is sometimes called the road between the old and new training field; correspondence with Charles Crowley, 1992.

13. Samuel Hopkins Emery, *History of Taunton, Massachusetts* (Syracuse, N.Y.: D. Mason & Co., 1893), 90.

14. Ibid., 99.

15. *Quarter Millennial Celebration of Taunton, Massachusetts* (Taunton, Mass.: Taunton City Government, 1889), 38.

16. Emery, *History of Taunton,* 403. The rectory is also known as the McKinstrey House.

17. Drake, ed., *Old Indian Chronicle,* 70.

18. Warner, *Spirit,* 72.

19. *Quarter Millennial Celebration of the City of Taunton,* 223.

20. Emery, *History of Taunton,* 203.

21. Ibid., 204.

22. Ibid.

23. *Quarter Millennial Celebration of the City of Taunton,* 223.

24. Baylies, *New Plymouth,* 19.

25. Ibid., 384.

26. Drake, ed., *Old Indian Chronicle,* 71.

27. Hubbard, *History,* vol. 1, 55.

28. Emery, *History of Taunton,* 93.

29. Hubbard, *History,* vol. 1, 84.

30. Local historian Charles Crowley believes that a fourth garrison ("the Powderhouse") may have been located on Powderhouse Hill, on the east side of the Taunton River in the Weir section of town, between Plain Street and Berkley Street, east of Beacon Street; correspondence with Charles Crowley, 1992. However, no record of this structure was found until after the Revolution. Emery, *History of Taunton,* 595.

31. Emery, *History of Taunton,* 403.

32. Ibid.

33. Ibid.

34. James Phinney Baxter, "Early Voyages to America," *Collections of the Old Colony Historical Society,* no. 4 (Taunton, Mass.: C. H. Buffington, 1889), 64.

35. Warner, *Spirit,* 82.

36. Pere Forbes, "A Topographic Description of Raynham, In the County of Bristol, February 6, 1793," *Collections of the Massachusetts Historical Society for the Year 1794,* vol. 3, 1st series, Boston, 172. In 1835, a nonagenarian remembered fishing there as a boy; Fanny Leonard Koster, *Annals of the Leonard Family* (Taunton, Mass.: self-published, 1911), 59. Taken together, these two reports suggest a rather dramatic transformation of the pond from being a fish-bearing body of water in 1769 to having fifty-foot pines and cedars in 1794.

37. Emery, *History of Taunton,* 384.

38. Ibid., 387.

39. Ibid., 405.

40. Ibid., 388.

41. Ibid., 405.

42. Hubbard, *History,* vol. 2, 42.

43. Bodge, *Soldiers,* 405–406.

44. James Bell, [first name unknown] White, Israel Dean, and William Hoskins are also

listed as Taunton residents participating in the Great Swamp Fight; see Emery, *History of Taunton*, 386.

45. Ebenezer W. Peirce, *Indian History, Biography and Genealogy* (North Abington, Mass.: Zerviah Gould Mitchell, 1878), 122.

46. *Quarter Millennial Celebration of the City of Taunton*, 226–229.

47. William Bradford Browne, *The Babbit Family History* (Taunton, Mass.: n.p., 1912), 23.

48. Vicki-Ann Gay, "City Crews Put Chain Saws to Ancient King Philip Oak," *Taunton Daily Gazette*, February 1, 1983, 1.

49. Ibid.

50. Bob Williams, "Son of King Philip's Oak Thriving at Church Green," *Taunton Daily Gazette*, February 9, 1983, 1.

51. Personal communication, Taunton Parks and Recreation Department, 1991.

52. Hubbard, *History*, vol. 1, 62.

53. Ibid.

54. Ibid.

55. Ibid., 63.

56. Thomas Weston, *History of the Town of Middleboro, Massachusetts* (Cambridge, Mass.: Riverside Press, 1906), 17.

57. Newspaper clipping, no date or source, Old Colony Historical Society, Box 68.

58. Peirce, *Indian History*, 215–216.

59. Warner, *Spirit*, 87. Wampanoag tribal historian Russell Gardner notes that a number of Massasoit's descendants, through Lydia Tuspaquin and her son, Benjamin, live in the Saundersville, Rhode Island, area. Gardner calls this an "absolute, unquestionable connection" from Massasoit to the twenty-first century.

60. Personal correspondence with Helen Pierce, 1991.

61. Job Winslow's property is described in the *Proprietors Records for the Town of Swansea*. A description of the Ennis property is found in the *Town of Warren Land Records*, Book 26, page 406. The land was purchased by Ennis in 1884. These two documents clearly describe the same location, and agree with Ellis and

Morris's contention that Job Winslow's home was on the property "now the farm of Mr. Edward Ennis" (see George W. Ellis and John E. Morris, *King Philip's War* [New York: Grafton Press, 1906], 57).

62. John Raymond Hall, *In a Place Called Swansea* (Baltimore: Gateway Press, 1987), 116.

63. Ibid., 121.

64. Correspondence with Helen Pierce, 1991. The site of the garrison is based on tradition. Also see Otis Olney Wright, ed., *History of Swansea, Massachusetts 1667–1917* (published by the town of Swansea, 1917), 7–8.

65. Ellis and Morris, *King Philip's War*, 59.

66. Hall, *Swansea*, 103.

67. Hubbard, *History*, vol. 1, 187.

68. Hall, *Swansea*, 124.

69. Hubbard, *History*, vol. 1, 71.

70. Benjamin Church, *Diary of King Philip's War, 1675–76* (1716; reprint with an introduction by Alan Simpson and Mary Simpson, Tiverton, R.I.: Lockwood, 1975), 34–35.

71. Ellis and Morris, *King Philip's War*, 66. Also see Benjamin Church, *The History of King Philip's War*, with an introduction and notes by Henry Martyn Dexter (Boston: John Kimball Wiggin, 1865), 23–24. Guy Fessenden is more precise in saying that the remains were "doubtless near the Pound, on Kickemuit River. The pound did not then exist, but was first built, as it now stands in 1685" (Guy M. Fessenden, *History of Warren, R.I.* [Providence, R.I.: H. H. Brown, 1845], 70).

72. Hubbard, *History*, vol. 1, 71.

73. Correspondence with Helen Pierce, 1991.

74. Ibid.

75. As the marker at the site of the Miles garrison indicates, the names of the men who died are now known.

76. Justin Winsor, ed., *The Memorial History of Boston*, vol. 1, (Boston: James R. Osgood, 1882), 250.

77. This story may be more fiction than fact; see George Sheldon, "The Traditional Story of the Attack Upon Hadley and the Appearance of Gen. Goff, Sept. 1, 1675: Has It Any Foun-

dation in Fact?," *New England Historic Genealogical Register* 28 (October 1874), 389. Douglas Wilson disputes Sheldon and offers his own interpretation; see Wilson, "Web of Secrecy: Goffe, Whalley, and the Legend of Hadley," *New England Quarterly* 60, no. 4 (December 1987), 539ff.

78. Annie Haven Thwing, *The Crooked Narrow Streets of the Town of Boston, 1630–1882* (Boston: Marshal Jones, 1920), 5.

79. Ibid.

80. Winsor, ed., *Memorial History of Boston*, 246.

81. Ibid., 250–251.

82. Thwing, *Boston*, 7.

83. Laurie Weinstein-Farson, *The Wampanoag* (New York: Chelsea House, 1989), 33.

84. Thwing, *Boston*, 7.

85. Ibid., 198.

86. Ibid., 18.

87. Abel Bowen, *Bowen's Picture Book of Boston* (Boston: P. Otis, Broaders, and Co., 1838), 238.

88. Ibid., 52.

89. Winsor, ed., *Memorial History of Boston*, 231.

90. Ibid., 237.

91. Ibid., 537.

92. Thwing, *Boston*, 135.

93. Bodge, *Soldiers*, 59.

94. David Arnold, "The Island's Gone Inside Out," *Boston Globe*, July 24, 1991, 65. "Native Americans gathered on Deer Island yesterday to honor the memory of ancestors who were imprisoned there and voice opposition to MWRA construction over the sacred burial ground. Musketaquid Remembrance Day marks the 318th anniversary of the closing of the internment camp at Concord (formerly Musketaquid) and the forcible transfer of Native American internees to Deer Island said members of the Muhheconneuk Intertribal Committee. Sam Sapiel, a member of the Penobscot Indian Nation, said over 3,000 Indian people died while interned on the island.

The remembrance is about 'the history and all the things that were done to Indian people in the 1600s—all of the catastrophe the Indian people had to go through,' said Sapiel . . . During yesterday's ceremonies, the committee hosted a series of commemorations and retraced the route of the internees from Musketaquid through Charlestown to Deer Island. Native Americans have lobbied against construction of the Massachusetts Water Resources Authority sewage treatment plant because of Deer Island's historical significance. Native Americans countered that the Island is the site of burial grounds." Julie Ross, "Native Americans Honor Ancestral Deer Isle Victims," *Boston Herald*, February 22, 1994, 11.

95. Bowen, *Picture Book of Boston*, 271.

96. Winsor, ed., *Memorial History of Boston*, 552.

97. James Raymond Simmons, *The Historic Trees of Massachusetts* (Boston: Marshall Jones, 1919), 3.

98. Hubbard, *History*, vol. 1, 200. Also see Winsor, ed., *Memorial History of Boston*, 553.

99. Samuel Barber, *Boston Common* (Boston: Christopher Publishing House, 1914), 29.

100. Ellis and Morris, *King Philip's War*, 164.

101. Hubbard, *History*, vol. 1, 200.

102. Barber, *Boston Common*, 37.

103. National Register of Historic Places document, 1990.

104. *Attleborough Bi-Centennial Anniversary, Official Souvenir Programme* (October 18–19, 1894), 17.

105. John Daggett, *A Sketch of the History of Attleborough* (Boston: Samuel Usher, 1894), 97.

106. Ibid., 98.

107. Ellis and Morris, *King Philip's War*, 144.

108. National Register of Historic Places document, 1990.

109. Ibid.

110. Eugene Aubrey Stratton, *Plymouth Colony: Its History and People, 1620–1691* (Salt Lake City, Utah: Ancestry Publishers, 1986), 109.

111. Daggett, *Attleborough*, 91.

112. Their main campsite is known as Wapnucket and has yielded artifacts from the Paleo-Indian, Archaie, and Woodland Periods; see Weinstein-Farson, *The Wampanoag*, 12–14.

113. Ellis and Morris, *King Philip's War*, 47. The precise location is known but not usually publicized to avoid vandalism.

114. Church, *Diary*, 144.

115. Hubbard, *History*, vol. 1, 275.

116. Ibid.

117. Church, *Diary*, 146.

118. Ibid.

119. Weston, *History of the Town of Middleboro*, 86.

120. Stratton, *Plymouth Colony*, 101.

121. Weston, *History of the Town of Middleboro*, 74. The Middleboro Historical Society reported forty-eight men living in Middleboro at the time of King Philip's War (personal correspondence with MHS, 1992).

122. Stratton, *Plymouth Colony*, 101.

123. Weston, *History of the Town of Middleboro*, 74.

124. Thomson, with Benjamin Church's father, built the first framed meetinghouse in Plymouth. Thomson arrived in Plymouth in August 1623, one of the "First Comers"; see Elroy S. Thompson, *History of Plymouth, Norfolk, and Barnstable Counties, Massachusetts*, vol. 1 (New York: Lewis Historical Publishing Company, 1928), 107.

125. Hubbard, *History*, vol. 2, 41.

126. Thompson, *History*, vol. 1, 110.

127. "The Story of the Thompson Gun," undated letter from Warren and Marion Whipple to the Old Colony Historical Society, Taunton, Massachusetts.

128. Thompson, *History*, vol. 1, 112.

129. There is a story told about an almost identical event which was supposed to have taken place in Dartmouth during the war; see below, "Attack on Old Dartmouth, Massachusetts." Visitors to Buckman Tavern in Lexington, Massachusetts, can also see "Long John," a gun attached to yet a third, nearly identical story, this one set on the Sudbury River a half-century later.

130. Thompson, *History*, 112.

131. Travel three-tenths of a mile east on Sachem Street from Route 105. Walk along the right-of-way cut for the power lines, past the large metal pole where the lines intersect, to pole E33. Here, the path narrows and turns right. Follow this directly to the rock.

132. Thompson, *History*, vol. 1, 109.

133. Hubbard, *History*, vol. 2, 40. Recent research indicates that the story of Danson's death is inaccurate. In fact, Danson not only survived the war, but lived for many years afterwards in Boston as a "loaf bread baker" (personal communications with Russell Gardner, 1999).

134. Church, *Diary*, 115.

135. *Mattapoisett and Old Rochester, Massachusetts*, 3rd. ed., 1907 (produced by the Mattapoisett [Mass.] Improvement Association, 1950), 17.

136. Church, *Diary*, 119.

137. Ibid.

138. Franklyn Howland, *A History of the Town of Acushnet* (New Bedford, Mass.: self-published, 1907), 17.

139. *Our Country and Its People: A Descriptive and Biographical Record of Bristol County, Massachusetts*, prepared and published under the auspices of the *Fall River News* and *The Taunton Gazette* with the assistance of Hon. Alanson Borden of New Bedford (Boston: Boston History Co., 1899), 39.

140. George H. Tripp, "The Town of Fairhaven in Four Wars," *Old Dartmouth Historical Sketches*, no. 5 (June 27, 1904), 9.

141. Donald R. Bernard, *Tower of Strength: A History of Fort Phoenix* (New Bedford, Mass.: Reynolds-DeWalt, 1975), 16.

142. James L. Gillingham et al., *A Brief History of the Town of Fairhaven, Massachusetts* (1903), 12.

143. Howland, *Acushnet*, 21.

144. Ibid.

145. Church, *Diary*, 51. Compare this to a similar event in Middleboro; see below, "Attack on Middleboro, Massachusetts."

146. Church, *Diary*, 89–90.

147. Ibid., 91.

148. Ibid., 92.

149. *Mattapoisett and Old Rochester*, 14. Also see Dexter in Benjamin Church, *History*, 96.

150. Maurice Robbins, "The Sandwich Path: Church Searches for Awashonks," Pathways of the Past, no. 3 (Attleboro, Mass.: Massachusetts Archaeological Society, 1984), 8.

151. Ibid., 8–9.

152. Hubbard, *History*, vol. 1, 84.

153. Richard LeBaron Bowen, *Early Rehoboth*, vol. 3 (Rehoboth, Mass.: privately published, 1948), 73.

154. Hubbard, *History*, vol. 1, 87.

155. Bowen, *Early Rehoboth*, vol. 3, 73.

156. Dexter in Benjamin Church, *History*, 43–44.

157. *A Patchwork History of Tiverton, Rhode Island,* Bicentennial Edition (Tiverton, R.I.: Tiverton Historical Society, 1976) 4.

158. Peirce, *Indian History*, 46.

159. Ibid., 255.

160. *Tiverton, Rhode Island*, 11–12.

161. Ellis and Morris, *King Philip's War*, 77.

162. *Fall River in History*, compiled by the Tercentenary Committee of Fall River (Fall River, Mass.: Munroe Press, 1930), 5.

163. Ellis and Morris, *King Philip's War*, 77.

164. Hubbard, *History*, vol. 1, 88.

165. Mather, *History*, 61.

166. Drake gives the location as "two Miles from the Village of Plymouth, at a Place called Eel River" (see Hubbard, *History*, vol. 1, 179).

167. Douglas Edward Leach, *Flintlock and Tomahawk: New England in King Philip's War* (1958; reprint, New York: Norton, 1966), 166.

168. Victoria B. Engstrom, *Eel River Valley,* Pilgrim Society Notes, no. 23 (Plymouth, Massachusetts: Pilgrim Society, March 1976), 6.

169. Dexter in Benjamin Church, *History*, 70.

170. Ellis and Morris, *King Philip's War*, 187.

171. Conversation with staff at Plimoth Plantation and Pilgrim Memorial Hall, 1991.

172. William S. Russell, *Pilgrim Memorials, and Guide to Plymouth* (Boston: Crosby, Nichols, 1855), 37.

173. Hubbard, *History*, vol. 1, 272.

174. Samuel Adams Drake, *Nooks and Corners of the New England Coast* (New York: Harper & Brothers, 1875), 278.

175. Nahum Mitchell, *History of the Early Settlement of Bridgewater* (1840; Baltimore: Gateway, 1970), 38.

176. Mitchell, *Bridgewater*, 41.

177. Katherine M. Doherty, ed., *History Highlights: Bridgewater, Massachusetts: A Commemorative Journal*, a publication of the Bridgewater Bicentennial Commission (1976), 28.

178. Mitchell, *Bridgewater*, 41.

179. William Latham, *Epitaphs in Old Bridgewater, Massachusetts* (Bridgewater, Mass.: n.p., 1882), 239–240.

180. Conversation with Ken Moore, *Bridgewater Independent*, 1991.

181. Nathaniel Morton, *New England Memorial*, 5th ed., edited by John Davis (Boston: Crocker and Brewster, 1826), 454.

182. Ibid.

183. Ibid., 455. The traditions associated with the fate of Philip's son are many, according to Wampanoag tribal historian Russell Gardner, though none can be supported by historical record. There is a strong tradition that James Keith and his family took Philip's son into their home for a period of time to shield him from authorities. From there, he may have been smuggled to Martha's Vineyard, at that time a part of New York. A second tradition—nothing more than speculation, according to Gardner—has Philip's son being

sold into slavery in Bermuda or the West Indies. A third tradition finds Philip's son having made his way to Canada: a family in present-day Battle Creek, Michigan, has a family Bible that indicates that members of the "Philips" family are direct descendents of King Philip through his son. An entire "House of Seven Crescents" has arisen around the belief that Philip's son survived and has living descendents to this day. Gardner notes that these traditions are undocumented and unproven, and the best we really know comes from the simple, final line, "Philip's boy goes now to be sold" (personal communications with Russell Gardner, 1999).

184. Peirce, *Indian History*, 49.

185. Mather, *History*, 191.

186. Hubbard, *History*, vol. 1, 264.

187. Mather, *History*, 191.

188. See Hubbard, *History*, vol. 1, 264, and Mather, *History*, 191.

189. Tercentenary Committee, *Fall River in History*, 6. Warner, *Spirit*, 84.

190. Peirce, *Indian History*, 50. Twice elsewhere in the book, however, Peirce writes that Weetamoo's body was discovered on the Swansea-Somerset side of the Taunton River.

191. Warner, *Spirit*, 84.

192. Church, *Diary*, 133–134.

193. Ibid., 124.

194. Ibid., 125.

195. Ibid., 132.

196. Ibid., 136–137. See Drake's note for a description of the swamp.

197. Ibid., 127.

198. Ibid., 131.

199. Ibid., 134.

200. Ibid., 136–138.

201. Mather, *History*, 180. It is perhaps only a coincidence that Drake visited Anawan Rock on the 150th anniversary of Anawan's capture.

202. Dexter in Benjamin Church, *History*, 175.

203. Mather, *History*, 137.

204. Obviously with permission, since Bliss

acknowledged Drake's assistance in preparing the *History of Rehoboth*.

205. Ibid., 104.

206. Dexter in Benjamin Church, *History*, 166–167.

207. Peirce, *Indian History*, 19.

208. Ibid., 207. Peirce goes on to challenge Church's story in total, saying that "this overestimate of the peril in descending was probably on a par with the bragging indulged in when describing the other details of the feat of capturing Annawon, who with his company were very poorly supplied with both arms and ammunition, reduced to a comparative handful in numbers, distressed, dispirited, and every day growing more feeble by constant and continual capture by the enemy and desertions to the English" (see Peirce, *Indian History*, 208).

209. James C. O'Connell, *Inside Guide to Springfield and the Pioneer Valley* (Springfield, Mass.: Western Massachusetts Publishers, 1986), 9.

210. James H. McDonald, "Doubts Raised About Indian Site," *Providence Journal*, November 26, 1990. Dexter's account is more accurate when he estimates the rock at 125 feet in length and 75 feet in width, and notes the huge boulders lying at the base; see Dexter in Benjamin Church, *History*, 167.

211. Bob Sharples, "Anawan Rock Location Under Question," *Rehoboth Reporter* 2, no. 9 (October 1990), 10.

212. McDonald, "Doubts."

213. Conversation with Bob Sharples, 1991.

214. Correspondence with E. Otis Dyer Jr., 1992.

215. Leonard Bliss Jr., *History of Rehoboth, Bristol County, Massachusetts: Comprising a History of the Present Towns of Rehoboth, Seekonk and Pawtucket, from Their Settlement to the Present Time, Together with Sketches of Attleborough, Cumberland, and a Part of Swansey and Barrington, to the Time That They Were Severally Separated from the Original Town* (Boston: Otis, Broaders, and Company, 1836), 104.

216. Book 5, page 97, *Rehoboth Proprietors*

Land Records. This is the only time Anawan Rock is mentioned in these records.

217. Benjamin Church, *History,* 142.

218. Dexter finds no evidence that Church kept the belts; see Dexter in Benjamin Church, *History,* 174.

219. *Catalog of State Papers, Colonial Service, Whitehall, London, England for 1677–1680,* no. 314.

220. Ibid., no. 1131.

221. Ibid., no. 1349.

222. Notes from Maurice Robbins, given to the author by Bob Sharples, 1991.

223. Personal communication with Bob Sharples, 1991.

224. Benjamin Church, *History,* 141.

225. Personal communications with Linda Eppich, Rhode Island Historical Society, 1991.

226. Personal communications with Ruth Warfield, Massachusetts Archaeological Society, 1992.

CHAPTER 5: KING PHILIP'S WAR
IN CENTRAL AND WESTERN
MASSACHUSETTS

1. William Hubbard, *The History of the Indian Wars in New England from the First Settlement to the Termination of the War with King Philip in 1677, from the Original Work by the Rev. William Hubbard* (1677), vol. 1 (reprint, edited by Samuel G. Drake,1865; Bowie, Md.: Heritage Books, 1990), 168.

2. George Madison Bodge, *Soldiers in King Philip's War* (1906; Baltimore: Genealogical Publishing Co., 1991), 34–36.

3. Henry Stedman Nourse and John Eliot Thayer, eds. *The Narrative of the Captivity and Restoration of Mrs. Mary Rowlandson* (Cambridge: J. Wilson and Son, 1903), 95. Local historians Nourse and Thayer, quoted in Mary Rowlandson, *The Narrative of the Captivity and Restoration of Mrs. Mary Rowlandson* (1682; reprint edited by Robert Diebold, Lancaster, Mass.: Town of Lancaster, 1975), 74. Mary Rowlandson added that they left this camp at Wachusett and "went about three

or four miles, and there they built a great wigwam, big enough to hold a hundred Indians, which they did in preparation to a great day of dancing" (see Rowlandson, *Narrative,* 46). Thayer and Nourse place this second site near the southern end of Wachusett Lake; quoted in Rowlandson, *Narrative,* 76. This is probably the site mentioned by Leach; see Douglas Edward Leach, *Flintlock and Tomahawk: New England in King Philip's War* (1958; reprint, New York: Norton, 1966), 199.

4. George W. Ellis and John E. Morris, *King Philip's War* (New York: Grafton Press, 1906), 86.

5. Personal communications with Jeff Fiske, 1991; Jeffrey H. Fiske is the author of *Wheeler's Surprise: The Lost Battlefield of King Philip's War* (Worcester, Mass.: Towaid Printing, 1993), cited below.

6. J. H. Temple, *History of North Brookfield, Massachusetts* (published by the Town of North Brookfield, 1887), 33.

7. Ibid.

8. Ibid. Ellis and Morris believed that the middle camp was the site of Rowlandson's third remove; see Ellis and Morris, *King Philip's War,* 86.

9. Temple, *Brookfield,* 30.

10. Levi Badger Chase, *Interpretation of Woodward's and Saffrey's Map of 1642, or the Earliest Bay Path* (Boston: David Clapp & Son, 1901), 4.

11. Temple, *Brookfield,* 27.

12. Ibid., 30–31.

13. Fiske, *Wheeler's Surprise,* 33.

14. Temple, *Brookfield,* 27.

15. Ibid., 29.

16. Hubbard, *History,* vol. 1, 86.

17. Increase Mather, *The History of King Philip's War* (1676; reprint, edited by Samuel G. Drake, 1862; Bowie, Md.: Heritage Books, 1990), 63.

18. John G. Metcalf, *Annals of the Town of Mendon, from 1659 to 1880* (Providence, R.I.: E. L. Freeman, 1880), 62.

19. Samuel Drake, ed., *Old Indian Chronicle: Being a Collection of Exceeding Rare Tracts, Written and Published in the Time of King Philip's War* (Boston: Samuel G. Drake, 1867), 142.

20. Temple, *Brookfield*, 92.

21. Ibid., 93.

22. Louis E. Roy, *Quaboag Plantation Alias Brookfield: A Seventeenth Century Massachusetts Town* (Worcester, Mass.: self-published, 1965), 153. Speaking in 1828, Joseph Foot noted an older tradition: "According to all tradition this place is the hill at the north end of Wickaboag Pond. This Hill appears to have been used as an Indian Cemetery. When it was cultivated by the English after their return, great numbers of Human bones were exhumated" (see Foot, *An Historical Discourse Delivered at West Brookfield, Mass., Nov. 27, 1828* [West Brookfield, Mass.: Merriam & Cooke, 1843], 56).

23. Ebenezer W. Peirce, *Indian History, Biography and Genealogy* (North Abington, Mass.: Zerviah Gould Mitchell, 1878), 196.

24. Emphasis mine. This is one of the most hotly debated parts of Wheeler's description: Did "a swamp where the natives then were" refer to the camp that Ephraim Curtis had visited on August 1, ten miles from Brookfield? Or did it refer to some second location where the Nipmuc could now be found? The following sentence implies the latter—"near the said swamp"—but there is no consensus.

25. Thomas Wheeler's narrative, as quoted in Lucius R. Paige, "Wickaboag? Or Winnimisset?: Which Was the Place of Capt. Wheeler's Defeat in 1675," *New England Historic Genealogical Register* no. 38 (1884), 396.

26. A contemporary account noted that "Captain Hutchinson died, when his wife and son were within twelve miles of him in their journey to see him"; Drake believed the son to be Elisha Hutchinson, grandfather of Thomas Hutchinson, future governor of Massachusetts; see Drake, *Old Indian Chronicle*, 143.

27. Temple, *Brookfield*, 94.

28. Paige, "Wickaboag?" 398.

29. Temple, *Brookfield*, 94.

30. Foot, *Historical Discourse*, 56.

31. D. H. Chamberlain, "Wheeler's Surprise, 1675: Where?" A paper read before the Quaboag Historical Society at New Braintree, September 12, 1899, and before the Worcester Society of Antiquity at Worcester, November 14, 1899, held by the Massachusetts Historical Society.

32. *Proceedings of the Massachusetts Historical Society*, 2nd series, vol. 8 (Boston: Massachusetts Historical Society, 1899), 280.

33. Paige, "Wickaboag?" 396.

34. Ibid., 397.

35. Hubbard, *History*, vol. 1, 98.

36. *Proceedings*, 2nd series, vol. 8, 279–280.

37. Bodge, *Soldiers*, 111.

38. *Proceedings*, 2nd series, vol. 8, 280–281.

39. Temple, *Brookfield*, 96.

40. Ibid., 95.

41. Ibid.

42. A contemporary account of the event noted that "the guide that conducted men through the woods, brought them to a swamp not far off the appointed place" (see Drake, ed., *Old Indian Chronicle*, 142). This description of a site just a short distance from the meeting place also favors Temple's conclusion. See Temple, *Brookfield*, 94–95.

43. Temple, *Brookfield*, 97.

44. Bodge, *Soldiers*, 66.

45. Hubbard, *History*, vol. 1, 98–99. Hubbard wrote: "until they came to the place appointed; and finding no Indians, so secure were they, that they ventured along further to find the infidels as their chief town, never suspecting that least danger, but when they had rode four or five miles that way, they fell into an ambush." Note that Hubbard's estimated distances are sometimes inaccurate, like when he wrote that the distance from Providence to Nipsachuck was twenty-two miles, more than twice the correct distance.

46. Bodge, *Soldiers*, 111.

47. Roy, *Quaboag Plantation*, 154. Roy de-

scribed it as a point one thousand feet north-west of the present home (in 1964) of Ernest Waterman.

48. We sometimes become so locked into geography by the paths of modern roads that we fail to find the most logical, direct route that a seventeenth-century woodsman might have cut; personal communications with Jeff Fiske, 1991.

49. Fiske, *Wheeler's Surprise;* 42–43.

50. Hubbard, *History,* vol. 1, 100.

51. Leach, *Flintlock,* 78.

52. Hubbard, *History,* vol. 1, 100.

53. Ellis and Morris, *King Philip's War,* 94.

54. Hubbard, *History,* vol. 1, 104.

55. Mather, *History,* 68.

56. Ellis and Morris, *King Philip's War,* 94.

57. Mather, *History,* 68.

58. Drake writes that Willard and his men had been joined at this point by forty-six troopers under Captain James Parker of Groton, making the total force ninety-four men; see Hubbard, *History,* vol. 1, 103.

59. Foot, *Historical Discourse,* 56–57.

60. Mather, *History,* 76–77.

61. Bodge, *Soldiers,* 129.

62. The author visited the area with local historian Byron Canney in 1992. There is no convincing local tradition placing the battle.

63. Ellis and Morris, *King Philip's War,* 104.

64. J. H. Temple and George Sheldon, *History of the Town of Northfield, Massachusetts For 150 Years, with An Account of the Prior Occupation of the Territory by the Squakheags and With Family Genealogies* (Albany, N.Y.: Joel Musell, 1875), 74. Temple also described the camp as being near Pine Meadow; see *Pocumtuck Valley Memorial Association Proceedings,* vol. 2, Field Meeting 1872, 121.

65. Ibid., 75.

66. Personal communication with Rosa Johnston, 1992.

67. This is present-day Maple Street; see Herbert Collins Parsons, *A Puritan Outpost: A History of the Town and People of Northfield,*

Massachusetts (New York: Macmillan, 1937), 44. Epaphas Hoyt wrote that "for some distance the ravine extended along the right of the route, and at the place where it was to be passed it made a short turn to the left, continuing directly to the river. Discovering Beers' approach, a large body of Indians formed an ambuscade at this place" (see Hoyt, *Antiquarian Researches: Comprising A History of the Indian Wars in the Country Bordering Connecticut River and Part Adjacent, and Other Interesting Events* [Greenfield, Mass.: Ansel Phelps, 1824], 104).

68. Temple and Sheldon, *Northfield,* 75. Temple added that "Capt. Beers' baggage wagon was left about midway of the plain and nearly opposite the present house of T. J. Field, and perhaps marks the spot reached by the rear of the column."

69. Ibid.

70. The stone markers in town were placed in the mid-nineteenth century under the direction of historian George Sheldon. Their location was based partly on family traditions passed down to Phineas Farm, who owned the land on which the ambush took place. The newer Massachusetts state markers are probably less accurate.

71. Temple and Sheldon, *Northfield,* 20.

72. Ibid., 75–76. In his 1835 speech at Bloody Brook, Edward Everett noted that no monument marked the site of Beers' fall, and that only tradition "will hand it down to the latest posterity." Everett did not mention head and foot stones; see Everett, *Orations.*

73. Personal communication with Rosa Johnston, 1992.

74. Temple and Sheldon, *Northfield,* 76.

75. Hoyt, *Antiquarian Researches,* 104.

76. Temple and Sheldon, *Northfield,* 77.

77. Ibid., 23.

78. Hubbard, *History,* vol. 1, 111.

79. Temple and Sheldon, *Northfield,* 22. This is along present-day Orange Road in Warwick State Forest. The precise location is unknown; personal communication with Rosa Johnston, 1992. Mary Rowlandson's captors passed

north through Northfield on their sixth and seventh removes, and south on their fourteenth remove, although this latter site may have been farther north in New Hampshire.

80. Temple and Sheldon, *Northfield*, 13.

81. Ibid., 13.

82. *Pocumtuck Valley Memorial Association Proceedings,* Field Meeting 1897, 445–446.

83. Hubbard, *History,* vol. 1, 1112.

84. Mather, *History*, 85.

85. Everett, *Orations,* 653–654.

86. Mather, *History*, 85. The figure commonly used is seven to eight hundred Indians as judged by those few English who escaped; see Hubbard, *History*, vol. 1, 115. Such a figure was almost certainly overstated.

87. Mather, *History*, 85.

88. Ellis and Morris, *King Philip's War,* 112. Edward Everett quoted a Newbury, Massachusetts, tradition which claimed that a man who died there in 1824, at the age of ninety-seven, was acquainted with two of the three men from Lathrop's company said to have survived the Bloody Brook massacre. Henry Bodwell, his left arm broken by a musket ball, fought his way clear of the ambush. John Tappan hid in a watercourse covered by grass. Robert Dutch of Ipswich, also said to have survived the massacre, was wounded and left for dead but was rescued by Moseley's troops; see Everett, *Orations, 655–656.*

89. Ellis and Morris, *King Philip's War,* 113.

90. Ibid., 112.

91. Hoyt, *Antiquarian Researches,* 109.

92. There is some confusion on this point. Hoyt wrote in 1824 that the first monument erected near the place of attack was now decayed, with "two plain stone flags, lying near the front of the house . . . its only remains. Several gentlemen have it in contemplation to repair the old, or erect a new monument, near the same spot with an appropriate inscription" (see Hoyt, *Antiquarian Researches,* 109–110). Whether the current stone slab is one of the original "plain stone flags," or a second, new memorial is unknown.

93. John Warner Barber, *Historical Collections, Being a General Collection of Interesting Facts, Traditions, Biographical Sketches, Anecdotes, etc. Relating to the History and Antiquities of Every Town in Mass.* (Worcester, Mass.: Dorr, Howland, 1839), 247–248. Everett reported in 1835 that "the spot has recently been identified by excavation on the roadside, directly in front of the house of Stephen Whitey, Esq., of South Deerfield." (See Everett, *Orations,* 656).

94. Barber, *Historical Collections,* 248.

95. Ibid.

96. Mather, *History,* 86.

97. Barber, *Historical Collections,* 248. One wonders if the committee wasn't counting with history in mind. This number matches precisely Increase Mather's report of ninety-six Indians killed; see Mather, *History,* 86.

98. Everett, *Orations,* 655.

99. This site should not be confused with King Philip's Stockade, adjacent to Forest Park where Route 5 enters Longmeadow. King Philip's Stockade was named for the sachem centuries after his death and has no relevance to King Philip's War.

100. Mason A. Green, *Springfield, 1636–1886: History of Town and City* (Springfield, Mass.: C. A. Nichols, 1888), 160–161.

101. John P. Pretola, "The Springfield Fort Hill Site: A New Look," *Archaeological Society of Connecticut,* Bulletin, no. 48, 37.

102. Personal communications with John Pretola, 1992.

103. Pretola, "Springfield Fort Hill Site," 38–40.

104. Ibid., 42–43.

105. Ellis and Morris, *King Philip's War,* 117–118.

106. Ibid., 118.

107. Ibid.

108. Ibid., 120. Hubbard estimated "300 of Phillip's Indians" were admitted into the fort; see Hubbard, *History,* vol. 1, 120. An Agawam scout captured at the time estimated

the total force to be 270, but others in Springfield felt the force was not more than 100, most of them being Agawam; see Bodge, *Soldiers*, 145.

109. Ellis and Morris, *King Philip's War*, 119.

110. Hubbard, *History*, vol. 1, 122.

111. Ellis and Morris, *King Philip's War*, 119.

112. Hubbard, *History*, vol. 1, 123.

113. Ibid., 206.

114. Mather, *History*, 253.

115. Ellis and Morris, *King Philip's War*, 193. The settlers were said to be descending Pecowsic Hill; *Proceedings at the Centennial Celebration of the Incorporation of the Town of Longmeadow, October Seventeenth, 1883* (1884), 29.

116. A. Cory Bardswell et. al., *The Hatfield Book* (Northampton, Mass.: Gazette Printing Co., 1970), 3-4.

117. Ibid., 7.

118. Hubbard reported seven hundred, but few later historians use this number; see Hubbard, *History*, vol. 2, 44.

119. Ibid., 124.

120. Ibid., 125.

121. Daniel White Wells and Reuben Field Wells, *A History of Hatfield, Massachusetts* (Springfield, Mass.: F. C. H. Gibbons, 1910), 82.

122. Ibid.

123. Ibid.

124. Bardswell et. al., *Hatfield*, 8.

125. Ibid.

126. Hubbard, *History*, vol. 2, 234. The number sometimes reported is seven hundred and perhaps confuses the first and second attack.

127. Wells and Wells, *Hatfield*, 90.

128. Bardswell et. al., *Hatfield*, 8.

129. Wells and Wells, *Hatfield*, 90.

130. Francis Jennings, *The Invasion of America: Indians, Colonialism, and the Cant of Conquest* (New York: Norton, 1975), 313.

131. Ibid., 314. This was probably overstated. A better estimate might have been four

to five hundred; see Ellis and Morris, *King Philip's War*, 165-166.

132. Jennings, *Invasion*, 315.

133. Ibid., 316.

134. Personal communication with Christina Kelly, Schaghticoke town historian, 1991.

135. Ibid.

136. New York had been officially opened to native refugees in May 1676.

137. Personal communication with Christina Kelly, 1991

138. Jennings, *Invasion*, 323.

139. Hubbard, *History*, vol. 1, 223.

140. William Barry, *A History of Framingham, Massachusetts* (Boston: James Munroe, 1847), 24.

141. Hubbard, *History*, vol. 1, 223.

142. Barry, *Framingham*, 27-29.

143. Ibid., 24.

144. Rowlandson, *Narrative*, 3-4.

145. Ibid., 371.

146. Personal communication with Herbert Hosmer, 1991.

147. Leach, *Flintlock and Tomahawk*, 159.

148. Rowlandson, *Narrative*, ix.

149. Ibid., 7.

150. Ellis and Morris, *King Philip's War*, 172.

151. Personal communication with Herbert Hosmer, 1991.

152. Rowlandson, *Narrative*, 63.

153. *Exercises at the Bi-Centennial Commemoration of the Burning of Medfield by Indians in King Philip's War* (Medfield, Mass.: George H. Ellis, 1876), 15.

154. The natives wrote: "We come 300 at this Time," but Hubbard estimated their number to be 500; see Hubbard, *History*, vol. 1, 171.

155. Ibid., 168.

156. Ibid., 169.

157. Kenneth A. Lockridge, *A New England Town: The First Hundred Years* (New York: Norton, 1970), 95.

158. Hubbard, *History*, vol. 1, 169.

159. Ibid.

160. William S. Tilden, ed., *History of the Town of Medfield, Massachusetts, 1650–1886* (Boston: Geo. H. Ellis, 1887), 82.

161. Ibid., 83.

162. Hubbard, *History*, vol. 1, 170.

163. Tilden described the location as "about fifth rods eastward of the junction of Main and Pound Streets" (see Tilden, *Medfield*, 83).

164. Conversation with the staff, Medfield Historical Society, 1992.

165. Like most structures of its age, Peak House is not without its controversies. Tilden wrote that Peak House was an addition to Benjamin Clark's second house and was not built until 1762. "After the decay of the old part, it was moved to its present location" (see Tilden, *Medfield*, 348). However, Paul Hurd, president of the Medfield Historical Society, wrote in 1991: "The foundation upon which it [Peak House] is built is unarguably of early 18th century construction . . . However, Abbot Lowel Cummings, formerly of the SPNEA [Society for the Preservation of New England Antiquities], swears it [Peak House] was built in the 17th century, and has included its architecture in his book about 17th century framed houses in Massachusetts . . . In researching the building for application to be included in the National Register of Historic Places all deeds, possible to be located, were checked out, and no evidence was found of Benjamin Clark having built another house to replace the one burned by King Philip's Indians on February 21, 1676, except Peak House."

166. *Bi-Centennial Commemoration of the Burning of Medfield*, 16.

167. Ibid., 22.

168. Conversation with the staff, Medfield Historical Society, 1992.

169. Ibid.

170. Ibid.

171. Richard Desorgher, *A Short History of the Indian Attack on Medfield, February 21, 1676* (1976), 5–6.

172. Desorgher, *A Short History*, 6.

173. Hubbard, *History*, vol. 1, 171.

174. Tilden, *Medfield*, 85.

175. Mather, *History*, 120.

176. Hubbard, *History*, vol. 1, 170. Tilden reported about thirty-two houses burned and about thirty-two left standing; see Tilden, *Medfield*, 84.

177. Desorgher, *A Short History*, 8.

178. Ibid., 9.

179. Ibid.

180. Hubbard, *History*, vol. 1, 171.

181. *Bi-Centennial Commemoration of the Burning of Medfield*, 16.

182. Ibid.

183. Personal communication with Paul Hurd, 1992.

184. Hubbard, *History*, vol. 1, 171.

185. Rowlandson, *Narrative*, 13.

186. Mortimer Blake, *A History of the Town of Franklin, Mass.* (Franklin, Mass.: Committee of the Town of Franklin, 1879), 17–18.

187. Michael J. Puglisi, *Puritans Besieged: The Legacies of King Philip's War in the Massachusetts Bay Colony* (Lanham, Md.: University Press of America, 1991), 110.

188. Ibid., 109.

189. Hubbard, *History*, vol. 1, 196–197.

190. Caleb Butler, *History of the Town of Groton* (Boston: T. R. Marvin, 1848), 82.

191. Personal communication with Robert Beal, 1992.

192. Ibid.

193. Hubbard, *History*, vol. 1, 196.

194. Ibid.

195. Butler, *Groton*, 83.

196. Ibid.

197. Hubbard, *History*, vol. 1, 198.

198. Ibid.

199. Ibid., 200.

200. Ibid.

201. Ibid., 199.

202. Ibid., 194–195.

203. Butler, *Groton*, 82.

204. Virginia May, *A Plantation Called Peta-pawag* (Groton, Mass.: Groton Historical Society, 1976), 69.

205. Personal communication with Robert Beal, 1992.

206. Puglisi, *Puritans Besieged*, 99.

207. Bodge, *Soldiers*, 235.

208. The Reverend John Russell of Hadley estimated one thousand; see Bodge, *Soldiers*, 236.

209. James Russell Trumbell, *History of Northampton, Massachusetts*, vol. 1 (Northampton, Mass.: n.p., 1898), 306.

210. Bodge, *Soldiers*, 236.

211. Hubbard, *History*, vol. 1, 132.

212. Bodge, *Soldiers*, 236.

213. Mather, *History*, 122.

214. Trumbell, *Northampton*, vol. 1, 268.

215. Personal communication with Terrie Korpita, 1992.

216. Trumbell, *Northampton*, vol. 1, 269.

217. Personal communication with Terrie Korpita, 1992.

218. Ellis and Morris, *King Philip's War*, 128.

219. Trumbell, *Northampton*, vol. 1, 269.

220. Ibid.

221. Jacqueline Van Voris, *The Look of Paradise* (Canaan, N.H.: Phoenix, 1984), 83.

222. Ellis and Morris, *King Philip's War*, 128.

223. Hubbard, *History*, vol. 1, 132.

224. Ibid.

225. Van Voris, *The Look of Paradise*, vol. 1, and correspondence with Terrie Korpita, 1992.

226. Trumbell, *Northampton*, vol. 1, 276–277.

227. Ibid., 308. Trumbell wrote that "it is comparatively easy to name the point of each assault," but gives no clues as to his sources.

228. Ibid., 306.

229. Bodge, *Soldiers*, 236.

230. Puglisi, *Puritans Besieged*, 98.

231. Ibid., 98.

232. Ella A. Bigelow, *Historical Reminiscences of the Early Times in Marlborough, Massachusetts* (Marlboro, Mass.: Times Publishing Company, 1910), 8.

233. Charles Hudson, *History of the Town of Marlborough, Massachusetts, from Its First Settlement in 1657 to 1861* (Boston: T. R. Marvin, 1862).

234. Personal communications with Gary Brown, 1991.

235. Bigelow, *Marlborough*, 6.

236. Ibid.

237. Ellis and Morris, *King Philip's War*, 189.

238. Bigelow, *Marlborough*, 5.

239. Leach, *Flintlock and Tomahawk*, 172, 175.

240. Mather, *History*, 127.

241. Hubbard, *History*, vol. 1, 247.

242. Hudson, *Marlborough*, 74.

243. Bigelow, *Marlborough*, 9.

244. Personal communication with Gary Brown, 1991.

245. Hudson, *Marlborough*, 82.

246. Personal communication with Gary Brown, 1991.

247. Hudson, *Marlborough*, 82.

248. Bigelow, *Marlborough*, 9.

249. Ellis and Morris, *King Philip's War*, 208.

250. Laura Scott, *Sudbury: A Pictorial History* (Norfolk, Va.: Donning, 1989), 31.

251. John C. Powers, *We Shall Not Tamely Give It Up* (Lewiston, Maine: John C. Powers, 1988), 63.

252. Ellis and Morris, *King Philip's War*, 208.

253. Powers, *We Shall Not Tamely*, 65.

254. Alfred Sereno Hudson, *The History of Sudbury, Massachusetts, 1638–1889* (Sudbury, Mass.: Town of Sudbury, 1889), 198–200.

255. Ibid., 199.

256. Many of the Sudbury monuments incorrectly list the date of the Sudbury Fight as April 18. This stemmed from William Hubbard's history of the war, which incorrectly gave the date of the battle; Drake, ed., *Old Indian Chronicle*, 233.

257. Scott, *Sudbury*, 31.

258. Ellis and Morris, *King Philip's War*, 209. Other reports indicated that two survived, making their way successfully to the Haynes garrison; see Powers, *We Shall Not Tamely*, 64.

259. Hudson, *Sudbury*, 199, and Ellis and Morris, *King Philip's War*, 210.

260. Hudson, *Sudbury*, 235.

261. Hubbard, *History*, vol. 1, 210.

262. Drake, ed., *Old Indian Chronicle*, 235.

263. Powers, *We Shall Not Tamely*, 73.

264. Ellis and Morris, *King Philip's War*, 213.

265. Scott, *Sudbury*, 33 (from Hudson).

266. Ibid., 31.

267. Hudson, *Sudbury*, 200.

268. Scott, *Sudbury*, 30.

269. Hudson, *Sudbury*, 198–200.

270. Ibid., 200.

271. Rowlandson, *Narrative*, 45.

272. Bodge, *Soldiers*, 238.

273. Ibid., 237.

274. Ibid., 244.

275. Ibid., 242.

276. Personal communication with Richard Colton, 1991.

277. Ellis and Morris, *King Philip's War*, 226, and Bodge, *Soldiers*, 243.

278. Ellis and Morris, *King Philip's War*, 227–228, and Bodge, *Soldiers*, 244. Turner himself doubted the estimate of only sixty or seventy warriors; see Bodge, *Soldiers*, 244.

279. Ellis and Morris, *King Philip's War*, 229.

280. Ibid., 230.

281. Ibid.

282. Ralph M. Stoughton, *History of the Town of Gill* (published by the town as a bicentennial project, 1978), 7.

283. Ellis and Morris, *King Philip's War*, 230.

284. Hubbard, *History*, vol. 1, 230.

285. Ellis and Morris, *King Philip's War*, 233.

286. Bodge, *Soldiers*, 247.

287. Personal communication with Crawford, 1992.

288. Lucy Cutler Kellogg, *History of Greenfield, 1900–1929*, vol. 3 (Greenfield, Mass.: Town of Greenfield, 1931), 1400.

289. Ellis and Morris, *King Philip's War*, 233.

290. Hubbard, *History*, vol. 1, 233.

291. Ellis and Morris, *King Philip's War*, 234. Hubbard thinks that no fewer than two or three hundred must have perished; see Hubbard, *History*, vol. 1, 231.

292. Ellis and Morris, *King Philip's War*, 235.

293. Mather, *History*, 149.

294. Stoughton, *Gill*, 34.

295. Rita Reinke, "Seventeenth-Century Military Defenses Uncovered," *Journal of the Massachusetts Historical Commission* (fall, 1990), 3.

296. Mather, *History*, 155.

297. Ibid., 156.

298. Hubbard, *History*, vol. 1, 245.

299. Mather, *History*, 156.

300. Ibid., 157.

301. Russell Bourne, *The Red King's Rebellion: Racial Politics in New England, 1675–1678* (New York: Atheneum, 1990), 140.

302. In 1660, forty-one of the fifty-nine members of the High Court of Justice were still alive. Fifteen fled abroad. Nine were captured and put to death; see John Cannon and Ralph Griffiths, *The Oxford Illustrated History of the British Monarchy* (Oxford, U.K.: Oxford University Press, 1988), 385.

303. Ellis and Morris, *King Philip's War*, 103.

304. Mather, *History*, 72.

305. George Sheldon, "The Traditional Story of the Attack Upon Hadley and the Appearance of Gen. Goffe, Sept. 1, 1675: Has It Any Foundation in Fact?" *New England Historic Genealogical Register* 28 (October 1874), 379.

306. Thomas Hutchinson, *The History of Massachusetts from the First Settlement Thereof in 1628, Until the Year 1750*, 3rd ed., vol. 1 (Boston: Thomas Andrews, 1795), 201.

307. Sylvester Judd, *History of Hadley* (Springfield, Mass.: H. R. Hunting, 1905), 139.

308. Sheldon, "Attack Upon Hadley," 380.

309. Ibid., 381.

310. Ibid., 382.

311. Ibid., 383.

312. Judd, *Hadley*, 137.

313. Sheldon, "Attack Upon Hadley," 388.

314. Ellis and Morris, *King Philip's War*, 104.

315. Leach, *Flintlock and Tomahawk*, 267.

316. Bourne, *The Red King's Rebellion*, 140.

317. Douglas Wilson, "Web of Secrecy: Goffe, Whalley, and the Legend of Hadley," *New England Quarterly* 60, no. 4 (December 1987), 539–541.

318. Ibid., 542–543.

319. Ellis and Morris, *King Philip's War*, 282. Hubbard states that forty-five were killed or captured, and that others died of wounds or sickness after reaching New York; see Hubbard, *History*, vol. 1, 279.

320. Hubbard, *History*, vol. 1, 280.

321. Hubbard, *History*, vol. 1, 279. The modern spelling of Ausotunnoog is Housatonic. The Dutch River is the Hudson River.

322. Charles J. Taylor, *History of Great Barrington, (Berkshire County) Massachusetts* (Great Barrington, Mass.: Clark W. Bryan, 1882), 8.

323. Ibid., 10.

324. Personal communications with Lila Parrish, 1992.

CHAPTER 6: KING PHILIP'S WAR IN RHODE ISLAND AND CONNECTICUT

1. This spring is sometimes confused with the spring by which Philip was shot and killed. The two are not the same; Philip was killed farther south near Mount Hope.

2. Susan G. Gibson, ed., *Burr's Hill: A Seventeenth-Century Wampanoag Burial Ground in Warren, R.I.* (Providence, R.I.: Haffenreffer Museum of Anthropology, 1980) 24.

3. Guy M. Fessenden, *History of Warren, R.I.* (Providence, R.I.: H. H. Brown, 1845), 71–72.

4. George W. Ellis and John E. Morris, *King Philip's War* (New York: Grafton Press, 1906), 68.

5. While lost to nineteenth-century Americans, the site of this burying ground was apparently known to seventeenth-century English settlers. Benjamin Church, ranging about Warren in search of Anawan near the war's end, wrote that "they heard another gun, which seemed toward the Indian burying place" (see Thomas Church, *The History of Philip's War, Commonly Called the Great Indian War of 1675 and 1676* [1717; reprint, edited by Samuel G. Drake, 1829; Bowie, Md.: Heritage Books, 1989], 130).

6. Laurie Weinstein-Farson, *The Wampanoag* (New York: Chelsea House, 1989), 39.

7. Gibson, ed., *Burr's Hill*, 22.

8. *A Patchwork History of Tiverton, Rhode Island* (Tiverton R.I.: Tiverton Historical Society, 1976), 11, and Rhode Island Historical Preservation Commission, *Tiverton, Rhode Island: Statewide Historical Preservation Report*, Preliminary (1983), 4.

9. Church wrote that these tracks were discovered near "the brook that runs into Nunnaquahqat neck." Drake identifies the brook as "that which empties into the bay nearly a mile southward from Howland's ferry. The road to Little Compton, here, follows the shore of the bay, and crosses said brook where it meets the bay" (Thomas Church, *History*, 39).

10. *A Patchwork History*, 11.

11. Thomas Church, *History* (ed. Drake), 40.

12. Benjamin Church, *The History of King Philip's War*, with an introduction and notes by Henry Martyn Dexter (Boston: John Kimball Wiggin, 1865), 31.

13. Thomas Church, *History*, 41.

14. Ibid., 42.

15. James E. Holland, "How The Four Corners of Puncatest Came to Be," *Old Rhode Island* 5, no. 2 (1995), p. 18.

16. Dexter in Benjamin Church, *History*, 34.

17. *A Patchwork History*, 12.

NOTES TO PAGES 241–251

18. Thomas Church, *History*, 46.

19. Benjamin Church, *History* (ed. Dexter), 36.

20. Ibid.

21. Ibid.

22. Ellis and Morris, *King Philip's War*, 76.

23. Richard LeBaron Bowen, *Early Rehoboth,* vol. 3 (Rehoboth, Mass.: privately published, 1948), 79. One of Philip's captains killed was Nimrod. A simple gravestone—probably unrelated but intriguing nonetheless—marked "Nimrod, An Indian" sits on a farm near the old Taunton Dog Track off Route 44 in Taunton, Massachusetts.

24. From a report by the Christian Indian George; see Thomas Hutchinson, *The History of Massachusetts from the First Settlement Thereof in 1628, Until the Year 1750,* 3rd ed., vol. 2 (Boston: Thomas Andrews, 1795), 267.

25. William Hubbard, *The History of the Indian Wars in New England from the First Settlement to the Termination of the War with King Philip in 1677, from the Original Work by the Rev. William Hubbard* (1677), vol. 1 (reprint, edited by Samuel G. Drake, 1865; Bowie, Md.: Heritage Books, 1990), 90.

26. William Hubbard estimated twenty-two miles.

27. Reprinted in Increase Mather, *The History of King Philip's War* (1676; reprint, edited by Samuel G. Drake, 1862; Bowie, Md.: Heritage Books, 1990), 228–229.

28. Hubbard, *History*, vol. 1, 94.

29. On September 3 Richard Smith Jr. reported that the Indians had killed some of his cattle, but in none of his subsequent letters to the commissioners does he suggest that he and his family were seized or in any way molested by the Narragansett.

30. Nathaniel B. Shurtleff and David Pulsifer, eds., *Records of the Colony of New Plymouth in New England,* vol. 5, *1674–1686* (Boston: 1854), 357.

31. Ibid., 361.

32. Daniel Berkeley Updike, *Richard Smith* (Boston: Merrymount Press, 1937), 110.

33. Ibid., 110–111.

34. Ibid., 111.

35. Ibid., 111–112.

36. Ibid., 112.

37. Ibid., 113.

38. Shurteleff and Pulsifer, eds., *Records*, 359.

39. Ibid., 457.

40. J. Hammond Trumbull, *The Public Records of the Colony of Connecticut* (Hartford, Ct.: F. A. Brown, 1852), 387.

41. W. Noel Sainsbury, ed. *Calendar of State Papers, Colonial Series, America and West Indies, 1675–1676* (London: Eyre and Spottiswoode, 1893), 442.

42. Ibid., 158.

43. Personal visit, 1991. A second site in Warwick related to King Philip's War concerns the death of John Wickes, killed by Narragansett in 1676 when he left the safety of the so-called Stone Castle. The Stone Castle, built entirely of stone in 1649, was located on the site of the present-day Elks Lodge parking lot on West Shore Road. The structure survived King Philip's War but was demolished in 1795. "Wickes' decapitated body was found by his companions and buried; his head was found a few days later and was buried in a smaller, separate grave" (see Rhode Island Historical Preservation Commission, *Warwick, Rhode Island: Statewide Historical Preservation Report,* Preliminary [April 1981], 7). Wickes' grave can still be seen in the Stone Castle Cemetery off West Shore Road, west of the Elks parking lot and directly north of Webster Street. An overgrown path leads from the parking lot to the cemetery, which is in a state of disrepair.

44. Ellis and Morris, *King Philip's War*, 145.

45. The precise site of Pumham's death is unknown. Guesses include present-day Medfield, or even farther southwest in present-day Bellingham. Personal communication with Robert Hanson.

46. Hubbard, *History*, vol. 1, 259.

47. Mather, *History*, 183.

48. Rhode Island Historical Preservation

Commission, *North Kingstown, Rhode Island: Statewide Preservation Report* (November 1979), 6.

49. Shurteleff and Pulsifer, eds., *Records*, 412.

50. Howard Millar Chapin, *The Trading Post of Roger Williams with Those of John Wilcox and Richard Smith* (Providence, R.I.: Society of Colonial Wars, 1933), 13. "The Narragansett sachems invited him [Roger Williams] to establish a post among them. Shortly thereafter, he began trading out of Cocumscossoc, a sheltered cove on the west side of the bay (now Wickford, Rhode Island) (Bailyn 1955:59; Chapin 1931:31; Woodward 1971). While maintaining his Providence residence, Williams was joined by two other traders. John Wilcox soon became William's partner and resident manager (Bailyn 1955:59; Chapin 1931:31, 1933:25). Richard Smith, Sr., eventually bought out both men's operations, becoming the primary trader in the region after 1651" (see William A. Turnbaugh, "Assessing the Significance of European Goods in Seventeenth-Century Narragansett Society," in *Ethnohistory and Archaeology: Approaches to Postcontact Change in the Americas*, edited by J. Daniel Rogers and Samuel M. Wilson [New York: Plenum, 1993], 141). The Brown University Department of Anthropology was actively examining the site in 1991.

51. Rhode Island Historical Preservation Commission, *North Kingstown*, 7.

52. Ibid., 6.

53. Quoted in William S. Simmons, *The Narragansett* (New York: Chelsea House, 1989), 89.

54. John Talcott, "A Letter Written by Maj. John Talcott from Mr. Stanton's at Quonocontaug to Govr. William Leete and the Hond. Council of the Colony of Connecticut" (July 4, 1676), (reprint, Providence, R.I.: Society of Colonial Wars, 1934), 11.

55. Ellis and Morris, *King Philip's War*, 249.

56. Talcott, "A Letter," 7.

57. The number of wigwams and population density is unclear. Joseph Granger wrote that "the 500 wigwams would yield a general figure of approximately 1,000 families, a number translated to produce a population estimate of nearly 4,000 persons . . . even with refugee populations, a figure of 2,000 individuals seems to be a high estimate for the Great Swamp winter site" (from Joseph E. Granger, "The 'Brumal Den': An Archaeological and Ethnohistorical Study of the 'Great Swamp Fort' of the Narragansetts" [unpublished], quoted with permission of the author, 42–43).

58. Patrick M. Malone, *The Skulking Way of War: Technology and Tactics Among the New England Indians* (Lanham, Md.: Madison Books, 1991), 73. Perhaps Stonewall John was active in the design or construction of the fort; ibid., 75.

59. This view was challenged by Welcome Arnold Greene in an 1887 analysis of the battle, one of the first critical evaluations of historical accounts. "The term block house may apply to a building no larger than a dog kennel, and that of a flanker, to a rail fence . . . It is a misnomer to call the affair a fort in any sense. It was simply a densely crowded Indian Village, with a line of fence and brush around it" (see Greene, "The Great Battle of the Narragansetts, Dec. 19, 1675," *Narragansett Historical Register* 5, no. 4 [December 1887], 333).

60. Stonewall John's prior relationship with Richard Smith Jr. probably made the Narragansett an ideal ambassador for his people. However, if Stonewall John was the most gifted military engineer among the Narragansett, and Canonchet's Fort was still in an unfinished state (which the English would supposedly exploit in their attack a few day's later), one wonders why he was not in the Great Swamp supervising construction activity.

61. Hubbard, *History*, vol. 1, 128. Hubbard reported that the natives killed "10 Englishmen and 5 women and children but two escaped in all."

62. Ebenezer W. Peirce, *Indian History, Biography and Genealogy* (North Abington, Mass.: Zerviah Gould Mitchell, 1878), 196.

63. Quoted in Norman M. Isham, "Preliminary Report to the Society of Colonial Wars of Rhode Island on the Excavations at the Jireh Bull Garrison House on Tower Hill in South Kingstown," *Rhode Island Historical Society Collections* 11, no. 1 (January 1918), 2.

64. Mather, *History,* 105.

65. Isham, "Excavations at the Jireh Bull Garrison House," 3, 5. Directions are given: "If one follows the Middle Bridge or Tower Hill road down into the valley of the Narrow River and turns to the right, or toward the south, he will see, just before the turn to the bridge, a triangular piece of meadow in the southwest corner of which is a bar-way. Beyond this an old road zig-zags up the hill. By following this road up to and beyond the stone way, one will find a trail toward the left or south which will bring him to the site." Today, the old road and trail have been replaced by modern homes.

66. Ibid., 5, 7.

67. Ibid., 9, 10.

68. "Report Upon the Objects Excavated at the Jireh Bull House and Now in the Museum of the Rhode Island Historical Society," *Rhode Island Historical Society Collections* 18, no. 3 (July 1925), 83 ff.

69. Society of Colonial Wars, *A Plat of the Land of Capt. Henry Bull, Drawn by James Helme, Surveyor, January 8, 1729* (Providence, R.I.: E. L. Freeman, 1927).

70. A marker placed to commemorate the garrison had been removed at the author's visit in 1991.

71. Hubbard bemoaned the fact that "there was no Shelter left either for Officer or private Soldier" (see Hubbard, *History,* vol. 1, 143). Peirce wrote that "(their provisions being exhausted and the supply that they had expected to find in Bull's garrisoned house destroyed by the Indians) the wearied, frost bitten and hungry column recommenced its march" (see Peirce, *Indian History,* 128–129). However, Winslow knew of the garrison's destruction well before the march commenced and must have realized that his troops would be exposed to the elements and without additional supplies. Had the Bull garrison remained completely intact and welcomed the soldiers with open arms, there would still have been many hundreds left to sleep in the cold and snow.

72. Society of Colonial Wars, *A Record of the Ceremony and Oration of the Occasion of the Unveiling of the Monument Commemorating The Great Swamp Fight, December 19, 1675, in the Narragansett Country of Rhode Island* (1906), 31.

73. Thomas Hutchinson, *The History of the Colony and Province of Massachusetts Bay* (1765; reprint, Cambridge, Mass.: Harvard University Press, 1936), 302.

74. George Madison Bodge, *Soldiers in King Philip's War* (1906; Baltimore: Genealogical Publishing Co., 1991), 174.

75. Among firsthand accounts, neither Captain James Oliver, Joseph Dudley, nor Benjamin Church estimate the distance of the march from Pettaquamscutt to the fort.

76. Hubbard, *History,* vol. 1, 143.

77. Hutchinson, *History of the Colony and Province of Massachusetts Bay,* 253.

78. Ellis and Morris, *King Philip's War,* 149.

79. Bodge, *Soldiers,* 185.

80. Ibid., 173.

81. Leach, *Flintlock and Tomahawk,* 128.

82. In the 1906 oration that highlighted the dedication of the Great Swamp Fight monument, speaker Rowland G. Hazard noted that the freezing of the swamp so that it would bear the soldiers was "a thing almost unheard of before or since" (Society of Colonial Wars, *A Record of [. . .] the Great Swamp Fight,* 32).

83. Thomas Church, *History,* 58.

84. Bodge, *Soldiers,* 186. Welcome Arnold Greene noted in 1887, "From the northward the firm land projects into the swamp to within a distance of about a mile from the island . . . and if an attack were made on the fort it would probably be from the northern side" (see Greene, "The Great Battle of the Narragansetts," 335).

85. Bodge, *Soldiers,* 186. If other reports were true, of course, this water would have been frozen and passable without the log.

86. Samuel Drake, ed., *Old Indian Chronicle: Being a Collection of Exceeding Rare Tracts, Written and Published in the Time of King Philip's War* (Boston: Samuel G. Drake, 1867), 182. Were this literally true, Moseley probably would not have been left to report it.

87. For instance, not many months later at Turner's Falls, Massachusetts, a poorly prepared group of colonial soldiers experienced initial success in attacking an Indian camp, only to take terrible losses on their retreat home.

88. Joshua Tefft, quoted by Roger Williams, "The Winthrop Papers," *Collections of the Massachusetts Historical Society*, 4th series, vol. 6, 309.

89. Bodge, *Soldiers*, 193.

90. Thomas Church, *History*, 58.

91. Bodge, *Soldiers*, 193.

92. William Hubbard described Tefft as a "Renegade English man of Providence, that upon some Discontent amongst his Neighbors, had turned Indian, married one of the Indian Squaws, renounced his Religion, Nation and natural Parents all at once, fighting against them" (Hubbard, *History*, vol. 1, 162). Tefft may have worked as a miller with his father at Pettaquamscutt, though contemporary historians believed he had become a member of the Pokanoket in 1662, marrying a Pokanoket woman. Contemporaries also believed that he assisted the Narragansett with construction of their fort and fought on their side in the Great Swamp Fight. Tefft denied these charges, but after his capture on January 14 was executed as a traitor by the English; see Roger Williams, *The Correspondence of Roger Williams*, vol. 2 (1654–1682), Glenn W. LeFantasie, ed. (Hanover, N.H.: University Press of New England, 1988), 715.

93. Williams, "The Winthrop Papers," 310.

94. "James Quanapaug's Information," *Collections of the Massachusetts Historical Society*, 1st series, vol. 6, 206.

95. Ibid., 207. Quanpohit would also estimate that the Narragansett had "seven hundred fighting men, well armed, left" (ibid., 208). This would have meant that the Narragansett had 740 warriors before the Great Swamp Fight.

96. Bodge, *Soldiers*, 174.

97. *A Continuation of the State of New England, Being a Further Account of the Indian Warr.* London: Dorman Newman, 1676.

98. *News from New-England* (London: J. Coniers, 1676; reprint, Boston: Samuel G. Drake, 1850), 7. "Their own confession" probably refers to the Narragansett sachem Potuck, quoted by William Hubbard below.

99. Mather, *History*, 108–109.

100. Hubbard, *History*, vol. 1, 151–152. One of the factors mitigating the loss of so many Narragansett was the mobile nature of their camps. Patrick Malone wrote: "Warfare often required movement of the entire population of a village or camp with very little notice. Sachems, warned of a possible attack could gather separate groups into one or more easily defensible positions or temporarily scatter their people into mobile bands capable of avoiding their enemies. Southern New England Indians were not nomads, but they were used to seasonal moves and could pack their belongings quickly. Within a few hours' notice, an entire village could be broken up and the inhabitants on their way to one or more places of refuge" (see Malone, *Skulking*, 13–14). Hubbard noted that "it seems that there was but one Entrance into the Fort, though the Enemy found many Ways to come out" (see Hubbard, *History*, vol. 1, 145). Based on accounts of the battle, it would seem that most Narragansett women, children, and old men would have had the opportunity and the ability to flee the village before the wigwams were set on fire.

101. Bodge, *Soldiers*, 193.

102. Ibid., 174.

103. Thomas Church, *History*, 61.

104. Malone, *Skulking*, 10.

105. Granger writes in "The 'Brumal Den,'" 40–41, "As for the reliability of participants observing placement of provisions, it is probable that the three foot high doorways would have deterred colonial soldiers familiar with low fortified doorways and 'murderer's holds' from close inspection, and more consistent to believe that pit storage was practiced."

106. Personal communication with Joseph Granger, 1994.

107. Drake, ed., *Old Indian Chronicle*, 183. Drake noted that this seemed "like a rather

large story; especially as the fire was in a dense wilderness, and a great snow-storm was all the time prevailing."

108. Bodge, *Soldiers*, 174.

109. Douglas Leach wrote, "On the day after the Great Swamp Fight the English troops buried thirty-four of their dead at Wickford, while in the following days still others of the wounded succumbed. A month after the battle the total number of dead was approaching seventy, and both Hubbard and Mather subsequently placed the figure at more than eighty" (see Leach, *Flintlock*, 132).

110. Many survivors carried reminders of the battle for the rest of their lives. Increase Mather reported that Major William Bradford, age seventy-three in 1697, "hath worn a bullet in his flesh above 20 of them" (see Mather, *History*, 109). John Bull of Hingham petitioned the Massachusetts legislature for a pension in 1703, explaining that "in the yere 1675 your humble petisinor was impresed in to His magistis servis and marched to Naregansit fort fight under ye Command of Cap Johnson who was there slaine in Battel myself sorely wounded by A bulet being shot into my back aftor I was wounded I was caried some twenty mils in a very could Night and laid in A could chamber, a wooden pillo my covering was ye snow the wind drove on me a sad time to war in to be wounded the (then) in a lettle time I was moved to Rodisland from thence hom to Hingham where I remained two yers and upward helples my diit and tendance cost the cuntery not one peny after I came home had I not bin helped by my Naighbors and frinds I had perished before this day but in time through gods goodness to me I atained to so much strengh that I came to do some small labor thow with much pain by reson the bullit is in my body to this day but now age coming on and natorall forse begin to abate my former pains do increas upon every letel could or chang of wether by reson of my wound" (see Bodge, *Soldiers*, 484). Dr. Simon Cooper, a resident of Newport, was responsible for attending to many of the men wounded in the Great Swamp Fight. In a letter written to the governor and council at Hartford, written shortly after the fight in 1676, Cooper detailed

his work: "Captain Mason of Norredge his skull broken I did for him & took out many pieces not Cured & accommodated him. Edward Shippey of Say Brooke shot through ye mouth his upper Jaw broke which the Surgeons would not dress because ye said he was a dead man. Cured. Jacob Perce: wounded in ye Leg & Joshua Basham wounded in ye breast which belongs to your Colony but I do not know what towns almost Cured went home. Mark Makins of Stratford his shoulder blade shot to pieces Cured. Joseph Ginings of Wetherfeeled shot into the head. his Ja[w] broken & many pieces taken out Cured. Joseph Wheeler of Milford wounded in ye arm Cured. John Seargant of Gilford wounded in ye back: Cured. For which I demand 8 pounds sterling money: or money's worth" (Simon Cooper, "A Letter Written by Dr. Simon Cooper of Newport on the Island of Rhode Island to the Governor and Council of the Connecticut Colony" [June 17, 1676, reprint, Providence, R.I.: Society of Colonial Wars, 1916], 21).

111. Bodge, *Soldiers*, 174.

112. Quoted in Peirce, *Indian History*, 135.

113. Ibid., 175.

114. Williams, "The Winthrop Papers," 308. If Trumbull's numbers of Mohegan dead are accurate, then clearly the Narragansett were unaware of any such agreement.

115. "James Quanapaug's Information," *Massachusetts Historical Society*, 207.

116. Michael J. Puglisi, *Puritans Besieged: The Legacies of King Philip's War in the Massachusetts Bay Colony* (Lanham, Md.: University Press of America, 1991), 22.

117. Justin Winsor, ed., *The Memorial History of Boston*, vol. 1 (Boston: James R. Osgood, 1882), 91. More than a century before, the Reverend Samuel Niles reported, "The English set the wigwams on fire soon after they entered the fort, so that not only their houses but their treasure also was quickly turned into ashes, and their corn and beans were turned into coal, and great quantities of them remain to this day in their full proportion at a small depth under the surface of the earth" (Samuel Niles, "A Summary Historical Narrative of the Wars in New-England with

the French and Indians, in Several Parts of the Country," *Collections of the Massachusetts Historical Society,* 3rd series, vol. 6 [Boston: American Stationers', 1837] 154). Niles was born on May 1, 1674, just a year before the start of King Philip's War, and died in 1762 at the age of eighty-eight.

118. J. R. Cole, *History of Washington and Kent Counties, R.I.* (New York: W. W. Preston, 1889), 20.

119. Bodge, *Soldiers,* 184–185.

120. Ellis and Morris, *King Philip's War,* 149.

121. In 1887 Welcome Arnold Greene gave this account of the site: "The accounts given of it are, in many respects misleading. The site of the 'Fort,' (so called) on which the assault was made is spoken of by some historians, as a 'hill' rising in a swamp; by other, and more cautious ones, as 'a rising ground.' Now in a swamp any land, to be dry, must be 'rising,' above the water line, and in fact the island on which this 'fort' stood appeared to be, when standing upon it, to rise just about fifteen inches above the Highwaterline. In June 1885, a party of six of whom the writer was one, rode through the swamp onto the island, and we could not appreciate just where the wheels left the wet grass at the edge of the swamp and entered on the dryland. Of course an area of three or four acres would not be dead level, but not one of us estimated the highest part of the island to be more than three feet above highwater level. My own estimate was as stated, about fifteen inches" (Greene, "The Great Battle of the Narragansetts," 331). The weakness in Greene's analysis, of course, is that while he might have described the site of the memorial with great accuracy, he may not have been describing the site of the Great Swamp Fight.

122. Thomas Church, *History,* 57.

123. *News from New-England,* 6.

124. *A Continuation of the State of New England.* Greene commented: "To speak of a clay wall on the island seems to one standing upon it an absurdity. There is no clay on the island. It is a mile through an almost impassable swamp to the nearest dry land, and there is no clay bed known to exist for miles

around. To suppose that the Narragansett indians dug that clay miles away, and 'packed' it on their backs across the swamp in order to make that clay wall, requires an estimate of Indian character that is based purely on imagination" (see Greene, "The Great Battle of the Narragansetts," 332).

125. Roger Williams to John Leverett, "The Winthrop Papers," 307–311.

126. Ezra Stiles, *The Literary Diary of Ezra Stiles,* vol. 3, 1782–1795 (New York: Scribners, 1901), 23.

127. Granger, "The 'Brumal Den,'" 14.

128. Personal communication with Carl Congdon, 1994.

129. Paul G. Martasian, "Unearth Historic Indian Relics," unknown publication, September 10, 1959 (held by Rhode Island Historical Society, F.F. Subj. K540, King Philip's War, 1675–1676).

130. Erwin H. Johnson, "Digging Into the Great Swamp Mysteries," *Alumni Bulletin* (University of Rhode Island) 40, no. 1 (January–February 1960) (held at Rhode Island Historical Society, V.F. Subj. K540, King Philip's War, 1675–1676).

131. Granger, "The 'Brumal Den,'" 27.

132. Ibid., 31, and personal communication with Paul Robinson (Rhode Island Historic Preservation Commission) and E. Pierre Morenon (Rhode Island College), 1991.

133. Personal communication with Paul Robinson, E. Pierre Morenon, Mary Soulsby (University of Connecticut), and Carl Congdon, 1994.

134. Simmons, *The Narragansett,* 91, and personal communication with Paul Robinson and E. Pierre Morenon. Many local residents have preserved artifacts from the Great Swamp, though only a small percentage relate to the historic period; see David George et al., *Report Archaeological Reconnaissance Survey,* (South Kingstown, R.I.: Public Archaeology Survey Team, August 1993), 37.

135. Simmons, *The Narragansett,* 91.

136. George et al., *Report,* 1–3.

137. Ibid., 40–41.

138. This site is away from the memorial but, for purposes of preservation, has not been identified.

139. George et al., *Report*, 41.

140. Ellis and Morris, *King Philip's War*, 189.

141. Noah A. Phelps, *History of Simsbury, Granby, and Canton from 1642 to 1845* (Hartford, Conn.: Case, Tiffany and Burnham, 1845), 21.

142. Ibid., 23.

143. Ibid., 24.

144. Ibid., 25.

145. Mather, *History*, 165.

146. Phelps, *Simsbury*, 26.

147. Leonard Bliss Jr., *History of Rehoboth, Bristol County, Massachusetts: Comprising a History of the Present Towns of Rehoboth, Seekonk, and Pawtucket, From Their Settlement to the Present Time, Together With Sketches of Attleborough, Cumberland, and a Part of Swansey and Barrington, to the Time That They Were Severally Separated From the Original Town* (Boston: Otis, Broaders and Company, 1836), 93. Hubbard's account of whether Canonchet led the attack or not is unclear. Shortly before Canonchet was captured in April 1676, Hubbard wrote that he was "at that Moment divertising himself, with the Recital of Capt. Pierces Slaughter, surprised by his Men a few Days before." Some take this to mean Canonchet was hearing about the story (for the first time) from men who were actually there; others that he was simply basking in a Narragansett victory. See Hubbard, *History*, vol. 2, 57.

148. John G. Erhardt, *Rehoboth, Plymouth Colony, 1645–1692* (Seekonk, Mass.: John G. Erhardt, 1983), 332.

149. Rhode Island Historical Preservation Commission, *Pawtucket, Rhode Island: Statewide Historical Preservation Report P-PA-1* (October 1978), 4.

150. Erhardt, *Rehoboth*, 328.

151. Bliss, *History of Rehoboth*, 88.

152. Rhode Island Historical Preservation Commission, *Survey of Central Falls* (January 1978), 6.

153. Ibid.

154. Bliss, *History of Rehoboth*, 89.

155. Ibid.

156. Ibid.

157. Hubbard, *History*, vol. 1, 174, and Mather, *History*, 127.

158. *Survey of Central Falls*, 3.

159. Ibid., 5.

160. Bliss, *History of Rehoboth*, 90.

161. Ibid., 91.

162. Ibid., 84.

163. *Attleborough Bi-Centennial Anniversary Official Souvenir Programme,* (October 18–19, 1894), 18.

164. Patrick T. Conley, *An Album of Rhode Island History, 1636–1986* (Norfolk, Va.: Donning, 1986), 28.

165. *Attleborough Bi-centennial Programme,* 19.

166. Personal communication with Albert Klyberg, 1992.

167. Patrick T. Conley and Paul R. Campbell, *Providence: A Pictoral History* (Norfolk, Va.: Donning, 1982), 73.

168. Ibid., 14.

169. Ibid., 15.

170. Rhode Island Historical Preservation Commission, *Downtown Providence, Rhode Island: Statewide Historical Preservation Report,* (May 1981), 41.

171. Samuel Greene Arnold, *History of the State of Rhode Island and Providence Plantations*, vol. 1 (New York: D. Appleton, 1859), 408.

172. Ibid., 408–409.

173. Mather and Hubbard both reported thirty houses burned in their first accounts of the war. Later, Hubbard adjusted this number to eighteen houses burned on June 28, 1675, and fifty-four burned on March 29. He also reported that "most of the rest" were burned when the residents of Providence abandoned the town. See Mather, *History*, 132, and Hubbard, *History*, vol. 1, 181, and vol. 2, 47.

174. Leach, *Flintlock and Tomahawk*, 168.

175. Isaac Backus, *A History of New England, with Particular Reference to the Denomination of Christians Called Baptist*, 2nd ed., with notes by David Weston, vol. 1 (Newton, Mass.: Backus Historical Society, 1871), 337.

176. *Old Providence: A Collection of Facts and Traditions relating to Various Buildings and Sites of Historic Interest in Providence*, printed for the Merchants National Bank of Providence, Providence, R.I., 1918, 2.

177. Rhode Island Historical Preservation Commission, *Downtown Providence*, 42.

178. Conley and Campbell, *Providence*, 17.

179. Arnold, *Rhode Island*, 409.

180. Hubbard, *History*, vol. 1, 90.

181. Bowen, *Early Rehoboth*, vol. 3, 94.

182. Rhode Island Historical Preservation Commission, *East Providence, Rhode Island: Statewide Historical Preservation Report* (September 1976), 7.

183. Bliss, *History of Rehoboth*, 78.

184. See Erhardt, *Rehoboth*, 337–338.

185. Richard LeBaron Bowen, *Early Rehoboth*, vol. 2 (Rehoboth, Mass.: privately published, 1946), 8.

186. Ibid.

187. Ibid., 9.

188. Peirce, *Indian History*, 181.

189. Erhardt, *Rehoboth*, 337. This was probably exaggerated.

190. Mather, *History*, 131

191. Erhardt, *Rehoboth*, 340. Kingsley's gravestone, which resembles a hitching post, was moved from his farm to the Newman (or Hurst) Cemetery, located at the intersection of Route 114 (Pawtucket Avenue) and Route 152 (Newman Avenue) in East Providence. The stone sits near a tall Newman marker in the north end of the cemetery near the parking lot across from the Newman Church.

192. Personal communication with E. Otis Dyer Jr., 1992.

193. E. Otis Dyer Sr. "Like North, Rehoboth Had Its Garrisons," *Attleboro Sun Chronicle*, December 9, 1990, 41.

194. Ibid.

195. Ibid.

196. Sue Ellen Snape, *Rising from Cottages* (Taunton, Mass.: William S. Sulwold, 1990), 71.

197. Hubbard, *History*, vol. 2, 56.

198. Ibid., 56–57.

199. Ibid., 57.

200. Ibid., 58.

201. Ibid., 59.

202. Ibid.

203. Ibid., 60.

204. Ellis and Morris, *King Philip's War*, 202.

205. Hubbard, *History*, vol. 1, 265.

206. Church, *History* (ed. Drake), 121.

207. Ellis and Morris, *King Philip's War*, 271.

208. Church, *History* (ed. Drake), 123.

209. Mather, *History*, 194. Ellis and Morris believed he was a "subject of Awashonks" (see Ellis and Morris, *King Philip's War*, 272).

210. Church, *History* (ed. Drake), 125.

211. Ibid.

212. Church, *History* (ed. Dexter), 150.

213. Church, *History* (ed. Dexter), 150.

214. Church, *History* (ed. Drake), 126.

215. Mather reported that Philip's hands were sent to Boston; see Mather, *History*, 195.

216. Church, *History* (ed. Drake), 127.

217. Rowlandson, *Narrative*, 3.

218. Files of the Fruitlands Museums.

219. From the *Utica* (?) *Daily Gazette* (1842), in the files of the Fruitlands Museums.

220. A letter from Mrs. James to the Historical Society of Connecticut in 1876 attempted to retrieve the items; see the files of the Fruitlands Museums.

221. Checkley's memoirs were published in 1897 when the objects were "said still to remain" at the Connecticut Historical Society; see John Checkley, *Memoirs of the Rev. John Checkley*, ed. Edmund F. Slafter, in *Publications for the Prince Society: John Checkley*, 2 vols. (John Wilson, 1897).

222. Lydia Black, "Valuable Indian Relic Stolen from Fruitlands," *Nashoba Free Press*, July 2, 1970.

223. Joseph P. Kahn, "Wampanoag War Artifact Finds Trail Back Home," *Boston Globe*, June 7, 1995, pp. 1, 16.

224. Checkley, *Memoirs*, 119.

225. Church, *History* (ed. Drake), 123.

226. Benjamin Church, *Diary of King Philip's War, 1675–1676* (1716; reprint, with an introduction by Alan Simpson and Mary Simpson, Tiverton, R.I.: Lockwood, 1975), 17–19.

227. Stratton, *Plymouth Colony*, 127.

228. Little Compton (R.I.) Historical Society, *Indians of Little Compton* (1988), 3. The report continues: "We do not think that Pocasset lands came any further south than the marshy cove below today's Seapowet Avenue."

229. Little Compton Historical Society, *Indians of Little Compton*, 5. Awashonks' descendents, however, did not. Wampanoag tribal historian Russell Gardner notes that Awashonks' son, Peter, was settled after King Philip's War on the old Watuppa reservation on the east side of Watuppa Pond. This reservation was created in 1686, and Peter's descendents were still living there when the reservation was repartitioned in 1763. Eventually Massachusetts took the reservation for a watershed area for the city of Fall River. The old reservation is remembered in the name of a nearby road, Indian Town Road. (Personal communications, 1999.)

230. Little Compton (R.I.), Historical Society, *Notes on Little Compton* (1970), edited, annotated, and arranged by Carlton C. Brownell, from records collected by Benjamin Franklin Wilbour.

231. Church, *Diary*, 76.

232. Ibid., 77.

233. Ibid., 78.

234. Ibid., 80.

235. Rhode Island Historical Commission, *Little Compton, Rhode Island: State Preservation Report, Preliminary* (1990), 73.

236. Personal communication with Carlton Brownell, 1991.

CHAPTER 7: KING PHILIP'S WAR IN MAINE AND NEW HAMPSHIRE

1. William Hubbard, *The History of the Indian Wars in New England from the First Settlement to the Termination of the War with King Philip in 1677, from the Original Work by the Rev. William Hubbard* (1677), vol. 2 (reprint, edited by Samuel G. Drake, 1865; Bowie, Md.: Heritage Books, 1990), 100.

2. Ibid.

3. Ibid., 101.

4. *Brunswick, Maine: Two Hundred Years a Town*, published by the town of Brunswick (1939), 17.

5. Ibid.

6. Increase Mather, *The History of King Philip's War* (1676; reprint, edited by Samuel G. Drake, 1862; Bowie, Md.: Heritage Books, 1990), 202.

7. Hubbard, *History*, vol. 2, 104.

8. Ibid.

9. Mather, *History*, 89.

10. George W. Ellis and John E. Morris, *King Philip's War* (New York: Grafton Press, 1906), 295.

11. Ibid., 303.

12. Personal communication with Emerson Baker III, 1991.

13. *Portland City Guide* (Portland, Maine: City Printing Company, 1940), 281.

14. Ellis and Morris, *King Philip's War*, 306. James Andrews' Island is now Cushing Island.

15. Hubbard, *History*, vol. 2, 170.

16. *J. B. Stuart and Co. Atlas of the State of Maine* (1901); notation made by former city historian on a map held by the York Institute, Saco, Maine.

17. Hubbard, *History*, vol. 2, 105.

18. Roy P. Fairfield, *Sands, Spindles, and Steeples: A History of Saco, Maine* (Portland, Maine: House of Falmouth, 1956), 11.

19. Hubbard, *History*, vol. 2, 106.

20. Ibid., 108.

21. Ibid., 109.

22. Personal communication with Emerson Baker III, 1991.

23. Ellis and Morris wrote that "a large body of Indians" attacked the home; see Ellis and Morris, *King Philip's War*, 298.

24. Hubbard, *History*, vol. 2, 114.

25. Ibid., 115.

26. Personal communication with Emerson Baker III and visit to site, 1991.

27. Hubbard, *History*, vol. 2, 121.

28. Ibid.

29. An old photograph shows three gravestones at this location. Only one survives today.

30. Ellis and Morris, *King Philip's War*, 302.

31. Hubbard, *History*, vol. 2, 157.

32. Russell Bourne, *The Red King's Rebellion: Racial Politics in New England, 1675–1678* (New York: Atheneum, 1990), 227.

33. Ellis and Morris, *King Philip's War*, 303.

34. Hubbard, *History*, vol. 2, 163.

35. Emerson W. Baker, *The Clarke and Lake Company: The Historical Archaeology of a Seventeenth-Century Maine Settlement*, Occasional Publications in Maine Archaeology, no. 4 (Augusta, Maine: Maine Historic Preservation Commission, 1985), 61.

36. Hubbard, *History*, vol. 2, 72.

37. Russell Bourne wrote that an Abenaki woman seeking shelter was allowed into the fort, and waited until late at night to open the gates; see Bourne, *The Red King's Rebellion,* 227.

38. Hubbard, *History*, vol. 2, 159.

39. Ibid.

40. Ibid., 160.

41. Ibid., 161.

42. Personal communication with Emerson W. Baker III, 1991.

43. Hubbard, *History*, vol. 2, 224.

44. Ibid., 164.

45. Baker, *The Clarke and Lake Company,* 17.

46. Ibid., 18.

47. Ellis and Morris, *King Philip's War*, 304.

48. Baker, *The Clarke and Lake Company,* 17.

49. Ibid., 21.

50. Ibid., 39.

51. Ibid., 49.

52. Hubbard, *History*, vol. 2, 130.

53. Ibid., 187.

54. Edward M. Cook Jr., *Ossipee, New Hampshire 1785–1985: A History,* vol. 1 (Ossipee, N.H.: Peter E. Randall, 1989), 12.

55. Ibid.

56. Hubbard, *History*, vol. 2, 187.

57. Ibid., 188.

58. Personal communications with Ruth Loring, Ossipee Historical Society, 1992.

59. Cook, *Ossipee,* 12.

60. Ellis and Morris, *King Philip's War*, 307.

61. Hubbard, *History*, vol. 2, 172.

62. Ibid.

63. William S. Southgate, *The History of Scarborough from 1633 to 1783,* vol. 3, (1853), in *Collections of the Maine Historical Society,* 109.

64. Ibid., 111.

65. Hubbard, *History*, vol. 2, 232.

66. Ibid.

67. Ibid., 234.

68. Ibid.

69. Ibid., 235.

70. Ellis and Morris, *King Philip's War*, 312.

✦ BIBLIOGRAPHY ✦

READERS WISHING A DETAILED ACCOUNT OF THE WAR should begin with Douglas Edward Leach's *Flintlock and Tomahawk,* published in 1958 and still considered by many to be the single best history of the war. Another excellent retelling of the war, *King Philip's War,* was authored in 1906 by respected Connecticut River valley historians George W. Ellis and John E. Morris. While somewhat dated in its interpretations, *King Philip's War* has the advantage of covering the war in Maine in the years after King Philip's death. Readers lucky enough to own the original Grafton Press edition— still available in antiquarian bookstores—will be treated to a number of early twentieth-century photos of important sites related to the war, many of which are reproduced in this book.

There are four important texts written by participants and observers of King Philip's War, all of which are still quite readable despite their age. Boston's minister Increase Mather and Ipswich's minister William Hubbard published histories of the war in 1676 and 1677 respectively, each racing their texts to the sole printer in Cambridge. Mather's *The History of King Philip's War* is the quintessential Puritan interpretation of events and is both fascinating and insufferable because of that. Hubbard's *The History of Indian Wars in New England* is of the same school, but includes more detail and benefits from Hubbard's firsthand interviews of many of the war's participants, including his friend and neighbor Major Samuel Appleton. A careful reading also shows that Hubbard was not above criticizing colonial leaders' handling of the war effort, though his text needed to pass muster with Massachusetts Bay authorities and hence its criticisms are well veiled. Because both works were written while the war was being fought, there is some confusion as to dates and events; therefore, they should be tackled after a reading of Leach or Ellis and Morris.

Benjamin Church published his *Entertaining Passages Relating to Philip's War* in 1716, and it is truly a soldier's tale, dictated from the memory (and perhaps the field notes, too) of an old veteran to his son, some forty years after the end of the war. Numerous editions of Church's work have been published over the years, but those edited and annotated by antiquarians Samuel Drake in 1829 and Henry Martyn Dexter in 1865 are by far the best. The notes that each write about the people, events, and sites of the war are treasures in themselves. More recently, the 1975 edition of the *Diary of King Philip's War 1675–76,* published by the Little Compton Historical Society and introduced by Alan and Mary Simpson, is an outstanding summary of Church's life and times, and of the way his work has been presented and interpreted through the years.

The fourth work by an observer of the war is *The Narrative of the Captivity and Restoration of Mrs. Mary Rowlandson,* which Rowlandson published in Boston, Cambridge, and London in 1682. Few American colonial texts gained the popularity of Rowlandson's narrative, which related events from the time of her capture by Indians at Lancaster in February 1676 to her release at Redemption Rock in Princeton, Massachusetts, some three months later. Dozens of editions have been published throughout the centuries; however, perhaps the easiest to secure is one published by the town of Lancaster in 1975, including a helpful set of notes by Robert Diebold.

The single book that perhaps best helps interpret and synthesize the writings of Mather, Church, and Rowlandson, as well as a handful of other contemporaries, is Richard Slotkin and James K. Folsom's 1978 *So Dreadful a Judgment: Puritan Responses to King Philip's War, 1676–1677.* Slotkin and Folsom's analysis—widely quoted—pits the real events of the war against the Puritan's written responses. By analyzing the distortions that appear in the latter, the editors highlight the crisis that the war brought to Puritan New England, and the many changes in society that it forced upon its participants.

For genealogists, and for those interested in the firsthand letters of English soldiers reporting on events from the field, George Madison Bodge's 1906 *Soldiers in King Philip's War* is a delight. Bodge had access to the account books of John Hull, treasurer-at-war of Massachusetts Bay colony from 1675 to 1678. Not only are Hull's many lists reprinted and preserved, but Bodge includes sections on the postwar tribulations of King Philip's War veterans attempting to hold Massachusetts to its wartime promises.

Contemporary analysis of King Philip's War is limited to a handful of excellent texts, all written since 1980. Patrick Malone's 1991 *The Skulking Way of War* examines the technology and tactics of both the natives and the English in the seventeenth century, with particular emphasis on how the Indians came to adapt various aspects of English technology to their own traditions, creating a potent military force in the process. Malone's book is also full of wonderful nineteenth-century sketches of the war.

Three texts are fascinating for their examination of the period after King Philip's War: Michael Puglisi's 1991 *Puritans Besieged*, Daniel R. Mandell's 1996 *Behind the Frontier*, and a collection of articles edited by Colin Calloway and published in 1997 entitled *After King Philip's War*. Unlike the traditional histories, where events often end abruptly with the death of Philip, these texts see King Philip's War as a transition event to a new period in New England colonial history. Puglisi focuses on the impact of the war in Massachusetts Bay Colony; Mandell examines the lot of the Indians in eighteenth-century Massachusetts; and Calloway edits a collection of articles that range from the myth of the disappearing Abenaki in Maine, to the relationship between the Narragansett and the state of Rhode Island during the Revolutionary period, to the impact of the nineteenth-century Massachusetts Indian Enfranchisement Act.

Finally, Jill Lepore's 1998 *The Name of War*, while not a blow-by-blow retelling of the war, is an exceptionally well researched, detailed analysis of how the brutality and hatred of King Philip's War influenced the relationships between Indians and Anglos in the United States for the next three hundred years.

Adams, Charles J. *Quabaug 1660–1910.* Worcester, Mass.: Davis Press, 1915.

Allen, Wilkes. *The History of Chelmsford.* Haverhill, N.H.: P. N. Green, 1820.

Apes, William. *Eulogy on King Philip.* Boston: Self-published by Apes, 1836.

Arnold, David. "The Island's Gone Inside Out." *The Boston Globe,* July 24, 1991, front page.

Arnold, Samuel Greene. *History of the State of Rhode Island and Providence Plantations,* vol. 1. New York: D. Appleton, 1859.

Attleborough Bi-Centennial Anniversary, Official Souvenir Programme (October 18–19, 1894). Attleborough, Mass.: Bi-Centennial Committee.

Axtel, James. *The Invasion Within.* New York: Oxford University Press, 1985.

Backus, Isaac. *A History of New England, With Particular Reference to the Denomination of Christians Called Baptist,* 2nd ed., with notes by David Weston, vol. 1. Newton, Mass.: Backus Historical Society, 1871.

Bailey, Sarah Loring. *Historical Sketches of Andover, Massachusetts.* Boston: Houghton, Mifflin and Company, 1880.

Baker, Emerson W. *The Clarke and Lake Company: The Historic Archaeology of a Seventeenth-Century Maine Settlement.* Occasional publications in Maine archaeology, no. 4.Augusta, Maine: Maine Historic Preservation Commission, 1985.

Barber, John Warner. *Historical Collections, Being a General Collection of Interesting Facts, Traditions, Biographical Sketches, Anecdotes, etc. Relating to the History and Antiquities of Every Town in Mass.* Worcester, Mass.: Dorr, Howland, 1839.

Barber, Samuel. *Boston Common.* Boston: Christopher Publishing House, 1914.

Bardswell, A. Cory et. al. *The Hatfield Book.* Northampton, Mass.: Gazette Printing Co., 1970.

Barry, William. *A History of Framingham, Massachusetts.* Boston: James Munroe, 1847.

Baxter, James Phinney, A.M. "Early Voyages to America," *Collections of the Old*

Colony Historical Society, no. 4. Taunton, Mass.: C. H. Buffington, 1889.

Baylies, Francis. *An Historical Memoir of the Colony of New Plymouth,* Part III. Boston: Hilliard, Gray, Little, and Wilkins, 1830.

Bernard, Donald R. *Tower of Strength: A History of Fort Phoenix.* New Bedford, Mass.: Reynolds-DeWalt, 1975.

Bicknell, Thomas Williams. *A History of Barrington, Rhode Island.* Providence: Snow and Farnham, Printers, 1898.

Bigelow, Ella A. *Historical Reminiscences of the Early Times in Marlboro, Massachusetts.* Marlborough, Mass: Times Publishing Company, 1910.

Black, Lydia. "Valuable Indian Relic Stolen from Fruitlands." *Nashoba Free Press,* July 2, 1970.

Blake, Mortimer. *A History of the Town of Franklin, Mass.* Franklin, Mass.: Committee of the Town of Franklin, 1879.

Bliss, Leonard, Jr. *History of Rehoboth, Bristol County, Massachusetts: Comprising a History of the Present Towns of Rehoboth, Seekonk and Pawtucket, From Their Settlement to the Present Time, Together With Sketches of Attleborough, Cumberland, and a Part of Swansey and Barrington, to the Time That They Were Severally Separated From the Original Town.* Boston: Otis, Broaders and Company, 1836.

Bodge, George Madison. *Soldiers in King Philip's War.* 1906. Reprint, Baltimore: Genealogical Publishing Co., 1991.

Bourne, Russell. *The Red King's Rebellion: Racial Politics in New England, 1675–1678.* New York: Atheneum, 1990.

Bowen, Abel. *Bowen's Picture Book of Boston.* Boston: P. Otis, Broaders and Company, 1838.

Bowen, Richard LeBaron. *Early Rehoboth,* vol. 2. Rehoboth, Mass.: privately published, 1946.

———. *Early Rehoboth,* vol. 3. Rehoboth, Mass.: privately published, 1948.

Bradford, Laurence. *Historic Duxbury in Plymouth County, Massachusetts.* Boston: The Fish Printing Company, 1900.

The Bridgewater Book. Boston: George H. Ellis, 1899.

Brown, Abram English. *History of the Town of Bedford.* Bedford, Mass.: published by the author, 1891.

Browne, William Bradford. *The Babbitt Family History.* Taunton, Mass.: n.p., 1912.

Brunswick, Maine: 200 Years a Town. Published by the Town of Brunswick, 1939.

Burrage, Henry S. *The Beginnings of Colonial Maine.* Portland: State of Maine, 1914.

Butler, Caleb. *History of the Town of Groton.* Boston: T. R. Marvin, 1848.

Byrne, Terence G., and Kathryn Fairbanks. "Sunconewhew: 'Philip's Brother'?" *Bulletin of the Massachusetts Archaeological Society* 57, no. 2 (fall 1996).

Calloway, Colin G. *The Abenakis.* New York: Chelsea House, 1989.

———, ed. *After King Philip's War: Presence and Persistence in Indian New England.* Hanover: University Press of New England, 1997.

Cannon, John, and Ralph Griffiths. *The Oxford Illustrated History of the British Monarchy.* Oxford, U.K.: Oxford University Press, 1988.

Catalog of State Papers, Colonial Service, Whitehall, London, England for 1677–1680, #1349. "Answer to the Inquiries of the Committee for Trade and Plantations about New Plymouth." Also #314, #1131, #1349.

Chamberlain, D. H., "Wheeler's Surprise, 1675: Where?" A paper read before the Quaboag Historical Society at New Braintree, September 12, 1899, and before the Worcester Society of Antiquity at Worcester, November 14, 1889. Massachusetts Historical Society.

Chapin, Howard Millar. *The Trading Post of Roger Williams With Those of John Wilcox and Richard Smith.* Providence, R.I.: Society of Colonial Wars, 1933.

Chase, George Wingate. *The History of Haverhill, Massachusetts.* 1861. Reprint, Somersworth, N.H.: New England History Press, 1983.

Chase, Levi Badger. *Interpretation of Woodward's and Saffrey's Map of 1642, or the Earliest Bay Path.* Boston: David Clapp & Son, 1901.

Checkley, John. *Memoirs of the Rev. John Checkley.* Edited by Edmund F. Slater.

Church, Benjamin. *Diary of King Philip's War, 1675–76.* 1716. Reprint, with an introduction by Alan Simpson and Mary Simpson, Tiverton, R.I.: Lockwood, 1975.

———. *The History of King Philip's War.* Introduction and notes by Henry Martyn Dexter. Boston: John Kimball Wiggin, 1865.

Church, Thomas. *The History of Philip's War, Commonly Called the Great Indian War of 1675 and 1676.* 1717. Reprint, 1829, edited by Samuel G. Drake. Bowie, Md.: Heritage Books, 1989.

Cogswell, Hon. John B.D. "Bradford, Mass. from its settlement to 1888." *History of Essex County, Mass.,* vol. 2. Compiled under the supervision of D. Hamilton Hurd. Philadelphia: J.W. Lewis and Co., 1888.

Cole, J. R. *History of Washington and Kent Counties, R.I.* New York: W. W. Preston, 1889.

Coleman, Jack. "Setting the Stage for Conflict." *Middleborough Antiquarian* 24, no. 1 (spring 1991), 8.

Conley, Patrick T. *An Album of Rhode Island History, 1636–1986.* Norfolk, Va.: Donning, 1986.

Conley, Patrick T. and Paul R. Campbell. *Providence: A Pictoral History.* Norfolk, Va., Donning, 1982.

A Continuation of the State of New England, Being a Further Account of the Indian Warr. London: Henry Oldenburg, 1676.

Cook, Edward M., Jr. *Ossipee, New Hampshire 1785–1985: A History,* vol. 1. Ossipee, N.H.: Peter Randall, 1989.

Cooper, Simon. "A Letter Written by Dr. Simon Cooper of Newport on the Island of Rhode Island to the Governor and Council of the Connecticut Colony" (June 17, 1676). Providence, R.I.: Society of Colonial Wars, 1916.

Cronon, William. *Changes in the Land: Indians, Colonists, and the Ecology of New England.* New York: Hill and Wang, 1983.

Daggett, John. *A Sketch of the History of Attleborough.* Boston: Samuel Usher, 1894.

Daniel, Clifton. *Chronicle of America.* Mount Kisco, N.Y.: Chronicle Publishing, 1989.

Davis, William T. *Ancient Landmarks of Plymouth, Damrell and Upham.* Boston: 1887.

Deetz, James. *In Small Things Forgotten: The Archaeology of Early American Life.* New York: Anchor Books/Doubleday, 1977.

Delaney, Edmund. *The Connecticut River: New England's Historic Waterway.* Chester, Ct.: Globe Pequot Press, 1983

DeLue, Willard. *The Story of Walpole, 1724–1924.* Norwood, Mass.: Ambrose Press, 1925.

Denison, Rev. Frederic. *Westerly (Rhode Island) And Its Witnesses.* Providence, R.I.: J. A. and R. A. Reid, 1878.

Desorgher, Richard. *A Short History of the Indian Attack on Medfield, February 21, 1676.* Unpublished paper held by the Medfield Historical Society, May 1976.

Doherty, Katherine M., ed. *History Highlights: Bridgewater, Massachusetts: A Commemorative Journal.* Bridgewater, Mass.: Bridgewater Bicentennial Commission, 1976.

DownEast Enterprises. *Maine: A DownEast Vacationtime Guide.* Rockport, Maine: DownEast, 1991.

Drake, Samuel Adams. *Nooks and Corners of the New England Coast.* New York: Harper & Brothers, 1875.

Drake, Samuel G., A.M. *The History and Antiquities of Boston.* Boston: Luther Stevens, 1856.

———, ed. *Old Indian Chronicle: Being a Collection of Exceeding Rare Tracts, Written and Published in the Time of King Philip's War,* Boston: Samuel G. Drake, 1867.

Dyer, Otis E., Sr. "Like North, Rehoboth Had Its Garrisons." *Attleboro Sun Chronicle,* December 9, 1990, 41–42.

Easton, John. *A Relation of the Indyan Warr.* Albany, N.Y.: J. Munsell, 1858.

Ellis, George W., and John E. Morris. *King Philip's War.* New York: Grafton Press, 1906.

Emery, Samuel Hopkins. *History of Taunton, Massachusetts.* Syracuse, N.Y.: D. Mason & Co., 1893.

Engstrom, Victoria B. *Eel River Valley.* Pilgrim Society Notes, no. 23. Plymouth, Massachusetts: Pilgrim Society, March 1976.

Erhardt, Dr. John G. *Rehoboth, Plymouth Colony, 1645–1692.* Seekonk, Mass.: John G. Erhardt, 1983.

Everett, Edward. *Orations: Speeches on Various Occasions,* 7th ed., vol. 1. Boston: Little, Brown, 1865.

Exercises at the Bi-Centennial Commemoration of the Burning of Medfield by Indians in King Philip's War. Medfield, Mass.: George H. Ellis, 1876.

Facaros, Dana, and Michael Pauls. *New England: A Handbook for the Independent Traveler.* Chicago: Regnery Gateway, 1982.

Fairfield, Roy P. *Sands, Spindles and Steeples: A History of Saco, Maine.* Portland, Maine: House of Falmouth, 1956.

Feld, Jane. *A Brief History of Georgetown, Massachusetts 1838–1963.* Georgetown, Mass.: Georgetown Historical Commission, 1988.

Fessenden, Guy M. *History of Warren, R.I.* Providence, R.I.: H. H. Brown, 1845.

Fiske, Jeffrey H. *Wheeler's Surprise: The Lost Battlefield of King Philip's War.* Worcester, Mass.: Towaid Printing, 1993.

Foot, Joseph I. *An Historical Discourse Delivered at West Brookfield, Mass, Nov. 27, 1828.* West Brookfield, Mass.: Merriam & Cooke, 1843.

Forbes, Allan. *Some Indian Events of New England.* Boston: State Street Trust Company, 1934.

Forbes, Pere. "A Topographic Description of Raynham, In the County of Bristol, February 6, 1793." *Collections of the Massachusetts Historical Society for the Year 1794,* vol. 3, 1st series, Boston.

Gay, Vicki-Ann. "City Crews Put Chain Saws to Ancient King Philip Oak." *Taunton Daily Gazette,* February 1, 1983.

George, David, Brian Jones, and Ross Harper. *Report Archaeological Reconnaissance Survey.* South Kingstown, R.I.: Public Archaeology Survey Team, August 1993.

Gibson, Susan G., ed. *Burr's Hill: A Seventeenth-Century Wampanoag Burial Ground in Warren, R.I.* Providence, R.I.: Haffenreffer Museum of Anthropology, 1980.

Gillingham, James L. et al. *A Brief History of the Town of Fairhaven, Massachusetts.* 1903.

Granger, Joseph E. "The 'Brumal Den': An Archaeological and Ethnohistorical Study of the 'Great Swamp Fort' of the Narragansetts." Unpublished paper, 1992.

Green, Mason A. *Springfield, 1636–1886, History of Town and City.* Springfield, Mass.: C. A. Nichols, 1888.

Greene, Arnold. "The Great Battle of the Narragansetts, Dec. 19, 1675." *The Narragansett Historical Register* 5, no. 4, (December 1887).

Griffith, Henry S. *Mystery of Carver, Massachusetts.* New Bedford, Mass.: E. Anthony & Sons, Inc., Printers, 1913.

Gurney, Judith Jenney. *Tales of Old Rochester.* Baltimore: Gateway Press, 1990.

Haley, John Williams. *"The Old Stone Bank" History of Rhode Island,* vol. 4. Providence, R.I.: Providence Institution for Savings, 1944.

Hall, John Raymond. *In a Place Called Swansea.* Baltimore: Gateway Press, 1987.

Hannah, William F. *A History of Avon, Massachusetts, 1720–1988.* Avon, Mass.: Avon Centennial Committee, 1989.

Hayward, John. *The New England Gazetteer.* Boston: Otis Clapp, 1857.

Historical Celebration of the Town of Brimfield. Brimfield, Mass.: Town of Brimfield, 1879.

Holland, James E. "How The Four Corners of Puncatest Came to Be." *Old Rhode Island* 5, no. 2 (1995).

Howe, George. *Mount Hope: A New England Chronicle.* New York: Viking, 1959.

Howe, M. A. DeWolfe. *Bristol, Rhode Island: A Town Biography.* Cambridge, Mass.: Harvard University Press, 1930.

Howland, Franklyn. *A History of the Town of Acushnet.* New Bedford, Mass.: Self-published, 1907.

Hoyt, Epaphas. *Antiquarian Researches: Comprising A History of the Indian Wars in the Country Bordering Connecticut River and Part Adjacent, and Other Interesting Events.* Greenfield, Mass.: Ansel Phelps, 1824.

Hubbard, William. *The History of the Indian Wars in New England from the First Settlement to the Termination of the War with King Philip in 1677, from the Original Work by the Rev. William Hubbard* (1677), vol. 1. Reprint, edited by Samuel G. Drake, (1868). Bowie, Md.: Heritage Books, 1990.

Hudson, Alfred Sereno. *The History of Sudbury, Massachusetts, 1638–1889.* Sudbury, Mass.: Town of Sudbury, 1889.

Hudson, Charles. *History of the Town of Marlborough, Massachusetts, From Its First Settlement in 1657 to 1861.* Boston: T. R. Marvin, 1862.

Hutchinson, Thomas. *The History of the Colony and Province of Massachusetts Bay.* 1765. Reprint, Cambridge: Harvard University Press, 1936.

———. *The History of Massachusetts from the First Settlement Thereof in 1628, Until the Year 1750,* 3rd ed., vol. 1. Boston: Thomas Andrews, 1795.

Irving, Washington. *Rip Van Winkle and Other Stories.* Garden City, N.Y.: Doubleday, 1955.

Isham, Norman M. "Preliminary Report to the Society of Colonial Wars of Rhode Island on the Excavations of the Jireh Bull Garrison House on Tower Hill in South Kingstown." Providence: *Rhode Island Historical Society Collections* 11, no. 1, 2. January 1918.

"James Quanapaug's Information." *Collections of the Massachusetts Historical Society,* 1st series, volume 6.

Jamieson, Louise. "Unlocking the Cache." *The Region* (Ipswich, Mass.) July 17, 1991.

Jennings, Francis. *The Invasion of America: Indians, Colonialism, and the Cant of Conquest.* New York: Norton, 1975.

Johnson, Erwin H. "Digging Into the Great Swamp Mysteries." *Alumni Bulletin* (University of Rhode Island) 40, no. 1 (January–February 1960). Held at Rhode Island Historical Society, V. F. Subj. K540, King Philip's War, 1675–1676.

Johnson, Steven F. *New England Indians.* Pawtucket-Wamesit Historical Association, 1980.

Jorgensen, Harvey C., and Alexander G. Lawn. "The Development of the Narragansett Confederacy: An Economic Perspective." *Bulletin of the Massachusetts Archaeological Society,* 44, no. 1 (April 1983).

Judd, Sylvester. *History of Hadley.* Springfield, Mass.: H. R. Hunting, 1905.

Kahn, Joseph P. "Wampanoag War Artifact Finds Trail Back Home." *The Boston Globe,* June 7, 1995.

Kellogg, Lucy Cutler. *History of Greenfield, 1900–1929,* vol. 3. Greenfield, Mass.: Town of Greenfield, 1931.

Kingsbury, J. D. *Memorial History of Bradford.* Haverill, Mass.: C. C. Morese & Son, 1883.

Know Rhode Island. Compiled by the State Bureau of Information, Office of the Secretary of State, State of Rhode Island and Providence Plantations, 1927.

Koster, Fanny Leonard. *Annals of the Leonard Family.* Taunton, Mass.: self-published, 1911.

Krusell, Cynthia Hagar. *Map of Early Indian and Pilgrim Trails of Old Plymouth Colony.* Copyright 1978 by Cynthia Hagar Krusell.

Krusell, Cynthia Hagar, and Betty Magoun Bates. *Marshfield: A Town of Villages 1640–1990.* Marshfield Mills, Mass.: Historical Research Associates, 1990.

Kull, Andrew. *New England Cemeteries: A Collector's Guide.* Brattleboro, Vt.: Stephen Green Press, 1975.

Lane, Helen. *History of the Town of Dighton, Massachusetts.* Dighton, Mass.: Town of Dighton, 1962.

Latham, William. *Epitaphs in Old Bridge water, Massachusetts.* Bridgewater, Mass.: n.p., 1882.

Leach, Douglas Edward. *Flintlock and Toma-hawk: New England in King Philip's War.* 1958. Reprint, New York: Norton, 1966.

———. "A New View of the Declaration of War Against the Narragansetts, November, 1675." *Rhode Island History* 15, no. 2 (April 1956).

Lepore, Jill. *The Name of War: King Philip's War and the Origins of American Identity.* New York: Knopf, 1998.

Lindberg, Marcia Wiswall, ed. *Genealogists Handbook for New England Research,* 2nd edition. Boston: New England Historic Genealogical Society, 1985.

Little Compton Historical Society. *Indians of Little Compton.* Little Compton, R.I.: Little Compton Historical Society, 1988.

———. *Notes on Little Compton.* From records collected by Benjamin Franklin Wilbour, edited, annotated, and arranged by Carlton C. Brownell. Little Compton, R.I.: Little Compton Historical Society, 1970.

Lockridge, Kenneth A. *A New England Town: The First Hundred Years.* New York: Norton, 1970.

Maine Atlas and Gazetteer, 13th edition. Freeport, Maine: DeLorme, 1988.

Maine Catalog: Historic American Buildings Survey. Lewiston, Maine: Maine State Museum, 1974.

Malone, Patrick M. *The Skulking Way of War: Technology and Tactics Among the New England Indians.* Lanham, Md.: Madison Books, 1991.

Mandell, Daniel R. *Behind the Frontier: Indians in Eighteenth-Century Eastern Massachusetts.* Lincoln: University of Nebraska Press, 1996.

Marshfield: The Tale of a Pilgrim Town. Marshfield, Mass.: Marshfield Tercentenary Committee, 1940.

Martasian, Paul G. "Unearth Historic Indian Relics." Unknown publication, September 10, 1959, held by Rhode Island Historical Society, F.F. Subj. K540, King Philip's War, 1675–1676.

Mather, Increase. *The History of King Philip's War, 1676.* Reprint, edited by Samuel G.

Drake, 1862. Bowie, Md.: Heritage Books, 1990.

Mattapoisett and Old Rochester, Massachusetts, 3rd ed. 1907. Produced by the Mattapoisett [Mass.] Improvement Association, 1950.

May, Virginia. *A Plantation Called Petapawag.* Groton, Mass.: Groton Historical Society, 1976.

McDonald, James H. "Doubts Raised About Indian Site." *Providence Journal,* November 26, 1990.

McIntyre, Ruth A. *William Pynchon: Merchant and Colonizer.* Springfield, Mass.: Connecticut Valley Historical Museum, 1961.

Merchant, Carolyn. *Ecological Revolutions: Nature, Gender, and Science in New England.* Chapel Hill: University of North Carolina Press, 1989.

Merrill, Joseph. *History of Amesbury.* Haverhill, Mass.: Franklin P. Stiles, 1880.

Metcalf, John G. *Annals of the Town of Mendon, From 1659 to 1880.* Providence, R.I.: E. L. Freeman, 1880.

Middleborough Historical Commission. *Middleborough Historical Commission Presents Old Middleborough Founders Day, June 1, 1669.* Middleborough, Mass.: Middleborough Historical Commission, 1991.

Mitchell, Nahum. *History of the Early Settlement of Bridgewater.* 1840. Baltimore: Gateway, 1970.

Morison, Samuel Eliot. *Historical Markers Erected by Massachusetts Bay Colony Tercentenary Commission.* Boston: Commonwealth of Massachusetts, 1930.

Morris, Gerald E., ed. *Maine Bicentennial Atlas: An Historical Survey.* Portland, Maine: Maine Historical Society, 1976.

Morton, Nathaniel. *New England Memorial,* 5th ed. Edited by John Davis. Boston: Crocker and Brewster, 1826.

Munro, Wilfred H. *The History of Bristol, R.I.: The Story of the Mount Hope Lands.* Providence, R.I.: J.A. & R.A. Reid, 1880.

The Narragansett Dawn: We Face East 2, no. 6 (October 1936).

New England Historic Genealogical Register,

vol. 28 (October 1874); vol. 38 (1884); vol. 144, no. 575 (July 1990).

News from New-England. London: J. Coniers, 1676. Reprint, Boston: Samuel Drake, 1850.

Niles, Samuel. "A Summary Historical Narrative of the Wars in New-England with the French and Indians, in Several Parts of the Country." *Collections of the Massachusetts Historical Society,* 3rd series, vol. 6. Boston: American Stationers', 1837.

O'Connell, James C. *Inside Guide to Springfield and the Pioneer Valley.* Springfield, Mass.: Western Mass. Publishers, 1986.

Official Souvenir Programme, Attleborough Bi-Centennial Anniversary, October 18 & 19, 1894.

Old Colony Historical Society archives, Box 68; VC 473 B.

Old Providence: A Collection of Facts and Traditions relating to Various Buildings and Sites of Historic Interest in Providence. Providence, R.I.: Merchants National Bank of Providence, 1918.

Our Country and Its People: A Descriptive and Biographical Record of Bristol County, Massachusetts. Prepared and published under the auspices of the *Fall River News* and *The Taunton Gazette* with the assistance of Hon. Alanson Borden of New Bedford. Boston: Boston History Company, 1899.

Paige, Lucius R. "Wickaboag? Or Winnimisset?: Which Was the Place of Capt. Wheeler's Defeat in 1675." *New England Historic Genealogical Register* no. 38 (1884).

Paradise, Scott H., ed. *The Story of Essex County,* vol. 1. New York: American Historical Society, 1935.

Parsons, Herbert Collins. *A Puritan Outpost: A History of the Town and People of Northfield, Massachusetts.* New York: Macmillan, 1937.

A Patchwork History of Tiverton, Rhode Island. Tiverton, R.I.: Tiverton Historical Society, 1976.

Pattee, William S. *A History of Old Braintree and Quincy.* Quincy, Mass.: Green and Prescott, 1878.

Peirce, Ebenezer W. *Indian History, Biography and Genealogy.* North Abington, Mass.: Zerviah Gould Mitchell, 1878.

Perley, Sidney. *The History of Salem, Massachusetts,* vol. 3, Salem, Mass.: S. Perley, 1928.

Perry, Gardner B. *History of Bradford, Massachusetts.* Haverhill, Mass.: C.C. Morse and Son, 1872.

Phelps, Noah A. *History of Simsbury, Granby, and Canton From 1642 to 1845.* Hartford, Conn.: Case, Tiffany and Burnham, 1845.

Pillsbury, Katherine H., Robert D. Hale, and Jack Post, eds. *The Duxbury Book, 1637–1987.* Duxbury, Mass.: Duxbury Rural and Historical Society, 1987.

Plymouth Guide, April–July 1991. S. Yarmouth, Mass.: Prescott Visitor Magazines, Inc.

Pocumtuck Valley Memorial Association Proceedings, vol. 2. Field Meeting, 1870.

———. Field Meeting, 1897.

Portland City Guide. Portland, Maine.: City Printing Company, 1940.

Powers, John C. *We Shall Not Tamely Give It Up.* Lewiston, Maine: John C. Powers, 1988.

Pretola, John P. "The Springfield Fort Hill Site: A New Look." *Archaeological Society of Connecticut,* bulletin no. 48.

Proceedings at the Centennial Celebration of the Incorporation of the Town of Longmeadow, October Seventeenth, 1883. Longmeadow, Mass.: Published by the Secretary of the Centennial Committee, Under Authority of the Town, 1884.

Publications for the Prince Society: John Checkley, 2 vols. John Wilson, 1897.

Puglisi, Michael J. *Puritans Besieged: The Legacies of King Philip's War in the Massachusetts Bay Colony.* Lanham, Md.: University Press of America, 1991.

Quarter Millennial Celebration of the City of Taunton, Massachusetts. Taunton, Mass.: Taunton City Government, 1889.

Reinke, Rita, "Seventeenth-Century Military Defenses Uncovered." *Journal of the Massachusetts Historical Commission,* Fall 1990.

"Report Upon the Objects Excavated at the Jireh Bull House and Now in the Museum of the Rhode Island Historical Society," *Rhode Island Historical Society Collections* 18, no. 3 (July 1925).

Rhode Island Historical Preservation Commission. *East Providence, Rhode Island: Statewide Historical Preservation Report.* September 1976.

———. *North Kingstown, Rhode Island: Statewide Preservation Report.* November 1979.

———. *Pawtucket, Rhode Island: Statewide Historical Preservation Report P-PA-1.* October 1978.

———. *Survey of Central Falls.* January 1978.

———. *Tiverton, Rhode Island: Statewide Historical Preservation Report* (Preliminary). 1983.

———. *Warwick, Rhode Island: Statewide Historical Preservation Report* (Preliminary). April 1981.

Richard, Lysander Salmon, *History of Marshfield.* Plymouth, Mass.: The Memorial Press, 1901.

Robbins, Maurice. *The Indian History of Attleboro.* Attleboro, Mass.: Attleboro Historical Commission, September, 1969.

———. *The Monponset Path.* Pathways of the Past, no. 4. Attleboro, Mass.: Massachusetts Archaeological Society, 1984.

———. *The Sandwich Path: Church Searches for Awashonks.* Pathways of the Past, no. 3. Attleboro, Mass.: Massachusetts Archaeological Society, 1984.

Robinson, Brian. *A Guide to Rhode Island Archaeological Collections.* Providence, R.I.: Haffenreffer Museum of Anthropology, 1986.

Rodman, Capt. Thomas R. "The King Philip War in Dartmouth." *The Old Dartmouth Historical Sketches* #3 (December 29, 1903).

Rowlandson, Mary. *The Narrative of the Captivity and Restoration of Mrs. Mary Rowlandson.* 1682. Reprint, edited by Robert Diebold, Lancaster, Mass.: Town of Lancaster, 1975.

Roy, Louis E. *Quaboag Plantation Alias Brook-field: A Seventeenth Century Massachusetts Town.* Worcester, Mass.: self-published, 1965.

Russell, William S. *Pilgrim Memorials, and Guide to Plymouth.* Boston: Crosby, Nichols, 1855.

Sainsbury, W. Noel. *Calendar of State Papers, Colonial Series, America and West Indies, 1675–1676.* London: Eyre and Spottiswoode, 1893.

Schroeder, Betty Groff. "The True Lineage of King Philip (Sachem Metacom)." *New England Historical and Genealogical Register* 144, no. 575 (July 1990).

Scott, Laura. *Sudbury: A Pictorial History.* Norfolk, Va.: Donning, 1989.

Sharples, Bob. "Anawan Rock Location Under Question." *Rehoboth Reporter* 2, no. 9 (October 1990).

Sheldon, George. "The Traditional Story of the Attack Upon Hadley and the Appearance of Gen. Goff, Sept. 1, 1675: Has It Any Foundation in Fact?" *New England Historic Genealogical Register* 28 (October 1874).

Shurtleff, Daniel B., and David Pulsifer, eds. *Records of the Colony of New Plymouth in New England,* vol. 5 (1674–1686). Boston: W. White, 1854.

Simmons, James Raymond. *The Historic Trees of Massachusetts.* Boston: Marshall Jones, 1919.

Simmons, William S. *The Narragansett.* New York: Chelsea House, 1989.

Slotkin, Richard, and James K. Folsom, eds. *So Dreadful a Judgment: Puritan Responses to King Philip's War, 1676–1677.* Middletown, Ct.: Wesleyan University Press, 1978.

Smith, Chad Powers. *The Housatonic: Puritan River.* New York: Rinehart & Company, 1946.

Snape, Sue Ellen. *Rising from Cottages.* Taunton, Mass.: William S. Sullwold, 1990.

Snow, Caleb M., M.D. *The History of Boston.* Boston: Abel Powers, 1825.

Snow, Edward Rowe. *The Islands of Boston Harbor, 1630–1971.* New York: Dodd,

Mead & Company, 1936.

Society of Colonial Wars. *A Plat of the Land of Capt. Henry Bull, Drawn by James Helme, Surveyor, January 8, 1729.* Providence, R.I.: E. L. Freeman, 1927.

———. *A Record of the Ceremony and Oration of the Occasion of the Unveiling of the Monument Commemorating The Great Swamp Fight, December 19, 1675, in the Narragansett Country of Rhode Island.* Society of Colonial Wars, 1906.

Southgate, William S. *The History of Scarborough From 1633 to 1783,* vol. 3. Collections of the Maine Historical Society, 1853.

Steinberg, Sheila, and Cathleen McGuigan. *Rhode Island: An Historical Guide.* Providence: Rhode Island Bicentennial Foundation, 1976.

Stiles, Ezra. *The Literary Diary of Ezra Stiles,* vol. 3. New York: Charles Scribner's Sons, 1901.

Stoughton, Ralph M. *History of the Town of Gill.* Gill, Mass.: Town of Gill, 1978.

Stratton, Eugene Aubrey. *Plymouth Colony: Its History and People 1620–1691.* Salt Lake City, Utah: Ancestry Publishers, 1986.

Swan, Bradford F. *An Indian's an Indian.* Providence, R.I.: Roger Williams Press, 1959.

Talcott, John. "A Letter Written by Maj. John Talcott from Mr. Stanton's at Quonocontaug to Govr. William Leete and the Hond. Council of the Colony of Connecticut (July 4, 1676)." Reprint, Providence, R.I.: E. L. Freeman, 1934.

Taylor, Charles J. *History of Great Barrington, (Berkshire County) Massachusetts.* Great Barrington, Mass.: Clark W. Bryan, 1882.

Temple, J. H. *History of North Brookfield, Massachusetts.* North Brookfield, Mass.: Town of North Brookfield, 1887.

Temple, J. H., and George Sheldon. *History of the Town of Northfield, Massachusetts For 150 Years, with an Account of the Prior Occupation of the Territory by the Squakheags and With Family Genealogies.* Albany, N.Y.: Joel Musell, 1875.

Tercentenary Committee of Fall River. *Fall River in History*. Fall River, Mass.: Munroe Press, 1930.

Tercentenary History Committee. *History of Hatfield, 1670–1970*. Hatfield, Mass.: Town of Hatfield, 1970.

Thompson, Elroy S. *History of Plymouth, Norfolk, and Barnstable Counties, Massachusetts*, vol. 1. New York: Lewis Historical Publishing Company, 1928.

Thurlby, Hope A. *Picture Guide to Historic Plymouth*. Plymouth, Mass.: Pilgrim Society, 1990.

Thwing, Annie Haven. *The Crooked & Narrow Streets of The Town of Boston 1630–1882*. Boston: Marshal Jones Company, 1920.

Tilden, William S., ed. *History of the Town of Medfield, Massachusetts 1650–1886*. Boston: Geo. H. Ellis, 1887.

Tripp, George H. "The Town of Fairhaven in Four Wars." *Old Dartmouth Historical Sketches* no. 5 (June 27, 1904).

Trumbell, James Russell. *History of Northampton, Massachusetts*, vol. 1. Northampton, Mass.: n.p., 1898.

Trumbull, J. Hammond. *The Public Records of the Colony of Connecticut*. Hartford, Ct.: F. A. Brown, 1852.

Turnbaugh, William A. "Assessing the Significance of European Goods in Seventeenth-Century Narragansett Society." *Ethnohistory and Archaeology: Approaches to Postcontact Change in the Americas*. Edited by J. Daniel Rogers and Samuel M. Wilson. New York: Plenum, 1993.

———. "Community, Commodities, and the Concept of Property in Seventeenth-Century Narragansett Society." *Archaeology of Eastern North America: Papers in Honor of Stephen Williams*. Archaeological Report no. 25, edited by James B. Stoltman. Jackson, Miss.: Mississippi Department of Archives and History, 1993.

Updike, Daniel Berkeley. *Richard Smith*. Boston: Merrymount Press, 1937.

Utley, Robert M., and Wilcomb E. Washburn. *Indian Wars*. Boston: Houghton Mifflin, 1977.

Van Dusen, Albert Edward. *Connecticut*. New York: Random House, 1961.

Van Voris, Jacqueline. *The Look of Paradise*. Canaan, N.H.: Phoenix, 1984.

Wagenknect, Edward. *A Pictorial History of New England*. New York: Crown, 1976.

Warner, Joseph Everett. *Spirit of Liberty and Union, 1637–1939*. Taunton, Mass.: Joseph Everett Warner, 1947.

Waters, Thomas Franklin. *Ipswich In the Massachusetts Bay Colony*. Ipswich, Mass.: The Ipswich Historical Society, 1905.

Webb, Stephen Saunders. *1676: The End of American Independence*. New York: Knopf, 1984.

Weinstein-Farson, Laurie. *The Wampanoag*. New York: Chelsea House, 1989.

Wells, Daniel White, and Reuben Field Wells. *A History of Hatfield, Massachusetts*. Springfield, Mass.: F. C. H. Gibbons, 1910.

Weston, Thomas. *History of the Town of Middleboro, Massachusetts*. Cambridge, Mass.: Riverside Press, 1906.

Whipple, Chandler. *First Encounter: The Indian and the White Man in Massachusetts & Rhode Island*. Stockbridge, Mass.: Berkshire Traveller Press, 1974.

Whipple, Warren and Marion. "The Story of the Thompson Gun." Undated Letter sent to the Old Colony Historical Society, Taunton, Mass.

Wiencek, Henry. *The Smithsonian Guide to Historic America: Southern New England*. New York: Stewart, Tabori & Chang, 1989.

Williamson, William D. *The History of the State of Maine; From its First Discovery, A.D. 1602, to the Separation, A.D. 1820, Inclusive*. Hallowell, Maine: Glazier, Masters & Co., 1832.

Williams, Bob. "Son of King Philip's Oak Thriving at Church Green." *Taunton Daily Gazette*, February 9, 1983.

Williams, Roger. "The Winthrop Papers." *Collections of the Massachusetts Historical Society*, 4th series, vol. 6.

Williams, Roger. *The Correspondence of Roger Williams*, vol. 2 (1654–1682). Edited by

Glenn W. LeFantasie. Hanover, N.H.: University Press of New England, 1988.

Wilson, Douglas. "Web of Secrecy: Goffe, Whalley, and the Legend of Hadley." *New England Quarterly* 60, no. 4 (December 1987).

Winsor, Justin, ed. *The Memorial History of Boston*, vol. 1. Boston: James R. Osgood and Company, 1882.

Winthrop, Wait. "A Letter Written by Capt. Wait Winthrop from Mr. Smiths in Narragansett to Govr. John Winthrop of the Colony of Connecticut." Issued at the General Court of the Society of Colonial Wars in the State of Rhode Island and the Providence Plantations by its governor, Henry Dexter Sharpe, and the council of the society, August 8, 1919, Providence. Printed for the society by the Standard Printing Co., from the original manuscript in the archives of the State of Connecticut.

Woodcock Garrison House Historic District. National Register of Historic Places registration form, May 31, 1990.

Wright, Otis Olney, ed. *History of Swansea, Massachusetts 1667–1917*. Published by the Town of Swansea, 1917.

The Yankee Compass: A Visitor's Guide to Sturbridge and Environs. Sturbridge, Mass.: Sturbridge Area Tourist Association, 1991.

❧ INDEX ❧

413